THE DARKEST PERIOD

The Civilization of the American Indian Series

THE DARKEST PERIOD
The Kanza Indians and Their Last Homeland, 1846–1873

Ronald D. Parks

University of Oklahoma Press : Norman

Library of Congress Cataloging-in-Publication Data

Parks, Ronald D., 1949–
   The darkest period : the Kanza indians and their last homeland, 1846–1873 /
Ronald D. Parks.
      pages cm. — (Civilization of the American Indian series ; volume 273)
   Includes bibliographical references and index.
   ISBN 978-0-8061-4430-6 (cloth)
   ISBN 978-0-8061-4845-8 (paper)
1. Kansa Indians—History—19th century. 2. Kansa Indians—Government
relations. 3. Kansa Indians—Social conditions. I. Title.
   E99.K2P37 2014
   305.897'525—dc23
                              2013038462

The Darkest Period: The Kanza Indians and Their Last Homeland, 1846–1873 is
Volume 273 in The Civilization of the American Indian Series.

The paper in this book meets the guidelines for permanence and durability of
the Committee on Production Guidelines for Book Longevity of the Council
on Library Resources, Inc. ∞

To the Kanza people, past and present

Contents

ILLUSTRATIONS

FIGURES

MAPS

TABLES

Acknowledgments

Among the many individuals and institutions providing assistance in the preparation of this book, the Kaw Nation has been especially generous and hospitable in offering me access to the tribe's resources and expertise. I am grateful to the Kaw Nation chairman and CEO, Guy Munroe, the tribe's executive councils both past and present, and many staff members for making the tribe's collection of documents and photographs available to me at its headquarters in Kaw City, Oklahoma. Among the tribal leaders who offered their friendship and support are revered elder Luther Pepper and the chair of the Cultural, Museum, and Library Committee, Donna Villa. I also want to recognize the contributions of tribal members Lonnie Burnett and Jim Pepper Henry. Justin McBride, the first director of the Kanza Language Project, and former and present staff members Jennie Baker, Betty Durkee, and Thomas Firme all provided invaluable assistance. I am forever indebted to CML Committee member Pauline Sharp and her husband, Doug, for their generous contributions of hundreds of hours of research in Kansas newspaper archives and Kanza-related Civil War materials.

Many Council Grove–area organizations and individuals extended assistance during the time I prepared this book. I am especially grateful for the generous financial contributions of the Friends of Kaw Heritage, Inc.; Oscar and Ina Nystrom Foundation; John E. Trembly Foundation; and the Arthur and Ethel Hylton Trust. Much support and encouragement has been offered by Mary Honeyman, site administrator, Kaw Mission State Historic Site; Fay Laughridge, past president, Friends of Kaw Heritage, Inc.; FKH board members Peg and Don Jenkins, Ken Stiebben, and Margy Stewart; local historians Ken and Shirley McClintock, David Aspelin, Derrick Doty, and Don and Doris Cress; and Lee Dobratz, director, Council Grove Public Library, and Dobratz's assistant, Kathy Avers.

The historical Kanza homeland covers a large area of eastern and central Kansas, and I received the support of many people in the region, including Joyce Mathies, director of the Alma Branch, Pottawatomie Wabaunsee Regional Library; Michael Stubbs and Michael Nelson, Wabaunsee County; Jan Huston and Don Schiesser, Lyon County; Don Huber, Shirley Unruh, and Randy Norland, McPherson County; Jettie Condray, curator, Ottawa County Historical Museum; Gaylinn Childs, director, Geary County Historical Museum, and GCHM volunteer Ron Harris; Deb Pryor, Manhattan; and Nona Barton, government documents librarian, Fort Hays State University.

I appreciate those who assisted in finding and preparing images for the book, including Katy Haun of Council Grove, map illustrator; Tom Jonas of Phoenix, Arizona, cartographer; Nancy Sherbert, photographic archivist, Kansas State Historical Society; Rachel Mossman, photographic archivist, Oklahoma Historical Society, and her assistant, Jon May; JoAnn Monroe O'Bregon, Ponca City, Oklahoma; Joe McKenzie, director, Salina Public Library; Sharon Haun, archivist, Morris County Historical Society; Scott Brockelman, Haslet, Texas; and Crystal Douglas, Kanza Museum director, Kaw City, Oklahoma.

Others providing significant support during the time I researched and wrote this book include historians Ramon Powers of Topeka, Kansas, and Leo Oliva of Woodston, Kansas; Dr. Robert L. Rankin, professor of linguistics (retired), University of Kansas; Dr. Lauren Ritterbush, associate professor of anthropology, Kansas State University; Robert C. Stevens, Pittsford, New York; Rita Shelley, Omaha, Nebraska; Shirley Gilpin, Davidson, North Carolina; and especially Clark Sexton, Lawrence, Kansas, who devoted many hours applying his editorial and technical talents in preparing the manuscript.

The staff members at the University of Oklahoma Press have been exceptionally helpful in every phase of the book project. I will always be grateful for the hard work, expertise, common sense, and good will of Alessandra Jacobi Tamulevich, Emily Jerman, Emmy Ezzell, Tom Krause, Kathleen Kelly, Anna María Rodríguez, Tony Roberts, Sandy See, and Amy Hernandez. I deeply appreciate the penetrating analyses and enormously beneficial criticisms of my manuscript offered by distinguished scholars William E. Unrau and James N. Leiker. I also want to recognize the invaluable contributions of the copyeditor, Chris Dodge, of Kalispell, Montana.

I especially want to thank members of my family for their moral support during the five years or more this book has been in progress. These include my brother, William Parks of Portland, Oregon; my son Casey, and his partner, Sara, of Phoenix, Arizona; daughter Toni and her husband, Brett, and grandchildren Jackson and Sophie, of Oklahoma City. Finally, I want to express my gratitude to my wife, Judy.

Demonstrating the resiliency and strength of the Kanza people over time, the Kaw Nation in 2000 reclaimed ownership of approximately 160 acres of former reservation land near the historical Kanza Agency a few miles southeast of Council Grove, Kansas. As owners of the Allegawaho Memorial Heritage Park, the Kanzas are now a welcome presence in their "final" Kansas homeland.

The Darkest Period

INTRODUCTION

In October 1852, Wilson Hobbs, a Quaker medical doctor and mission school superintendent assigned to the Shawnee tribe, "desired to make a trip to Council Grove" to observe the Kanza Indians, a tribe he considered—compared to the Shawnees—"wilder" and "entirely uncivilized."[1] To reach his destination, Hobbs traveled about one hundred miles west by horseback on the Santa Fe Road across present-day eastern Kansas. En route, he observed many buffalo wallows that were "but memories of the past, as no hoof had lately been upon them." The Quaker doctor's assessment of the prairie he traversed reflects the conventional Euro-American view of the presettlement Kansas landscape: "It was a day of wonder to me why God had so long allowed so much wealth and beauty to lie waste."[2]

Hobbs's description of Council Grove and the Kanzas is sketchy, with one exception. As he stood on the west bank of the Neosho River near Seth Hays's trading post, the Quaker looked back east across the river at a party of Kanzas preparing to cross the ford. The men quickly disrobed to their breechcloths and boldly waded through the waist-deep water. Hobbs's attention, however, was focused on the women:

> They carefully lifted their skirts, as they waded in, to suit the depth, and as carefully dropped them as the water grew shallower toward the other shore. I carefully watched one who approached the crossing with two children in her arms, as her hands and arms were already employed. She

stood the little ones in the shallow water near the shore and waded in the deeper water in front of them, where she squatted down in the water and fastened her clothing high up on her shoulders. She then reached for the children and moved on, gradually rising as the water grew deeper. When the water became shallower, near the other shore, she began to squat, and came lower and lower down until she could safely land the children, when she put them down in the water and loosed her skirts and let them drop as she straightened herself up, and waded out without having wet her clothing or exposed her person.[3]

Thanks to Hobbs—and without knowing what prompted his fascination—we are left with a description rare among Kanza-related historical records: a detailed account of a Kanza person engaged in a necessary act of daily life. The event itself, fording the stream, is deceptively simple. In fact, the young mother confronted a number of important considerations requiring her to make intelligent decisions regarding how to keep her clothing dry on a cool October day, provide for the safety of her children while moving through a waist-deep current (which required physical strength and agility), and fulfill the cultural requirements of feminine modesty. At first glance, this scene is alien to the modern experience. After all, within a hundred feet of this same crossing, young mothers today effortlessly drive over the Neosho River on a concrete bridge, their children strapped into the safety seats of SUVs. But the crossing of the young Kanza woman resonates with the experience of many modern women who each day protect their children, invent solutions to overcome myriad obstacles, and oblige cultural precepts of femininity. Her situation stirs our imaginations because it is both different and, in a broader sense, similar to that of our own.

This book, *The Darkest Period: The Kanza Indians and Their Last Homeland, 1846–1873*, is my attempt to tell the story of the Kanzas' final years in Kansas so that the skeleton of historical data is animated with the heartbeat of its human participants. To see the Kanzas clearly requires an attempt to extract from sources—albeit almost exclusively the writings of Euro-American government officials, journalists, travelers, missionaries, teachers, and diarists—details that illuminate the humanity, and in some cases inhumanity, of the Kanzas and their

Euro-American neighbors. The ability to fully realize this intention is limited by a formidable obstacle that has been acknowledged by other researchers: the dearth of information about this tribe. Nevertheless, historical records yield, in my estimation, sufficient material to construct a narrative illuminating the lives of ordinary Kanzas while featuring the Kanza nation's most prominent events, personalities, customs, and subsistence strategies from 1846 to 1873 when the Kanzas were forced to move to Indian Territory, now Oklahoma. Kanza agency cannot be understood in isolation. It was realized through relationship to various entities: the tribe's internal social and political structure; other tribes, friendly and hostile; the all-encompassing deity, Wakanda; Anglo and Hispanic travelers on the Santa Fe Road; and their Euro-American neighbors. Council Grove, especially, is inextricably linked to the Kanzas so that neither the town nor the tribe can be clearly understood exclusive of the other.

The thematic emphases of this book do not negate the fact that the Kanzas were, indeed, dominated by powerful Euro-American cultural, political, and economic forces during their last years in Kansas. Government officials and their policies, Protestant educators and missionaries, predatory economic interests, and national events such as the Mexican-American War, two economic depressions, the Colorado gold rush, American Civil War, and postwar industrialization all profoundly affected the tribe. The tribe's afflictions were also magnified by a set of unfortunate geographical circumstances. Created by the federal government in November 1847, the twenty-mile-square Kanza Reservation at its inception contained the seeds of Kanza destruction as it was bisected by a vector of whiskey and contagious diseases—the Santa Fe Trail—and encompassed the ambitious and soon-to-be thriving trade center of Council Grove. On a larger scale, the location of the reservation between the advancing population of land-hungry white settlers to the east and the powerful and hostile Plains tribes to the west diminished the tribe's capacity to subsist by the traditional means of small-scale horticulture and hunting. During the twenty-six years the Kanza occupied the reservation on the Neosho River, this small, impoverished "border tribe" became increasingly dependent on the federal government to provide the material necessary for existence.

These themes are delineated in considerable detail by a distinguished historian, William E. Unrau, in *The Kansa Indians: A History of the Wind People, 1673–1873*. In this 1971 work, Professor Unrau presents an overview of the Kanza culture and thoroughly explicates the machinations of government policy, powerful economic forces, and land-hungry frontiersmen in usurping the Kanza's land. In his *The Kaw People*, published four years later, Unrau sketches the Neosho reservation period while presenting the Kanza view of the tribe's history from the time of European contact through the early 1970s. Relations between the mostly white community of Council Grove and the Kanzas are briefly and crudely rendered in two books reprinted by the Morris County [Kansas] Historical Society. Still sold in Council Grove retail stores as of 2013, the books are *The History of Morris County*, a compilation of a series of articles written by Council Grove newspaperman John Maloy from the mid-1870s through 1890, and *The Story of Council Grove on the Santa Fe Trail*, by Lalla Maloy Brigham, published in 1921.

These works provide important material. However, they leave implicit something I seek to make explicit in this book, and that is the importance of place. A foundational theme of this story is the dynamic interaction between the weather, plants, animals, waters, and landforms of the Kanza homeland (now northeastern and central Kansas) and its human inhabitants. In 2003, Australian environmentalist and philosopher Glenn Albrecht introduced the term *solastalgia* to describe the psychological illness experienced by humans who, while living in their homeland, witness its physical desolation. The Kanzas' prairie homeland was plowed, game disappeared, ancestor's graves were violated, and groves were cut down. Seeing this—seeing grass overgrazed, holy sites desecrated, their freedom of motion constricted, the Kanzas' *solacium* ("comfort or consolation") derived from the emotional and spiritual bond with their land was replaced with *algia*—"pain, suffering, or sickness."[4]

In May 1871, Kanza head chief Allegawaho pronounced that moment "the darkest period in our history." As one feature after another of the tribe's cultural landscape was damaged or destroyed by an aggressive Euro-American civilization hell-bent on "improving" the land, the attendant psychological debilitation enfeebled the physical health of the tribe. When the Kanzas came to the Neosho reservation in 1847, the tribe numbered sixteen hundred; when they left twenty-six years later there were fewer than six hundred. Speaking at the Kaw Mission in Council Grove in 1996, one of the tribe's last remaining "full-bloods" at that time, Johnny Rae McCauley, provided an eloquent, heart-felt diagnosis of his ancestors' malaise: "They died of a broken heart; they died of a broken spirit."[5]

Although during this period the health and vitality of the tribe were badly damaged through contact with powerful and mostly corrosive Euro-American forces, the complete Kanza story should not be reduced to a study of how hapless Indian victims were traduced by the juggernaut of industrial civilization. For, while government neglect, white encroachment, disease, the ambitions of a burgeoning Council Grove, environmental deterioration, and other forces inimical to the tribe's well-being exerted enormous pressure on tribal cohesion, the Kanzas persisted in their struggle to exercise political autonomy while maintaining traditional social customs and subsistence strategies up to the time of their removal to Indian Territory in 1873. On the level of the public record, this resistance is evident in the statements of Kanza chiefs, most prominently Ishtalasea and Allegawaho, who sought to bend government policy to serve the best interests of their people by means of treaty negotiations, letters, councils with government officials, and speeches.

"Frontiers are messy," wrote historian Elliott West, "and so are their legacies." West's "messy" implies complexity, and understanding that complexity requires looking at how nineteenth-century white Americans viewed themselves, which in turn shaped how they viewed the indigenous people they were supplanting. Two interrelated precepts that governed the attitudes and actions of Euro-Americans of all classes and regions in mid-nineteenth century America were the doctrine of Manifest Destiny and the deeply ingrained notion of white racial supremacy. Coined in 1845, the phrase "Manifest Destiny" expressed the conviction that God wanted white Americans to go forth in conquest of the American West. The pervasive and profoundly racist beliefs implicit in this doctrine found expression in the multivalent forms of violence Euro-Americans inflicted on the Kanzas and their homeland during the tribe's occupancy of the Neosho reservation. "Events in Kansas suggest that although settlers may have battled over the status of African Americans," writes Kristen Tegtmeier Oertel in her *Bleeding Borders: Race, Gender and Violence in Pre-Civil War Kansas*, "they simultaneously united on the ground of white supremacy over Indians."[6]

Dehumanization of despised "Others" and blindness to Others' humanity are endemic to the practice of racism in any time or place. As this book will demonstrate, the historical record is chock-full of commentary relegating the Kanzas to a position abysmally inferior to white Americans. This relentless dehumanizing of the Kanzas in the third quarter of the nineteenth century challenges us today to confront our own messy legacy. We cannot alter the events of the past, but we can, to the best of our ability, come to know stories that tell what really happened. To that end, the vignette of the young mother and her children crossing the Neosho River in the early 1850s is emblematic of the purpose of this book: a necessary reenvisioning of the Kanza people of that time as valued companions in our deeply flawed human journey.

CHAPTER 1

A New Home for the Kanzas

When the ten men reached the confluence of the Smoky Hill and Republican Rivers, the six Kanzas of the exploring party became apprehensive. Despite the warm June nights, the Indians slept with their leggings and moccasins on and tied their horses at their heads to be ready to run while others kept an overnight watch. In 1847 white people called this place—known today as Junction City, Kansas—Grand Point. The Kanza Indians knew it as Minghoci Oizkanka, or "The Fork Where the Ducks Dwell." A few days before, Kanza scouts had spotted their powerful enemies, the Comanches, near Minghoci Oizkanka. The Kanzas told the party's leader, U.S. Indian agent Richard W. Cummins, that they did not wish to go farther west. Recent events validated the Indians' fears. The previous July the Comanches and Kanzas had battled near the Pawnee Fork (west of present-day Larned, Kansas), both tribes suffering heavy losses. Cummins insisted that the little expedition push farther out into the plains. If detected they would have been cut off easily by the Comanches, although Cummins thought at least some of the Kanzas could have escaped. Not far west of Grand Point, the agent concluded that it was too dangerous to proceed any farther and ordered a halt. After another deliberation, the anxious men retreated east down the Kansas River valley.[1]

The mission of the little expedition was to reconnoiter the proposed new homesite for the Kanzas in the vicinity of present-day Minneapolis, Kansas. To get there, they traversed on horseback a vast

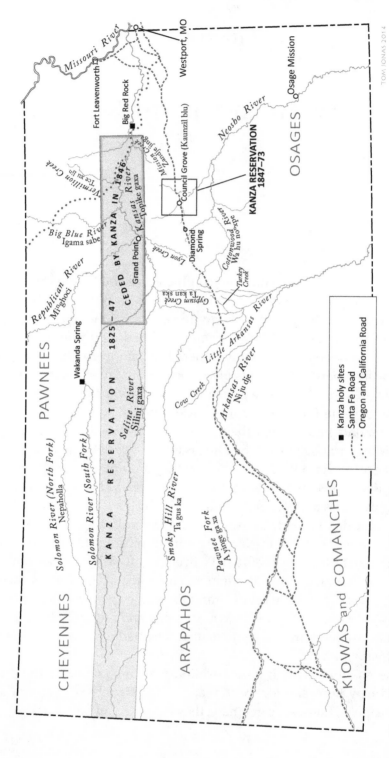

Kanza Homeland, 1847. © 2014, University of Oklahoma Press.

Map labels:

Missouri River

Westport, MO

Osage Mission

OSAGES

Neosho River

Fort Leavenworth

Big Red Rock

Mission Creek Zintke juñe

Council Grove (Kaunzil blu)

KANZA RESERVATION 1847–73

Vermillion Creek Tce xu lin

CEDED BY KANZA IN 1846

Kansas River

Topike gaxa

Big Blue River Igama sabe

Grand Point

Lyon Creek

Diamond Spring

Cottonwood River Wa hu no xpe

Republican River Mi'nghoci

Gypsum Creek Ta kan ska

Turkey Creek

PAWNEES

Wakanda Spring

KANZA RESERVATION 1825–47

Little Arkansas River

Arkansas River Ni ju dje

Saline River Silimi gaxa

Cow Creek

Solomon River (North Fork) Nepaholla

Solomon River (South Fork)

Smoky Hill River Ta gus ka

Pawnee Fork A'yinge gaxa

CHEYENNES

ARAPAHOS

KIOWAS and COMANCHES

Legend:
■ Kanza holy sites
--- Santa Fe Road
··· Oregon and California Road

TOM JONAS 2014

10

grassland expanse over a rolling terrain to about 150 miles west of present-day Kansas City. Here, flanked by a broad, tall grass–covered valley floor, the Solomon River, known by the Kanzas as the Nepaholla, snaked its way from the northwest to the southeast across the prairie landscape. In June 1847, two decades before the arrival of the plow, these grasslands were resplendently green—a new growth of bluestem, Indian grass, and switchgrass mixed with shorter grasses sprinkled profusely with wildflowers, all having been nurtured by a moisture-laden winter of abundant snowfall.[2]

The party had reluctantly probed west up the Kansas River valley because the treaty signed by U.S. commissioners and Kanza chiefs on January 14, 1846, required an assessment of "a sufficiency of timber" in this area. If Cummins's party found a supply of hardwood timber adequate to support the Kanzas in farming, the government would assist the Indians in establishing permanent villages there. Under the treaty scenario, the tribe was to abandon its villages in the Kansas River valley between present-day Wamego and Topeka, and move about one hundred miles west to the Solomon. In their new homes the Indians would continue their traditional forms of subsistence, hunting bison on the adjoining plains and raising corn and other vegetables in the stream bottoms, while nearby groves of oak and walnut would supply sturdy timber for rail fences to protect their fields from marauding livestock. Here, under the protective and benign guidance of an Indian agent, the tribe would be supported by federal financial and infrastructural assistance. Under the tutelage of government hirelings, Kanza children would attend school while Kanza adults learned modern agricultural practices. As the bison herds disappeared, agriculture would supplant the hunt, confinement would replace mobility, and civilization would supersede "savagery."[3] The underpinnings of the government's reservation policy were articulated by the commissioner of Indian Affairs, Luke Lea, in 1850. Filled with "haughty pride," as Lea put it, the Indians considered labor degrading and cared only for war, the hunt, and eloquence in council. In response, the government should subdue the "wild energies" of its untutored wards and train them, Lea said, "to the more ennobling pursuits of civilized life" by means of confinement and control until the Indians were "compelled by sheer necessity to resort to agricultural labor or starve." To this end, each tribe should be assigned a permanent home of limited extent that was well adapted to agriculture, and here the tribe "should be compelled constantly to remain" until it demonstrated improvement.[4]

Implicit in Lea's statement are assumptions shared uncritically by almost all policy makers and many members of the general public in the mid-nineteenth-century United States. Civilizations existed within a hierarchical "chain of being," with white Christians at the apex and others arranged at various lower positions. As an enlightened people, Euro-Americans bore the responsibility of guiding the benighted "savages" into the "ennobling pursuit of civilized life" before the oncoming tide of white immigration destroyed them. Obviously, due to their ignorance, racial inferiority, and overweening pride, the Indians could not govern themselves. Therefore, the U.S. government, in order to fulfill its altruistic aim of elevating its misguided, undisciplined, and childlike charges, would have to resort to compulsion. Above all, it was necessary to confine the wandering tribes. Once fixed into place, the Indians could no longer elude the administration of civilizing agents such as government-funded bureaucrats, teachers, missionaries, tradesmen, and farmers. The installation of Euro-American ways into the hearts and minds of the Indians would dissipate primitive beliefs and customs, and Indians would assimilate into the dominant society as educated, property-owning, Christian tillers of the soil.[5]

What the Kanzas or other Native people thought of this program designed for their "improvement" was of little consequence to policy makers. Fortunately for our purposes, a record exists of an unidentified Kanza chief stating the advantages of Indian life over Euro-American while addressing U.S. military officers in 1818. Though the translation of the chief's talk is laden with the conventional expressions of the Romantic Age, the Kanza speaker addresses the issues of confinement and compulsion, illuminates for his audience the limits of the chiefs' authority, and conveys why the disciplined Euro-American way of life is so unappealing to him:

> Father—your young men are prescribed within certain bounds. Not one of them can pass that chain of sentinels without your permission. Thus

ever within your power you govern them with ease. But my warriors[,] impatient of restraint as the wild horse in the toils of the hunter, brook no controul. Free as the air which they breathe, light and impetuous as the Antelope, they bound Mountains and moor in pursuit of pleasure which nature has ordained they should enjoy. To confine them to one vally would deprive them of their subsistence; they would pine and die in penury and want.

. . . Should we then who are Lords of the Forests quit the pleasures and the adventures of the hunt, and like you, confine ourselves to one solitary valley, to practice discipline and subordination . . . No, father.[6]

Seven years later, in 1825, Kanza chiefs journeyed to St. Louis where in the office of Superintendent of Indian Affairs William Clark they signed a treaty establishing the tribe's first reservation: a thirty-mile-wide tract extending from near present-day Topeka about three hundred miles west to the headwaters of the Smoky Hill River, a point about forty miles inside modern-day Colorado's eastern border. The reservation would be home to about sixteen hundred Kanzas. The eastern one-third of this reservation—two million acres of rich and productive Kansas River valley land—would be ceded by the Kanzas to the United States in the treaty of 1846.

The Kanzas had compelling reasons to reduce the size of their reservation. On January 23, 1844, the two principal Kanza leaders, Hard Chief and Fool Chief, wrote a letter addressed to "My Father" stating the tribe's willingness to sell a forty-five-mile-long section on the east end of the reservation. On a modern map of Kansas, this segment of the reservation extends from Topeka to near Manhattan. Describing their tribe as "very poor and needy," the chiefs said their tribe's next annuity payment—$3,500 as stipulated by the 1825 treaty—would be their last, and $1,500 of this would go to cover debts owed to their trader, Frederick Chouteau. The Kanzas ordinarily paid their traders' debts with robes upon returning from a hunt, but the winter hunt of 1843–44 had been unsuccessful. Poverty and debt created an urgency to generate cash, and the fastest way was to sell tribal land. The chiefs' asking price was $61,000.[7]

The tribe's predicament was compounded by one of the most horrific floods in Kansas history in the summer of 1844. Kanza women farmed plots of corn, potatoes, beans, melons, and other vegetables on the bottomlands of the Kansas River. That summer the valley overflowed from bluff to bluff, the flood sweeping off all of the Indians' fencing, houses, and crops. Another flood in late spring the next year destroyed the Kanzas' early crops. Later that summer sickness struck the villages, killing about two hundred people, two-thirds of them children. At the same time a disease, characterized by swelling under the chest, killed many of the tribe's horses and area deer and raccoons. Reeling from these disastrous events, the Kanza chiefs assembled on January 14, 1846, at Mission Creek just west of present-day Topeka were eager to make a deal.[8]

Sitting across the table from the chiefs were the two Indian Office bureaucrats who drafted the treaty document: Kanza agent Cummins and his St. Louis–based supervisor, Superintendent of Indian Affairs Thomas Harvey. Nineteen Kanza chiefs and headmen signed the treaty, the order of signature indicating hierarchical status. The first Kanza listed was Kihigawahchuffe, or Hard Chief, the principal chief of the tribe. Among the signatures appearing on the 1846 treaty document were those of men who were to play prominent roles in the tribe's future, Ishtalasea and Seth Hays. The fourth Kanza listed, Ishtalasea, or Speckled Eyes, would succeed Hard Chief, and Hays, one of the eight witnesses to sign the document, would soon operate a trading post at Council Grove.[9]

Two million acres, the 104-mile-long eastern section of the reservation, were ceded to the United States effective May 1, 1847, at the rate of ten cents per acre. In exchange, the Kanzas received eight thousand dollars each year in the form of "annuities," interest payments on the initial payment of $202,000. Other treaty provisions required the government to spend annually one thousand dollars on the tribe for education and one thousand dollars for agricultural assistance. Additionally, the Indian Office would erect a mill near the new Kanza villages, provide a blacksmith, and send a sub-agent to reside among the Kanzas and oversee the tribe's farming operations and "general improvement."[10]

The sticking point in negotiations was where to relocate the tribe. It was presumed that the Kanzas would establish their villages near the eastern boundary of their newly truncated reserve, the same locale the Cummins party was supposed to survey to determine sufficiency of timber. But the Kanzas would not settle this area for the same reason that Cummins had not reconnoitered it: doing so would have delivered the overmatched tribe into the jaws of their implacable enemies. Not just the Comanches, but more prominently the Pawnees and Cheyennes, powerful tribes hostile to the Kanzas, contested this area as their bison hunting grounds.[11]

The U.S. government could not fulfill its treaty obligations in 1847 because it could not protect the Kanzas at the proposed place of re-settlement. The new eastern margin of the reservation was over 140 miles from the nearest military post, Fort Leavenworth. Coauthor of the treaty Richard Cummins summed up why his own plan would not work: "The Camanches & the Pawanees, to say nothing about other tribes, have been at war with the Kansas for a long time. Either of these tribes greatly out number the Kansas, the country left them by their session is occupied a portion of almost every year by these tribes, particularly by the Pawanees [and] without constant protec-tion the Kansas could not live their." The proposed Kanza home-land was virtually unexplored by Americans. At that time no viable wagon road extended from present-day Kansas City to the Solomon River valley, and such a road would have been necessary to effect communication and supply linkage between the Office of Indian Affairs and its Kanza charges. Finally, Indian Office officials never addressed the imposing, if not impossible, task of securing, then retaining the required agent, blacksmith, farmer, and missionary/teacher for deployment at this isolated and precarious post.[12]

When discussing the proposed treaty, the Kanza chiefs protested that "they could not live on the Kansas River or its watters, any where west of the Grand point," because there was no timber there "except cotton wood & some very short scattering timber of other kinds." In response, Cummins and Harvey inserted into article five of the treaty this qualifier: "the President of the United States shall be satisfied that there is not a sufficiency of timber, he shall cause to be selected and laid off for the Kansas a suitable country, near the west-ern boundary of the land ceded by this treaty, which *shall remain for their use forever*" [my italics]. In fact, in the area proposed for Kanza resettlement, today's Ottawa and Lincoln Counties, the banks of the

Solomon River and its tributaries, including Salt and Pipe Creeks, were timbered with scattered groves of hardwoods such as bur oak and walnut. Government officials did not know this, but the Indians did, having hunted here for generations.[13]

During the summer of 1847, Cummins investigated at least two more alternative reservation locations: the country adjacent to the western boundary of the Shawnee Reservation in present eastern Dickinson County and the divide between the Kansas and upper Neosho valleys in present northern Morris and southern Geary Counties. Both locations, the Kanza agent declared, lacked sufficient timber for agricultural purposes. What then, to do? "I then examined," wrote Cummins, "the country known as the Council Grove on the head waters of the Neosho."[14]

Although their villages had been situated in the Kansas River valley since at least the late eighteenth century, the Kanzas had long maintained hunting camps in the Council Grove area and near the Santa Fe Road in present eastern and central Kansas. In 1807, explorer Zebulon Pike was informed by his Indian guides that he was entering Kanza hunting territory when approaching the Cottonwood River, about forty miles southwest of Council Grove. In early August 1825, U.S. official George C. Sibley intended to meet with Kanza chiefs at Council Grove, but as the tribe was hunting bison to the west, his party parleyed with Kanza chiefs a few days later on Turkey Creek near present-day McPherson, Kansas, seventy miles west of Council Grove. At this time the Kanzas, as had their Osage allies a few days before in Council Grove, signed a treaty guaranteeing safe passage for wagon trains and providing a right of way to Santa Fe in exchange for eight hundred dollars worth of cash and merchandise.[15]

Throughout the 1830s and early 1840s, travelers on the Santa Fe Trail reported friendly encounters with the tribe in that vicinity. One afternoon in late November 1845, a small group of Kanza men rode into a camp of freighters at the Big John Creek crossing of the Santa Fe Road two miles east of Council Grove. The Indians invited James Josiah Webb and companions to visit their village two or three miles downstream. Here a "swap" would take place, Webb trading a blanket coveted by one of the Kanzas for a pail full of honey. The next morning the freighters enjoyed a sweet breakfast in a Kanza lodge, dipping a spoon fashioned from part of a buffalo horn into a wooden bowl filled with honey, and passing the spoon back and forth "Indian fashion." Afterward, one of the Kanzas warmed a honey-filled rawhide bag in front of the fire, occasionally kneading it, then filled a pail to be carried on horseback to the Big John Creek campsite, where that evening Webb once again indulged in copious amounts of honey, in consequence suffering a stupendous bellyache.[16]

The tribe suffered intensely during the two-year interim between signing the Mission Creek treaty in January 1846 and their final relocation to Council Grove, a period when they were essentially homeless. Described by their agent as "very poor and indigent," Kanza bands scattered across the territory, a long-established survival strategy employed in times of extreme need. In early February 1846, some of the tribe arrived at their Fort Leavenworth Agency (located four miles west of Westport, Missouri, just inside the present Johnson County line) in a destitute condition. According to Cummins, the Kanzas had "nothing to eat, and were the most greedy people for provisions I ever saw, the little meat I gave them only served to make them howl and beg for more; it was painful to my feelings that I could not give them enough to do them some good." Anticipating that the Indians would be compelled to subsist on roots and the sap of trees, Cummins supplied the tribe with 1,818 bushels of corn, 2,513 pounds of bacon, and 466 pounds of fresh pork. The desperate Kanzas brought bags for provisions and as many horses and mules they could find, and left with as much corn as their animals could bear. Those men and women without pack animals departed with packs on their own backs. In late February Cummins reported some improvement in Kanza health and spirits. At about the same time, they visited their neighbors, the Sac and Fox Nation, who, seeing the Kanzas' distress, gave them about fifty guns, seventy horses, and a considerable quantity of clothing, blankets, household goods, and calico fabric.[17]

Many Euro-American writers heaped scorn on the Kanzas for the tribe's habit of wandering and begging. Traveling through Kansas in 1846, historian Francis Parkman described most Kanzas as beggars and "ragged vagabonds, with bad or vacant faces, and a very mean

Kanza family, sketch by George Catlin, 1832. Courtesy Kansas State Historical Society.

appearance." The Kanzas were a "filthy, lazy, thieving, worthless set of beings," Augustus Heslep wrote after camping at Council Grove in June 1849. Such contemptuous and racist judgments—and there were many—obscure a perception of the humanity of the Kanza. Begging was a means of survival for a hungry people unable to secure subsistence because their command of resources was rapidly dwindling. But perhaps more importantly, white Americans could not see that the Kanzas and other tribes behaved within a deeply seated cultural precept that embraced not only asking for assistance in times of need but also giving to needful others if they were not enemies.[18]

The hospitality of the Kanza is well documented. Their agent for almost a decade, Richard Cummins reflected on the tribe's deeply ingrained behavior: "I consider them the most hospitable Indians that I have any knowledge of. They never turn off hungry white or red, if they have anything to give them, and they continue to give as long as they have anything to give." Such generosity is given credence by no less a luminary than William Becknell, "father of the Santa Fe Trail." Returning in January 1822 from his historic trade expedition to Santa Fe, Becknell described the Kanzas as "hospitable." In February 1847, the Kanzas assisted two parties of white travelers incapacitated by severe weather. Having lost their mules, eight men headed by Thomas Boggs wandered the prairie "half frozen and nearly starved." They found their way into a Kanza village where two boys offered to guide them cross country to Fort Leavenworth. At about the same time, the Kanza found two "half starved and frozen" white men on the prairie and brought them into their village where the two rested and revived before being retrieved a few days later by an escort from Fort Leavenworth.[19]

In the summer of 1846, a large crop of corn was raised on 115 acres near the Kanza village on Mission Creek under the direction of a government-appointed farmer. After harvest, a portion of this corn was distributed to the tribe. On January 14, 1847, Cummins wrote to Harvey confirming the tribe's homeless status and reminding his supervisor that by May 1 the Kanzas "have to go some where." By late April the Kanzas' new reservation was still undetermined, and it was too late in the season to prepare new fields for planting. Cummins hastily advised the tribe to plant crops in their old Kansas River valley fields. At this time, Superintendent Harvey described the Kanza as "the most meek agreeable Indians in the superintendency." The 1847 crop was probably a failure, judging by the tribe's miserable condition the following winter. During the year, out of his own pocket Cummins purchased $333 worth of hoes for the Kanzas, only to discover in September that, in contradiction to the terms of the new treaty, no money had been appropriated for agricultural expenditures. On October 30, 1847, Cummins reported that of the tribes under his jurisdiction—Kanzas, Shawnees, Delawares, Kickapoos, Stockbridge Indians (Mahicans), Munsee Indians, and Christian Munsee people—all were doing well, "except the Kansas."[20]

By that time, as several eyewitnesses attest, some Kanza bands were already established on the Neosho River. It is plausible that some of the tribe, after waiting while the government dithered for almost two years about relocation, preemptively decided the question themselves, possibly with the tacit approval of Cummins and

Harvey, who had a contingency plan to relocate the Kanzas to the Neosho as early as July 1846. At that time—about one year before the Cummins party's expedition to the confluence of the Smoky Hill and Republican Rivers—Harvey suggested the possibility of placing the Kanzas on the upper Neosho where the tribe would be near their Osage allies and farther from their enemies, especially the Pawnees.[21]

A year later and well past the May 1, 1847, deadline set by the treaty, the problem of finding suitable land for the reservation remained unresolved. At this time the Indian Office officials finally took definitive action. Cummins and the Kanza chiefs examined the Council Grove area, finding a beautiful country, plenty of rocks and good water, and an abundance of hardwoods such as walnut, oak, hickory, and elm, suitable for their agricultural purposes. The Kanzas accompanying Cummins expressed a great desire to be located here.[22]

On August 11, 1847, Harvey explained to William Medill, then-commissioner of Indian Affairs, that by locating the Kanzas in the vicinity of Council Grove, the government would be spared the time and expense of building a fort to protect whites in that region. The superintendent then advised Cummins to establish the southern reservation boundary at least eight miles north of Council Grove to place the Kanzas "beyond the interruption of the whites passing on the road to New Mexico." Cummins ignored this directive because a reservation located eight miles north of the Santa Fe Road would overlap far into the Shawnee Reservation and, as he had previously reported, there was no timber in this area.[23]

The Kanza agent outlined the new reservation boundaries, encompassing four hundred square miles: "To commence at a point ten miles due north of the Trading house of Boon & Hamilton and the Government blacksmith shop, both of which are on the bank of council grove creek at the crossing of the santife road, from thence due west five miles, to corner, thence due south twenty miles to corner, thence due east twenty miles to corner, thence due north twenty miles to corner, thence due west fifteen miles to the place of beginning."[24]

On September 8, Superintendent Harvey endorsed his subordinate's selection, praised the upper Neosho region, and noted that the Kansas "after having sold a large portion of the best country on the Missouri should not be asked to receive as their *permanent home* [my emphasis] . . . any but what is good." On October 29, presumably having received no response from the authorities in Washington, D.C., Harvey desperately concluded a letter to Commissioner Medill: "<u>What Shall be done with the Kansas Indians?</u>"[25]

In November, the president of the United States, James Polk, accepted the proposed boundaries of the new Kanza Reservation recommended by Cummins, Harvey, and the Kanza chiefs. Finally the tribe's confused, prolonged, and painful move from the Kansas River was mercifully ending. But the Indians would not find the Neosho valley a secluded country in which to regroup and revitalize their culture and economy unfettered by outside influences. Instead, the Kanza came to live in a place irrupting with the energies of white people's commercial and imperial ambitions.

Prior to 1846, Council Grove was notable mainly as a "rendezvous point" on the Santa Fe Road where, guided by the principle of safety in numbers, smaller wagon trains were formed into larger caravans before proceeding west. Here amidst the extensive grove of hardwood timber, freighters prepared for the journey to come by organizing their caravans and repairing wagons and equipment. Men harvested logs of oak, walnut, and hickory, attaching them to the underside of wagons in anticipation of inevitable breakdowns. To replace broken axles, spokes, tongues, yokes, and other parts, the freighters required hardwood logs, none of which were available on the trail west of Council Grove, where only "softwood" trees grew, such as cottonwood, willow, and hackberry.[26]

Council Grove loomed large in the mind of trader and historian Josiah Gregg, who made several trips between Independence and Santa Fe in the 1830s. In his classic *Commerce of the Prairies*, Gregg lent this prophetic commentary about the future of Council Grove: "All who have traversed these delightful regions, look forward with anxiety to the day when the Indian title to the land shall be extinguished, and flourishing 'white' settlements dispel the gloom which at present prevails over this uninhabited region."[27]

Beginning in May 1846 and terminating February 1848, the Mexican-American War transformed both Council Grove and the

Santa Fe Road. Before the war, the eight-hundred-mile trail was an international route of commerce extending across the plains from western Missouri to Santa Fe. Both Anglo and Mexican freighters hauled merchandise, principally cloth, by means of wagon caravans southwest to Santa Fe. After 1830, most of these goods were shipped south to cities in the interior of Mexico. On the return trip east, freighters hauled donkeys, furs, and silver to markets in the United States. In 1843, 230 wagons and 350 men traveled westward on the route to Santa Fe, carrying a total of $450,000 in merchandise.[28]

When war commenced three years later, traffic on the road exploded. In November 1847, Quartermaster General Thomas Jessup reported that 459 horses, 3,658 mules, 14,904 oxen, 1,556 wagons, and 516 pack saddles had moved over the road to Santa Fe to supply the U.S. Army in the Southwest. In late July 1846, the Fort Leavenworth quartermaster sent two men to Council Grove to perform "such repairs as the wagoners, or troops might require." This blacksmith station was important to the functioning of this critical supply line because at the time it was the last permanent station for repairs until New Mexico. It also marked the beginning of the permanent U.S. occupation of Council Grove.[29]

When hostilities terminated in 1848, the United States had gained five hundred thousand square miles, or about one-half of Mexico's national territory. Following the cessation of war, the high volume of military-related trail traffic through Council Grove persisted, the wagon trains transporting men and supplies to the new forts protecting the vastly expanded U.S. territories in the Southwest. At the same time, commercial trade increased as merchants responded to the demand for goods in the burgeoning southwestern settlements. Indelibly linked by geography to these powerful economic and political forces unleashed by war, Council Grove had undergone a transformation.[30]

By late June 1847, six Euro-Americans inhabited Council Grove: a blacksmith, his wife and son, a wagon maker and repairer, and two Indian traders: Seth Hays and Charles Chouteau. The blacksmith, William H. Mitchell, had been the government-hired farmer for the Kanzas before assuming the blacksmith position for the tribe from 1846 through 1848. Mitchell's wife had lived among the Potawatomies for several years. Described as "sprightly and good-natured," Mrs. Mitchell spoke the Kanza language and was held in high esteem by the Indians. She was the first among several white women in the Council Grove area able to win the respect, if not affection, of their Kanza neighbors. By July 1847, twenty to thirty Kanza "wigwams" and three log houses had appeared in Council Grove. The Kanzas' "doleful songs at night disturbed my slumbers," lamented a soldier encamped at Council Grove that summer.[31]

The Kanzas experienced great difficulties during the winter of 1847–48. Bands of the tribe scattered throughout the Kansas River valley in January 1848. They were returning from the fall hunt and had no corn. The previous spring the women had been late in planting the crops because at that time the government still had no place for them to go. Now the Kanzas headed toward the Shawnee, Delaware, and Ottawa reservations and nearby white settlements to beg for provisions. The Kanzas told Superintendent Harvey that they were anxious to go to work in their new country but could not do so without subsistence. In February most of the tribe congregated in Westport where their new agent, Solomon Sublette, issued six pounds of bacon and one-half bushel of corn to each individual. Harvey encouraged the Kanzas to go to the new reservation on the Neosho, plant and cultivate their corn, then go to the buffalo country (in present central Kansas) as soon as they could.[32]

When encamped at Council Grove on May 23, 1848, Lieutenant George Gibson and his men were visited by several Kanzas. At the end of the visit, the soldiers gave the Kanzas all of their spare coffee. It had been twenty-two months since Gibson's unit had passed through Council Grove en route to the Mexican campaign. Gibson observed that the settlement had changed greatly, writing that "[it] now presents a novel appearance to men from Mexico with its Log Cabins and Rail Fences and is an important point to Travellers." A few miles east of Council Grove, Gibson met a large number of Kanzas whose provisions were packed on their animals.[33]

In 1849, Council Grove witnessed an influx of a new kind of emigrant, the gold seekers who would become known as "49ers." Between April and September 1849, an estimated twenty-five hundred emigrants left western Missouri for the California goldfields via the

Santa Fe road. Other gold seekers came up the Neosho valley from the Fort Scott area, turning west when intersecting the trail at Council Grove. One member of a party that had stopped to secure timber for wagon repairs praised Council Grove as "an oasis in the wilderness." He noted that although Council Grove was in Indian country and was the "headquarters" of the Kanzas, the white inhabitants of the six houses and three or four shops lived in safety and comfort. The large number of travelers proceeding west on the trail, and their propensity to slaughter buffalo and other game, dismayed plains tribes such as the Cheyennes.[34]

Stimulated by the 1849 gold rush, a monthly stage in May began to operate from Independence, Missouri, to California via Santa Fe. Consequences for Council Grove were immediate. The mail contractors established a station at Council Grove, staffed by a blacksmith and men to cut and cure hay. The new establishment brought more provisions, animals, and grain, and an attendant farming operation. These developments brought more Euro-Americans. Stationed in Council Grove in September 1849 were fourteen men employed by three merchant outfits licensed to trade with the Kanzas. Among the "employed" were African American slaves.[35]

In three years Council Grove transformed from a campsite to a settlement. No longer "nothing more than a grove of timber," it had become a vital outlier of the advancing frontier, its beginnings not coincidentally intersecting with the burgeoning of trail traffic and arrival of the Kanzas. In transitioning from a rendezvous point to a trade center, Council Grove afforded both whites and Indians not only a commercial venue, but also a stage on which events during the ensuing twenty-five years would shape the destiny of the Kanza people.

In the meantime, the Kanzas were engaged in matters of both peace and war. In October 1848, ten tribes convened a council on the Delaware Reservation near Fort Leavenworth. Seven of these tribes—Delaware, Shawnee, Miami, Wyandot, Potawatomie, Ottawa, and Chippewa people—were members of the "Northwestern Confederacy," an alliance organized at least a century before, when these "emigrant tribes" still occupied their homelands in the region east of the Mississippi and north of the Ohio River. Between 1825 and 1845 these tribes and others were relocated at the behest of the

U.S. government to present-day eastern Kansas, then part of the region known as Indian Territory. The Kanzas accepted an invitation to join the confederacy and spent the first night of the week-long council "in a bustle, making preparations for a grand dance." In council, the Indians considered the best measures for promoting peace among themselves and discussed the efforts underway in the U.S. Congress to organize Nebraska Territory, an area that included all the tribes' reservations. The tribes were fully aware that the government's conferring territorial status on an area was tantamount to its ensuing settlement. A government official who witnessed the congress was impressed with the "the social and friendly feeling exhibited amongst the people there congregated, the enjoyment of the dance, and the great numbers engaged in them."[36]

That same year a moment of prospective peace turned suddenly into war. In July 1848, a large band of Kanzas hunting bison on a tributary of the Kansas River were joined by smaller parties of Sacs, Potawatomies, and Kickapoos. All was well until a Pawnee hunting party showed up. The outnumbered Pawnees sent a messenger offering the pipe of peace. Reciprocating the overture, Keokuk, chief of the Sacs, was handing the pipe back to the Pawnees when a Kanza fired, and a Pawnee fell dead. A fight immediately erupted during which at least five Pawnees were killed and scalped.[37]

The Pawnees and the Kanzas had been bitter enemies for longer than anyone could remember. From the sixteenth century, if not earlier, the diverse ancestors of the Pawnees had lived and hunted in present-day Nebraska and Kansas. The Kanzas had migrated from the Midwest, and by the early 1700s they were established on the west bank of the Missouri River in present Doniphan County, Kansas. The dominant power on the central plains by the early nineteenth century, the Pawnees were the larger of the two tribes, with a population of 6,244 in 1840, according to the Office of Indian Affairs, compared to a Kanza count of 1,588 in 1843. The tribes contested the prime bison hunting grounds on the Smoky Hill, Saline, Solomon, and Republican Rivers in present north-central and central Kansas. For the first six decades of the nineteenth century, the essence of the Pawnee-Kanza relationship was relentless warfare, interrupted by short-lived peace agreements.[38]

Fueling the conflict were cultures that encouraged the young men of both tribes in the practice of warfare. Those warriors demonstrating courage in battle and stealing horses from the enemy won honors and gained status in their tribe. The Pawnees were especially renowned and feared as exceptional horse thieves. Their victims, including the Kanzas, designated them "snakes in the grass." They were said to be able to sneak up, cut the rope by which a Kanza was holding his pony, mount the steed, and ride away. Enemy tribes suspected them of practicing sorcery, their medicine making the nights darker, bringing storms, putting guards to sleep, and frightening horses. In fact, Pawnee "doctors" were said to be advanced in hypnosis and other forms of mind control.[39]

A Kanza fighter, Necaquebana, was said to have run down and killed eighteen Pawnees with a knife at different times. When Necaquebana returned from a raid on the Pawnees, he would drive a herd of stolen horses before him. One time he rode into the Kanza villages with 150 stolen horses, promptly distributing them to chiefs Hard Chief, Fool Chief, and Broken Thigh. Vengeance was a pervasive motivation for both tribes. When his brother Sans Oreilles was killed by the Pawnees, Hard Chief commanded his warriors to attack the Pawnees and not return until they had taken one hundred scalps. Led by Hard Chief's brothers, the war party returned a few weeks later bearing only one scalp. The indignant Hard Chief ordered the party to go out again, exclaiming, "[D]o not stop until you have got 100 scalps!"[40]

One of the most noted Kanza men was Wahobake, his name meaning "carries the sacred bundle on his back." He was chosen by his band to carry the medicine bundle on war and hunting expeditions, an exalted position requiring the bearer to be in good standing with Wakanda, the all-powerful divinity animating the universe, as the bundle's powerful medicine brought success in the hunt and war. One time when on a bison hunt Wahobake went alone to a creek to bathe. There two Pawnees surprised him, each shooting him with .32 caliber bullets. He fell into the water and floated downstream. His assailants waded in after him and clubbed him. A blow on his head brought him back to consciousness, at which point he sprang to his feet, startling the Pawnees, who fled in a panic, leaving Wahobake's

INDIAN RECORD of a Battle between the PAWNEES and KONZAS delineated on a BISON ROBE.

Sketch by Titian Ramsay Peale of a Pawnee bison robe painting of a Pawnee-Kanza battle that occurred sometime prior to 1819. While approaching a Pawnee village, a raiding party of eighteen Kanzas was discovered by a larger band of mounted Pawnees. All of the Kanzas were killed. Courtesy Kansas State Historical Society.

horse behind. Seriously wounded, he mounted his horse and rode back to the Kanza hunting camp where he fell to the ground exhausted. Eventually Wahobake was brought back to Fool Chief's village, where he lay in his lodge near death for a long time. Assuming he was about to die, Wahobake asked to ride his favorite hunting horse one more time, and so it was brought to his lodge. He was so weak and emaciated that he could not sit unsupported, so his friends strapped his legs under the horse's belly and tied him onto the saddle. With little or no guidance from its unresponsive rider, his pony began to race across the prairie, agitating Wahobake's body, bursting an abscess caused by his wounds. The discharge apparently released toxins from his system. Returning to his lodge, he immediately began to recover and within days his health was fully restored.[41]

Raiding their enemies was a way the Kanzas propitiated Wakanda. A displeased Wakanda could visit misfortune upon the tribe in the form of death of relatives, scarcity of game, failure of crops, or defeat in battle. In 1839, missionary William Johnson witnessed the Kanzas preparing to send a war party consisting of nearly every warrior in the tribe against the Pawnees. "They must shed blood or commit depredations upon some other tribe, as a satisfaction for the loss which the Great Spirit has caused them to sustain," Johnson wrote. This warfare had strategic consequences. In the early 1830s repeated attacks by the Kanzas and their Osage allies forced the Kitkehahki band, one of the four Pawnee bands, to abandon its village in the Republican River basin and to rejoin the other Pawnee bands north in present-day Nebraska. Recently scholars have debunked the notion that nineteenth-century Plains Indian wars consisted mostly of bloodless jousts between warriors exhibiting their battlefield derring-do by such acts as counting coup. Instead it has been characterized as a "bloody street fight for survival" pitting tribes desperately competing for hunting grounds and dwindling resources.[42]

A brief summary of hostilities in the 1840s conveys the ferocity of the intertribal conflict. In June 1840, the Pawnees stole sixty horses from a Kanza hunting camp near the Arkansas River. That December a war party of sixty-five Kanzas fell upon an undefended Pawnee village, its warriors absent on a hunt. The assailants killed and scalped over seventy women and children and three men, burned the village, took eleven prisoners, and stole ten horses. After returning to their villages on the Kansas River, the tribe suspended all other activities while, according to William Johnson, the Kanzas, in their elation, did "little else but dance." Thereafter the missionary made little headway in educating and Christianizing his charges, who, besides dancing, became preoccupied with the anticipated Pawnee reprisal. His effort to reform the tribe, Johnson wrote, "is truly gloomy at present." In spring 1842, the Pawnees attacked and burned the vacant village of Hard Chief on Vermillion Creek near present-day Belvue, Kansas. In both June 1843 and September 1844, Oregon Trail migrants in eastern Kansas met war parties of Kanzas returning south from fights with the Pawnees. In May 1846, the Pawnees attacked the Kanzas, killing several and burning one of their villages. In 1849, Kanza warriors seized a Pawnee girl who was riding in a carriage of white persons on the Oregon Trail, then butchered her in front of the horrified passengers.[43]

Violence between these tribes continued after the Kanzas' removal to the Neosho reservation. The Pawnee made as many as a dozen horse-stealing raids on the Kanzas and nearby whites, some with disastrous consequences for the failed thieves. In 1860, a Pawnee attempting to steal horses from a Kanza encampment on the Smoky Hill River near present-day Enterprise, Kansas, was discovered and killed. The subsequent celebratory dance was witnessed by a large crowd of whites, one of whom supplied whiskey to the Kanza celebrants. In 1859, a Pawnee man was wounded while attempting to steal horses from a white farmer in what is now southwest Wabaunsee County, Kansas. The farmer, thinking the incapacitated Indian lying in a haystack was a Kanza, sent word to the latter tribe that they should come to reclaim one of their own. When about thirty Kanza warriors showed up, they swiftly dispelled any confusion about the wounded man's tribe by scalping him alive and leaving him to die a lingering death. Outraged, the farmer caught up with the Kanza party and demanded that they return to put the man out of his misery. They obliged by cutting the Pawnee's throat. Then they tied the corpse to the tail of a wild pony, pricked the animal with their spears to provoke it into a fast run, then celebrated as it bolted across the stony prairie, strewing pieces of flesh in its wake. Finally, the Kanzas used the victim's skull as a football.[44]

The point in recounting the grisly details of this encounter is to add one more layer to the complex texture inherent in the story of the Kanzas and their homeland. To understand that this tribe could be both exceedingly generous and kind to suffering wayfarers and brutal, if not sadistic, to their enemies is to shatter the old reductive, dehumanizing myths of Indians as essentially either savage or noble. Under varying circumstances, the Kanzas manifested behaviors that could be accurately characterized as savage or noble. "However cruel they may be to their foes," wrote Father Pierre De Smet, "the Kansas are no strangers to the tenderest sentiments of piety, friendship and compassion."[45]

Superintendent Harvey described the Kanzas as "the most docile Indians of my acquaintance" soon after the tribe was situated on the upper Neosho reservation. At this time, administrators in the Office of Indian Affairs praised the Kanzas for orderly conduct and confidently predicted that the Indians would protect the whites wherever they met on the plains. In October 1848, agent James S. Rains reported that the Kanzas were anxious for a farmer and a missionary to arrive and had assured Rains of their intention of working like their white neighbors. According to the agent, the Kanzas "wanted their children to learn to read and write, and to work like white men, and not live, as their parents are, like wolves." In his 1848 annual report, Commissioner Medill credited the tribe for the commendable way they had removed themselves "from their old country on the Kanzas river" and settled in their new "better location."[46]

Optimistic reports replete with self-congratulation and wishful thinking have always been standard fare for bureaucrats trying to look good. In fact, the Indian Office had failed to fulfill its treaty obligation to place a sub-agent on the new reservation to look after Kanza interests. Indeed, the government had neglected to provide an escort to guide the tribe in determining where to establish their villages on the upper Neosho. When Superintendent Harvey was confronted near Westport with desperate Kanzas beseeching him for assistance, the best he could do was to counsel them to go to the Neosho reservation, plant corn, and head west to hunt bison. With the exception of distributing small amounts of food to the tribe, most officials held themselves emotionally and geographically aloof from the grim reality the Indians faced.

Years of homelessness, government neglect, and disease had taken a toll. In September 1845, agent Cummins reported the tribe's population at 1,607. At the time, Cummins described the Kanzas as "very poor," but he also characterized them as "a stout, active lively people" who had more children proportionately than any other tribe he knew. In October 1849, the Kanza population, as counted by the tribe's new agent, Charles Handy, stood at 1,300, which, if accurate, would have meant a 19 percent decline. There were other ominous signs. The tribe Harvey described a year earlier as "the most docile" was by October1849, becoming, in the government's view, "trouble-some." The Kanzas were accused of acts of theft and plunder and of passing themselves off for Pawnees while committing depredations upon the whites. The small enclave of white people in Council Grove, having been subject to Kanza threats, was "in a state of much uneasi-ness." While acknowledging that the Kanzas were still friendly and respectful to him, agent Charles Handy judged it imprudent to go to the Kanza Reservation to compel the Indians "to do right" unless backed by a sufficient military force. Apprehensions were also felt by Santa Fe Trail travelers. One 49er who passed through Council Grove described the Kanzas as "a great pest to a camp in their vi-cinity," saying that "constant vigilance is necessary for the safety of your property."[47]

In May 1848, Superintendent Harvey went to Council Grove to distribute a one-half annuity payment of $4,000 to the Kanzas. While there, he learned that a Kanza had been assaulted by a white man attached to one of the Santa Fe wagon caravans. Harvey investi-gated and concluded that the white man had not been justified in striking the Indian. The owner of the train paid the Indian several dollars as compensation for his injuries. Before he departed, Harvey ordered the Kanzas not to visit the freighters' camps and instructed the freighters "to be careful in their conduct to the Indians." Such admonishments, of course, were to be ignored by both sides. In 1847, Harvey had wanted the new reservation to be located at least eight miles from Council Grove so the Kanzas would be "beyond the in-terruption of the whites passing on the road to New Mexico." This had not been possible, and now he had witnessed one of his worst apprehensions portending a future fraught with conflict between Euro-Americans and the Kanzas, a future not long in coming.[48]

The smoldering Kanza hostility of 1849 is best understood when viewed against a background of other developments. The govern-ment's plans to establish productive farms on the new reservation had not gone well. The capricious weather had not helped. Kansas was in the grip of a drought when in the spring of 1848 the Indian Office contracted with Pierre Chouteau to break and plant in corn three hundred acres of prairie on the new reservation. Chouteau's men arrived in Council Grove in early May with six heavy teams prepared to bust sod. No ground was broken, however, despite the ample animal power, on account of the ground being too dry.[49]

The drought yielded to heavy rains that summer, and grass and water on the Santa Fe Road were reported to be more abundant than within the recollection of the oldest traders. But the winter of 1848–49, the first experienced by the Kanzas in their new Neosho valley home, was ferocious in its severity. It arrived in October and got worse. Relentless cold and snowstorms in December caused havoc in eastern Kansas. For ten days in mid-December, temperatures were consistently below zero, on December 23 plummeting to minus twenty-nine degrees Fahrenheit. That month an estimated sixteen hundred oxen belonging to U.S. government trains perished on the Santa Fe Road east of Council Grove. The following spring, travelers passed "immense numbers" of dead oxen, and in some places as many as thirty skeletons lay in piles.[50]

A global climate phenomenon affected the local and seasonal weather. From roughly 1600 to 1850, the "Little Ice Age" lowered temperatures and elevated precipitation throughout the northern hemisphere. Among its consequences, some historians and biologists have theorized, was the explosion of the bison population on the Great Plains. After the mid-nineteenth century, more heat and less rain stressed plants, animals, and humans inhabiting the central plains. Local conditions accurately reflected the larger patterns. The summer of 1849 was dry, particularly along the Arkansas River. In October, grass had been entirely burned off along the Santa Fe Road from Council Grove eighty-five miles west to the Little Arkansas crossing. The winter of 1849–50 was normal, the following spring wet, but the next summer another tremendous drought withered the plains, lasting until the spring of 1851. In February 1851, the Kansas River was described as "about run dry."[51]

In April 1849, the government once again hired a contractor, this time Alexander Majors, to plow and plant three hundred acres for the Kanzas near Council Grove, paying Majors fifteen hundred dollars. However, whatever the Kanza produced on this acreage was subject to another drought and predation from transient whites. In a letter written at Council Grove on June 7, 1849, a journalist offered this assessment of his fellow travelers on the Santa Fe Road: "From the spirit of the emigrants, it is not to be wondered at that the Indians are hostile and treacherous. It is perfectly outrageous to see how the poor Indians' fences, chickens, pigs, sheep, corn, potatoes, onions, &c. are stripped from them without even saying 'by you[r] leave, if you please.'"[52]

This flurry of migration coincided with a horrific cholera outbreak on Missouri River steamboats and the overland trails in eastern Kansas and western Missouri. By May 1849, cholera was raging among white travelers on the Oregon Trail and Indians in the region. By mid-summer, over one hundred Kanzas had succumbed to the disease and died. In a study of cholera among Plains Indians, historians Ramon Powers and James N. Leiker found that the tribes living closest to the trails—such as the Kanzas—were the most devastated. Among the factors that reduced the tribe's resistance to cholera were the stresses of chronic malnutrition, geographic dislocation, chronic homelessness, poor sanitation, whiskey consumption, conflicts with whites, and other diseases. And the Indians' traditional response to epidemics—flight—meant that white migrants found Indian property easy pickings that summer in eastern Kansas.[53]

The Kanzas had no honeymoon period in their new home. Barely settled in, they already had been besieged by disease, bad weather, and hostile white people. The early optimistic reports of Indian Office officials were replaced by gloomy assessments. In September 1850, the Kanza agent, Handy, accused the tribe of committing many depredations on the Santa Fe Road, stealing horses from neighboring tribes, and becoming great whiskey drinkers and sellers. As for the three hundred acres of ground broken for them, he predicted "they will not till this land in future." These numerous and seemingly intractable problems hampered Indian Office efforts to impose its assimilation policy on the tribe. At the same time, the government and its religious allies were putting into place on the Neosho reservation an institution designed to overcome Kanza resistance to Christian civilization. In September 1850, the Methodist Episcopal Church South, chartered by the federal government, began to erect buildings on the west bank of the Neosho River in Council Grove. Kanza children were soon to have a school.[54]

*

The relocation of the Kanzas from the Kansas River valley to the Neosho reservation was a result of the federal government's policy of constricting the land holdings of the native tribes of Kansas, the impoverished tribe's dependence on the U.S. government, and the availability of natural resources in the upper Neosho valley. In addition, the government placed the Kanzas on the Neosho reservation in part because this location provided a buffer from the predations of their Pawnee, Cheyenne, and Comanche adversaries. Implied in this arrangement for the Kanzas was a precarious trade-off: less exposure to Indian enemies meant more contact with white people. The new reservation was bisected by the Santa Fe Road and contained the small trade settlement of Council Grove. The Kanzas' arrival coincided with the War with Mexico, an expression of Manifest Destiny that quickly transformed both the Santa Fe Road and Council Grove into dynamic features of a rapidly expanding Euro-American frontier. The Kanzas' arrival also intersected with a deadly cholera epidemic and the onset of hot, dry weather adverse to the practice of agriculture. The reservation rapidly became a cauldron of seething hostilities between the Kanzas and a Euro-American population steeped in the consciousness of white racial superiority. By 1850 this arrangement's downside was becoming readily apparent to all concerned.

CHAPTER 2

One of the Most Difficult Tribes

Picture the scene in autumn 1850 from the west bank of the Neosho River overlooking the Santa Fe Road ford. A large military supply train is moving southwest on the road to the newly acquired territories. As dozens of the wagons creak and rumble slowly past, men curse, bullwhips crack, oxen bawl, and mules snort and squeal. There's no escaping the dust; it gets into the eyes and nose and mouth and leaves a gritty film on hands and faces. Hundreds of fresh manure piles litter the road, baking and stinking in the sun. Below in the streambed, a narrow ribbon of water trickles over the flat, stony surface of the Neosho River crossing. For many weeks the country has been dry and hot. Across the Neosho to the east, hundreds of oak, hickory, and walnut trees stand tall. Over the past three decades men with axes and saws have nibbled at the famous grove, opening gaps here and there for their campsites and wagons and animals, but most of the huge forest canopy has survived intact, offering sun-weary travelers a respite of cool shade.

To the west is a tiny settlement with six houses and three "shops" scattered along both sides of the road. At the location of today's Farmers and Drovers Bank in Council Grove squats a crude log supply depot flanked by haystacks and a split-rail-fenced corral containing a dozen horses and mules. This is the Waldo & Hall mail station where each month one eastbound and one westbound eight-passenger, six-mule-drawn stagecoach, "beautifully painted" and "water-tight," thunders in carrying mail between Santa Fe, New

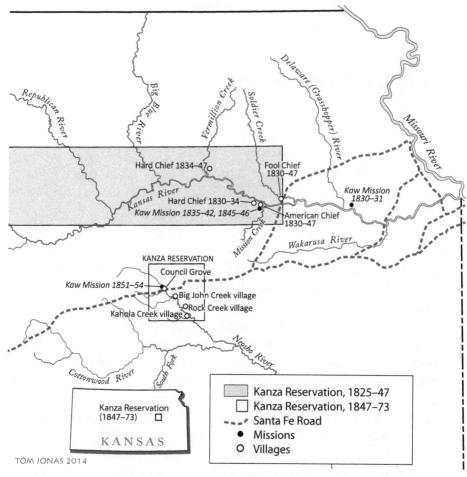

Villages, Missions, Reservations, 1830–60. © 2014, University of Oklahoma Press.

Mexico, and Independence, Missouri. From dawn to dusk the clink-clang of a blacksmith's hammer reverberates through the valley. Nearby on the north side of the road, Seth Hays operates a trading post in a modest log building. According to one of his customers, Hays is "making money hand over hand" wheeling and dealing with his Kanza and Santa Fe–bound customers.[1]

From the middle of the road, looking west over ground overlain today by Main Street, a rough dirt surface about one hundred feet wide stretches out in a broad swath across the prairie. Along the edge of the road are dusty clumps of grass and weeds. Farther out on the margins short-cropped grasses predominate, here hardly recognizable as "tall grass" prairie. To the southwest a thin, broken tree line traces the meandering course of Elm Creek. Beyond the trees loom the grassy hills, stretching for miles beneath the southwest horizon in clean, sinuous lines.

To the northwest an imposing north-trending ridge, now Belfry Hill, towers over the valley, its steep slopes covered by a winey, russet-toned carpet of grass, splotched gray with rocky outcrops. There's movement on the slope's lower half. About twenty men and five teams of mules are working there. Wielding shovels, sledgehammers, saws, chisels, and drills, the men work briskly at scraping dirt and gravel to expose underlying rock, then hacking and sawing and drilling into the gray limestone, removing chunks that other men swinging stone hammers shape into rough cubes. These stones, some weighing as much as three hundred pounds, are hoisted onto flatbed wagons which the mules haul about three hundred yards northeast to a point on the west bank of the Neosho River where a stone building large enough to accommodate fifty Kanza students and their teacher is under construction.[2]

By the end of February 1851, the construction of the Kaw Mission was complete. Supervised by an employee of the Shawnee Mission near present-day Kansas City, Kansas, Allen T. Ward, the masonry crew had finished the stone walls by Christmas. Carpenters had then made the house ready for occupation by installing floors, stairway, and trim made of walnut supplied from the local grove. The men labored and lived in primitive conditions through a Kansas winter, although the weather had been mild. They constructed the thirty-five-by-fifty-foot, two-story mission, erected a nearby log workshop and log kitchen, and dug a twenty-seven-foot well lined with rock.[3]

The project was supposed to cost $3,452, to be paid by the U.S. government to the Missionary Society of the Methodist Episcopal Church South. This society was headed by Ward's supervisor, Thomas Johnson, who as superintendent of the Shawnee Mission about 110 miles away was responsible for overseeing the construction and operations of the Kaw Mission. The Methodists also fenced and plowed one hundred acres and fenced thirty acres for pasture on the east side of the river. Johnson presented the government with a bill totaling $4,325.05, proving cost overruns for government work existed long before the modern era.[4]

In the spring of 1851, the Kaw Mission stood on the Neosho's west bank, 120 miles west of the frontier. It was an imposing sight, a stately, elegantly crafted edifice, a portentous outlier of Euro-American civilization rapidly advancing into the interior of that region then known as Indian Country.

"We must look to the missionary and the schoolmaster as the most reliable means of effecting the improvement," wrote Indian Office superintendent Thomas Harvey in 1846. "The improvement" Harvey spoke of was the elevation of Indians from what was seen as pagan barbarism to a state of Christian civilization through the acceptance and practice of Euro-American values. The most prominent of these values were piety, learning, and industry. These ideals were to be realized through the agencies of school, church, home, farm, and the trading house. Sharing identical viewpoints on the "Indian question," the Indian Office and Protestant missionary societies formed contractual arrangements to establish schools such as the Kaw Mission that would impart, in the words of historian Francis Paul Prucha, "practical, moral, and religious education of the Indians."[5]

A summation of the attributes of civilization that government policy makers, missionaries, and educators sought to impose on Indians in the last half of the nineteenth century is provided by David Wallace Adams, author of *Education for Extinction: American Indians and the Boarding School Experience, 1875–1928*. These were, wrote Adams, "a commitment to the values of individualism, industry, and private property; the acceptance of Christian doctrine and morality, including the 'Christian ideal of family'; the abandonment of loyalty to the tribal community for a higher identification with the state as an 'independent citizen'; the willingness to become both a producer and consumer of material goods; and finally, an acceptance of the idea that man's conquest of nature constituted one of his noblest accomplishments."[6]

This, then, is the ideological basis for the Kaw Mission and other government measures intended to implement assimilation on the

Kanza Reservation. Schools would help to solve the "Indian problem" because they would impart to Indian children the knowledge, skills, values, and beliefs to survive in the white world. What the Indians thought of this program did not matter to bureaucrats and missionaries because as savages they were incapable of knowing what was best for them.[7]

In the years preceding the construction of the Kaw Mission, Indian Office officials labored to convince themselves and their superiors that the Kanzas really wanted a school for their children. In February 1848, Thomas Harvey reported that the Kanzas were anxious to have their school in operation. "The civilization of the Indians is no longer a mere speculative idea," wrote Harvey. "Remove from among them bad white men and their contaminating influence, and substitute an efficient administration among them, aided by energetic missionaries, with the manual school system, and it will be found entirely practicable."[8]

In reality, "bad white men" continued to associate with the Kanzas and the Indians did not embrace white schools. By the time the Kaw Mission had been constructed in Council Grove, the tribe had already resisted for over two decades missionary efforts to educate their children and convert Kanzas of all ages to Christianity. The Catholics had been the first to try. Joseph Anthony Lutz was appointed "missionary priest" for the tribe in the spring of 1828. By September, the disillusioned Lutz decided not to offer baptism to any of the adults because "[t]he superstition of the Kanzas tribe is more gross than any one could believe." By December the young priest had retreated to his diocese headquarters in St. Louis.[9]

The Methodists opened a mission and school for the Kanzas in 1830 on the north side of the Kansas River seven miles upstream from present-day Lawrence, Kansas. Two years later, the Methodists withdrew, having accomplished very little. Many obstacles hindered progress: cold weather, remoteness of the largest Kanza villages, the language barrier, and the Kanzas' extreme poverty. Attendance was also severely hampered by the tribe's practice of leaving their Kansas River villages twice a year for several weeks at a time to hunt buffalo on the plains. The missionaries were also dogged by the hostility of some government Indian agents. One of them, Kanza agent Marston

Clark, denounced the missionaries for sapping "the foundations of our Republican Institutions" by being "only interested in patronage, power and money."[10]

In September 1835, Thomas Johnson's brother, William, returned to work with the Kanzas as their missionary and teacher. This time he established his residence and built a school near the Mission Creek villages a few miles west of present-day Topeka. In June 1836, William wrote to his brother: "If they only knew Jesus and would worship in His name with the same promptness that they attend to their own ceremonies, they would doubtless be a happy people." In 1843, Johnson's lament was echoed by the chairman of the Methodist Kansas Mission who found the Kanzas "one of the most difficult tribes to operate upon we have tried in all this vast field of missionary operations." The missionaries' bafflement about the Indian's unyielding adherence to their own forms of worship reveals a universal shortcoming of Christian missionaries of that period: they never comprehended that the Kanzas had their own complex and meaningful spiritual life deeply rooted in tribal culture and the physical environment.[11]

The Kanzas were a deeply religious people who through symbolic expressions such as sacred bundles, prayer, myths, ritual, dance, and vision quests continually sought unity with Wakanda, the mysterious, pervasive, and all-powerful divinity animating the universe. This spiritual sensibility was infused into every major event of their lives and provided guidance in making decisions and taking actions. If a Kanza man prospered, he expressed his gratitude to Wakanda, saying, "Wakanda has indeed been looking at me!" Religious leadership was provided by shamans, called *Wakandagi*, who had accessed the superhuman dimension through dreams, visions, and spirit possession. Specific clans performed certain duties in ceremonials to maintain the delicate harmony between the Kanzas, the natural world, and Wakanda. For example, members of the Lo, or Thunder Being clan, would at the time of the first spring thunderstorm put green cedar on a fire to protect against violent storms. Because Wakanda infused the manifest universe, the Kanzas offered prayers to the rising sun in the morning and the setting sun in the evening as well as to the other stars, the hills, the four winds, the Thunder Being, and the morning star. The earth was alive and relationships between humans, other creatures, and plants were dynamic and full of mystery. Unlike in the world of Christian dogma, the gap between the human and the supernatural was narrow and permeable, a condition requiring an attentive and worshipful sensibility as one went about everyday activities.[12]

Oblivious to, if not contemptuous of what they were up against, the Methodists convinced themselves that they were making some inroads among the Kanzas until irruptions of smallpox in 1839 and a subsequent series of bloody encounters between the Kanzas and Pawnees. By December 1840, William Johnson reported that his efforts among the Kanzas were paralyzed. Faced with the tribe's intransigence, the Methodists began to remove Kanza children from their villages to educate them at the Shawnee Mission. In the spring of 1841, while escorting eleven Kanza boys to the Shawnee Mission, William Johnson became critically ill. He never recovered, dying in April 1842. The Kanza boys were returned to their villages, and several died soon after their arrival home. Following these deaths, Hard Chief forbade Kanza children to go with the Methodists, saying, "They at the mission smelled the big knife so much that when they came back to the tribe they soon died." Two more attempts were made by the Methodists to establish a missionary presence at Mission Creek, but both ended in failure. The last effort was abandoned in 1846.[13]

Tall and slender, Thomas Sears Huffaker first set his eyes on the Kaw Mission in April 1851. Huffaker's bearded face wore a serious expression, his eyes exuded a cool intelligence, and his receding hairline and dignified stature conferred maturity beyond his twenty-six years. He had come to Council Grove via the Santa Fe Road, having departed a few days earlier from the Shawnee Mission, where since 1849 he had been employed as a teacher. A few weeks earlier he and his partner, H. W. Webster, had subcontracted with the Methodist Episcopal Church South for the management of the school and farm of the Kaw Mission, sometimes called the Kansas School. Huffaker was to be in charge of the school, Webster would supervise the farm.[14]

Thomas Sears Huffaker, teacher at the Kaw Methodist
Mission, businessman, and politician. Courtesy Morris
County Historical Society.

Thomas had deep roots in the Methodist Episcopal Church
South. His father, George Smith Huffaker, was a Kentucky-born, ordained minister of the Methodist Church South, having established
churches in several Missouri towns. Born on March 30, 1825 in Clay
County, Missouri, Thomas Sears was the second-oldest child of a
brood of thirteen. His father's Kentucky upbringing undoubtedly
influenced Thomas's attitudes toward the leading ecclesiastical and
political questions of the day, foremost of which was the issue of
slavery. This question split the Methodists in 1845, the position of the
Church South being that slavery was strictly a political question that
required no doctrinal response from the Methodist Church.[15]

Thomas Huffaker embraced slavery, as had his Shawnee Mission employer, Thomas Johnson, the owner of several slaves. Two years after he came to the Kaw Mission, Huffaker purchased "a certain Negro woman named Cynthia aged about thirty years" for six hundred dollars. When Huffaker brought Cynthia to Council Grove, her bondage would have been neither conspicuous nor unique. The 1855 census counted forty-five of eighty-three Council Grove residents as emigrating from proslavery Missouri. One of the village's leading citizens, Missouri-born Seth Hays, owned a slave known as Aunt Sally. In fact, ten of Council Grove's eighty-three inhabitants in 1855 were slaves. No records indicate Cynthia's existence in Council Grove, but the census does list a twenty-one-year-old Negro slave named Lucinda Huffaker. Whatever her identity, Cynthia or Lucinda was probably used as a domestic servant in the Kaw Mission. She would have augmented the "mission family," which included the wife of Huffaker's partner, Mrs. H. W. Webster, who was in charge of the school's kitchen. After a year, the Websters returned to their home in Iowa, dissatisfied with the lonely and difficult life so far from civilization.[16]

Two other Euro-Americans resided at the Kaw Mission: a widow named Agnes Baker and her daughter, fifteen-year-old Eliza Ann. Agnes worked at the school as housekeeper, seamstress, matron, and teacher. One observer claimed that she "had probably done more for the Kansas Indians than any other person on the Reservation; She had toiled for them from morning till night." Thomas courted Eliza and on May 6, 1852, they were wed in the Kaw Mission.[17]

From the beginning the Kaw Mission was beset with problems. In January 1852, Thomas Johnson provided a bleak report: only fifteen Kanza children attended the school, a large number of the Indian children and all of the "mission family" were sick, and the Kanzas had insisted on taking their children with them on a buffalo hunt. The buffalo hunts were semiannual treks to a region in present-day central Kansas about one hundred miles west of Council Grove. Ordinarily, after harvesting their crops in early October, the entire tribe journeyed west to their hunting grounds. Here the Kanzas would spend several weeks killing bison and processing the meat and robes, then return to the reservation, arriving sometimes as early as

Christmas. In the spring the Kanzas would repeat the cycle: plant their crops in early May, then travel west en masse to hunt buffalo, returning by late June or early July. Although enjoyed by Kanzas of all ages, these communal hunts were the bane of the teachers' existence, disrupting the continuity of their instruction and reinforcing cultural forms the Euro-Americans were seeking to destroy.[18]

Descriptions of the actual operations of the Kaw Mission are sketchy. According to Huffaker, average attendance during the three years the school operated was about thirty. All pupils were boys, and they received instruction in spelling, reading, writing, and arithmetic, but none in the trades, and "the boys worked well on the farm." Describing himself as a teacher, never a minister of the gospel, Huffaker imparted religious instruction to his students but did not attempt to conduct religious observances among Kanza adults. Until he learned the language, Huffaker was assisted by an interpreter, a "fine looking, intelligent" full-blood named William Johnson, who, like all of the Kanza students, would have been assigned a Euro-American name after entering the school. Four upstairs rooms served as a dormitory. The downstairs rooms were classrooms and living quarters for the teacher, farmer, and their families.[19]

Unfortunately, no description exists of the daily routine at the Kaw Mission. However, in 1855 a visitor outlined a school day at the Shawnee Mission, the Kaw Mission's parent institution, where Huffaker had received his training as schoolmaster. At 5:00 A.M., a bell was rung to awaken the students, who did farm work until breakfast at seven. Studies began at nine and with the exception of one brief recess, halted at noon for lunch, then resumed from one to four in the afternoon. Tea was at six, followed by a meal, then students did their homework until eight. After thirty minutes of indoor recreation, the Indian scholars were sent to their dormitories for the night. During the week, religious instruction consisted of reading the Bible followed by prayer before the morning and evening meals. Saturday mornings were set aside for work, Saturday afternoons were holidays, and Saturday evenings were spent cleaning up for Sunday, the day of devotional services. Upon entering the school, the children were immediately instructed in English. "If they misbehave," wrote the observer, "the system of discipline is nearly the same as formerly in vogue in New England. They do not, however, care much for any species of punishment, save that of the rod."[20]

At the same time he launched the school for the Kanzas, Huffaker found time to open a school in the Kaw Mission for the children of the small but growing enclave of Euro-Americans living in Council Grove. These government employees, licensed traders, and mail contractors conducted business with the Kanzas and served the needs of Santa Fe Road freighters and merchants. From twelve to fifteen of their children attended this elementary school, which operated for six years in the Kaw Mission. The children received instruction almost year-round, with only brief summer vacations.[21]

The "mission family" also provided hospitality to travelers. Staying overnight in the Kaw Mission in September 1851, Harriett Bidwell Shaw described the Kanzas as "thick as bees" around the yard. At dark, however, the Indians were ordered to leave, and at this time the large mission watchdog was turned out for the night. In the morning, the Shaw party found that their carriage, mules, and other property had not been disturbed. Travelers frequently described the mission as "large" or "substantial." After encountering a Kanza village on the east bank of the Neosho, a Quaker visitor noted the stone building on the west bank "with a considerable farm attached." Another observed that the mission was surrounded by hedged-in fields. However, the hospitality of the Methodists was not extended indiscriminately. In 1854, New Mexico territorial governor David Meriwether and his traveling companions, including Mrs. Louis Smith, wife of a Baptist missionary, stopped at the Mission but were turned away by the Mission family because of, in Meriwether's view, Mrs. Smith's Baptist affiliation.[22]

This fierce interdenominational rivalry doubtlessly helped to shape the views of the Baptist minister C. B. Boynton during his autumn 1854 visit. Boynton was not favorably impressed with either Council Grove or the Kaw Mission. The "few log-cabins" and the mission constituting the whole of Council Grove seemed a "confused huddle" and the site "not very happily chosen." The Methodist mission was attended irregularly by a few Kanza children but "little or nothing" was being done in the school. "The name of 'Mission,'" wrote Boynton, "does not very well describe the thing."[23]

In early November 1854, the first territorial governor of Kansas, Andrew Reeder, stayed overnight at the Kaw Mission while on an excursion throughout the territory. Reeder's agenda included ascertaining the best location for the temporary seat of government for Kansas. Council Grove received high marks in a Leavenworth newspaper article about Reeder's trip. The writer noted the fine body of timber on the stream, good springs, and soil equal to any of the territory. In regard to Reeder's visit, John Maloy, whose version of early-day Morris County history was informed by Thomas Huffaker, identified the one crucial factor working against Council Grove's interests: "Had the Indian lands here been open for settlement and sale, our city would undoubtedly have become the capital of the Territory."[24]

The one successful aspect of the school's operation identified by Huffaker—the boys' work on the farm—required the Kanzas to realign their traditional gender roles. Indeed, the agricultural revolution that the Methodists and government officials sought to impose on the Kanzas implied radical social, technological, and economic changes. For generations Kanza women had practiced horticulture, utilizing hoes to raise corn, beans, pumpkins, squash, potatoes, and melons in small fields. Under the new regime, Kanza men were to labor in large fields day after day, guiding plows powered by draft animals. In 1853, a few Kanza men told their agent, John W. Whitfield, that they were willing to "quit the hunt, and turn their attention to farming, if they could be protected" from other Kanza men. According to the agent, when the government plowed the three hundred acres in 1849, a few Kanza men went into the fields and began to prepare the ground for planting. Declaring that these men were disgracing themselves because the women alone should do the work, the chiefs sent men into the field, where they cut up harnesses, broke plows, and whipped the would-be farmers. In Whitfield's version, "these poor unfortunate beings [Kanza women] do all the work, and, from their education, believe it right. You would be surprised to see the amount of corn they raise with the hoe alone."[25]

In addition to subsisting on their corn and other vegetables, the Kanzas were instructed to sell their crop surpluses on the commercial market. Having participated in the fur trade for over a hundred years, the Kanzas were not unfamiliar with the machinations of a market economy. Indeed, in 1853 the tribe had sold one thousand bushels of corn to a local trader at sixty-six cents per bushel. However, channeling surplus agricultural "commodities" to the marketplace did not square with the Kanzas' deep-seated and, from the viewpoint of Indian Office officials, imprudent practice of sharing their corn supply with most any tribe that asked for it. Notwithstanding Kanza agent Richard Cummins's pronouncement that the Kanzas were "the most hospitable Indians I have any knowledge of," the Indians were encouraged to forsake their traditional economy of reciprocal gifting that established social bonds and instead sell surplus grain in exchange for cash. Indian Office bureaucrats and missionaries never doubted that this seismic cultural shift was necessary for the Kanzas to ascend from "savagery" to civilization.[26]

By July 1851, the Kaw Mission's corn crop was thriving because the drought of 1850 had given way to abundant rains in the spring and summer of 1851. This auspicious event had far-ranging consequences for agriculture in this region. The mission's successful crop was the area's first, overturning the widely held view that large-eared corn grown by Euro-Americans could not be produced in this drought-prone region of the Great Plains. Henceforth, other area farmers were induced to plant corn. What is not clear is how much corn was actually harvested in the late summer of 1851. Thomas Johnson painted a bleak picture of Kanza ineptitude and lack of self-restraint, accusing the tribe of stealing nearly all of the mission's potatoes and garden vegetables when they were half-grown and a considerable amount of corn when it was still green. The following year, the crops were good again, both on the mission farm and in the small fields tended by Kanza women. Again Johnson excoriated the Kanzas, dismissing them as "reckless creatures" who sold their corn for a mere trifle, "and so in a few months they will be begging and stealing again, just as bad as if they had made nothing."[27]

Johnson's description underscores the difficulty of looking through the lens of one's own culture at the motives and actions of those from a radically different culture. The questions vexing the whites were two: Why were the Kanzas seemingly compelled to harvest crops prematurely? And how could impoverished Kanzas be generous to a fault in giving away their corn but also be such incorrigible thieves? While living on the Neosho reservation, the Kanzas were often stalked by hunger. Additionally, to the Kanzas and most tribes in the region, gift exchanges were extremely important, implying friendship and obligations to give protection to and maintain harmony with their benefactors. Gift exchange created relatives, and its absence opened the door to a spectrum of hostile behaviors. While one would always be generous to one's friends and family, it was acceptable for a Kanza to steal from enemies. Most Euro-Americans understood crops as commodities best retained as property by the owner until exchanged at the highest cash value. What they saw as the common sense of the marketplace was a negation of an ancient form of bonding practiced by the Indians. The rigid adherence of most Euro-Americans to the inviolable principle of private property placed them outside the circle of kinship created by reciprocal gift exchange and its attendant harmonious solidarity. This principle, however, was selectively applied. As will be demonstrated in great detail, when it came to trespass on the property of the Indians, white Americans felt little or no compunction.[28]

As early as January 1852, Methodist officials acknowledged that the Kaw Mission project was in trouble. Thomas Johnson described himself as "at a loss" on how to sustain the school. Compounding the ongoing problems of sickness and absenteeism, he wrote, was the tribe's "habit of stealing from every body in their reach." Eight months later Johnson's outlook was at best ambivalent: "Sometimes we have encouraging hopes, and at other times the prospects are very gloomy." Once again Johnson mentioned considerable sickness in both the mission family and some of the Kanza boys. The previous spring, one of the sick Kanza boys was treated by a whiskey bath, the whiskey furnished by the trading post of Seth Hays. At the same time the agent, Francis W. Lea, averred that it would take time to operate on the Kanza prejudices against schools.[29]

Government documents of the period are filled with reports blaming the failure of schools on the Indians. Less common, however, was an articulation of the reasons for the Indians' disaffection. When Superintendent David D. Mitchell urged the "border tribes" such as the Kanzas to turn to agriculture and mechanical pursuits, invariably they replied, "What is the use of it? In a few more years we will be driven back into the plains, or the Rocky Mountains; and what will our knowledge of agriculture, or the mechanic arts, avail us on the prairies, or in the Rocky Mountains?" Mitchell pronounced the effort to civilize and Christianize the border tribes "a signal failure."[30]

In 1853, agent Whitfield reported that as soon as the boys were large enough to go on the hunt, the Kanza adults removed them from school. When they returned to the reservation, instead of furthering their education, the boys invariably opted for the Kanza way, shaving their heads except for a strip of hair on the back, painting faces, and dressing in full Indian costume, these appearances reflecting their determination, according to Whitfield, "to excel in being of less account than any Indians in the nation." Two years later the same point was made by another Kanza agent, John Montgomery, observing that the former Kaw Mission students were "common Kaws in dress, manners, and everything else."[31]

One of the persistent problems experienced by on-reservation boarding schools such as the Kaw Mission was absenteeism. Teachers and Indian Office officials frequently complained of the difficulty of first obtaining, then keeping the children at school because of the children's desire to be free and unrestrained. Much of this truancy can be attributed to the students' discomfort in being forced to adapt to unfamiliar customs, as illustrated by a description of newly arrived Kanza boys at the Shawnee Mission in the early 1840s: "poor fellows, when it came to dressing themselves the next morning, they were at their wits end; for, when discovered, they were busily engaged in arranging their pantaloons, wrong side out, and the forepart behind. The next thing was to give them names."[32]

White authorities frequently complained of the disposition of parents to indulge the children. The affection of Indian grandparents and parents for their children impressed a number of observers, including Thomas Say who visited the Kanzas' Blue Earth village in 1819. Say observed that while the girls respected and obeyed their parents, "the males are very disobedient, and the more obstinate they are and the less readily they comply with the commands of their parents, the more the latter seem to be pleased, saying, 'He will be a brave man, a great warrior—he will not be controlled.'"[33]

Headstrong and aggressive, dismissive of adult authority, this behavior is the opposite of what would be required of Kanza boys in the Kaw Mission. A Quaker teacher provided this description of the tensions pervasive in Indian schools in the 1850s in what is now Kansas: "Unused to restraint at home, the discipline of school life was very irksome to the children, and not easy for us, especially out of school and in winter when they could not exercise out of doors. A room full of lively children, jabbering an unknown tongue, was very trying on one's nerves." Noted for their restraint, nonviolence, and respect for native peoples, the Quakers resorted to such disciplinary measures as tying the Indian children's hands behind their backs, blindfolding them, placing chips between their teeth, and making unruly boys stand on stumps. These measures would be exceeded by the Methodists, whose preferred punishment was that of the rod. The firmly entrenched practice of corporal punishment was regarded by most Indians as abhorrent and degrading. This was one of many cultural dislocations compounding the difficulties faced by both the Kanzas and their white supervisors at the Kaw Mission.[34]

The Kanzas responded to government pressure to enroll students in the Kaw Mission by withholding girls and sending the boys the tribe held in lowest esteem. Kanza agents and teachers attributed the school's struggles to the tribe's not permitting girls to attend because of the tribe's practice of having them marry at a very early age. George Morehouse wrote that "the pure Indian type of that wild tribe" refused to send their children to the mission school, and as a rule only allowed "the orphans and a few dependents" of the tribe to attend. "They considered it very degrading and a breach of true, old Indian dignity and aristocracy to adopt and follow the educational methods of their white brothers."[35]

The Kanzas, like all Indians, were never a static cultural entity, especially by the time of their residency in the upper Neosho valley. By 1851, the tribe had been influenced for over a century by intensive Euro-American contact, undergoing profound cultural changes throughout this period, a process that continued, if not accelerated, in their new home near Council Grove. That the Kanza response to the Euro-American challenge was not uniform is cited as a cautionary principle against attributing conflicts between whites and

Indians exclusively in terms of the Indians' reactionary adherence to their traditional forms. Nevertheless, the Kanzas' rejection of the government's efforts to acculturate them through the instruments of schooling and agriculture is in part a function of the tribe's enduring cultural conservatism. To paraphrase Willard Hughes Rollings, author of a study of the Osage response to missionaries, the Methodists could never understand that they were asking the Kanzas to stop being Kanza. To some extent, this allegiance to their traditions had been solidified by the Kanzas' long exposure to the ways of whites on the Kansas frontier, a familiarity that bred some forms of emulation but more often disillusionment. "Permit me to say," wrote a Kanza agent, "that this tribe . . . have been so badly dealt with in former years—that they have but little confidence in white men of any class."[36]

Huffaker's performance at the Kaw Mission received mixed reviews. Agents Whitfield and George W. Clarke praised Huffaker, Clarke maintaining that the Kaw Mission had done as well as it could among the Kanzas, "a people who are averse to education and wholly opposed to all efforts to civilize them." But some of the tribe criticized Huffaker for his management of the farm and the school. Speaking to Commissioner of Indian Affairs James Denver in 1857, a Kanza chief accused Huffaker of working the Kanza boys "all the time at the plough and in the fields. Didn't teach them any thing." When asked about the boys at the Kaw Mission, the chief said, "At first he [Huffaker] had about fifty children, but didn't learn them much. . . . They were engaged in nothing. They don't study any thing." These accusations echo the statements of both Indians and whites about how Thomas Johnson, Huffaker's mentor and the Kaw Mission's superintendent, operated his Shawnee Mission school. A group of Shawnee headmen charged that the Methodists had "departed from their legitimate office" to become "money changers." In 1851, a visiting Indian Office official, while impressed with the size and productivity of the Shawnee Mission farm, noted that its profits, "which are very great," enriched the managers of the institution instead of going to the Indians.[37]

After three years of operating the Kaw Mission, the Methodists and their government sponsors conceded failure. When on October

30, 1854, Kanza agent Clarke arrived in Council Grove to distribute annuities to the tribe, Huffaker informed him "that the school would be discontinued at this time and until the next spring or perhaps later." It is revealing of where the power lay that the teacher informed the government official in charge of Kanza affairs of the decision to close the Kaw Mission, surely an indication of Thomas Johnson's enormous influence with government officials. And there never was a "later," as the Methodists terminated their twenty-four-year effort among the Kanzas. Three years after the school closed, Huffaker cited its "failure for want of means to support it."[38]

A gloomy assessment of the Kaw Methodist Mission was pronounced by agent John Montgomery in 1855: "at present [the Kanzas] have no school, and it seems that what they have had has been only a dead expense to the government." A more vituperative appraisal, replete with racism and certainty about where to place the blame, was offered by visiting Baptist minister Boynton soon after the school was closed:

> I had never before seen a community of real, absolute heathen, for such these Kaws are, permitting no Christian teaching among them, except some trifling instruction in reading and writing, to a few of their children. They are among the lowest and poorest of the Indian tribes—guilty of all the vices that Paul ascribes to heathenism, in the first chapter of Romans—and if any new wickedness has been invented since Paul wrote, they doubtless have learned even that. In observing these miserable creatures, I was moved, sometimes to laughter and sometimes with pity, for their ignorance of all good, and consequent wretchedness. In them, sin had wrought out, without much restraint, its legitimate consequences, and they afforded the most fearful evidence of its nature and its power.[39]

The failure of the Kaw Mission is best understood within a broader context of the overall deterioration of Kanza-white relations during the school's 1851–54 period of operation. In January 1851, seven Santa Fe Road merchants wrote to the president of the United States pleading for an Indian agent to be assigned to the Kanzas at Council Grove. The traders were concerned that the Kanzas, having previously been peaceful and quiet, recently were "in the daily commission of depradations upon all parties of traders and others who are passing." A recent example was cited: a Kanza had confronted a government train near Council Grove, demanding a present of sugar, powder, and lead. The freighters refused, whereupon the Indian shot and killed one of their oxen and rode away. This was cited by the merchants as typical of many recent incidents involving Indian molestation of peaceable travelers, these reflecting "the growing insolence of these Indians." Their patience with the obstreperous tribe nearly exhausted, the letter writers warned of impending bloodshed that would put the government "to much cost and trouble."[40]

A few weeks later, a force of fifty dragoons commanded by Major Robert H. Chilton marched 120 miles from Fort Leavenworth to the Kanza Reservation. Following a "big talk" with Kanza chiefs, Chilton arrested the principal chief, Hard Chief, and his two brothers, then journeyed back through severe weather to Fort Leavenworth where the Indians were imprisoned for about a month. The army held the incarcerated chiefs responsible for thievery committed by the young men in the tribe. Especially egregious was the stealing of horses from white people, including U.S. Army soldiers, who traveled the Santa Fe Road. Not surprisingly, Hard Chief intensely disliked his imprisonment, which he called "sleeping between logs." Described as being "very sore" when released, he vowed to kill any Kanza who stole any more horses.[41]

Despite Hard Chief's threat, complaints against the Kanzas persisted. In July 1851, Abraham R. Woolley, an Indian agent assigned to New Mexico, wrote from Council Grove about frequent Kanza depredations in the area. Warning that such incidents were likely to increase, Woolley too pleaded for the appointment of an agent to reside in Council Grove to protect "the safety of the property & persons of individuals travelling or sojourning."[42]

In the autumn of 1852, Major Chilton's company of mounted troops again confronted the Kanzas. This time the cavalrymen (then known as dragoons) were camped near Diamond Spring about fifteen miles west of Council Grove. The October days had been sunny, the nights frosty, the grass tall and dense, ideal conditions for prairie fires. During the day groups of Kanzas had shadowed Chilton's men. A couple of hours before sunset, fire broke out in a circle all around within a mile of the camp. Strong winds drove the flames, some twenty feet high, toward the camp. The cavalrymen were forced to fight for their lives, suffering, in the words of Sergeant Percival G. Lowe, "burned hands and faces, many of us terribly blistered." The next day they marched to Big John Spring, two miles east of Council Grove, where they established another camp. At this time they made plans to force the return of five horses the Kanzas had allegedly stolen from a party of mounted rifles in the spring.[43]

Lowe's orders were to present Chilton's demands to a Kanza chief to bring the stolen horses into the Big John Spring camp that night. Written fifty years later, Lowe's description of the locations of the Kanza villages is confusing and he was unable to recall the name of the chief, although he did say that he had been one of Chilton's Kanza prisoners in 1851. Lowe found him lying ill on a willow mattress inside a round lodge of mud and willows. The chief, recalled by Lowe as a "sensible, good man," was embarrassed. After tense discussions with the Indians and a return to the Big John Spring camp to consult with Chilton, Lowe led a party of troops back to the chief's village, where they kidnapped the chief, precipitating chaos. Amid howling men, women, and children, warriors rushed out of their lodges with weapons drawn for battle. The hostage chief turned on his mount and rode backward, "gesticulating and talking at the top of his voice." Lowe warned the interpreter that if the Indians fired a shot, both the interpreter and the chief would be killed, a message the two Indian captives repeated "vigorously and continually" to their people until they had ridden out of sight.

Around the time the cavalrymen and their prisoners reached the hills east of Big John Creek, Lowe met a messenger hastily sent by Chilton ordering him to return to camp, as the Kanzas had already returned three of the horses and promised the speedy return of the other two. Later, at the camp, Chilton conducted a council with the chief and other Kanza headmen, during which he threatened their "young bucks" with extermination if he had to come from Fort Leavenworth another cold winter to punish them. Reflecting on this event over fifty years later, Lowe expressed profound regret: "I became convinced that I had been guilty of an outrage on a man who had been guilty of no wrong, in order to recover some horses that had been stolen by some thieves of his tribe."

Implicit in Lowe's remorseful reflection is the recognition that Kanza chiefs could not assert absolute control over the actions of their warriors, a familiar theme in many accounts of Indian-white conflicts in North America, of which the Kanza pattern is one variation. During his visit to the Blue Earth village in 1819, Thomas Say observed that a chief "possesses nothing like monarchical authority, maintaining his distinction only by his bravery and good conduct. There are ten or twelve inferior chieftains, or persons who aspire to such dignity, but these do not appear to command any great respect from the people." Not understanding that chiefs did not rule their people in a chain-of-command system of authority but rather exerted influence by force of character, military authorities frequently held the chiefs accountable for the hostile acts of their men. As a result, the chiefs were subject to humiliating punishment while the transgressions of their warriors persisted unabated.[44]

Some of the challenges a Kanza chief faced during a time of great change and stress for his people are illustrated by tracing the life of Hard Chief, the principal chief of the Kanzas from 1846 until his death in 1861. Given the paucity of historical records featuring any Kanza individual, no matter how prominent, such a reconstruction must be based on scattered bits of data and is but a crude biographical sketch. Hard Chief's Kanza name was subject to a multitude of spellings assigned by agents, travelers, and traders, among them "Kihegawachuckee," "Kahegahwahcheha," "Kahhegawatchee," and "Kahegawachuffee." A translation of his name is "Difficult to Endure Chief." It was Hard Chief who in the 1840s declared his opposition to Kanza children attending mission schools because those who did so returned to the tribe weakened and prone to die. In 1846, Oregon Trail traveler Edwin Bryant estimated the chief's age at about fifty-five years. Bryant found him "of commanding figure, and of rather an intellectual and pleasing expression of countenance." A less complimentary description of the chief was provided by historian George Morehouse, who wrote that Hard Chief possessed an ordinary intellect and was not a great warrior.[45]

Unidentified Kanza brother chiefs, relatives of Maggie Ah-Sis-Sa Mehojah (to whom the photograph belonged). Early in the Kanzas' occupation of the Neosho reservation three brothers—Hard Chief, Pegahoshe, and Ishtalasea—were the chiefs of three villages. Courtesy JoAnn Monroe O'Bregon.

Unlike many Euro-Americans travelers in Indian Country, Bryant, whose party was encamped near Hard Chief's village, understood the necessity of giving gifts to the Kanzas to ensure harmony. When he gave Hard Chief's wife a dozen strings of glass beads, the couple both said "Good! Very good!" As Bryant describes it, the Kanza chief wore a turban, a soiled damask dressing gown, buckskin leggings, and moccasins. His face was painted vermillion and he wore "bone and tin ornaments about his ears and neck, and the little jingling buttons or bells on his legs." Hard Chief promised the Bryant party that none of his people would steal from them that night in camp. The next morning Hard Chief and his wife sat on the ground near Bryant's tent, awaiting a contribution in exchange for the kept promise. He was given a large quantity of flour, bacon, and other articles, which he then distributed among his people. A chief gained great favor among his people by allotting goods to them in this way. It marked him as a generous leader, a man who could be trusted.[46]

Hard Chief had emerged as a prominent Kanza chief in the 1820s. As "Ky-he-ga-wa-che-he" he was the third chief to sign the St. Louis Treaty of 1825. By 1830 the tribe had fragmented into three bands, and Hard Chief had established a village of about five hundred Kanzas south of the Kansas River on high ground over a mile west of Mission Creek (near present-day Valencia, Kansas). A mile downstream on Mission Creek was American Chief's village of about twenty lodges, and about seven miles east of the two Mission Creek villages, located north of the river, was Fool Chief's village of eight hundred Kanzas. By January 1835, Hard Chief had moved his village twenty-three miles west to the east bank of Vermillion Creek near present-day Belvue. Perhaps not coincidentally, Hard Chief and his band moved west just before the Methodists reestablished a Kanza school and mission on Mission Creek in 1835.[47]

In spring 1831, Hard Chief and his brother, Gray Eyes, traveled to Fort Leavenworth, where they admitted to agent John Dougherty that the Kanzas over the previous twelve months had scalped fourteen Pawnees and stolen twenty to thirty of that tribe's horses. Hard Chief returned to Fort Leavenworth in 1833 with ten other Kanza headmen to attend a peace council of fourteen area tribes, including the Pawnees. The Kanza representatives signed a treaty pledging to cease all hostile acts against other tribes and to take no private or personal revenge. The Kanza delegation was headed by White Plume, Fool Chief, and Hard Chief, whose name appeared on the treaty document as "Ky-he-ga-war-che-ha." Five years after signing the nonaggression pact, Hard Chief, recognized by the government as "the third Chief of the nation," headed a war party of twenty Kanzas against an unspecified enemy, most likely the Pawnees. In the 1843 tribal census, "Ki e ga wah chah he" is listed as a male over the age of forty sharing a lodge with a female under forty.[48]

When explorer John C. Fremont moved up the Kansas River valley in June 1842, he encountered Hard Chief's "large but deserted" village near the mouth of Vermillion Creek. Some of the huts clustered along the east margin of the stream had been burned and others were blackened by smoke, signs of a devastating Pawnee attack earlier that spring. Although he noted that weeds were already claiming the open spaces, Fremont admired the village location, noting that it had been "chosen with the customary Indian fondness for beauty of scenery." By May 1845, Hard Chief and his band had returned to reinhabit the site, and they resided here through May 1846.[49]

Hard Chief's ascendancy to the head chief position followed the deaths of White Plume in 1838 and Fool Chief in January 1845. For the next fifteen years his name appeared first among Kanza chiefs signing government documents such as treaties, annuity rolls, and statements acknowledging debts to traders. Although he did not possess absolute authority, a strong head chief commanded considerable respect from his people. Frederick Chouteau, an intimate associate of the Kanzas as trader from 1829 through the early 1850s, later claimed that tribe members regarded their chiefs "as characters of great dignity," and any social interaction with them was regarded as a great favor. Chouteau frequently observed the Kanza practice of presenting gifts to their chiefs as a way of currying favor.[50]

While Chouteau in his later years reminisced about "great dignity," during his years as a trader he diminished the dignity of the Kanza chiefs by his violent methods of imposing his will on the tribe. The trader's primary instrument of control was a brutal Kanza henchman named Necohebra. According to Chouteau, Necohebra was called Wacondagatonga, or "Big Medicine Man." The Kanzas believed that he possessed immense powers, including "the power to kill or save as he might choose." Necohebra's authority was augmented by his possession of a little red morocco box containing vials of medicine, an object inspiring awe and fear among the Kanzas. Chouteau claimed that he had Necohebra physically whip Hard Chief, Fool Chief, and others who were negligent in paying their debts. The trader said that he had also ordered Necohebra to beat up Kanza women who annoyed him by leaving large tree limbs in inconvenient places around his store and that he had Necohebra assault young men who picketed their horses on Chouteau's favorite feeding grounds. "I had the big medicine man teach them better manners," recalled Chouteau. "He was exceedingly useful to me." Although possibly exaggerating his own power, Frederick Chouteau's brutally graphic reminiscences expose the debilitating impact of influential traders on the self-confidence and social cohesion of the Kanzas. Knowledge of Chouteau's ruthless methods provides insight into why Hard Chief and Fool Chief initiated government negotiations that culminated in the 1846 treaty. Among the chiefs' reasons for proposing a land-for-money swap was the tribe's debt of $1,500 owed Frederick Chouteau.[51]

Chouteau followed the Kanzas to Council Grove, where he remained until the early 1850s. The Chouteau company was but one of many licensed by the government to trade with the Kanzas at their new reservation. After coming to Council Grove, the tribe continued to be plagued by mounting debt. From 1849 through 1860, the Kanzas accumulated a debt total of $36,494.47 owed to twenty-three individuals, mostly traders. By 1862, the year the traders received their total payment, the per capita debt shared by 807 Kanzas, each of whom received an annual annuity payment of $10, was $45.22.[52]

Hard Chief and other notable Kanzas helped to incur this debt. From May 1852 through August 1853, Hard Chief purchased eight items from trader Christopher Columbia totaling $33.75. The acquisitions included coffee, sugar, flour, cloth, and a bell. In the credit column: Hard Chief paid $8.75 cash and traded Columbia ten deer skins, one otter, three wolves, and six coons valued at $15.25. With credits at $24, Hard Chief owed Columbia $9.75. Some chiefs had not been so frugal. The son of the deceased Fool Chief, also named Fool Chief, owed Columbia $137.50. Among other prominent Kanza debtors were Pegahoshe at $285.80 and Wahobake at $143.50. A total of 202 Kanzas purchased on credit from Columbia. On the credit side, the Kanzas supplied Columbia with 265 buffalo robes, receiving in exchange an average of $4.29 credit each and thirty horses at an average of $36.40 each.[53]

Trade had long been viewed by federal authorities as an effective way of controlling Indians and getting access to their lands because such commerce inevitably produced Indian indebtedness. Writing to Indiana governor William Henry Harrison in February 1803, President Thomas Jefferson outlined how the Indian trade helped Americans to achieve their expansionary ambitions: "we shall push our trading houses, and be glad to see the good and influential individuals among them [Indians] run in debt, because we observe that when these debts get beyond what the individuals can pay, they become willing to lop them off by a cession of lands." Jefferson preferred government over private enterprise but either would produce the same desirable outcome: financial destruction of the Indians. Jefferson's plan was sound because all the whites—government officials, settlers, speculators, and merchants—stood to gain by its implementation, and the losers, as the traders' ledgers revealed, had been apparently willing accomplices. The whole disenfranchising process was aimed at what everyone valued the most—land—and with Kansas declared a territory in May 1854, Euro-Americans would soon be casting their hungry eyes in the direction of the 256,000-acre "permanent home" of the heavily indebted Kanzas.[54]

*

One of the fundamental underpinnings of federal Indian policy at this time was that the "Indian problem" could be resolved through a process of assimilating the "savages" into the dominant white society. As mentioned above, churches, schools, and commerce were instrumental in the process. Operating from 1851–54, the Methodist school for the Kanzas in Council Grove failed to achieve its educational and religious missions in part because the Kanzas preferred their own religious traditions and ways of instructing children. Efforts of the Indian Office to change Kanza men from hunters and warriors into disciplined agrarians similarly failed. However, the machinations of Indian traders did succeed in shattering tribal social cohesion and plunging the Kanzas into a prison of debt. In those instances when Kanzas challenged American dominance, both the U.S. Army and traders exercised brutal means of suppression. Implicit in the attempts to inculcate Euro-American cultural and economic forms was an assault on the Kanzas' deepest values and beliefs, those which gave shape to their fundamental identity, how they understood themselves as human beings in relation to the rest of the universe. That this transformation was to be effected in the classroom, fields, and trading houses rather than the battlefield makes it no less violent. Indeed, in the sense of violence as a violation, infringement, or profanation, the colonialist enterprises unleashed on the Kanzas on their new reservation were acts of violence, whatever the good intentions of some of the propagators.

CHAPTER 3

WHITE MEN NOW LIVING
AMONGST US

One morning in late July 1858, when touring the countryside, an Emporia, Kansas, newspaper editor crossed into the Kanza Reservation. After leaving the tiny settlement of Americus, the editor rode his pony up the east side of the Neosho River, heading northwest toward where Rock Creek joins the Neosho. Recent heavy rains had softened the ground and the air was still cool and fresh before the onset of afternoon heat. Although contemplating the expanses of upland prairie was pleasant enough, what really thrilled him was that everywhere he looked people had "improved" the land. Where a year before along the same route there were but few settlers, now he witnessed countryside transformed by an ambitious population of settlers working feverishly to establish farms and build cabins. Large fields of grain checkered the Neosho valley. The recent wheat harvest was a bountiful one, with winter wheat yielding better than the spring variety. The corn was doing well, and the potato crop would be large.[1]

At the mouth of Rock Creek near present-day Dunlap, Kansas, the newspaperman stopped at Elisha Goddard's place. The sheriff of Breckinridge County, Goddard had settled at this location over two years before. Among his improvements were a house valued at $1,000, well, privy, stable and corn crib, chicken house, corral, five hundred rods of fencing, and sixty acres of broken ground, all this valued at $2,113 including the house. Not far from the Goddard farmstead was the village site of the Kanzas' Rock Creek band, then

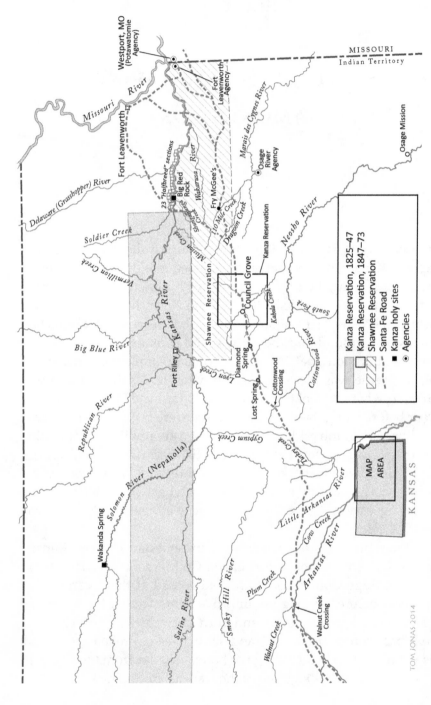

Kanza Homeland, 1848–54. © 2014, University of Oklahoma Press.

headed by Chief Ishtalasea. Next the editor rode eight miles up Rock Creek to a tiny settlement called Agnes City. Here he visited Judge Arthur I. Baker, who lived in a fine new limestone house near where the Santa Fe Road crossed the creek. Baker's place, like Goddard's, was located on the reservation.[2]

Noting that settlers now occupied every timbered claim on the Kanza Reservation, the editor was delighted with "the evidences of thrift and enterprise" he saw everywhere he looked. Notably absent in his description of the Kanza Reservation was any mention of the Kanzas. After all, it was inevitable that the Indians' "illegal claim" would soon be set aside and the settlers allowed to preempt the land. Despite the many signs of progress, the editor admitted that the uncertain legality of the settlers' claims retarded improvements of all kinds. Nevertheless, he celebrated the rapid progress he had witnessed that day, declaring, "Even to one who has witnessed it all as it has been made piece by piece, the aggregate is astonishing."[3]

Among those witnesses, of course, were the Kanzas, but what the Indians thought of their reservation being overrun by white squatters was of little concern to the editor. Less sanguine about the situation on the Kanza Reservation was the new governor of Kansas Territory, James W. Denver. In March 1858, Denver warned the Office of Indian Affairs that if prompt measures were not taken, "you will find yourself compelled to subsist these Indians during the coming season or pay for their depredations on the surrounding whites." Denver urged Indian Office officials to buy out the Indians or to rigidly enforce the law—that is, to evict the illegal squatters.[4]

Historian Paul Wallace Gates observed that "Sooners," the term later applied to illegal squatters in Oklahoma, "were found on every reservation in Kansas before the Indian lands were officially sold or open to settlement." The U.S. government was obligated to prevent whites from taking over land "reserved" for the Kanzas by the treaties of 1825 and 1846. However, from the time Kansas became a territory in May 1854, whites built cabins, cut timber, grazed their cattle, and raised crops on Kanza reservation land. The initial invasion took place on the well-timbered and fertile land on the north bank of the Kansas River stretching from present-day Topeka to a few miles downriver of present-day Lecompton. The Kanza Treaty of 1825 had assigned 640-acre parcels of this land to each of twenty-three "half-breed" Kanzas, who retained ownership of this property even after the tribe had been relocated to the Council Grove area in 1847. But because these lands were highly desirable and their property lines had not been surveyed, the "half-breed" allotments were among the first to be overrun by squatters. In June 1856, Kanza agent John Montgomery attempted to evict the encroachers. After several unsuccessful appeals to the military for support, twelve men of the First U.S. Cavalry from Fort Riley were assigned to assist him, and for a few days the task of removing the whites was undertaken.[5]

As compensation for doing his job, Montgomery was arrested by territorial Kansas officials on charges of arson, abandoned by the military, condemned by Kansas newspaper editors, ignored by his supervisors in the Office of Indian Affairs, and threatened by a mob with tarring and feathering. He also witnessed the intruders' successful occupation of the mixed-blood allotments. In July 1856 Montgomery wrote to his supervisor in St. Louis that "after several weeks of fatiguing and exciting exertions to carry out the instructions of the Department, I am compelled to give it up and return to Council Grove where my other duties require my attention."[6]

He had jumped out of the frying pan and into the fire. By late summer 1856, the reservation on the Neosho was being invaded by white squatters. They settled primarily in the Neosho valley in the vicinity of Council Grove, although there was a smaller concentration of settlement seven miles east along Rock Creek. Squatters found the Council Grove vicinity most desirable because of the safety of a relatively compact population, abundant timber, rich bottomland, and the convenience of a nearby trade center. Montgomery reported between fifty and seventy-five families on the reservation. Once again, Montgomery's supervisor ordered him to evict the encroachers. On October 9, the Kanza agent posted "Notices to Intruders" ordering them to leave the reservation within twenty days. The ensuing outcry of protest from outraged citizens was amplified by newspapers and channeled into the corridors of power by politicians, the effect being the negation of the Indian Office's policy and yet another humiliation for the Indian agent, who contemplated moving with his family out of the territory because of "threats of personal violence made in regard to myself, by those white people."[7]

Paradoxically, the same John Montgomery persecuted for attempting to enforce the law was accused of fomenting this same kind of illegal encroachment. Most damaging to Montgomery was the July 1856 testimony of several leading citizens that the agent had sanctioned their land claims in the vicinity of Council Grove at locations well within the reservation boundaries. Worse yet, Thomas Huffaker testified that while in the company of Montgomery, Huffaker had made a claim for the agent about two miles southeast of Council Grove. If true, Montgomery had attempted to secure property for himself near the center of the Kanza Reservation.[8]

Although he apparently had compromised his responsibilities to his Indian wards, Montgomery was not the only Indian agent in Kansas Territory to get caught up in the powerful tide of land settlement and speculation that swept across Kansas Territory. One of his predecessors, John W. Whitfield, was elected delegate to Congress partly because he was thoroughly identified in his interests and sympathies with the squatters, he being one of them. The agents were under immense pressure to assist in the expansion of the frontier. In this they were abetted by the prevailing ethos of the period shaped by Manifest Destiny, which produced a system for Euro-Americans to advance unimpeded and acquire land. "While it was not to the agent's credit when he succumbed to the pressure of economic expansion," wrote historian William E. Unrau, "it is singularly unfair to shoulder him with most of the blame."[9]

From 1854 through 1856, Euro-American immigration into this area, then considered "Southwest Kansas," was a mere trickle. That changed in the spring of 1857, when immigrants flooded onto the Kanza Reservation, establishing their homes in the well-wooded and watered valleys. At least 90 percent of the settlers occupying the Kanza Reservation in 1859 had come onto the reservation after December 1856. The 1859 census counted 569 inhabitants of Morris County, 199 of whom were eligible to vote. Of those 199 white males over age twenty, only twelve had lived in Morris County prior to 1857. A Kansas City, Missouri, newspaper reported in June 1858, "From Council Grove to the mouth of the Cottonwood, the country is somewhat broken, but not too much, so to admit settlement; and upon every quarter section you may see a comfortable log house and a fence spread round a thrifty looking corn or wheat field, potato

patch and garden, which the hardy hands of industry have reared."
Left unsaid was that the northern segment of this swath cut through
the heart of the Kanza Reservation.[10]

At least four factors contributed to the floodgates of immigration
opening wide into this region in 1857. Much of the best land in Kansas Territory east and north of the upper Neosho valley had already
been claimed. Secondly, reaching its apex in 1856, the violence of the
"Bleeding Kansas" era had subsided by spring 1857, at which time
the free-state (antislavery) forces had clearly gained the upper hand.
("Bleeding Kansas" refers to the sometimes violent political conflict
during the territorial Kansas period [1854–61] between antislavery
Free State and pro-slavery forces over the question of whether Kansas would enter the Union as a free state or a slave state.) Thirdly,
the Panic of 1857 created massive unemployment and social un-
rest across the nation, prompting thousands of disenfranchised
Americans to seek their fortunes on the western frontier, a section
of which was then located in Breckinridge [now Lyon], Morris, and
Davis [now Geary] Counties. Indeed, the towns of Junction City and
Emporia, soon to become rivals of Council Grove, were both established in 1857. Finally, according to agent Montgomery, ambitious
men who had resided on the reservation since the early 1850s—led
by Thomas Huffaker and his brother-in-law Arthur I. Baker—had
spread false reports "to persuade people who are entirely ignorant
as to the disputed title of the Kansas Country to move and locate
around this point."[11]

Local promoters might have been the first to disseminate pro-
paganda in support of the illegal Euro-American occupation of the
Kanza Reservation, but their original arguments were repeated, amplified, and embellished by Euro-American squatters, land speculators, journalists, and politicians. Understandably, pro-encroachment
justifications have surfaced in the works of contemporary historians,
who, reflecting the literature of the period, and presumably aiming
to produce a "balanced" treatment of the subject, continue to repeat
some of these as fact, adding yet another layer to the already substantial body of work supporting encroachment. In view of these pervasive, lingering, and unresolved controversies, a summary follows of
the four major factors and justifications in support of encroachment,
along with an assessment of their legitimacy.

First, the Kanza Treaty of 1846 located the eastern border of the tribe's reservation many miles west of the reservation established in 1847 on the Neosho River. A detailed narrative on the decision to establish the reservation in the upper Neosho was provided in chapter 1, so only the most salient features of this process will be summarized here. The advocates for the squatters repeatedly seized on the following passage in article five of the Treaty of 1846 as proof that the Kanza Reservation belonged west of Council Grove: if the authorities determined that there was an insufficiency of timber on the new Kanza Reservation close to its eastern boundary [near Minneapolis, Kansas], then a "suitable country" near this boundary would "be selected and laid off . . . which shall remain for their use forever." This prescription proved impractical mainly because of the close proximity of enemy tribes in that area. Subsequently, after surveying other possible sites, in July 1847 agent Richard Cummins and the Kanza chiefs selected a well-timbered twenty-mile-square tract on the upper Neosho. On November 6, 1847, the new reservation—its boundaries a matter of public record as described by Cummins— was approved by President James K. Polk.[12]

Second, a large portion of the four-hundred-square-mile Kanza Reservation overlapped with the "Shawnee Purchase," a tract of the original Shawnee Indian Reservation open for settlement. This caused unwitting emigrants to settle on the Kanza Reservation. In 1847, the U.S. government did, in fact, mistakenly establish the northern three-tenths (120 square miles) of the Kanza Reservation on land already reserved for the Shawnee tribe, and this land became available for preemption in 1854, the Shawnee title having been extinguished. The southern boundary line of the Shawnee Purchase crossed east–west about four miles north of Council Grove. The southern boundary line was surveyed in 1833 by Isaac McCoy, who at the time marked the southwest corner of the Shawnee Reservation by erecting an eight-foot-square, five-and-one-half-foot mound of dirt, topped by a stone. This point is located about a mile and a half southwest of present Latimer in Morris County, Kansas.[13] However, as has been established, only a small number of settlers came to Morris County prior to the summer of 1856, at which time the boundaries of the Kanza Reservation were being surveyed and marked. Moreover, of these, only a small percentage settled on the northern three-tenths of the reservation because of the well-documented advantages offered by the Council Grove and Rock Creek settlements, both located well to the south of the Shawnee Reservation. Therefore, the Shawnee Purchase overlap had a negligible effect on causing immigrants to mistakenly settle on the Kanza Reservation.

A third factor involved in white encroachment is that settlers on the Kanza Reservation made their claims in accordance with the instructions of Kanza Indian agents John Whitfield and John Montgomery. On July 19, 1856, seventeen citizens appeared before a justice of the peace, Arthur I. Baker, to accuse Kanza agents Montgomery and, to a lesser extent, Whitfield, of misdirecting them to settle on the Kanza Reservation, especially in the Rock Creek area. The evidence is strong in support of the accusations against Montgomery. Newly appointed in the spring of 1855, the young agent was possibly ignorant of the actual reservation boundaries delineated by Cummins eight years before. More likely he submitted to the prevailing ethos of the time in support of aggressive economic expansion and yielded to the temptation to tell prospective settlers, especially well-connected ones like Huffaker, what they wanted to hear. It is even more likely—indeed, Montgomery says as much—that Huffaker, Columbia, Baker, and others knew the actual reservation boundaries but found it to their advantage to collude with the agent in the misinformation process about the same.[14] Sensing his predicament, in November 1855 Montgomery proposed a new twenty-mile-square reservation, its northeast corner to be located less than a mile southwest of Council Grove. To justify this move, he cited "a difference of opinion between the Indians and the Government as to the tract intended for them" and the overlap of the Kanza and Shawnee reservations. The agent's proposal was rejected by Robert McClelland, secretary of the Interior, who confirmed the existing boundaries, noting that the Kanzas had in fact settled on the reservation plotted by Cummins. In compliance with his supervisors' ruling and fortified by the survey completed that summer, Montgomery then made a serious but unsuccessful effort in the autumn of 1856 to remove the squatters from the Kanza Reservation.[15]

Fourth and finally, a Seth Eastman map certified as correct on August 5, 1854, by Commissioner of Indian Affairs George Manypenny, and "got up expressly for the guidance of settlers," located the Kanza Reservation west and south of Council Grove and off of the Santa Fe Road. The apologists for the squatters argued that one of the map's flawed representations—a nonexistent gap between the southern boundary of the Shawnee Reservation and the northern boundary of the Kanza Reservation—misled settlers into establishing their claims on land they later discovered was located on the Kanza Reservation. Additionally, the Eastman map was cited by a citizen petition as proof that the Kanza Reservation was intended to have been situated "fifteen miles further west and ten miles further south than at the present time." Another citizens' letter, written in May 1857, referred to the Eastman map as proof that the reservation should be located thirty-five or forty miles northwest of the surveyed boundaries. However, a careful study of the extant Eastman map refutes the settlers' allegations. Among the features on the map clearly located inside the reservation's boundaries are the two primary areas of early settlement—Rock Creek and Council Grove at the Santa Fe Road crossing of the Neosho River.[16]

Embodying the conventional wisdom of the region, these four factors and arguments buttressed the Emporia editor's confident and widely shared prediction that the Kanzas' claim to their reservation would soon be extinguished. For the most part, these formulations are specious, however. The settlers' presumed innocence rested on exploitation of the uncertainties of the situation, be they a map, agent instructions, or treaty interpretations. The overriding weakness of the squatters' position is that after the widely publicized government survey of reservation boundaries was completed on July 24, 1856, all ambiguity about the Kanza Reservation boundaries ended. From then on, every reasonably informed citizen knew the precise location of the Kanza Reservation, so that when they "settled" on the Kanzas' land, they knew they did so outside the law.[17]

We should consider what the most knowledgeable people—the Indians, traders, government officials, and missionaries—had literally put on the ground in the years following the 1846 treaty. Why, if the Kanza Reservation was actually located west of where the Kanzas had settled, did the Kanza establish their villages within an eleven-mile radius of Council Grove? Why did licensed Kanza

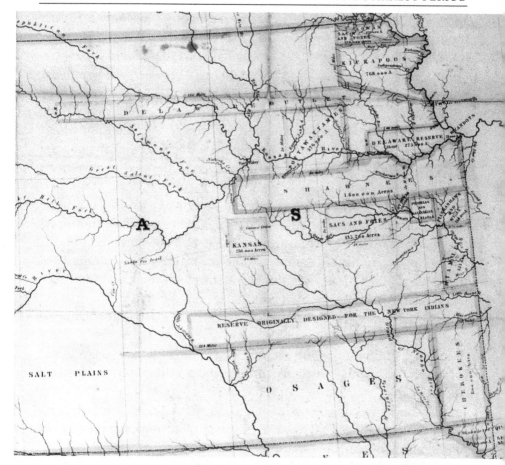

Controversial Seth Eastman map, 1854, endorsed as correct in regard to Indian reservation by the commissioner of Indian Affairs, George P. Manypenny. This map was frequently cite by defenders of the illegal occupation of the Kanza Reservation by white squatters. Courtes Kansas State Historical Society.

traders Boone, Hamilton, and Chouteau establish their posts in Council Grove in 1847? Why did the government fund the building of the Kaw Mission in Council Grove in 1850? Why did agent Montgomery establish his agency in Council Grove in 1855?

If ambiguities supporting the squatters' position and the invasion of Kanza land had not existed, it is safe to conclude that others would have been invented. Paul Wallace Gates says it best in his book, *Fifty Million Acres*: "Disregard of Indian rights was traditional on the frontier, and it did no violation to settlers' ethics to intrude on Indian lands, whether trust, allotments, or reserves."[18]

In a June 14, 1857, letter to the Indian Office, John Montgomery acknowledged the futility of continuing his efforts to evict the squatters. Nevertheless, he recommended that every settler should be promptly removed from the Kanza Reservation and that the government enter suit against one or two of them for trespass as a lesson to the others. In a detailed analysis of "the intrusions upon Indian lands carried on by the Whites," the Kanza agent observed that white squatters had organized and enlisted the support of territorial politicians and legal authorities. The settlers despised him, he said, because he "emphatically disapproved of their conduct in settling upon the lands which they have no right to," and due to threats from whites, the agent's personal safety was precarious. He also stated that permitting unlawful intruders to remain on the reservation had weakened the Indians' confidence in the government and that his utmost endeavors "to keep peace and harmony" had succeeded better with the Indians than with the whites.[19]

The encroachment had a devastating impact on the Kanzas, who, in their agent's words, "are now to be driven from the small space of Country reserved for them by the Government."[20] The Kanzas responded by sending a delegation to Washington, D.C., to protest the trespass upon their lands. On July 22, 1857, Commissioner of Indian Affairs John W. Denver (soon to be appointed governor of Kansas Territory) was visited by a Kanza delegation composed of Hard Hart, Wolf, White Hair, and five men, including three mixed-bloods, one of whom acted as interpreter. Referring to both the Neosho reservation and the twenty-three "half-breed" sections on the north bank of the Kansas River, the Kanzas presented

a statement of their grievous wrongs, sufferings and apprehensions to which they have been subject, in many and various ways at the hands of the whites who have trespassed upon their lands and wrested from them their possessions and property and excluded them from the quiet and peaceful enjoyment thereof as guaranteed to them by solemn treaty stipulations. . . . they as the rightful and sole owners thereof have been

ejected therefrom and driven off by the trespassing whites, their property taken [and] spoiliations [sic] committed, by cutting and destroying
timber & other and various ways. . . . First request is that the Government of the United States will reinstate them in the full and free possession & enjoyment of their reserved lands uninterrupted by the presence
of the whites within the limits of their reservation, and that the Government will adopt prompt and effectual measures to cause all and every
trespassing white man to be at once removed without the limits of the
reservation.[21]

The Hard Hart delegation also told Denver that they did not want
to make a treaty or sell their land. One of the Kanzas stated: "I have
got white men now living amongst us, and I suppose our father [the
agent] can do nothing with them, and I can do nothing myself; and
that is the reason I came to see my great father in Washington that
he might help us. . . . White men also live by me, and many of them
are worse than Indians." Near the end of the conference, Hard Hart
made this final appeal to Commissioner Denver: "I have several
children home, some high and some low, some big and some small,
who must be supported. There used to be plenty of game in our
country, but there is none, and my children must do something else,
besides hunting, to live. . . . white men on my reserve have some
good houses, and I want them moved off so that we may live in
them ourselves."[22]

Denver's response was to encourage the Kanzas to return to
their reservation and "imitate the whites, by cultivating the earth
and being industrious." Compelling the Indians to abandon the
hunt and become farmers was, of course, one of the underpinnings
of the Indian Office's civilization program. Fulfilling this prescription was impossible, however, given the conditions on the ground
of the Kanza Reservation, a conclusion Denver himself reached a
mere eight months after lecturing the Kanzas in Washington. Now
governor of Kansas Territory, Denver conversed with another Kanza
delegation in March 1858, this time in his office in Lecompton, the
territorial capital. Following the visit, Denver wrote to the Office of
Indian Affairs: "Their reserve is covered all over with white settlers,
who will not allow them to plant their corn this spring."[23]

"Hard Hart" and other Kanza chiefs in conference with Commissioner of Indian Affairs James Denver, 1857, published in *London Illustrated News*, April 25, 1857. Courtesy Kansas State Historical Society.

Denver's assessment was corroborated by others familiar with the situation on the Kanza Reservation. Indian traders Hiram Northrup and Joseph Chick advised the Indian Office that before the whites occupied the reservation, the Kanzas had raised crops. Northrup and Chick wrote to Indian Office superintendent Alfred Cumming, "They had small patches of Corn planted in secluded spots & from which they could guard their stock—But since the Whites have settled the Country having no fences the Indians can raise no crops— Hence the Buffalo is their only reliance against starvation." By the spring of 1858, the reservation squatters were busy breaking prairie, cutting timber, and fencing farms while the Indians, according to agent Montgomery, had been driven from their little farms.[24]

Given the political clout of the white encroachers, the threat of being forced to relocate to another reservation hung over the Kanzas.

Some Kanza chiefs told Huffaker that because "they must plant corn some where this spring," they needed to know where the "Great Father" intended for them to live. In March 1858, the leading Kanza chiefs—Hard Chief, Fool Chief, Pegahoshe, Allegawaho, Shomacossa, Cahegaotussa, and Washunga—wrote to Governor Denver, saying that the tribe "will not await any longer for some one to settle their land question[;] they say if the Government intends to give them other land than this they wish to know it now[.] They wish to plant corn this spring and if they are to be removed they do not wish to plant on this land. They depend a great deal on their little fields for subsistence."[25]

In March 1858, Quaker Thomas Stanley met with the Kanzas. He had come to the reservation with the intention of assisting the Kanzas in developing their agriculture. After the meeting, he changed his mind, declaring that "the present state of the reserve would forbid my doing any thing towards encouraging them to go to farming." If the Indians planted corn and other crops, they would be in danger of being destroyed by the settlers' livestock, and if the Indians tried to fence their fields, the settlers would have objected. Some Kanzas had planted corn but part of this had been destroyed by high water. "Three weeks ago," wrote Stanley, "quite a number of them with the Cheafs came to see me and informed me that they had nothing to eat."[26]

In assessing the whites' hostility toward the Kanzas, Montgomery addressed the Euro-Americans' most pervasive and bitter complaint about the tribe: "this ill will manifested on the part of the whites is attributable in some degree to the frequent petty depredations commited [sic] upon their property by the Indians, who do so under the belief that they are entitled to something for the use of their land and timber." Amid the documents of the period, this fair-minded explanation assigning white encroachment as a causal factor in Kanza thievery is a singular, contrarian rock located in the midst of an unrelenting stream of self-righteous abuse and resentment branding the Kanzas incorrigible thieves and beggars. That it was articulated by a government official who had facilitated such criminal trespass on the reservation is extraordinary. An irony implicit in the situation was that the whites damned the Indians for conduct that the aggressions of the whites made inevitable. Denying the Kanzas the means of raising corn on their own reservation, the encroachers were outraged when hungry Indians stole a chicken or two. "What whites saw as begging and thieving," wrote historian Elliott West, "can just as well be seen as Indians working within a delicate nexus of limited possibilities. . . . The elements of life were dwindling, hostile pressures were growing, the weather was worsening, and their options were narrowing."[27]

The scale of the white invasion precluded the tribe from employing one of its time-tested strategies for avoiding disaster—flight. Kanza agent Montgomery claimed that he alone had persuaded the Kanzas not to abandon their present home and seek "the distant wilds of the plains far beyond the intrusions of lawless white men." Despite the agent's rhetoric, by the late 1850s, the prospect of the Kanzas establishing a protective enclave in distant lands no longer existed. They were squeezed between the twin "hostile pressures" of whites invading their reservation homeland and enemy tribes such as the Cheyennes and Pawnees disputing their hunting lands. No longer permitted to raise crops near their villages, the Kanzas were forced during the encroachment period of 1856–62 to either wander among the Euro-American settlements begging and thieving or journey to the plains in pursuit of bison meat and robes while risking annihilation. Although conducting a few successful hunts during this period, the tribe's overall ability to garner subsistence from their environment continued to decline.[28]

Signs of those narrowing options were everywhere to be seen. The Kanza chiefs had complained to Denver in July 1857 that white traders were laying out a town on their lands. The Indians were right. Formed in March 1857, the Council Grove Town Company was granted a charter of incorporation by the territorial legislature and governor in February 1859. The fledgling town, as clearly established by the survey of 1856, was situated well within the bounds of the Kanza Reservation and so outside the sanction of federal law. In August 1859, an Emporia newspaperman was favorably impressed with Council Grove, "the county seat and chief town in Morris county," and one of the best business points south of the Kansas River. Observing that "several new and substantial buildings" had been erected that summer, the journalist mentioned what was obvious but rarely acknowledged: "there can be no doubt that if the Kaw Indian title was extinguished, Council Grove would speedily become a first rate town."[29]

One of the most substantial buildings recently constructed was the large frame store of Seth M. Hays and Company, its opening celebrated by a "grand affair" on July 21, 1859. Just after dark that day, thirty-eight couples assembled at Hays's new building where they danced until midnight. Everyone then gathered in the dining room of the Hays House, where they found the table loaded "with all the good things of this world." After the sumptuous meal, the revelers returned to the hall where some of them danced until daylight to music provided by Hall's Quadrille Band of Emporia. Noting that those attending were mostly residents of Council Grove, the Cottonwood Falls newspaper declared that "our neighbors are not behind older communities in all that tends to make life pleasant."[30]

Other observers were full of praise for Council Grove, the recent construction especially drawing favorable reviews: "Council Grove has improved considerably since I was there a year ago," wrote a reporter in the *Lawrence Republican* in September 1859. "Two of the most substantial and elegant buildings in the Territory are now on the town site. The cut-stone store of Messrs. Goddard & Sampson is a model building, and the large frame warehouse of S. M. Hays & Co., would do credit to Leavenworth or Lawrence." The "cut-stone store" had been built by Conn, Hill & Co. in 1858. Malcolm Conn, a native of Baltimore, Maryland, had come to Council Grove in 1856, and he competed with Seth Hays for the trade of the trail. He operated a lucrative mercantile operation out of this store, later known as the Pioneer Store, until the late 1860s.[31]

Why did Council Grove undergo a building boom at this time? Recent financial and political changes prompted a flurry of commercial construction. First, the Santa Fe Road trade in the late 1850s experienced enormous growth. According to scholar Craig Crease, the 1858 trade was worth $3.5 million, and that rose in 1859 to $10 million. In one day in October 1859, one Council Grove mercantile operation took in over $1,600 in gold and silver, and another store took in over $1,400. "We are selling over one hundred thousand dollars worth of goods per Annum," proclaimed Council Grove's newspaper, the *Kansas Press*, "and our trade is increasing." From April 24 to June 24, 1860, the amount of traffic passing through Council Grove was 1,400 wagons, 372 horses, 3,868 mules, 11,705 oxen, and 65 carriages bearing 3,562 tons (seven million pounds) of freight. Smart and experienced businessmen, Conn and Hays knew when conditions were right to expand their stores.[32]

Secondly, four villages—Council Grove and the Kanza villages on Big John, Rock, and Kahola Creeks—lay within the boundaries of the twenty-mile-square Kanza Reservation in 1859, but only the Indian villages had a legal basis for their existence as encoded by the Treaty of 1846. Realizing that the territorial government's charter granted in February 1859 would carry little weight when measured against federal Indian statute, town leaders sought to solidify their tenuous legal foundation by tipping the political scales onto their side. By 1859, prospects for this outcome looked good. Newspaper editor and town promoter Sam Wood, citing the political muscle supplied by eight hundred squatters, predicted that "a change must and will be effected" on the question of the Kanza Reservation, otherwise the Democratic administration would "reap the whirl wind." Wood counseled patience, his five years in Kansas having convinced him that "when whites got on to Indian Reservations that eventually they got their lands, it is only a question of time." Although Wood probably exaggerated the number of squatters, his assessment of future events soon proved correct.[33]

On October 5, 1859, incarnation of Wood's prophetic words appeared on the Kanza Reservation in the person of Alfred B. Greenwood, James Denver's replacement as commissioner of Indian Affairs. Without notifying agent John Montgomery, Greenwood met with twenty-eight Kanza chiefs at the recently constructed agency house three and one-half miles southeast of Council Grove. The Kanza delegation was led by Hard Chief, Ishtalasea, Neehoojainga, Fool Chief, and Allegawaho. Translation was provided by Joseph James, a mixed-blood recently appointed U.S. interpreter for the tribe.[34]

Greenwood came to Kansas to negotiate treaties with the Delaware, Sac and Fox, and Kanza tribes. For at least three decades federal Indian policy had reflected the official view that Indians should be encouraged to settle on reservations and there be prepared for assimilation into the dominant white society. Greenwood went one step further, endorsing the policy of "concentration," whereby the reservations would be made significantly smaller "for a limited period until they [the Indians] can be fitted to sustain themselves." This entailed allotting lands in the newly diminished reserves in farm-sized plots to individual Indians, thereby destroying the Indians' communal ownership of land, a policy advocated by Secretary of War James Barbour in 1828 and actually implemented in 1854 by Denver's and Greenwood's predecessor, George Manypenny.[35]

The chiefs meeting with the commissioner in 1859 learned that Greenwood sought their agreement to a reduction of their twenty-mile-square reservation assigned to the tribe by the Treaty of 1846. The "Diminished Kaw Reservation" was to be a nine-by-fourteen-mile tract located in the southwest corner of the original reservation, a reduction from 256,000 to 80,620 acres. The 175,380 acres of "surplus lands" were to be held in trust by the U.S. government. This land was to be sold at fair market price in 160-acre parcels to the highest bidder in cash for each parcel. The proceeds from these sales would pay off Kanza debts and be used for the betterment of the tribe.[36]

The chiefs signed the treaty, which stipulated that each member of the tribe would be assigned a forty-acre tract of land. This was necessary, the treaty proclaimed, because the Kanzas were "desirous of promoting settled habits of industry amongst themselves by abolishing the tenure in common by which they now hold their lands." The newly assigned lands were to be cultivated and improved for their individual use and benefit. A school for Kanza children would be established near the agency building. Houses would replace their bark-and-mat lodges and bison-skin tipis, and the government would furnish agricultural implements, stock animals, and other necessary aid so that the Kanzas could commence agricultural pursuits under favorable circumstances.[37]

The 1859 treaty, then, would be the legal mechanism for integrating the Kanzas into Euro-American culture. Members of the tribe would turn into property holders, the men becoming farmers and stock raisers, their children educated and Christianized. As a work ethic was firmly established in their minds and hearts, they would participate in society as U.S. citizens and function as producers and consumers in a market economy. "I am strongly impressed with the propriety and beneficial influences which would result to many of the members of the tribes," enthused Superintendent of Indian Affairs A. M. Robinson, "could lands be allotted to such as deserve them, with an assurance of permanent location and enjoyment of labor and products of soil. Certainly there could be no greater stimulus to industry."[38]

Article five of the 1846 treaty had stipulated that a new reservation "be selected and laid off for the Kansas a suitable country . . . which shall remain for their use forever." Thirteen years later this promise of permanency had proven ephemeral, a fact surely not lost on Hard Chief, the first chief to sign both treaties. Why then, given the radical cultural change imposed on their people by the terms of the agreement, did Hard Chief and the twenty-seven other Kanza chiefs "touch the pen" on the 1859 Treaty document?[39]

Debt, Thomas Jefferson's preferred strategy for tribal dispossession, was a compelling factor. By 1859, the Kanza owed $36,500 to traders, including Council Grove stalwarts Columbia, Hays, Conn, Simcock, and Huffaker. These men were influential both with the government and the Kanza chiefs, most of whom owed them money, and payment of these debts using proceeds from the sale of Kanza lands was guaranteed by the treaty. Secondly, although treaties were ostensibly made between sovereign nations, the Kanzas, like all tribes, occupied the status of a "domestic dependent nation" as defined by Chief Justice John Marshall in 1831. In relation to the United States, Marshall had declared, the position of the tribes resembled "that of a ward to his guardian." Finally, even more than in 1846, the Kanzas in 1859 were weakened not only by the tribe's debt, but also by military inferiority, vanishing game, reliance on annuity payments, the destitute condition of their people, and their own diminishing population. Commissioner Greenwood could dictate the terms of the treaty.[40]

By October 1859 illegal white squatters, their estimated numbers ranging from 250 to 800, occupied the most desirable sites on the

Kanza Reservation. As a result, the Kanzas became much-reviled refugees, described by agent Milton C. Dickey, Montgomery's replacement, as "roving from place to place not having so much as an acre of land they can call their own." Under these circumstances, Kanza chiefs must have found the language of article two of the proposed treaty most compelling: "no white person, except such as shall be in the employment of the United States, shall be allowed to reside or go upon any portion of said reservation." The only way Kanza chiefs could reclaim their Neosho valley homeland was to sign the Treaty of 1859.[41]

The Kanza chiefs' homecoming was not going to be easy, for the response of the white squatters and their many allies to the proposed treaty was emphatically negative. "We regard the so-called Kaw treaty an outrage upon the people of Morris county," proclaimed the Morris County Republican platform in October 1859. "This treaty is a direct attempt to ROB the settlers of their hard earnings, for the benefit of an Administration of speculators and land swindlers." Although the treaty stipulated that the ceded two-thirds of the reservation would soon be made available for settlement, the squatters were apprehensive that the sealed-bid process prescribed by the government would unfairly pit them against powerful outside speculators. They were also outraged that the new treaty recognized the Kanzas as the rightful owners of reservation land, gave no legal credence to the whites' land claims, and made no provisions for compensating the squatters for their "improvements" such as crops, fences, houses, and outbuildings. In sum, those who unlawfully occupied the Kanza Reservation saw themselves as victims.[42]

As the opposition party seeking to make electoral gains, the Republicans set their sights on the disgruntled voters occupying the reservation. Because the Democratic administration of President James Buchanan had negotiated the unpopular 1859 Kanza Treaty, Republicans could cast Democrats as Indian sympathizers out of touch with the legitimate concerns of the Neosho valley constituency. "We hold that every vote for the Democratic ticket, is an indirect vote for the Kaw Treaty, which was made by a Democratic Administration," declared Republican leader and Council Grove editor Sam Wood.[43]

Seventeen days after the Kanza chiefs put their X's on the Green-wood treaty, a meeting of reservation squatters was held in Council Grove for the purpose of taking measures to prevent the ratification of the treaty. A resolution committee including Thomas S. Huf-faker was appointed to draft a petition to the president of the United States "setting forth the facts of the case." This was the beginning of an intense, several-months-long campaign of resolutions, petitions, newspaper declamations, and lobbying seeking to influence Indian policy makers in Washington, D.C., to support the squatters' position. To this end the familiar arguments were repeatedly employed.[44]

For a time the outcome seemed uncertain. In early April 1860, Robert S. Stevens, a well-connected attorney and frontier entrepreneur, speculated fearfully that if the treaty was not ratified, the Office of Indian Affairs might clear the reserve of the squatters, which he thought would be "disastrous in the extreme." Stevens spoke to Commissioner Greenwood, who pledged that he would ask the Senate to amend the treaty "to do the settlers full & ample justice." These efforts paid off as the treaty ratified by the U.S. Senate on June 27, 1860, included an amendment providing compensation for the cost of improvements made by squatters who had settled on the reservation prior to December 2, 1856.[45]

Needing the signatures of Kanza chiefs, the Office of Indian Affairs sent the amended treaty document to the Kanza Reservation in July. At that time all of the chiefs and headmen who had signed the first document were over one hundred miles west in hunting camps on the Smoky Hill, Turkey Creek, and Cow Creek. The chiefs did not touch the pen on the amended treaty until October, when they returned to the reservation for their annuity payment. Finally, the Treaty of 1859 was proclaimed official on November 17, 1860.[46]

In early December the Kanzas met in full council with agent Dickey to express "their great desire to have the work entered upon" as stipulated by the new treaty. Foremost among the improvements enumerated by the chiefs were a sawmill, expanded agency, school, houses for each of their 152 families adjoined by ten-acre plowed and fenced fields, stock animals, and agricultural implements, all promised by Greenwood when meeting in person with the Kanzas in October 1859. The Kanzas reminded their agent that while persuading them to sign the treaty, Greenwood had drawn a compelling and pleasant picture of the tribe's improved condition once all the promises he made were fulfilled. The chiefs noted that their neighbors, the Sacs and Foxes, were already "having all these things done for them." Finally, the Kanzas requested that Dickey pose a question to the "Great Father," Greenwood, one that would persist over the remaining thirteen years of their occupancy of the now-diminished Neosho valley reservation: "ask him why they are neglected."[47]

At the same time that the Kanzas were compelled to forfeit two-thirds of their reservation, a distant event set in motion far-reaching consequences further constricting the tribe's access to land. The discovery of gold in July 1858 in the vicinity of Cherry Creek, thirty miles west of the future site of Denver, Colorado, was a transforming event not only for the Rocky Mountain eastern front region but for the central plains as well. By May 1860, Colorado rivaled New Mexico as the primary destination of most of the traffic on the Santa Fe Road, and many, if not most, travelers were gold seekers. Pike's Peak immigration through Council Grove at that time numbered about fifty wagons a day. In April, over 150 wagons bound for Pike's Peak had passed through Council Grove during a single day. The Council Grove newspaper described the mix of migrant and commercial traffic: "Walking up street the other day, we noticed five or six wagons of Pike's Peakers fitting out at each of our stores. Just then a new Mexican train of some thirty wagons, 40 men, and over 200 mules came in from the West, and another outgoing train about the same size, came in from the East. Our streets were a perfect jam. It was truly a great sight, and speaks volumes for the future of our place."[48]

The first massive wave of migration to the goldfields had come in 1859. During that year over one hundred thousand people journeyed across the plains en route to the Colorado diggings. Many traveled along the Platte River Road through Nebraska, but new trails popped up in the central and northern regions of Kansas heretofore relatively untrammeled by white people. The shorter but dangerous Smoky Hill Trail, short-lived Leavenworth and Pike's Peak stage line, and Parallel Road all had their champions as the best routes to the goldfields.[49]

The thousands who followed the well-established Santa Fe Road were still over five hundred miles short of their Colorado destination when they passed through Council Grove. One of these travelers, Charles C. Post, described Council Grove in May 1859 as "the last point where supplies can be had and there is everything here that a man wants if he has got money enough to buy it with." His description of the Kanzas reflects the attitude of many Euro-Americans moving along the trail: "Some of them [the Kanzas] are becoming a very little civilized, but most of them are mean, lazy devils. . . . We went to bed tonight and were lulled to sleep by the howls of wolves and yells of Indians, which is the only use or good or hurt they can be put to or do."[50]

At the time the Kanzas, as all the tribes of the central plains, were beginning to feel the ripple effect of the gold rush. Only two years earlier the Arapahos and Cheyennes occupied long-established winter villages in the goldfields region almost undisturbed by white presence. Now these tribes were forced to relocate their winter camps eastward onto the plains, especially in the valleys of the Smoky Hill, Solomon, and Republican Rivers, presumed remote from the transportation routes of the white invaders. But the massive influx of white migration, combined with the longstanding impacts of Indian pony herds and bison hunting for the robe trade, had degraded the plains environment, much to the Indians' despair. Buffalo herds had diminished, prairies were overgrazed, land surrounding streams had been stripped of timber, white hunters and trappers appeared in places previously considered inviolate, and there were the new trails to contend with.[51]

Some of the younger warriors, especially the band of Cheyenne and Cheyenne-Lakota Dog Soldiers, responded to the environmental degradation of their homeland with militancy, their aggression aimed not only at white intruders but other tribes competing for the dwindling supply of game.[52] Prominent among the latter were the Kanzas, who for many years had hunted bison and other game in what was soon to become central Kansas. Between 1859 and 1868, the Cheyennes were the scourge of the Kanzas. Because the Kanzas had "not able to cope with the wild Indians on the plains and by hunting obtain their living," reported agent Milton Dickey in February 1860, the tribe was in a "destitute condition."[53]

The devastating consequences of white migration on the Indians were of no concern to Pikes Peakers as they pushed through Council

Grove heading west. During one day in 1859, 325 vehicles bound for the gold mines crossed the ford on Elm Creek east of Wilmington (in western Osage County). By early May a reported one hundred to five hundred wagons per day were passing Diamond Spring headed for Pike's Peak. These migrants and their animals profoundly affected the plains environment. In May 1860 a traveler near Turkey Creek found grass along the Santa Fe Road "eaten off close by the numerous trains that have passed over it to and from Santa Fe and Pike's Peak." A couple days later, he reported from Cow Creek, the Kanzas' favorite hunting camp, that a large number of Pike's Peakers were "resting their teams and engaged in killing buffaloes."[54]

The Colorado gold rush transformed the way Euro-Americans understood the central plains they had traversed and their vision of this region's future. The explosion of commercial activity between the Missouri supply ports and the Rockies spurred white people to reimagine the plains less as a place to pass through and more as, in the words of Elliott West, "the middle ground of an economic whole, a vital membrane of exchange." For the first time, the central plains could be conceived as a destination where private property, shops, factories, ranches, farms, towns, and schools would flourish as expressions of industrial civilization.[55]

For this new dream to be manifest, the Indian vision of a meaningful existence lived in this place would have to yield. One way to graphically illustrate what was gained and lost as control of the central plains passed from the tribes to the whites is to examine the transformation of two landmarks that had a strong grip on the imaginations of both peoples. The Kanzas and Euro-Americans perceived these places through cultural prisms that were radically different, and how they saw the landmarks shaped how they were used, and this in turn determined what happened to the places as physical landmarks and as cultural icons.

In present-day north central Kansas, where, in the middle third of the nineteenth century, the Kanzas, Cheyennes, Pawnees, and other tribes hunted bison and fought each other, there was an Indian holy place. Today, about twenty miles west of Beloit, Kansas, just south of U.S. Highway 24, at a slightly elevated point overlooking the windswept waters of Lake Waconda, a large federal reservoir containing the stream flow of the Solomon River, a metallic historical marker announces the nearby presence of this place: Waconda Spring. Inundated by the lake, the spring can no longer be seen. For many years until a recent modification, the marker told this story:

> Many moons ago, so runs an Indian legend, Waconda, a beautiful Princess, fell in love with a brave of another tribe. Prevented from marriage by a blood feud, this warrior embroiled the tribes in battle. During the fight an arrow struck him as he stood on the brink of a spring and he fell mortally wounded into the waters. Waconda, grief-stricken, plunged after him. Believing her soul still lived in the depths, the tribes for countless ages carried their sick to drink the healing waters. Here they celebrated their victories and mourned their losses, never neglecting to throw into the spring some token for the Great Spirit.[56]

The story is a romance, a Romeo and Juliet in buckskins in the vein of Longfellow, Cooper, and many other writers of their ilk. Not a shred of evidence exists that this legend of Waconda, beautiful Indian "princess," stems from the oral traditions of the tribes of the central plains. Rather, the story is a fabrication of white people, steeped in the conventions of nineteenth-century romanticism, one of the most popular being the appropriating of Indians as objects to be woven into myths and legends, usually tragic in nature.[57]

Much more interesting and potent is the truth of Wakanda Spring, or at least its close approximate. The Kanzas named the Solomon River for this spring, calling it Nepaholla, meaning "Water on a Hill," an apt description of Wakanda Spring. The Nepaholla streambed of 150 years ago is about two hundred yards south of the spring, which is located three-fourths of a mile south of the highway marker. The size and shape of the "hill" never failed to impress early observers. It was a symmetrical cone 300 feet across at its base and 150 feet wide at the top, elevated 40 feet above the valley floor. Nestled in the center of the summit was a fifty-five-foot-wide circular spring basin. The pool's surface reached a few inches below the rim so that a strong wind from any direction splashed water over the rim on the opposite side. The water seeped through the porous encasement of travertine, a kind of limestone. The spring was deep: according to one measurement, thirty-five meters deep. Its water was heavily mineralized, especially high in salt and sodium sulfate, its source the underlying Dakota aquifer. According to one theory, the formative process began about eight thousand years ago when the water, elevated by artesian pressure, gradually deposited minerals, mostly calcium carbonate, that concreted into the mound. If this is true, it means, geologically speaking, that Wakanda Spring is an infant.[58]

In times before Euro-Americans settled in the region, it must have been extraordinary to come upon the spring, a stony mass rising up over the flat, grassy river bottom like a miniature volcano. It was a singular feature of the central plains, its size, symmetry, and mysterious pool of water a surefire way to evoke wonderment.

The Kanzas' veneration for the spring is reflected in the tribe's name for it: Ne Wohkondaga, or "Medicine Water." According to Isaac McCoy, who visited Wakanda Spring in 1830, "the singularity of this fountain" induced the Delawares and other eastern tribes relocated to Kansas to call it "Spirit Water" as well. The Pawnees' name was *kicawi caku*, or "Spring Mound." This tribe considered the spring a location of an important animal lodge "where mysterious powers were reputedly bestowed on individuals." McCoy wrote that the Kanzas, Pawnees, and Potawatomies "in passing by this spring, usually throw into it, as a kind of conjuring charm, some small article of value." The spring was held in great reverence and esteem by various Indian tribes. Many relics, including beads, medals, rifles, arrowheads, and bows and arrows, were, in fact, fished out of the pool.[59]

With Euro-American occupation, private property and entrepreneurship came to Wakanda Spring, starting in the 1870s with the bottling and national marketing of the spring's mineral waters under the moniker Waconda Water. In 1884, a health spa was established there, and over the years a complex of buildings was developed at the site, including a forty-eight-room, four-story stone sanitarium. In the late nineteenth century, dog and horse race tracks, a saloon, and a gambling house were located adjacent to the sanitarium. By the first decade of the twentieth century, the gambling and liquor dispensing had dissipated, but the health spa was revitalized, and it would flourish throughout the first half of the century. In 1965 the spa closed, its fate sealed by the impending construction of the Glen Elder dam that three years later impounded the Nepaholla waters. Prior to inundation, the sanitarium was bulldozed and its debris dumped into the spring, completing its transmutation from holy site to trash pit. Today, while recreationists and their boats periodically thrash across the lake's surface, the Spirit Water spring lies below in the still murk of its watery grave.[60]

Wakanda Spring is one of two known Kanza holy sites located within the borders of the state named for the tribe. One hundred eighty miles east of Wakanda Spring, near the eastern fringe of present-day Topeka, there once stood a large cube-shaped rock. Today located in a park in Lawrence, the rock is pink and about twice as tall as it is wide. It stands eleven feet high, has a circumference of about twenty feet and a diameter of seven, and weighs twenty-five tons. Before 1929, it stood for about 600,000 years or so on the south bank of the Kansas River just east of the mouth of Shunganunga Creek, on the edge of a village named Tecumseh. It is known as a glacial erratic, the name implying its itinerant origins, having traveled here from the eastern South Dakota area, pushed along by ice during a glacial period known as the Kansan, a time when ice penetrated as far south as the Wakarusa valley. After the ice receded north, hundreds of thousands of these rocks, also known as pink or red quartzite, were left strewn over the northeastern Kansas landscape. The rock is metamorphic and very hard (quartzite generally cannot be scratched by a knife or other sharp objects), a quality of some importance, as we shall see, to the Kanzas.[61]

During the more than two centuries the Kanzas inhabited the river valley bearing their name, this big red rock became sacred to the tribe. How it came to be venerated is not known, but the fact is that the rock became an object of worship. The Kanzas, according to historian George Morehouse, "regularly offered sacrificial prayers and offerings" at its site. Kanza chief Pahanle-gaqli drew a "prayer chart" for ethnologist James Owen Dorsey, depicting twenty-seven deities to whom the Kanzas offered prayer songs. Varying numbers of lines were drawn beneath each image as mnemonic devices identifying the number of songs addressed to each object. Among these "minor deities" were the four winds, the planet Venus, wolf, moon,

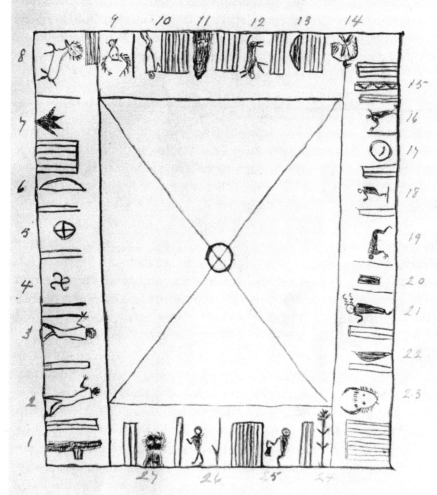

Song-prayer chart drawn by a Kanza elder in the early 1880s. The "Big Red Rock" is image number eleven. Courtesy Kansas State Historical Society.

buffalo bull, and corn. Number eleven on the chart, with five prayer marks beneath it, was the "The Big Red Rock Near Topeka," referred to by Morehouse as the "Prayer Rock."[62]

Morehouse, basing his translation on James Owen Dorsey's research, offered the following prayer chant verse:

"O Wakanda! O Wakanda!
We see the big, red rock;
It has a hard body,
Like that of Wakanda!
May we continue like it—
Like this big, red rock!"[63]

Wakanda, the entity to whom this prayer or petition is addressed, poses difficulties for minds steeped in the western traditions of monotheism. On one hand, according to Dorsey, "Wakanda" denotes superhuman beings or powers, and in that sense these twenty-seven venerated beings addressed in the prayer chart are all Wakandas. But on the other hand, Wakanda is also the pervasive, all-encompassing power investing the universe, impossible to diminish into any visual representation. According to Thomas Say, who visited the Kanzas at their Blue Earth village in 1819, the Kanzas said they had never seen Wakanda, so they "cannot pretend to personify him; but they have often heard him speak in the thunder."[64]

The Prayer Rock, however, was moved. In September 1929, a Topeka attorney proposed that it be removed to the statehouse grounds because "Topeka is holy ground of the glacial drift," the rock being a striking representation of that geological phenomenon. Meanwhile, twenty-five miles downriver, the city of Lawrence was preparing to celebrate its seventy-fifth year of existence. Like the quicker of two boys contesting a fumbled football, Lawrence swooped in and, with the help of a powerful hoist courtesy of the Atchison, Topeka, and Santa Fe Railway, scooped its heavy prize out of the river bank and hustled it back home. Here it was placed on edge atop a pedestal of rocks and cement in Robinson Park, located on the north end of Massachusetts Street, just south of the Highway 59 bridge over the Kansas River. Set into the rock are bronze plates memorializing the founders of Lawrence. Ruminating on the hardy pioneer forbearers who supplanted the Indians, however, requires ruminants to endure the incessant traffic noise of one of Lawrence's busiest intersections.[65]

*

Historian John H. Monnett wrote of the Cheyennes that the "visual landscape itself . . . was a fundamental element of Cheyenne cosmology as well as an economic base. To alter the relationships built into creation, by drastically and permanently changing the sacredness of the spiritual universe in physical ways through subdivision and private land ownership, was sacrilege to the Cheyenne religious belief system." Monnett's description of the Cheyennes' understanding of the sacred dimension of land is consistent with the beliefs of other central plains tribes, including the Kanzas. Inherent in Indian spirituality was a sensibility that place was elemental in the manifestations of the Great Mystery, an earth-based apprehension of the sacred that had no direct corollary in Christian traditions. By degrading both the material world and the spiritual dimension that infused all relationships within the physical environment, the transformations that white people imposed on the Kanzas' homeland threatened to destroy both the tribe's economic base and its spiritual belief system. Compounding the Kanzas' predicament was the increasing aggression of the Cheyennes and other nomadic tribes desperately competing for the diminishing resources available to them on the plains. Dispossessed of two-thirds of their reservation and no longer able to roam freely on their traditional hunting grounds in central Kansas, the Kanzas' grip on their land by 1860 was slipping away. More than just a temporary material and psychological setback, this new set of circumstances portended the end of a world.[66]

CHAPTER 4

THIS UNFORTUNATE AND
NEGLECTED TRIBE

When a journalist rode into Hard Chief's village on Kahola Creek in February 1857, he discovered a deserted town, burned lodges, piles of rubbish, and many graves "erected in a manner peculiar to the Indians." Instead of bark and mat lodges, he found himself surrounded by mounds of limestone rocks and slabs. Beneath the rock piles were layers of earth, bark, and timber covering the bodies of dead Kanzas lying in shallow trenches. Scattered up and down the Neosho valley and on nearby hillsides, such Kanza burial grounds left lasting impressions on whites passing by. A poem read by the president of Emporia's Fourth of July celebration in 1858 contained these lines: "The resting place of many a brave—Sad old Cahola's graves!"[1]

A contagious disease especially lethal to American Indians, smallpox struck the Kanzas in the summer of 1855. In mid-June, after the tribe received one thousand dollars in provisions from agent Montgomery, smallpox broke out and "continued fatally with the greater number of them" through the end of August. That summer, smallpox killed over four hundred Kanzas. In November 1854, the tribe's population had been 1,340. In November 1857 it was 1,015. A decade after 1,600 Kanzas moved to the upper Neosho reservation, their numbers had withered by six hundred, and the "peculiar" limestone mounds had erupted like pustules throughout the upper Neosho valley. In response, the tribe abandoned its villages and took flight. Later that summer of 1855, Hard Chief relocated his village to the

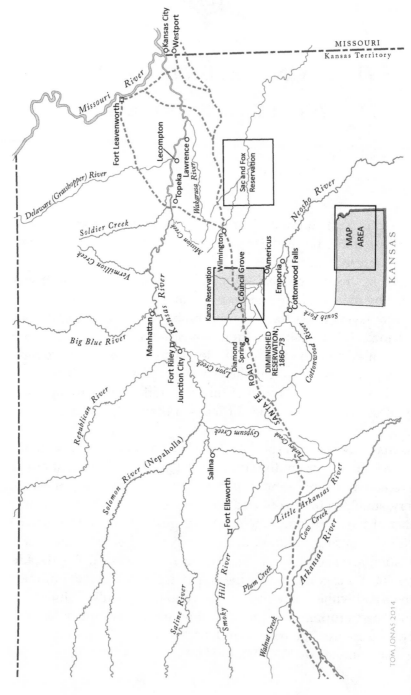

Kanza Homeland, 1855–64. © 2014, University of Oklahoma Press.

Neosho River near present-day Emporia, about ten miles southeast of the reservation.[2]

For at least one hundred years before the 1855 outbreak, the tribe had been subject to devastating outbreaks of smallpox and other epidemic diseases. For undetermined reasons, the government's smallpox vaccination efforts, the most recent conducted in 1838, had been ineffective. In the spring of 1855, smallpox pathogens from New Mexico moved northeast by means of a wagon train along the Santa Fe Road to Council Grove and the Kanza Reservation, where it exploded with fury among the Kanzas. The virus, *Variola major*, was highly contagious, capable of spreading through contact with the victims' bodies, cadavers, clothing, bedding, dust, or the infected person's objects. Initial symptoms were chills, pains, and high fever followed by pus-filled eruptions covering the hands, face, and sometimes the entire body. In its advanced stages, victims frequently experienced coma and delirium. Those fortunate to survive required a lengthy and precarious recuperation period.[3]

The loss of 30 percent of the tribe's population in a span of a few weeks profoundly affected the Kanzas' sense of well-being. "I believe, they have lost all confidence in each other," wrote Montgomery in 1855. The Kanzas' social disintegration in the wake of the smallpox epidemic is representative of what happened to all plains tribes that experienced a sudden and overwhelming loss of life due to disease. "Cholera and other diseases contributed to the disintegration of the southern Comanches and split the remaining northern and eastern bands into fragmented and confused groups," wrote Powers and Leiker. "Doubtless, many found their sense of place and political unity destroyed." The forms of consequent "social dysfunctionalism" identified by Powers and Leiker include the destruction of families and clans, shifts in marital customs, increased raiding and warfare, severing of relationships with the supernatural, loss of leadership, and an overall breakdown in morale.[4]

The 1855 smallpox epidemic is best understood as one of several pathogen-induced shocks suffered by the tribe during 1845–55. Recall that at least two hundred Kanzas died during an 1845 epidemic of an unidentified disease, and four years later over one hundred succumbed to cholera. Long-term chronic destitution and malnutrition contributed to the susceptibility of the tribe to these epidemics which, in turn, further escalated a downward spiral of the people's self-confidence, capacity to subsist, spiritual health, and ability to resist yet more outbreaks of contagious diseases. The collective physical and mental decline of native peoples threatened by "disintegrating forces" of civilization was described by contemporary ecologist and writer Paul Shepard. Among the forces Shepard listed were "sudden mass mortality, acute deprivation, alien invasion, unusual climatic events, widespread health or nutritional disorders," all conditions visited upon the Kanzas during their stay in the Neosho valley. To clearly understand the tribe's situation during "this dark period of their history" requires that we keep in mind that the Indians were continually under siege by these disintegrative forces from 1846 to 1873.[5]

In the summer of 1855, the government official assigned the responsibility of protecting and enhancing the tribe's well-being was newly appointed agent John Montgomery. Incredibly, in his August report, Montgomery celebrated the carnage that the epidemic had wrought on his Indian charges: "the smallpox broke out amongst them and has continued fatally with the greater number of them, it seems to the great satisfaction and admiration of all those who have any acquaintance with the Kaws." Warming to his theme, Montgomery elaborated: "I am constrained to say that the Kansas are a poor, degraded, superstitious, thievish, indigent, tribe of Indians; their tendency is downward, and, in my opinion, they must soon become extinct, and the sooner they arrive at this period, the better it will be for the rest of mankind." Montgomery's perverse elegy evoked a stinging rebuke from Commissioner of Indian Affairs George Manypenny, who instructed Montgomery's supervisor to inform the Kanza agent "that instead of designing their [the Kanzas'] extermination, he should employ the best means within his reach calculated to promote their welfare and improvement."[6]

Appointed by President Franklin Pierce in March 1855, Montgomery was the first Kanza agent expressly assigned to the tribe and actually stationed on the Neosho reservation. The absence of an agent during their first eight years on the new reservation created additional burdens for the tribe and contravened the Treaty of 1846. The treaty required the government to assign an agent to reside among the Kanzas, someone "charged with the direction of their farming operations, and general improvement."[7] In reality, a revolving door of agents assigned to multiple tribes and headquartered far from the Kanza Reservation ensured that for eight years the Kanza would suffer the consequences of government neglect.

Ten agents were assigned to the Kanzas over an eight-year span. Until April 1855, when John Montgomery established his office in Council Grove, the agency headquarters were never located within fifty-seven miles of Council Grove. Seldom would the agents visit the Kanzas for any other reason than to distribute annuities. In the 1840s these visits took place twice a year, but by the 1850s only one annuity visit was required each year, usually in September or October. Additionally, agents were to oversee the treaty-prescribed agricultural and educational revolutions, supervise employees such as farmers and blacksmiths, protect the Indians from white trespassers, investigate depredation claims filed by both Indians and whites, maintain peaceful relations between tribes, grant licenses to traders, and provide assistance to their tribes in times of deprivation. To fulfill these formidable responsibilities, the Kanza agent needed to understand the tribe's culture, closely monitor the health and safety of its people, and establish strong relationships with the chiefs. From 1847 through 1861, the actual performances of the Kanza agents never remotely resembled these modalities.

The already tenuous connection between the Kanzas and their agents was frayed even more when on May 31, 1854, Congress conferred territorial status on Kansas. The ensuing struggle between proslavery and antislavery forces affected the conduct of Kanza agents. The position of Indian agent was a highly sought political appointment made by the president of the United States. The agents were almost invariably members of the president's party, which in the 1850s meant they were proslavery Democrats. Kanza agents John W. Whitfield and George W. Clarke were both active proslavery partisans during the "Bleeding Kansas" period. After resigning as Kanza agent, Whitfield was elected in November 1854 as the proslavery delegate to Congress from Kansas Territory. Clarke of Van Buren, Arkansas, replaced Richard C. S. Brown, who died of cholera

TABLE 1. Kanza Agents and Agencies, 1847–55

Year	Agency	Distance from Council Grove (miles)	Agent	Tribes Represented by Agent
1847	Fort Leavenworth	118	Richard Cummins	6
1848	Osage River	57	Solomon Sublette, James S. Rains	10
1849	Osage River	57	Charles N. Handy (March)	8
1850	Osage River	57	John R. Chenault (October)	7
1851	Potawatomie (Westport)	122	Francis W. Lea (July)	2
1852	Potawatomie (Westport)	122	Francis W. Lea	2
1853	Potawatomie (Westport)	122	John W. Whitfield (June)	2
1854	Potawatomie (Westport)	122	Richard C. S. Brown (April), George W. Clarke (August)	2
1855	Kansas (Council Grove)		John Montgomery (April)	1

in June 1854. Clarke had worked on behalf of Democrat Franklin Pierce, who was elected president in 1852. A strong supporter of the proslavery cause, Clarke participated in several violent skirmishes before leaving Kansas in August 1858. John Montgomery, Kanza agent from 1855 through 1859, revealed where his sympathies lay in 1862, when he abandoned his family to join Quantrill's band of proslavery "Bushwhackers."[8]

In general, Indian agents of the 1850s operated in an Indian Office that failed to provide adequate means for its staff in Indian Country to carry out their responsibilities. Left to drift by the unresponsive bureaucracy of the Indian Office (itself chronically underfunded by Congress), geographically isolated, frequently undermined by Indian traders, and lacking the means to enforce laws, few agents proved equal to their tasks.[9]

Among the laws most difficult for the agents to enforce were the federal prohibitions against the sale of liquor to Indians. Already reeling from the effects of contagious disease and white encroachment, the Kanzas had long suffered from this pernicious invasion. Unfortunately for the Kanzas, inhabiting the Council Grove reservation meant living in close proximity to a whiskey pipeline. In 1855, Commissioner of Indian Affairs George Manypenny singled out the trading posts on the Santa Fe Road as places where the Kanzas could "procure intoxicating beverages from traders and emigrants passing through their country." Consequently, the Indians became "addicted to habits of intemperance and indolence, and the commission of such misdemeanors and crimes as usually follow in the wake of the liquor traffic." Exposure to such deleterious influences, wrote Manypenny, led the tribe to "depredations upon the property of emigrants on the great thoroughfare leading to Santa Fe.[10]

From 1854 through 1866, liquor was available to the Kanzas at trading posts and small stores, sometimes called ranches, at Fry McGee's 110 Mile Creek Station, Council Grove, Diamond Spring, Lost Spring, Cottonwood Crossing, Little Arkansas Crossing, Cow Creek Crossing, and Walnut Creek Crossing. Few travelers passed the store at the intersection of the Santa Fe Trail and Cow Creek, called a "whiskey shanty" by Santa Fe Road traveler Hezekiah Brake, "without doing ample justice to both viands and spirits." Brake described the cheap liquor's impact: "The stuff called whisky, furnished at Cow Creek sometimes made the camps worse than scenes where escaped lunatics give vent to unbridled noise and passion. . . . when all were fired with whisky, it was difficult to tell who were the worse men—Indians, Mexicans, Spaniards, or Americans.[11]

Prominent among these "justice doers" were the Kanzas. The tribe's favorite winter hunting camp was located five miles east-southeast of the whiskey shanty at the confluence of the two forks of Cow Creek (two miles south of present-day Lyons, Kansas). On December 23, 1858, about twenty mounted Kanza warriors led by

Chief Watianga raided the Cow Creek store then owned by Asahel Beach, carrying off cattle, horses, and "groceries." Among the latter was liquor, which more than likely provided both a motivation and the necessary disposition for Watianga and his warriors to plunder the store. When owner Asahel Beach prepared his depredation claim against the Kanzas, he informed his attorney of his quandary about whether to report the Indians' theft of the whiskey. After all, the sale of liquor in Indian Country was in violation of section 20 of the 1834 Trade and Intercourse Act. He decided to play it safe, listing only the livestock theft when he filed the actual claim.[12]

Kanza chiefs had recognized the problem of whiskey commerce prior to the tribe's arrival on the upper Neosho. In 1842, frontier entrepreneur George Ewing reported that one of the reasons the Kanzas were willing to sell their land was so they could put distance between themselves and Missouri whiskey merchants. In 1847, just as the tribe was becoming established on their new reservation, agent Richard Cummins reported that "large quantities of spirituous liquors and some wine" were being carried through Indian Country on the Santa Fe Road and that liquor was freely used on the road. That same year, Congress passed the most significant revision of the Indian alcohol code since the Trade and Intercourse Act of 1834. These changes called for imprisonment of any person selling liquor to an Indian in Indian Country. The change in the law also for the first time declared that Indians could be considered competent witnesses. Finally, the 1847 law stipulated that the annuity payments be issued to chiefs rather than to individual members of tribes, as an attempt to reduce the reckless expenditure of the monies to the ever-present whiskey vendors.[13]

The following year the St. Louis Indian Office superintendent, Thomas Harvey, reported that the new Indian liquor law had failed at its purpose of protecting the Indians. The tribes continued to smuggle in large quantities of liquor they procured in Missouri, and that state's laws were "so inefficient that it is difficult to convict the seller, or to punish him effectually if convicted." Cummins's plea to his Indian Office superiors in Washington to provide him with military assistance to enforce the laws illustrates the impotent position of Indian agents on the Kansas frontier. "What can an agent do," he asked, "with a trader after he has got 40 or 50 more miles into the

Indian country with his 20, 30 or more hands. Seize upon his wagons, no, he would be laughed at by them [and] perhaps taken to a hole of water and ducked."[14]

Cummins requested that at least thirty troops be stationed on the Santa Fe Road between Westport and Council Grove with orders to search all wagons heading west. By March 20, 1848, Cummins had heard nothing in response from his superiors in the Indian Office, but he did receive an answer from Colonel Clifton Wharton, commanding officer of Fort Leavenworth: he would receive no troops to stop the whiskey trade on the Santa Fe Road.[15]

As Commissioner Manypenny surmised, this unabated whiskey traffic on the Santa Fe Road profoundly affected the Kanzas. "They often travel a distance of two or three hundred miles for whiskey," wrote Kanza agent Charles Handy in September 1850, "making it convenient to steal a poney or two as they pass along, and exchange the same with these miserable whites along the line for whiskey." In July 1851, immediately following an annuity distribution on the nearby Kanza Reservation, Indians were observed openly purchasing whiskey at the store owned by Westport merchants Boone and Bernard, then managed by its future proprietor Seth Hays. By this time, the situation had clearly gotten out of hand on the reservation. A letter signed by a group of Council Grove traders in 1851 charged that the Intercourse Law was entirely disregarded and that many white men were among the Kanzas, "selling them liquor and otherwise encouraging them to mischief and robberies of which they are to reap the benefit."[16]

Whiskey consumption led not only to Kanza criminal acts targeting whites, but also to in-group brawling, sometimes with tragic consequences. A leading chief of the Kanzas from 1825 through 1845, Fool Chief was reputed to have killed at least two of his tribesmen while on drunken sprees. While encamped on the Shawnee Reservation near Westport in January 1845, Fool Chief, in a drunken rage, attacked a Kanza man, scalping him alive. The man, Wahobake, struck his assailant with a wooden club, killing the Kanza chief instantly. In January 1852, two or three Kanzas were killed during a drunken row about fifteen miles downstream from Council Grove. In the summer of 1857, a group of Kanza men returned to their camp south of the Smoky Hill River after "loading themselves with fire-water" near

Fort Riley. One of them assaulted his wife, who during the struggle killed him with a knife. The syndrome of whiskey-induced violence that victimized fellow tribe members is not unique to the Kanzas but is a well-chronicled phenomenon among neighboring tribes such as the Potawatomies and Sacs and Foxes.[17]

Indian officials both in and outside of Kansas frequently reported on how the tide of migrants sweeping across the territory left in its wake an increase in both whiskey consumption and social disorder among the tribes. In September 1854, the Sac and Fox agent attributed the unprecedented increase of liquor drinking among his tribe to "the fact of a portion of the Territory being open to settlement; the facility for obtaining it has thereby been greater." Kanza agent Montgomery concurred: "As the Territory of Kansas becomes populated, drunkenness and other vices become more prevalent." In each of his four annual reports, Montgomery railed against the devastating impact of the whiskey trade on his Kanza charges. In 1857, he reported that the whiskey shops "at almost every side and corner" of the reservation unfailingly captured a large percentage of the gold and silver coins issued to the Kanzas at the time of annuity payments. In 1858, the Kanza agent observed that the use of intoxicating liquors by the tribe continued unabated and that the laws to suppress the sale of liquor to Indians were insufficient. He also warned that if current liquor consumption persisted, in a few years it would "greatly diminish this very unfortunate and neglected tribe of Indians."[18]

Among the factors limiting the effectiveness of the Indian prohibition laws was how widespread and deeply rooted liquor commerce was among both Indians and whites. Early-day Kansas was a besotted frontier, Council Grove not excepted. Consumers and suppliers of ardent spirits got most of their liquor from distilleries in Missouri, where the production of alcohol was a big and profitable business. By 1840, Missouri produced one-half million gallons of whiskey annually. In 1857, whiskey sales in Kansas City, Missouri, population 1,500, totaled $135,000. Whiskey purchased at Leavenworth for twenty cents a gallon, after being watered down, was sold to Indians at from one dollar to five dollars per gallon. Most of this booze, however, was not being consumed by Indians. In 1860, the average

American fifteen and older annually consumed 2.16 gallons of alcohol in the form of "spirits" (whiskey, rum, gin, brandy), which is
three times today's per capita consumption of the same. The heavi-
est drinkers were white single males in their twenties working as
unskilled employees west of the Mississippi River. That this demographic profile fits most of the soldiers and freighters on the Santa Fe
Road and many residents of early-day Council Grove is confirmed
by the following statistical summary. A tally of traffic through Council Grove in 1859 counts 5,214 men and 220 women, almost all of
the men eighteen to forty years old. In 1855, eighty-three non-Indian
people lived in and near Council Grove; fifty-seven of them (67 percent) were males, only three of whom were over age forty. Of the
385 people living in the Council Grove Township in 1860, 219 were
males, and 153 of them were younger than thirty. Many of these
young men drank hard liquor and, as a consequence, behaved in
rowdy, sometimes violent, ways.[19]

This group's collective thirst translated into profits for proxi-
mate liquor dispensers. Council Grove merchant William Shamleffer recalled that when operating Malcolm Conn's Pioneer Store
in the early 1860s, within two years he sold over $12,000 worth of
whiskey and $15.20 worth of bibles. That some of this whiskey was
sold to the Kanzas is beyond doubt, as illustrated by a typically racist description of business as usual in Council Grove published in
the May 4, 1861 *Council Grove Press*: "A fat brave with his unctuous
better-half, and a pack of buffalo robes, all piled upon the back of a
small pony, is no uncommon spectacle. Being a man of business, the
Indian immediately proceeds to the store to trade, and by a series
of signs and grunts, manifests his desire to buy something. His first
demand is always whiskey." Earlier, the newspaper had denounced
white whiskey traders for selling liquor to the Indians while knowing "the damage it is liable to do, and that it is a palpable violation
of law." In September 1861, newly appointed Kanza agent Hiram W.
Farnsworth lamented, "Drunkenness is a common vice. Whiskey is
sold in many places in violation of law and all efforts to prevent it."[20]

Selling whiskey to Indians, however, was neither confined to the
proximity of the Santa Fe Road nor conducted exclusively by the
disreputable. In the winter of 1860, hunter and trader James R. Mead

was trading with the Kanzas on the "Big Bend" of the Smoky Hill River in present-day northwestern McPherson County. He noticed the Kanzas returning to their camp "full of booze." Investigating, Mead discovered a little shack hidden in an almost inaccessible gulch of a creek south of the Smoky Hill River. "Its stock in trade was booze and tobacco." The proprietor was none other than a future pillar of Council Grove society, Isaac Sharp, who went on to be the Democratic gubernatorial candidate in 1870.[21]

The traders defended themselves by arguing that they were exempt from the Indian intercourse laws because the Santa Fe Road was a public highway. The laws forbade selling liquor in "Indian Country," the boundaries of which remained nebulous and mutable in light of a number of factors, including land-cession and right-of-way treaties, statutory revisions affecting liquor laws, political infighting between politicians and government administrators, and development of settlements such as Council Grove along the overland trail corridors. Once Kansas Territory opened for settlement in 1854, the last vestiges of Indian Country as a zone of protection for Indians rapidly disappeared beneath waves of Euro-American land seekers.[22]

Many of these immigrants brought along a fondness for drink and a proclivity for intimidation and violence, a frequent subject of journalists touring the Kansas frontier. T. H. Gladstone, an Englishman headed to Leavenworth from Kansas City by steamboat in 1856, described his "border ruffian" traveling companions rushing to the bar "already maddened with whisky." The proslavery drinkers proceeded to vent a hateful rant aimed at their free-state enemies: "We ain't agoin' to stand their comin' and dictatin' to us with their nigger-worshipping, we ain't. I reckon we'll make the place hot enough for them soon that's a fact. Here, boys, drink. Liquors, captain, for the crowd. Step up this way, old hoss, and liquor."[23]

Perhaps less acknowledged is that in their indulgence in both "spiritous liquor" and the ensuing violence, Indians bore a strong resemblance to their white neighbors. "If Indians would only do what white men find so difficult, 'drink moderately,' it would not be so bad," lamented a Kansas Indian agent in 1862. Where men of any race or color gathered to drink, violence often erupted. Consider these extracts over a five-month period in 1860 from a Topeka news-paper, the *Kansas State Record*: In March, an old man who had come to Topeka to sell some vegetables was assaulted by some young men, who "being in liquor," beat him so severely he had to be carried off. In June, a man named Haley fatally stabbed a man named Burke in Kansas City: "Cause—whisky." One Sunday night in July a fracas took place in a "drinking saloon" in Atchison during which one man was killed and several wounded.[24]

Describing the drunkenness and violence of the Kanzas in terri-torial Kansas ostensibly reinforces the stereotype of the "drunken Indian." Regarded in the context of the times, however, it is obvious that the Kanzas were reflecting the behavior of the whites surround-ing them. "Everywhere on the frontier," wrote historian Robert Utley, "nearly all men drank nearly all the time, which made nearly all men more or less drunk most of the time. Drink enhanced self-importance, impaired judgment, generated heedless courage, and encouraged unreasoning resort to violence." It seems that the gov-ernment's policy of "assimilation" whereby the Kanza were edu-cated to adapt white men's attitudes and habits was successful in at least one area—the common vice of drunkenness.[25]

Inevitably, the presence of hard liquor on the Kanza Reservation was one of several catalytic factors stimulating the eruption of vio-lence between the Indians and whites in 1858 and 1859. In March 1858, territorial governor James Denver warned the Indian Office that the frustrated Kanzas were likely to commit depredations on the whites who had encroached on the reservation. In fact, even be-fore Denver's warning, the Kanzas were accused of various crimes. Dr. James H. Bradford, a Council Grove physician who resided east of the river, claimed that Kanzas robbed his house in the autumn of 1857. He had been treating Wahobake for dropsy (edema) by pre-scribing "medicinal brandy." Allegedly, the Kanzas broke into his house and stole ten gallons of brandy valued at forty-five dollars. Allen Crowley, a squatter in the Big John Creek area, attributed to the Kanzas a series of depredations starting in 1855 and extending through 1858: stealing household items such as flour, a mirror, blan-kets, one hoe, and gloves; burning a horse worth one hundred dol-lars; burning down his house and two thousand fence rails; killing an ox to provide food for a war party planning to raid the Pawnees; and taking one hundred bushels of corn from his fields.[26]

Mounting tensions on the reservation boiled over into actual physical violence on August 13, 1858, when a fracas broke out between a party of Kanzas and white squatters on Big John Creek near the northernmost of the Kanza villages. Some Kanzas entered P. D. Reed's cabin and became unruly. A struggle ensued during which several blows were struck. Having been summoned to the scene, Reed's neighbor Adam Helm shot a Kanza in the arm, whereupon the Indians struck both Mrs. Reed and Helm with a tomahawk, cutting his hand and head. With the enraged Kanzas in pursuit, Helm fled to a neighbor's. The Indians robbed his home, taking beds and bedding, clothing, meat, flour, sugar, coffee, one calf, poultry, beans, melons, pumpkins, corn, and potatoes worth $176. Reed's claim for stolen property was for $63.25.[27]

The day after the incident a delegation of whites including H. J. Espy met with Chief Pegahoshe at his village on Big John Creek, during which the Kanza chief presented a lengthy review "covering all the legal points in the Kaw land question." The following day the greater portion of the tribe, led by Hard Chief, Pegahoshe, and Fool Chief, met with area citizens in Council Grove. Thomas Huffaker and tribal member Sam Sampson acted as interpreters. Inexplicably absent was the man who should have been present to mediate the meeting as a function of his office—agent John Montgomery. The Indians admitted that their tribesmen had taken property from Reed and Helm and agreed to restore what was not destroyed or lost, and to pay for what they did not restore. In response, the whites' spokesman, Espy, informed the tribe that if the Kanzas were to ever again "imbrue their hands in the blood of a white man, the white people would exterminate their tribe."[28]

Another corrosive element in the deteriorating Kanza-white relations was the plague of horse stealing, the numerous perpetrators being both Indians and whites. One of many such instances took place in April 1859 when four white men lodged overnight in Council Grove. When they awoke next morning, nine of their horses, together valued at $525, were missing. During the men's ensuing investigation, the trail of the crime led to the Kanzas. The tribe admitted to the thievery and returned seven of the least valuable horses. However, a yellow mare worth $150 and a stallion valued at $200 were never recovered, the Kanzas having taken them to present-day Oklahoma, where they had sold them.[29]

As the tribe sank deeper into poverty, instances of horse stealing increased. In October 1859, agent Dickey reported "very bitter and hostile feeling against the Indians" in the settlements nearest the Kanza Reservation, especially for the theft of horses and cattle. The agent attributed the thievery to "hunger and extreme want." As a strategy of last resort, the destitute Kanzas would offer their ponies for sale to whites on the lookout for a bargain. A common Euro-American trade practice was to wait until late winter or spring when the Kanzas were especially needy and their ponies enfeebled by winter. In February 1858, a Cottonwood Falls man counseled settlers to buy Kanza ponies now "as it is a hard matter for them to keep their ponies from starving." The May 11, 1861, *Council Grove Press* advised that it was a propitious time to start a livery stable, as "Indian ponies can now be bought of the Kaws very cheap," meaning ten dollars a head. Dickey wrote that "the greater part of all the trouble" with the Indians was caused when the desperate Kanzas would steal horses from the settlements to replenish those they had previously sold in order to subsist.[30]

In September 1860, the 803 Kanzas, as counted by Dickey, possessed 350 horses, with an average value of forty dollars each. Worth fourteen thousand dollars in aggregate, their pony herd was by far the tribe's most valuable property. Beyond their trade value, horses were needed to enable the Indians to wrest subsistence from the land. Horses were used to transport the Kanzas to and from their bison hunting regions in central Kansas where they were mounted by the men during the actual hunts. Kanza women used them as pack animals in moving camp equipment and hauling meat and robes back to the villages. They also were indispensable to warriors combating their well-mounted enemies on the plains. By 1860, the Kanzas were utterly dependent on bison hunts because white encroachment had eliminated their practice of agriculture. "I can see no other way for them to live during the coming winter, but to return to their hunt," wrote Dickey.[31]

The Kanzas' destitution was compounded by white people steal-ing horses from the Indians. Dickey's successor as Kanza agent, Hiram Farnsworth, reported in June 1861 that the tribe could no lon-ger provide for their families by hunting buffalo because the "po-nies of many have been stolen." The agent spent much of his time traveling across the country assisting the Kanzas in locating horses stolen from them by white people. At about the same time, Kanza chiefs requested that power of attorney be granted to a Mr. Deming to recover about fifty ponies stolen from them and to identify the thieves.[32]

The Kanzas were not the only tribe in the region suffering from horse thievery by whites. A neighboring tribe located forty miles east, the Sac and Fox Nation, suffered from the depredations of horse thieves. In 1858, the tribal agent warned that if no means were de-vised to protect the Sacs and Foxes, "the only property on which they rely [horses] will soon all be taken from them." Adjoining the Sac and Fox Reservation on the east was the Ottawa tribe, who suf-fered the loss of many of their horses and ponies, stolen by "law-less and unprincipled white men," agent Perry Fuller reported in September 1860. Fuller had made several attempts to hunt down and arrest such men, but discovered that when closely followed, the thieves "leave for Pike's Peak, thus rendering pursuit useless." The potential for violence implicit in such criminal activity was realized in 1859 when four Potawatomies were murdered by horse thieves based in eastern Kansas.[33]

At the same time the far-flung nature of this phenomenon was vig-orously reiterated by the Pawnee agent J. L. Gillis, who declared the country from the Missouri River to the Rocky Mountains "infested with organized bands of daring and desperate horse-thieves, who have committed their depredations indiscriminately on the white man and the Indian." In June 1859, newspaper editor Sam Wood recommended vigilante violence as the only way to rid the country of horse thieves. "HANG EVERY ONE ENGAGED IN THE BUSINESS," he thundered. That same month nine alleged horse thieves, all of them white, were arrested and tried by a vigilante court in Council Grove. Three of the men were acquitted, two were whipped ten lashes and ordered to leave Kansas Territory, and four of the men received ten lashes, had one side of their heads shaved, and ordered to leave the country.[34]

Just as destitution contributed to Kanza thievery, so too did economic disaster drive some frontier white people to crimes such as horse thievery. The destructive and long-enduring effects of the Panic of 1857, which severely depressed wheat and corn prices, seriously affected Kansas Territory. In October 1857, a Lawrence newspaper observed that the crash among eastern banks had fallen severely upon the people of Kansas because the "country was full of Eastern exchange, which has become valueless. The times look dark and foreboding."[35]

Both whiskey and horse thievery triggered the tragic events of June 17, 1859. At about 8:00 A.M. that day, ninety-six Kanzas led by Allegawaho, armed and in full war regalia, rode up to the front of Seth Hays's store. Hays emerged and faced the Indians. According to one of four contemporary descriptions—that of Council Grove merchant Tom C. Hill—Hays did not give the mounted Kanzas an opportunity to explain why they appeared in such a manner. Instead, the merchant ordered them to leave. Indisposed to comply, the Indians lingered momentarily in the street. With little hesitation, Hays tried to frighten the Kanzas into leaving by firing two pistols into the air, one intentionally, the other accidentally. Rather than intimidating the Kanzas, Hays's shooting appeared to anger them. In the confusion, some Kanzas fired on nearby whites, wounding two men named Parks and Gilkey who lay wounded in the street, one shot through the neck with a bullet, the other hit in the side with an arrow. Holding his recently fired pistols, Seth Hays barricaded himself inside his store. In the meantime, the Kanzas fled, riding rapidly south to Four Mile Creek, where they gathered in council.[36]

Hill's version of the June 17 events was the most sympathetic to the Kanzas, possibly because he was a business rival of Seth Hays. Not so H. J. Espy, who, like Hill, had been both an eyewitness and participant in the day's events. Espy described the Kanzas' tone and manner as "bantering and insolent." Understanding most of the Indians' language and gestures, Hays was convinced that many were *much intoxicated* [emphasis mine] and their presence boded no good, so he "told them peremptorily to leave." After Hays's pistols went

Seth Hays, prominent Council Grove merchant. Arriving in Council Grove in 1847, Hays built a successful commercial operation trading with the Kanzas and freighters on the Santa Fe Trail. He died in 1873. Courtesy Morris County Historical Society.

off, Hard Chief raised his hand and spoke a few words to his men. The Kanzas then turned again to face the whites, "fired and then fled from the town at both outlets."[37]

A third perspective was offered by Thomas Huffaker, who stood by Hays's side translating the exchange: "They assembled at the door of Mr. Hays house and began to abuse Hays and other citizens," Huffaker wrote. The trader ordered the Indians to stop the verbal assault, but they continued, so he discharged two pistol shots over their heads. A fourth commentary appears in Kanza agent Milton Dickey's report to the Office of Indian Affairs. Dickey, who heard the Indians' side of the story during a June 22 council with Kanza chiefs, wrote that Hays had "acted hasty and to say the least improvidently by the premature discharge of his pistols until he had learned the intentions of the Indians."[38]

Hill, Espy, Huffaker, and Dickey all agreed on the facts of the precipitating event. On June 15, Kanza warriors had stolen two horses from the wagon train of R. Ortise, a Mexican commercial operator on the Santa Fe Trail. The importance of the Mexican freighters to local businesses is made clear by Seth Hays's register of all commercial trains passing through Council Grove from April 11 to June 6,

1859. Mexicans operated 17 of the 47 wagon trains, owned 184 of the 418 total wagons, and shipped 438.5 tons of freight out of a total of 1,070 tons. For Council Grove merchants it was a smart business practice to keep their Santa Fe Road clients happy, whether Mexican or American. So when Ortise complained about the June 15 thefts, Council Grove leaders immediately contacted the Kanza villages, demanding that the Indians return the stolen horses.[39]

According to Dickey, the Kanzas made a show of force at Hays's store because they were concerned that the whites would subject them to the same treatment they had administered a few days before on the party of white horse thieves. Of course, infusing venom into any white-Kanza contact was the bitter, unresolved dispute over possession of the Kanza Reservation. In particular, the ensuing events of June 17 can best be understood when viewed against the background of Espy's threat the previous August to exterminate the entire tribe should the Kanzas spill anymore white blood.[40]

Early in the afternoon of June 17, fulfilling this threat was foremost in the minds of Espy and his fellow citizens. Hill claimed that within six hours of the shooting over a hundred white men had gathered in town, "all perfectly blood thirsty." Disputing Hill's "blood thirsty" characterization, Espy described the people as calm as they quietly prepared to annihilate the tribe: "they spoke and acted as though a stern duty was staring them in the face, and they intended to acquit themselves like men." The practice of genocide, it seems, requires manly self-control.[41]

Meanwhile at their camp on Four Mile Creek, the Kanzas decided to send a small delegation into town to propose peace. Simultaneously, the citizens elected Espy to be their war leader, in his words, "not to make peace, but to chastise the Indians." Although chastising falls short of exterminating, choosing a leader obligated to fulfill his extermination threat signaled to the Kanzas that the tribe's survival was at stake. Espy's first act as captain was to send ten "spies" to reconnoiter the Kanzas' position. Half an hour later, fourteen Kanzas comprising the peace delegation were seen approaching the town from the south. Alone and unarmed, Espy went out to converse with them, but at this point the Indians saw the rapid approach of the ten spies, and, sensing an ambush, wheeled and retreated.[42]

Espy ordered his spies to intercept the party of Kanzas and bring them into town, a task they were unable to accomplish. It was only after the failure of the spy party to engage the Indians that a "peaceable adjustment" was first mentioned among the whites. A four-man committee including both Hill and Huffaker was appointed to confer with the Indians. The Kanzas, on the other hand, had concluded that bloodshed was inevitable, and so, in Huffaker's words, "they prepared to make a fight as they told us they supposed the whites would exterminate them."[43]

The citizen committee approached within a mile of the Kanza camp, giving signs of peaceful purposes. The Kanzas sent out a party of their own, and talks ensued. According to Hill, the Kanzas expressed their desire for a peaceful resolution. Hours of contemplating the real prospect of impending tribal annihilation no doubt had made the Kanza chiefs compliant. The Indians proposed two alternatives. They would either turn over the two men who had shot Parks and Gilkey or forfeit to the whites their eight thousand dollar annuity payment. Thomas Huffaker, again present as interpreter, recalled, "I was firm with the Kaw and resisted their attempts to bribe our people instead of turning over the braves." That the whites interpreted the offer of the annuity as an attempt at bribery reveals the cultural divide separating the adversaries. The Kanzas and many other tribes practiced a deep-seated tradition of resolving conflicts resulting from serious crimes such as murder by compensating the victims' kin and allies with gifts. Although the Indians adhered to their own doctrines of revenge, the preferred response in such situations was "to cover the dead" by presenting the relatives with gifts, and in this way circumventing the need to compensate death only by means of more death.[44]

Rejecting the money, the committee returned to Council Grove to report the Kanza concession proposals. Espy and his men were then sent to the Kanza position to take possession of the two prisoners. At the time it was presumed that Gilkey would survive but that Parks's wound was fatal. (Two days later it was reported that both men would recover, which they did.) Before sunset on June 17, Espy returned to Council Grove with the two Indian captives. Hill's letter provides the details about what happened next, although it is

Group of Kanzas during the time that the people were living on the Neosho Reservation. Courtesy Kansas State Historical Society.

important to note that Espy conceded the veracity of Hill's account of the subsequent events.[45]

Espy told the crowd that he had done all that he had been requested to, and that they were at liberty to do with the two Indians as they saw fit. After a few minutes, a citizen asked: "What disposition shall be made with these Indians?" Some men in the crowd shouted, "Hang them!" The prisoners were taken about a block west, where they were hung on the south side of Main Street in a livery stable. The bodies were left hanging until the next morning. Huffaker claimed that the Indians were hung only "after mature deliberation," and later in his life he said he believed that "justice was served." Hill's detailed narrative of the event suggests otherwise. In light of the actual outcome, perhaps Hill's charge that the whites were "all perfectly bloodthirsty" is not entirely without merit.[46]

A recurring justification for employment of vigilante violence is that citizens seeking to preserve public order had no viable recourse to normal legal channels. Police and courts were virtually nonexistent on the remote, sparsely settled, and "underdeveloped" frontier.

Indian agents, however, had the authority to intervene at the earliest possible moment to mitigate against violent incidents involving Indians and whites and to ensure that conditions were established for lawful resolution. This authority had been unambiguously given to them by the Indian Trade and Intercourse Acts. But just as agent John Montgomery was absent during the August 1858 incident at Big John Creek, so too was newly appointed Kanza agent Milton Dickey inexplicably a nonfactor on June 17, 1859. Ironically, one of the factors behind the Indian Office finally locating its agents on the Kanza Reservation in 1855 was pressure from Indian traders complaining about Kanza lawlessness. Agent proximity, however, had little effect when put to the test by actual events.[47]

Finally, it seems fair to ask why prominent Council Grove citizens such as Thomas Huffaker did not use their influence to persuade the June 17 mob that the Indian prisoners should be detained until the officials in the Indian Office were given an opportunity to exercise their authority. It may be that the mood of the crowd when they beheld the prisoners precluded any such possibility. It had been a long, frightening, and exhausting day, and darkness was rapidly approaching. These conditions alone make it plausible that the whites favored quick resolution delivered by violence rather than "mature deliberation" required by justice. When we consider that initially the citizens were committed to a plan for tribal obliteration, the execution of the two Kanzas seems a foregone conclusion. Upholding the law was irrelevant. Indians had to die so that white men who had promised massive violence in retaliation could save face. Finally, what mattered most was resolving the question lingering over the Kanza Reservation since the beginning of white encroachment: who could impose their sense of order on whom—that is, who had power and who had none.

The Kanza who had wounded Gilkey was a young chief. Because he was a warrior he did not wish to be hung, but preferred death by the hand of his victim. He requested that his execution be carried out by being shot by Gilkey. The wounded Gilkey was unable to execute the Kanza, and so he was hung. The man who had shot Parks was told that his victim was sure to die and that his life was about to be taken for it. He replied, "I am willing to give it, and will die like a brave man." A day after the hanging, the whites and Indians met together in council. The Kanzas, according to Hill, had left their camp on June 17 for the purpose of delivering up the two horses and having a talk with some of the citizens. But, according to Hill's version of events that day, "Hays had insulted them in the commencement and they had then done what they were sorry for."[48]

Hill concluded that the tribe had shown "a willingness to give up," and the trouble with the Kanzas was over. His assessment was corroborated by Dickey, who said that two days after the affair both whites and the Kanzas had expressed their regrets that it had happened, both had admitted to doing wrong, and the common desire was that the matter be allowed to drop. The Indians also promised not to steal any more from the Mexicans. Three months later Dickey reported that Kanzas had committed fewer depredations that summer than in previous years. The matter was not allowed to drop, however, as a number of Council Grove citizens were indicted for the hangings and tried in U.S. district court. They were "acquitted without much trouble," though, according to John Maloy, author of *History of Morris County, 1820–1890*. Records of this case have not surfaced and the identities of those facing charges are unknown.[49]

The "regretting" of the affair by white people is difficult to discern. Only contempt for the Indians is expressed in a letter ostensibly signed by "Fessor" from "Counsel Groave" in the July 11 issue of the *Kansas Press*, Sam Wood's Cottonwood Falls newspaper. Wood is likely the real author of this appalling parody: "Sense yu wor up hear times hey, bin poorty brisk, we hev haid one hangen, but the material warent good—nuthen but Cau Injens, you ort tu hev bin here to witnessed that. They gin them ar Caus one of thee jewhilicanest stretchens ever yu sou. They hung em tel they war ded ded, ef yu call a day and nite any thing."[50]

Arguably the most sensational and violent episode in Council Grove's history, the story has been kept alive by succeeding generations of writers, being treated in detail not only by Maloy (1890), but also by Andreas (1883), Brigham (1921), Alice Smith (1928), and Haucke (1952). One aspect of this story mostly absent in the accounts of the day, but featured in the later versions, is the dispensation of the bodies of the executed Kanzas. Whether fact or fantasy, these anecdotes indicate that the passage of time served to amplify a fascination with the morbid. For example, Andreas found it "a pitying sight to see the mother of the young chief cut and lacerate her head, neck and breast, and with the blood that flowed from her self-inflicted wounds rub the post on which her son had breathed his last." Of equal interest was the moment the bodies were returned to the tribe. In Lalla Maloy Brigham's *The Story of Council Grove on the Santa Fe Trail*, Brigham describes how Robert Rochford hauled the dead to the Kanza village in his ox-drawn wagon. Just as he arrived, the Indians "began their ceremony for the dead, which frightened the ox team. It was some time before they could be stopped, as the wagon was going around in a circle." Sixty-two years after the tragic event, Brigham felt it important to note that Mr. Rochford "could easily verify the statement that 'the only good Indian is a dead Indian.'"[51]

The emblem of Indian haters everywhere, the phrase "the only good Indian" expressed the same mind-set as Espy's pledge of extermination, the shouts of "hang them," Wood's disgusting "material warent good" parody, and the Kanza agent's satisfaction that smallpox would soon lead to the tribe's extinction. Embedded in a deeply felt sense of racial superiority pervasive throughout white America in the mid-nineteenth century, Indian hating had been the provenance of many generations of frontiersmen. In 1835, James Hall sketched the formation of the Indian hater's psyche: "Every child thus reared, learns to hate an Indian, because he always hears him spoken of as an enemy. From the cradle, he listens continually to horrid tales of savage violence, and becomes familiar with narratives of aboriginal cunning and ferocity. Every family can number some of its members or relatives among the victims of a midnight massacre. . . . With persons thus reared, hatred towards an Indian becomes a part of their nature, and revenge an instinctive principle." Indian haters viewed government policy makers, reformers, and philanthropists as deluded, "sickly sentimentalists" whose distant eastern domiciles insulated them from the stern realities of the western frontier. They believed, in Richard White's words, "that birth and race ought to make whites and Indians permanent strangers." Indians could not be civilized because being civilized meant becoming white. When a superior race collides with an inferior one, the latter must yield either by a regime of repression or by extermination.[52]

The racism and violence implicit in Indian hating propelled the events of June 17 to their tragic conclusion. It was an ideological construct licensing Euro-American men to regard the Kanzas as the alien "Other," an intrinsically inferior and irredeemable form of humanity. Particularly galling to the frontiersmen and, for them, a graphic demonstration of the Kanzas' essential depravity, was the tribe's habit of begging. "The Kaw Indians are known as the most ignorant and debased of the various aboriginal tribes on the eastern borders of Kansas," declared a Lawrence newspaper in 1857. "They are sunk in ignorance and degradation; are too indolent to labor, and too debased to be of service to themselves or to others. Unlike the Delawares or Shawnees, they do not engage in agriculture, but subsist almost wholly by the chase, by levying black mail on travelers, in stealing from the settlers, by the charities of the generous, or by annuities from government." Being dependent on others was anathema to white Americans who saw themselves as hardworking, self-sufficient, and ruggedly independent. A mark of their racial superiority was that, unlike the Kanzas, they could meet every challenge without succumbing to a condition of dependency.[53]

Within a year of the June 17 tragedy, this proposition was tested by one of nature's great levelers, weather. "Yesterday the wind was very high, and the stronger it blew the hotter became the temperature," reported the August 18, 1860, *Emporia News*. The air felt like it emanated from an oven and comfort was nowhere to be found. At three o'clock the thermometer stood at 110 degrees. The country was blasted by hot, withering winds several times in the summer of 1860. A Topeka newspaper reported in mid-July "the severest storm of wind ever known in this country" heated the air "almost to suffication. Penetrating every crevice, it was impossible to escape, entirely, its baleful effects." The terrible wind drove those working outdoors inside, prostrated farm animals, and burned young shoots of fruit trees. Although singular events, the desiccating winds were symptomatic of one of the most horrific droughts in Kansas history. The dry spell extending from June 1859 to February 1861 devastated both the Kanzas and their white neighbors.[54]

Reports of dry times first appeared in area newspapers in the spring of 1860. On March 3, the *Topeka Tribune* noted that the driest spring in five years had created a lack of moisture in the soil and caused farmers to lament "in right good earnest." Butler County was reported as parched and crisp. Over the next few months a drama unfolded in Kansas during which the state's newspaper editors and public officials slowly and reluctantly came to recognize that an insidious, life-sucking monster was in their midst and they needed help.[55]

Throughout late summer and early autumn 1860, a curious mix of denial and despair surfaced in the newspapers. The July 30 *Council Grove Press* rejoiced about "a very fine rain last Tuesday worth thousands to our farmers" while on the same page another column gloomily declared that area farmers were suffering intolerably with the drought, that the wheat and oat crops were entirely ruined, and that the corn appeared to be a failure. That July some Topeka citizens, concluding that they were being scourged by God for their wickedness, set apart "a day of fasting and prayer to the Giver of 'every good and perfect gift,' for rain." On August 6, the Council Grove newspaper celebrated "a perfect deluge" that would save some of the crops "that before were roasting with the drouth." Three weeks later, the paper both noted the "advancing vegetation" caused by recent "copious rains" and acknowledged that the corn crop would be a failure.[56]

By early autumn, denial became untenable. The monster, it was reluctantly conceded, was on the loose. "Disguise it as we may, this part of Kansas is suffering dreadfully with the drouth," conceded the *Council Grove Press* in late September. Nine-tenths of the settlers had exhausted their subsistence, crops were an entire failure, and business stood at a standstill. The people, according to the newspaper, "must do one of three things—have help, leave or starve."[57]

One eyewitness later provided this description: "Then everything was parched—literally burned up for want of water. Even our largest streams were dry, and the wells almost failed. The rays of the hot sun dazzled our eyes when we gazed out on the burning and dusty prairies. The hot winds and clouds of flying dust that rolled through our streets, and over our prairies, were almost suffocating. . . . The cattle lolled out their tongues and the poor animals of all kinds sought in vain for a cool place or a refreshing draught of water from the creeks. The leaves on the forest trees were shriveled, and fell to the ground in midsummer. Everything wore an air of feverish heat."[58]

The drought did not discriminate. The Kanzas' crop of corn, on which the tribe principally depended for food in midsummer, failed entirely in 1860. Agent Dickey worried that the suffering Kanzas would be forced to rove about looking for food, provoking hostile reactions from whites. As an antidote, the agent recommended an early annuity payment to the tribe. An unanticipated and favorable consequence of the drought was that, in the autumn, bison extended their range farther east than normal into the margins of the tallgrass region, significantly shortening the Kanzas' journey to their hunting grounds.[59]

Nevertheless, the tribe's situation remained desperate. In October, Dickey purchased four beef cattle for the Kanzas. On March 1, 1861, the agent cited the "unprecedented drought of the last year" as causing the tribe to "suffer to an extent beyond description." Unless assistance was soon forthcoming, Dickey warned, starvation would ensue. In early June, the government distributed to the eight hundred Kanzas eighteen hundred pounds of corn, five barrels of pork, and nineteen sacks of flour. The Kanza agent credited this relief with keeping the Kanzas from pilfering from their white neighbors.[60]

Meanwhile, the Kanzas' white neighbors also found themselves in desperate circumstances. The farmers, however, did not go down without a fight. When it was clear that their wheat crop had failed, they plowed it up and planted corn. When this crop withered, they plowed again and planted buckwheat. This too perished, but yet another plowing ensued, and turnip seeds were broadcast, but the dust yielded no turnips. By late summer desperate Kansans were writing to eastern newspapers and philanthropists describing the appalling conditions on the Kansas frontier and begging for relief.[61]

At first, Kansas editors were indignant. "The people repudiate, utterly, any such idea as begging, for the means of support from their Eastern friends," declared the *Emporia News*. The newspaper castigated those making such appeals as falsely representing the real sentiment of Kansans. Such beggars "belong to that class who ought to have remained at home tied to the apron strings of their mothers." As promotional organs seeking to attract newcomers to their communities, newspapers were especially outraged by the letter writers who, in the journalists' view, were frightening away thousands of timid settlers and keeping thousands more from immigrating here. The September 8 *Topeka Tribune* defiantly declared, "We as a people are entirely competent to take care of and provide for ourselves."[62]

This they could not do. Prominent citizens on an investigative tour of Kansas confirmed the desperate plight of the settlers. In the autumn a Territorial Relief Committee was formed to address the "Kansas famine." Penurious and facing the prospect of starvation, proud white Kansans were forced to beg for relief. "No one at a distance can form any idea of the actual condition of things here," conceded the *Council Grove Press* in early November 1860. "Those who could, many of them, have left the county to winter; others cannot leave, but by making sacrifices of property, can live until next year. But a large number have raised nothing, and have no means to buy with; and unless they have help, and that soon, they must starve." In fact, approximately one-third of the white population left Kansas during the period of drought.[63]

Contributions of provisions and money poured in from the East. From November 14, 1860, to March 15, 1861, Morris County received 62,180 pounds of donated food and clothing. The county's per capita distribution is difficult to determine. In August 1860, the census counted 694 residents of Morris County. By the winter a significant percentage had left. Some residents did not need assistance. Those who did and remained in the county probably received 150 to 200 pounds of provisions per person. These contributions undoubtedly saved many settlers from destitution and helped to stabilize the county's population. Conversely, the U.S. government provided 7,543 pounds of meat, grain, and flour to the eight hundred Kanzas, equating to 9.4 pounds per capita. There is no record of donated clothing.[64]

When the drought imposed the prospect of hunger on white Kansans, they were reduced to begging. In dependent circumstances, Kansans gladly accepted relief. The presumed yawning gap separating whites and Kanza proved delusional, the presumption of essential difference stripped away by the capricious assault of nature. But the weather turned more favorable. Starting in mid-January 1861, a series of strong storms dumped large amounts of snow on Council Grove and environs. Then on February 8 warm weather set in, followed by heavy rains that rapidly melted the snow. The *Council Grove Press* was unabashedly joyous: "The Neosho at the foot of Main street was fully capable of floating a seventy-four gunship. In all our uneventful life, high water had not such a pleasing effect on our feelings."[65]

*

While it is true that before 1855 the Kanzas had been ravaged by epidemics and the effects of whiskey, neglected by agents, plagued by skirmishes with Euro-Americans and the vagaries of weather, the tribe had never before experienced such a concentrated and relentless assault by inimical biological, political, cultural, and environmental forces that converged on their homeland from 1855 to 1860. Weakened by malnutrition, in 1855 the Kanzas suffered a severe smallpox epidemic that killed at least four hundred people. Kanza agents were remotely located, ineffective, and preoccupied with their own political and entrepreneurial schemes. The tribe was victimized by a brisk illegal whiskey trade and far-flung horse-stealing networks. The reservation rapidly became a cauldron of seething hostilities between the Kanzas and a Euro-American population steeped in the consciousness of white racial superiority. An armed confrontation between Kanza warriors and townspeople in Council Grove resulted in the hanging of two young Kanza men and the tribe's humiliation. Never again would the Kanza leaders employ armed confrontation as a tactic in dealing with the white people. The incredible drought of 1860 inflicted severe suffering on the Kanzas and white Kansans alike. Although it is doubtlessly true that tribal and governmental leaders could have been more effective in ameliorating the tribe's misery, the problems were so deep-seated and of such vast scale politically, socially, and geographically that even the strongest chiefs and agents would likely have failed. The ramifications of the doctrine of Manifest Destiny and many of its attendant pathologies—lawlessness, greed, whiskey, violence, and racism—were inevitably visited upon the vulnerable and marginalized Kanzas.

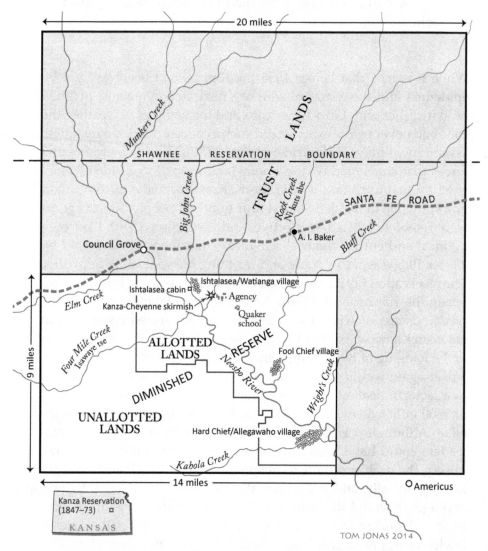

Kanza Reservation, 1860–73. © 2014, University of Oklahoma Press.

CHAPTER 5

Endless Trouble and Quarrels

In the early 1860s most of the approximately eight hundred Kanzas were organized into three bands, whose names reflected the creek valleys in which their villages were located. Ishtalasea's Big John Creek village was the largest, with a population of 271. Fool Chief's Rock Creek village had 247 people, and the Kahola Creek village, headed by Nopawia and Allegawaho, was inhabited by 257. The thirty-two remaining members of the tribe, listed by the Indian Office as "half-breeds," were not affiliated with any of the villages. Each village was periodically relocated to a site along the same stream providing good wood, water, and grass for the pony herds. Here a band would reside until the surrounding pastures were eaten down and filth accumulated, then once again the village would be relocated up or down stream. Until its disruption by the smallpox epidemic of 1855 and the white encroachment of 1856–62, this village arrangement provided the tribe with the means to adapt to the requirements of the land while maintaining its traditional social organization.[1]

Village life was communal, with social identities and functions organized according to an elaborate kinship system consisting of no less than sixteen clans, large extended families, each with its own name, traditions, rites, and responsibilities. For example, the Lo (or Thunder People) burned the prairie during a drought to cause rain. The Ta (or Deer People) were responsible for carrying messages and making announcements. Every Kanza belonged to a clan, membership determined at birth by the father's affiliation. Each clan owned a set of birth names conferred on its members by order of birth. Clan members considered their fellows as family, assuming a common ancestor. Although members of one clan might be found in all three villages, sometimes multiple families of the same clan occupied a common dwelling. The close proximity of lodges inherent in the village arrangement augmented the social cohesion afforded by the clan system. Obviously, this venerable, close-knit spatial and social system was antithetical to the dispersed, individualized farmsteads favored by white settlers and federal Indian policy.[2]

Reflecting declining Kanza economic fortunes and itinerant existence, Kanza huts around 1860 were rudimentary abodes compared to the large earth lodges they had lived in at the Blue Earth village on the Kansas River in the early nineteenth century. By the late 1850s their dwellings were reduced to little more than makeshift tents with frames of limber, eight-foot-long saplings stuck into the ground and arced over at the top. These frames were covered by multicolored canvases, hides, buffalo robes, and reed mats tied around the poles and drawn tightly together near the top, leaving an opening for smoke to escape. In 1862, Kanza agent Farnsworth described the lodges as "made of bark, grass, and skins. Some few have cloth tents."[3]

Providing a suitable habitat for the Kanza dwellings were the abundant, well-timbered streams bearing such names as Big John, Little John, Four Mile, Wright's, Rock, and Kahola. The Kanzas had their own names for these streams, although they too knew the north–south flowing creek passing two miles east of Council Grove as Big John. Four Mile was Isawaye ts'e, meaning "Where Hateful Died." Rock Creek was Nikuts'abe, or "The Creek in Which the Man Died." "Neosho" is a Kanza name meaning "Principal River." The Indians also called this river Watci^{n}cka tanga, or "Big River." A sample of translations of Kanza names for other reservation streams reveal a landscape laden with story and meaning: "War Road," "The Small Creek Where a Tree Was Broken by a Fall or Striking," "Where Kanika Farmed," and "The Lodge of Big Pawhuska."[4]

Although it did not resemble modern eco-romantic idealization of noble savages living in harmony with a benign nature, the Kanza way of life required an earth awareness that was time-tested, practical, nuanced, and cyclical. Early surveyors' maps indicate "Indian trails" wending along stream valleys and ridges both within and on the periphery of the reservation. To provide better forage for their ponies and to attract game to their Flint Hills hunting grounds, the Kanzas deliberately set fire to the prairie, thereby stimulating the earlier growth of more nutritious grasses in the spring. One way they set the prairie afire was by wrapping rawhide around a big ball of dead grass, lighting it, then pulling it behind a running horse. The Kanzas knew the locations of springs; the best water holes for bathing; meadows where "prairie turnips" could be dug; oxbow lakes where the women harvested large quantities of the nutritious, nut-like seeds of the American lotus plant; the most prolific berry and plum thickets; which tree hollows housed raccoons; and many other natural features and processes we can only guess at. The Kanza name for April was Tilling Moon; June was Buffalo Pawing Moon; September was Elk Rutting Moon; December was Bears Hibernating Moon. The organizing principle of this consciousness was the variegated land itself: its topography, waters, soils, plants, animals, and seasonal fluxes. This way of experiencing the earth was made all the more potent by a deeply ingrained sensibility that implicit in all places and beings was an invisible life and power called Wakanda.[5]

In 1861, this ancient way of living on the Kansas landscape was violently disrupted when the U.S. government imposed a linear grid on the Kanza Reservation in the form of the allotment system. In conformance with the Treaty of 1859, each member of the tribe was assigned a forty-acre parcel of land. The headman of each lodge was granted his forty-acre square near a stream where a stone hut was built. Frequently his wife, and perhaps a son or two, were assigned bottomland plots adjoining his, judged suitable for raising crops. Other members of the lodge were likely to be assigned their forty-acre parcel in the uplands within a mile or two of the headman's, where presumably livestock would be raised. For example, Ishtalasea was assigned an allotment just west of Big John Creek. His wives, who most likely were sisters—Wakopuzho and Asutungah—were each allotted a forty-acre plot of fertile valley land adjoining their husband's on the west. The seven other members of the lodge—two

men, one woman, and four children—were granted a block of adjoining allotments in the hills immediately east of the agency farm.
Each hut—each unit of land and family—was to sustain itself by producing crops and livestock both for its own subsistence and for the
marketplace.[6]

This system not only provided the means for impressing the Kanzas into the Euro-American economic and legal system, it also operated on peoples' imaginations in a nonverbal way. In establishing
the skeletal framework of grid-based land ownership, land surveys
and their derivative land allotments provided a symbolic means of
rationalizing the conquest of the land and its natives. In the words of
historian Julie Wilson, this system reduced "the unpredictable con-
tours of the land to a smooth sheet of paper crisscrossed with grids.
The bars of these grids serve to impose both a physical and moral
imperative on a landscape that, until mid-century, served as a richly
variable home for the Plains Indian tribes."[7]

The institution of land allotments on the Kanza Reservation represented a major shift away from the Indian Office's previous mode
of neglect and half-hearted policy implementation. From 1861 on,
the government shifted into a more aggressive mode of administration. At that time, Hiram Farnsworth replaced Milton Dickey
as the Kanza agent. Self-confident, energetic, and politically well-
connected, Farnsworth immediately initiated a series of councils
with Kanza leaders to learn the Indians' views on their situation. In
a June 13, 1861, letter, he summarized the contents of these councils
for Alfred Greenwood's replacement as commissioner of Indian Affairs, William Dole. The Kanzas, Farnsworth wrote, were anxious to
settle on their allotted lands, where they would live in comfortable
houses surrounded by fenced fields broken for cultivation, but none
of these improvements had been made. They had not been able to
plant that spring because no agricultural assistance had been forthcoming as promised by the treaty, and white squatters still occupied
their diminished reserve. The prospects for bison hunting, the other
primary means of subsistence, were greatly diminished because so
many of their ponies had been stolen. The remaining ponies often
starved in the winter and spring because the Kanzas did not put up
hay for them. As a remedy, Farnsworth's predecessor, Dickey, had

promised the tribe a mower, but none had yet arrived. The Kanzas emphasized the importance of an early annuity payment, preferably in early September, so that they might leave sooner for their autumn hunts on the plains. Finally, Farnsworth wrote, "The Indians profess the strongest loyalty to the Union and a determination to know no friends but those of the government."[8]

Six weeks later, having received no reply from the Office of Indian Affairs, the frustrated new agent decided to circumvent his supervisors and spell out the situation in a letter to U.S. senator Samuel Pomeroy. Caught in the middle of three forces vying for control of the diminished Kanza Reservation—the Indians, squatters, and Office of Indian Affairs—Farnsworth sought to enlist Pomeroy's assistance. The Kanzas had heard so many promises, wrote Farnsworth, "that they have little confidence in anything that is said." The Indians told their agent that they were anxious to see the promised houses and farms established soon so they might have shelter for the coming winter. The white squatters knew that the treaty concluded the previous November required their removal from the diminished reservation, but there was no certainty. "One week they hear the commissioners are coming on to locate the Indians, and the next that the Indians will be removed beyond the settlement." Especially aggravating was the Indian Office's silence. No clear policy had been articulated, so Farnsworth could "answer none of the numerous questions put to me by the Indians and settlers on Indian land."[9]

Farnsworth's predecessor had begun to implement the treaty provisions as early as January 1861, at which time he entered into a series of contracts with Robert S. Stevens for the building of a sawmill, agency house, dwelling houses, mission houses, and barn, the erecting of fences, and the plowing of fields. The work began with much fanfare in area newspapers. Employment-seeking men from all over Kansas flooded into Council Grove, and a large force of mechanics and laborers were engaged. By mid-March six buildings had been completed and the sawmill was turning out several thousand feet of lumber every day, an amount sufficient to build at least thirty houses. When Robert Stevens visited Council Grove in April, a "great crowd" gathered seeking to obtain work. This construction work, however, threatened the interests of the remaining

squatters in the diminished reservation, whose numbers were estimated as high as eighty-five. The newspaper counseled people to
keep cool. If the squatter opposition succeeded in stopping the construction, Stevens would by means of indemnification still collect
his money while no one else would benefit. Such a course would be
"suicidal," as Stevens had already let $21,000 worth of contracts to
local subcontractors.[10]

Within six weeks of Republican Abraham Lincoln's inauguration
on March 4, 1861, Democrat Stevens was ordered to cease his work
on the Kanza Reservation pending an investigation. Tensions surrounding the work on the diminished reservation had been mounting. On February 19, the irrepressible Sam Wood, a former ally of
Stevens, wrote to Republican congressman Martin Conway demanding that all work be halted, saying "we have allowed these Democrats to filch long enough." At the same time, a squatters' meeting
was held on the diminished reservation, and rumors circulated that
armed settlers had compelled Stevens to abandon his undertaking.
On March 30, Stevens's brother-in-law and business associate, Rufus
Briggs, visited the Kanza Agency, where he was informed that the
Kanzas had sent a delegation to the Sac and Fox Nation to "help
whip out the squatters on their Lands." Although skeptical of this
rumor, Briggs reported that the squatters forbade the contractors'
cutting of timber on the reservation. He followed with this extraordinary declaration: "They have no more right on these lands than I
have on any other mans Lands. I hope the Indians will demand their
rights and, if necessary, kill the last man."[11]

In his inspection of Dickey's plans and Stevens's work, Farnsworth
found much to criticize. Dickey had planned to place an eight-by-
nine-mile aggregate of Kanza allotments into the southwest corner
of the diminished reservation, thereby freeing some of the best agricultural land for white settlement. Both Farnsworth and a committee
of Quakers objected to this allotment location because of its short-
age of timber, water, and tillable land. Dickey planned to maintain
the three-village arrangement, establishing a fifty-five-acre fenced
field next to each village, the farm plots assigned to each household proportionate to the size of the families. The Kanzas were to

be housed in 138 wood-frame huts. Farnsworth, on the other hand, recommended spreading the houses along the streams throughout the diminished reservation and allotting forty adjoining acres to the headman of each house for purposes of tilled agriculture. Because Dickey's proposal seems more consistent with the communal, village-based culture of the Kanzas, perhaps he was influenced by tribal leaders during the planning process. Farnsworth's formula of breaking up villages and compelling the Indians toward the individuated practice of agriculture reflected the prevalent theory of Indian assimilation at the time and therefore was adopted. "If Indians are to be civilized," he wrote, "each family must be on its own land, and cultivate its own enclosed field." Farnsworth recommended that the houses and school buildings be constructed of stone, not wood; found the work on the agency house and mill "of the roughest and shabbiest kind"; and because the agent's house lacked shelves, closets, pantry, well, cistern, shed, or outhouse, declared that his family would not move into it.[12]

Despite the criticisms, the government retained Robert Stevens as its contractor, renegotiating two contracts with him on August 9 and December 28, 1861. During the fall, work progressed slowly and sporadically, the delays incurred in part because the Indian Office was slow in specifying the locations of the new buildings. During this time the Indian Office censured Farnsworth for approving construction of a council house and making improvements to his agency house without authorization. He protested his innocence, placing the blame on Robert Stevens. Finally, at the beginning of 1862, despite a cold, snowy winter, the political issues were somewhat muted, a survey marking off the allotments completed, and construction specifications put in place. Construction rapidly proceeded on the Kanza Reservation, and the work was completed that summer.[13]

By spring 1862, 138 stone huts had been erected throughout the diminished reservation in close proximity to the Neosho River and its tributaries. The twenty-four largest cabins, each built at a cost of $297.37, housed the lodges with the most occupants. The streams supplied water to the households with one exception—Ishtalasea's house one mile northwest of the agency was provided with a well. The total cost for all 138 structures was $33,135.98.[14]

A centerpiece of the construction activity was the agency-mission complex situated on a rise above the flood plains of nearby Little John and Big John Creeks, one-half mile east of where the latter joins the Neosho River. Before 1861, the Kanza Agency consisted of two small buildings closely spaced in a diagonal configuration. Constructed in 1858, for the next fifteen years this "agency house" with subsequent additions would serve as the home and office for six federal Indian agents. Two acres of surrounding ground were enclosed with oak or walnut rails, forming a fence eight rails high. Stevens's 1861 additions enlarged the agency house into a "commodious building." The two-story main building was divided into a parlor, dining room, and three bedrooms, with a spacious office attached on the east. The nearby "northwest building" housed a large kitchen, a bedroom above, and a cellar below, as well as icehouse, woodshed, toolhouse, and two privies.[15]

Directly east of the agency house was a two-story, limestone edifice with basement. Built to house the interpreter and his family, this structure was actually used as both a storehouse and a residence by agency employees and traders. The Indian Office strongly recommended that the interpreter be housed at the agency to facilitate communication between the agent and the Indians. However, records do not indicate that Joseph James, government interpreter from 1858 through 1871, ever lived in this house with his family. A few feet south of the interpreter's house stood the council house, one of about six buildings forming the agency complex. This small, one-story frame structure was where the agent and visiting government officials conducted formal meetings with the Kanza chiefs and headmen. According to local oral traditions, it also served as the "infirmary" or "drug store." East of the interpreter's house was a stable accommodating six horses, with a granary, overhead haymow, and wagon shed. At some point after 1861, a frame trader's store was built north of the interpreter's house, and one or two small limestone buildings of indeterminate use were added north of the agency house. These buildings were situated on the 160-acre "agency farm," including a 70-acre cultivated field.[16]

Four Kanza men and boys at the Kanza Agency, 1871. Courtesy Scott Brockelman collection of Morris County historical
photos and ephemera.

One-half mile southeast of the agency stood a pair of two-story,
frame "mission buildings." The eastern building housed two classrooms and apartments for the teacher and some of the students. The
western structure was designed as a boardinghouse. A barn, two
privies and a well were added, though the well proved dry. Although
the government set aside 160 acres for the school, the Quakers who
operated the school were plagued throughout its duration by the un-
availability of water on site, necessitating that they haul water from
the agency well. The school complex was designed to accommodate
eighty scholars. It was here in May 1863, after a nine-year hiatus in
educational endeavors among the tribe, that the Quakers reengaged
the task the Methodists had abandoned.[17]

For a little over a decade the agency and the adjoining school
formed the operational center of the diminished reservation. The
complex was designed as a place where the dominant culture would
transform the native people through instruments of policy implementation, technical assistance, education, and religious instruction. But it also was a middle ground where a myriad of difficult
and contradictory details of human coexistence were confronted.

For example, agent Hiram Farnsworth frequently functioned as a de facto physician and druggist for his tribe, tasks he performed without the benefit of a medical fund.[18]

Despite the frenzied pace of activity on the diminished reservation in the spring of 1862, one problem remained unresolved: many of the white squatters would not leave. Some of the squatters "refuse to remove until they are paid," wrote special commissioner Edward Wolcott on April 4, 1862. Wolcott warned the Indian Office that if the settlers were allowed to remain until receiving payment for their improvements, it would be too late for the Indians to make a crop and "moreover there will be endless trouble and quarrels between the two parties." The threat of violence, especially anticipated aggressions targeting Indians, was a major consideration for both the Kanzas and government officials as they sought to resolve the problems of encroachment on the reservation. As early as October 1861, Farnsworth recommended to Commissioner Dole that it was best for the Indians that the white settlers "be paid liberally" for their improvements, even if their claims were not legal, because any other course "will make most bitter enemies for the Indians and probably bring about a collision."[19]

Two months later, Kanza chiefs and headmen, concurring with the views of their agent, sent a petition to the Indian Office recommending that all settlers be paid for their improvements, without regard to the time when they were made. The petition illuminates the change in the balance of power on the reservation since the June 17, 1859 incident. No longer did the whites fear Kanza violence. Now it was the Kanzas who lived in fear of the whites, a situation leading to the effective practice of squatter extortion. The Kanza agent described the Indians as justifiably fearful that if the settlers were ejected by force, "the Indians will be annoyed by them and injured in their persons, stock and crops. They prefer to pay for these improvements in scrip receivable for their trust land, than be exposed to the vengeance of bad men for wrongs real or fancied." Farnsworth also warned that removing the squatters from the diminished reserve did not guarantee Kanza safety because many of them would settle on nearby trust lands where they "will not fail to improve every opportunity to vent their spite on the Indians."[20]

An unsigned column in the June 22, 1861, *Council Grove Press* validates the Kanza agent's assessment of white hostility. The newspaper's previous edition (no longer extant) quoted parts of a recent speech made by the Kanza chief Ishtalasea. In response, the writer makes an ad hominem attack guaranteed to play well with his readers: "Is-tal-a-sa, like all the members of the Kaw tribe, is a horse thief, a robber, a bandit and a liar; all of which we can prove before any Justice of the Peace in Kansas." The column contains the familiar arguments. The Kanza Reservation belonged seventy-five miles to the west, the Indians wasted their annuities and did not farm the land provided for them. "Whites, and not the Kaws, are entitled to every foot of land now claimed for them." It ends with a threat: "We unhesitatingly advise the settlers to keep up a *secret* organization, and if necessary resist to the death. Do not be afraid, others will come to your help when needed. *Vox populi. Vox Dei.*"[21]

One month later the Council Grove paper warned Farnsworth that to "conduce to the free circulation of his blood," he best arrange a speedy settlement of the "vexed reservation question." On March 13, 1862, the Kanza agent summoned Kanza chiefs to the agency for yet another treaty council. Ishtalasea's name topped the list of twenty-three chiefs and headmen marking their approval of a treaty document committing the Kanzas to compensate settlers on the diminished reservation for their improvements by means of "certificates of indebtedness," popularly known as "Kaw scrip." These certificates were to be receivable as cash for the purchase of both Kanza trust lands and unallotted parcels of the diminished reservation. The Treaty of 1859 provided compensation to those who settled on the diminished reservation prior to December 2, 1856, the certification date of the survey marking the reservation's boundaries. The new treaty expanded that commitment to compensate all who had settled on the diminished reservation before October 5, 1859, the date Kanza chiefs signed the treaty diminishing their reservation to one-third its original size. The money backing this Kaw scrip would come from the sale of the Kanza trust lands, the approximately 160,000 acres of the Neosho reservation the tribe had given up. In plain terms, subject to repeated threats of violence, the Indians agreed to pay the "settlers" for expenses they incurred while squatting on the diminished reservation. All of the parties—the white payees, government officials, and the Kanzas—were fully aware at the time that these encroachments were criminal acts of trespass.[22]

Article two of the treaty conveyed to Thomas Huffaker one-half section of land in the vicinity of the old Kaw Mission, the Huffaker family home since the school's closing in 1854. The Kanzas bequeathed this choice parcel of bottomland "for the many services rendered by said Huffaker as missionary, teacher, and friendly counselor of said tribe of Indians." Huffaker was to pay the tribe the appraised value of the land at a rate not less than $1.75 per acre. At the time, the Kanzas owed their ex-teacher $1,425 for having supplied the tribe with corn, potatoes, and cattle from 1851 through 1855. One observer of the treaty negotiations, special commissioner Edward Wolcott, objected to the secrecy of the talks and claimed that the Huffaker land deal was a swindle. Wolcott thought the tract was worth at least twenty dollars per acre, that the Indians knew nothing of the value of land, and that the matter should be investigated. Nevertheless, when the treaty was finally ratified in February 1863, the Huffaker land sale provision remained intact.[23]

One factor compelling the Kanzas to sign the treaty was Farnsworth's assurance that their consenting to extend payment of settlers' claims through October 1859 would result in the settlers' immediate removal. With the squatters finally out of the way, the Kanzas could proceed with the spring planting in time to raise corn and other crops. The settlers did finally leave in May when the commissioner of Indian Affairs promised them payment for their improvements. The recently appointed Kanza farmer, the ever-present Thomas Huffaker, reported that as the settlers left they had warned the Kanzas that if the government did "not pay them soon, they will return and again take possession of them. These circumstances all tend to disturb the peace and quiet of the tribe."[24]

The Kanzas were destitute in April 1862. The annuity payments had been delayed until late winter, the crucial winter hunt had failed, and it was uncertain whether the whites would leave their reservation. The Indians had no plows, draft animals, or any other means with which to begin their farmwork. During the winter and early spring, Farnsworth furnished provisions to some of the tribe

"Plowing on the Prairies beyond the Mississippi." Sketch by Theodore R. Davis, *Harper's Weekly*, May 9, 1868. Courtesy Kansas State Historical Society.

out of his own pocket and made arrangements with merchants—with the agent as security—for the Kanzas to buy on credit food and clothing "of which they stood in the most pressing need." On May 10, the government distributed to the tribe $2,500 worth of farming supplies, including twelve yoke of oxen, twenty-four plows, twelve dozen hoes, six dozen spades, five dozen axes, thirty harnesses, and seed corn and potatoes. Having been unable to farm for six years, the Indians immediately went to work, sowing 150 acres cultivated by the departed whites. Also, the government purchased for the Kanzas one hundred acres of wheat the whites had sown before departing, from which a good crop was harvested.[25]

After a six-year hiatus, the Kanzas faced difficulties in resuming farming on their reservation. The new fields had been broken so late that they produced few crops. An insufficient number of farming implements forced the Indians to wait their turn before tilling and planting their fields. A dry summer limited crop production by whites or Indians to about one-half of normal, excepting wheat. Finally, Farnsworth reported, he could not provide an accurate estimate of bushels of crops produced because the hungry Kanzas "commenced to live on the products of their land as soon as roasting ears, new potatoes, and vegetables were fit for use." Despite these limitations, the agent claimed that the Indians had done better than those most acquainted with them expected and that a "good number of their fields would do no discredit to white farmers."[26]

The weather improved in 1863, but the number of oxen, plows, and other agricultural implements remained inadequate. Of the 146 Kanza families in January 1863, 52 had no fields and 15 had fields without fences. Despite these disadvantages, with the assistance of the government-appointed farmer, Thomas Huffaker, the Kanzas cultivated three hundred acres that year, producing 9,000 bushels of corn, 1,000 bushels of potatoes, and 240 bushels of wheat. The Indians enclosed a considerable number of new fields and repaired fences around the old ones. In September 1863, Farnsworth reported the Kanzas had worked harder than ever before to be well fed and clothed. The Kanzas' disposition to work benefited their white neighbors who, according to Farnsworth, would have been unable to gather their crops in both 1862 and 1863 without the assistance of the Indians. In fact, some white neighbors had for years employed Kanzas to herd their cattle and do farm chores. Huffaker echoed Farnsworth's optimism, writing, "The Indians are well pleased with their new mode of life, and say they do not desire to exchange their present mode for their former."[27]

Initially, the Kanzas appeared satisfied with the new houses the government had built for them. In January 1863, Farnsworth reported that 137 of the 138 stone houses were occupied by Kanza families. Nine log houses built by the white occupiers were inhabited by nine Kanza families, but these houses needed considerable repairs. The Kanzas demanded that all members of their tribe be provided with houses and fields of equal quality. "They desire that all may be treated alike," wrote the agent. The Indians' communitarian concern that everyone in the tribe be treated "impartially and justly" contrasts with Farnsworth's succinct statement of the government's plan and its underlying individualistic philosophy: "to fence each man a field on his own land, believing that an Indian, as a white man, will take more interest in improving his own property, than in improving property held in common."[28]

The Kanzas told their agent that they wanted a carpenter, a blacksmith, a gristmill added to the sawmill, and a good physician to live among them as many in the tribe "are dying for want of good medical attention." Farnsworth warned the Indian Office that if his tribe continued to be neglected, they would lose confidence in the government. "Wicked men are not wanting in the vicinity of this Tribe, who are ever ready to aggravate the suspicions of the ignorant Indian," he wrote. "Now they express a strong desire to improve their condition. If this favorable feeling is permitted to die, a generation may pass away before it will revive."[29]

Prompting the Kanza agent's sense of urgency was a recent change in the tribe's leadership. On April 24, 1861, Hard Chief was murdered by a Kanza man. Succeeding him as head chief of the Kanzas was his brother, Ishtalasea. Vigorous, articulate, and capable, Ishtalasea was a commanding presence, a natural orator whose thunderous voice during tribal councils could be heard for at least a half mile, it was said. His name, translated as "Speckled Eyes," was derived from the peculiar black- and brown-dotted pupils of his eyes. Even when his older brother was the nominal head chief, Ishtalasea was said to have the most actual influence in the tribe. When meeting with government officials, the Kanzas put forth Ishtalasea as their spokesman because of his eloquence and strength of personality. He was tall and slender with a prominent Roman nose and high cheekbones. Although he was already in his seventies when ruling as head chief from 1861 to 1865, Ishtalasea always exuded a strong and sober dignity.[30]

As with all Kanza individuals, biographical details about Ishtalasea are few. His name first appears in the 1843 census, as "Ish tal la se," the only male over age forty, living in a lodge with one young man, two women, and three children. His is the fourth Kanza signature to appear on the 1846 treaty document, a position indicating his rank among chiefs and headmen. In 1862, "Ish ta lah see" is the first name listed on the tribal roll, a confirmation of his rank as head chief. At the time he shared a lodge with his two wives, two men, one other woman, and four children.[31]

Like most Kanza chiefs and headmen, Ishtalasea incurred debts to the traders. In July 1862, agent Farnsworth forwarded a list of debts, amounts unspecified, owed to William Mansfield by Ishtalasea and his band. According to Farnsworth, Ishtalasea had initially acknowledged the correctness of the Mansfield's accounts and assented to their payment by the tribe. Admonishing the chief and other Kanzas for incurring such debts, the agent declared that in the future he would not "forward them to the Department or make any effort to secure their payment." However, in May 1863, the Kanza chiefs in council instructed their agent that they would not consider Mansfield's claims, declaring, "They had signed all the papers they intended to sign from Washington."[32]

That defiant spirit persisted into the summer. These are the words that Ishtalasea and nineteen Kanza chiefs addressed to Commissioner of Indian Affairs William Dole on July 17, 1863: "My Great Father! White men tell us that you are going to drive us off to another place. We don't want to go. We want our children to have this place when we are dead." In the same letter Ishtalasea issued a demand that the amount of annuity payments be increased, saying, "Major Harvey told us we should have $12,000 as long as grass grows and the Kaw river runs; now we get only $8,000." Ishtalasea had other demands: Investigate allegations that agents Montgomery and Dickey stole the tribe's funds. Provide livestock and agricultural implements as promised by treaties. Compensate the tribe for 150 horses stolen by white people. Dismiss the current trader, hire a blacksmith and carpenter, repair log houses on the diminished reservation, and build a gristmill. Establish fields for men who have none. Deliver six medals to Kanza chiefs and nine smaller ones to Kanza men as promised a year before.[33]

On many previous occasions, Ishtalsea had asked government officials to bestow "peace medals" on the Kanza chiefs. When Commissioner Greenwood met with the Kanzas in October 1859, he promised to present the chiefs with six medals. During the ensuing three years the chiefs frequently reminded government officials of this promise but still no peace medals appeared. The United States followed the practice of European nations in giving Indians silver medals as tokens of friendship and garnering commitments of loyalty from the receivers. The medals had become a staple of U.S. Indian policy.[34]

Medals they had received previously were sacred to the Kanzas, among their most prized possessions, yielding the recipients great influence within their villages. When visiting Washington in 1857, Kanza chief Hard Hart submitted this request to Commissioner Denver: "I want a silver medal to show my people when I go home. It will make my children glad to see it. You always give a flag and a silver medal to your red children who come here to see you. These are great things among the Indian nations." The high status placed by the Kanzas and other tribes on such medals is a reflection of a culture valuing honors rather than material gain. These medals were seen as confirmations of Wakanda's esteem. In 1805, American Chief traveled to Washington, D.C., where he met with President Jefferson. Thirty-six years later, during a meeting with missionaries, the old chief proudly displayed his medal received on that occasion. By presenting status-laden medals, however, the government disrupted the ancient clan- and village-based traditions through which chieftaincies were conferred. In 1827, Chief White Plume complained bitterly to William Clark about "many men in our town who call themselves chief—they are not chiefs." Because the "great father" gave them medals, White Plume said, when they came home "they thought they were as big chiefs as me."[35]

In January 1863, Farnsworth recommended that two chiefs of each village receive a medal: Ishtalasea and the son of Pegahoshe from the first village; Fool Chief and Ebesunga from the second; and Nopawia ("Inspires Fear") and Allegawaho from the third. In May, the agent wrote again to remind the Indian Office of its medal commitment to the Kanzas. In July, Ishtalasea reminded "Great Father": "You owe us six medals which you promised me more than a year ago, and I have not received them yet." In the same letter the Kanza chief requested nine small ones for his men. Finally in September 1863, one large and five small medals were delivered to the Kanzas.

Presumably the large one afterward hung around Ishtalasea's neck and adorned his chest, softening his heart regarding the newly proposed treaty.[36]

In terms of an ability and willingness to vigorously advocate his position to the Indian Office, Farnsworth had met his match in Ishtalasea. Although the two men disagreed on several occasions, they did succeed in forging a bond never before achieved by a Kanza chief and agent. During the four years Ishtalasea and Farnsworth simultaneously held their respective positions, an unprecedented number of letters and petitions were produced containing forceful articulations of the Kanza perspective on the tribe's situation and government policies.

Farnsworth endorsed the Kanzas' request for an annuity payment increase from $8,000 to $12,000. Because the Treaty of 1846 stipulated an end to the annuity payments by 1876, this increase would exhaust the tribe's funds in little over a decade. Nevertheless, both Farnsworth and his supervisor, Harrison B. Branch, thought that the payments of $8,000 would keep the tribe suspended in poverty and that an infusion of additional cash, especially applied to agricultural development, was "the only plausible way of rendering them a self-sustaining people," as they wrote to Commissioner Dole. In this same letter, Farnsworth wrote that Ishtalasea had told him that he wanted a buggy because he was "getting too old to ride on horseback."[37]

By autumn 1863, Ishtalasea and some of the other Kanza headmen were no longer adamantly against a proposed new treaty requiring the removal of the Kanzas to Indian Territory (now Oklahoma). In October, Ishtalasea informed Farnsworth that he and a few principal chiefs wished to go to Washington that winter to negotiate a new treaty. In a letter to Dole, the agent quoted Ishtalasea as saying "that when they made their last Treaty they said they would never make another, but they were satisfied that their condition would be improved in some favorable location, more remote from white settlers." The Kanza head chief told Farnsworth that even though he was seventy-five years old he had never visited "the Great Father." He said that he was the only living Kanza present when the old treaties were made and that he knew that many provisions of those treaties had not been fulfilled. Farnsworth conveyed to Dole Ishtalasea's belief: if he could talk with you "in your own house, you will listen to his requests." This was a frequently expressed belief of the Kanza chiefs during their period of occupation of the Neosho reservation. If only they could bypass government underlings and speak directly to "the Great Father," then he would listen and cause the government to act justly in its treatment of the tribe. "They express great confidence in their Great Father in Washington, are apt to conclude that there must be some blame on the part of the agent if their reasonable requests are not acceded to," wrote Farnsworth.[38]

The composition of the Kanza delegation reflected the hierarchy in each of the three villages. Ishtalasea, Watianga, and Kehegasha represented Big John Creek village. Fool Chief and Pahdocahgahle ("Comanche Striker") were selected from the Rock Creek village, and the Kahola Creek village sent Allegawaho and Nopawia. Although U.S. interpreter Joseph James was a member of the delegation, Farnsworth designated Thomas Huffaker as the interpreter, noting that the mixed-blood James "has not comprehensive ideas enough" to interpret a treaty negotiation. The agent wanted him there, however, because he had Indian blood and would reassure the chiefs.[39]

It was June 1864 when the Kanza delegation finally arrived in Washington, D.C., to meet with Commissioner Dole. On June 11, the seven chiefs signed a treaty whereby they agreed to the sale of their Kansas reservation and the purchase of another tract of land "remote from the settlements of White men." Their Neosho reservation would sell for not less than sixty cents per acre and the Kanzas would not pay more than fifty cents an acre for their new reservation, most likely to be carved out of the Osage Reservation in present-day north central Oklahoma.[40]

The treaty document was generous to the Kanza chiefs and headmen. For example, houses were to be erected for Ishtalasea, Fool Chief, Allegawaho, and Nopawia, in addition to the agent. Chunks of land in the diminished reservation in Kansas were to become the property of Kanza leaders "for valuable services performed." Ishtalasea would own 320 acres; Fool Chief, Nopawia, Allegawaho, and Joseph James were allotted 160 acres each; ten headmen including Washunga and Watianga were allotted 60 acres each; and five others were granted 40 acres each. Ishtalasea was to be paid $18,520.93

to be spent at his discretion in establishing the Kanzas in their new home, this amount intended as full compensation for the funds and property allegedly stolen from the tribe by former agents Dickey and Montgomery. The treaty provided for the hiring of a physician and two hundred dollars worth of medicine for a three-year period. A school and a blacksmith shop were to be erected; flour, salt, and bacon would be distributed; sod would be broken and fields would be fenced. The government promised to investigate Kanza claims of horse stealing and unlawful timber destruction by whites. Once the losses were verified, the Kanzas were to be reimbursed.[41]

A few days after the treaty signing, the delegation met with President Lincoln in the White House. The contents of Ishtalasea's exchange with the president were summarized by the *Council Grove Press*:

> He said to the President, that ever since he was a boy he had heard of his Great Father at Washington, but that he had never got to see him till he became an old man. The Great Father was rich and he and his people were poor, and he had come all the way to Washington to get help from the great Father. His people had sold the Government a heap of land, and made the white people rich and the government should remember them kindly,—that they had done so much for the white men that the government should do something for his tribe. Their young men had gone into the army to fight the battles of the white men and nine of them had been killed, when they were fighting the battles of the white men and he thought it the duty of the Government to pay his tribe for them. He wound up by saying that he wanted to carry back presents to all his men, women, and children that they might all be pleased with his visit to the Great Father.[42]

Lincoln's response was cordial and vague, the paper reported. He wished Ishtalasea well and hoped the Kanzas had accomplished their intentions in Washington. The president suggested that Union forces had suffered greater proportionate losses than had the Kanzas in the war but pledged to deal with the Kanzas "as fairly and justly as with the white men."[43]

The single specific focus of this conversation—Kanza warrior enlistment in the Union army and their sacrifices—will be covered in the next chapter. But apropos of the Ishtalasea-Lincoln dialogue, by the war's end twenty-four of the eighty-seven Kanza soldiers in the Union army had died, a mortality rate of 28 percent. Of the estimated two million men serving the Union, approximately 350,000 died, a 17.5 percent rate.[44]

Ishtalasea ended the conference by turning to the audience and making a short speech. The *Council Grove Press* reported, "He said that it was once his delight to scalp his enemies and engage in savage dances over the scalps; but he has now endeavored to adopt the ways of the white men. He did not expect to come up to their standard but expects that his children will."[45]

The Kanza delegation returned west in late June. "The Indians are to go to the Indian Territory, south of Kansas, as soon as the state of the country will admit of it," announced the *Emporia News*. "This is good news." But U.S. Senate politics prevented such an expedient outcome. The Senate did not ratify the Kanza Treaty of 1864, a failure attributed in part to the ongoing struggle between squatters and well-connected speculators for control of Kanza lands. It is also possible that the extraordinarily low baseline price of sixty cents per acre and the liberal grants of property to the chiefs proved unsavory to the Senate leadership.[46]

Ishtalasea's trip to Washington, D.C., was not the only diplomatic mission undertaken by the venerable Kanza chief. About a year before meeting with the president, Ishtalasea and nine other Kanza chiefs had journeyed to the Arkansas River to meet with representatives of the Kiowas, bringing with them many gifts. Just before leaving their reservation, Ishtalasea and the chiefs had each purchased seventy-five dollars worth of goods from the Pioneer Store in Council Grove. Among the items purchased were flintlock rifles, cloth, brass kettles, bags of flint, lead bars, blankets, coffee boilers, and vermillion paints. The Kanza delegation would present these as gifts to the Kiowas, a time-honored means of diffusing tensions between tribes competing for bison in overlapping hunting grounds.[47]

Because the Kanza trade in the early 1860s continued to be profitable to Council Grove merchants, establishing trust with Indian customers was a necessity. According to Shamleffer, this required the ability to feel at ease inside a tipi, and "if invited, [to] sit in an Indian's banquet circle, where wombum, buffalo tongue, dried spotted corn, dog meat, and other delicacies were served." The Kanzas were frequent visitors to Council Grove. "They perambulate our streets in their blankets," wrote A. I. Baker, "with all the dignity of a Roman Senator in his toga." In February 1861, the *Council Grove Press* reported that the Kanzas were breaking up their hunting camps on the Smoky Hill River and preparing to return to their diminished reservation, where the "trade in robes and furs will be active after their arrival." Baker described his pleasure at watching the Kanzas through his newspaper office window as they bartered their robes at the Council Grove stores. The editor noted that both sides benefited from the trade. The Indians needed the provisions and clothing they got in the exchange. For the whites, "Furs and robes are associated with everything that is pleasant and refreshing. Just imagine that the robes," wrote Baker, "will next winter be wrapped around many happy loving hearts, swiftly gliding along with the merry sleigh bells." The newspaperman accurately identified the immediate fate of the Kanzas' hard-earned bison robes: use as sleigh, wagon, and bed covers.[48]

Although the 1861–62 winter hunt had been a failure, the Kanzas conducted a successful hunt in the winter of 1862–63, garnering enough bison for robes worth $8,000 in trade. The 1863–64 winter hunt was also a good one, partly because the Indian Office, after two successive years of delaying the tribe's annuity payment until February, had distributed the annuities in September 1863, giving the tribe ample time to conduct a hunt on the plains before severe weather set in. The Kanzas traded other commodities, most prominently ponies, by far the tribe's most valuable property as measured by the Euro-Americans. In both 1863 and 1864, the Kanzas owned five hundred horses, which the agent estimated as worth thirty dollars each. In the early 1850s, a leading Kanza trader paid an average of $36.40 per horse and $45.17 for each mule.[49]

The Kanzas also fabricated and sold horse accoutrements, including buffalo hide halters and lariats of horsehair. The hair was twisted into small strands, five or six of which would be braided into a rope three-fourths of an inch in diameter. They also made saddles of two forks joined by sidepieces and covered with rawhide, the whole highly ornamented with brass tacks. During an encounter with the Kanzas in spring 1834, author and naturalist John Kirk Townsend acquired hide halter ropes and leather saddle blankets in exchange for tobacco and bacon. The Indians frequently visited towns near the reservation, such as Emporia and Americus, to swap. A religious group in Americus attempted to stop the frequent and alarming practice of "trading with the Indians on Sunday." The Kanza trade network, however, extended far beyond the reservation's margins. For example, at Salina in February 1861, Luke Parsons "bought a Spanish bridle from a Kaw." Also documented is a Kanza visit to Junction City in January 1863, where they "indulged considerable in their propensity to 'swap.'" While near Fort Ellsworth in December 1866, a Kanza woman sold a white man an "Indian whip" studded with brass nails.[50]

Kanza women played a vital role in trade, especially in preparing robes and furs and processing buffalo meat. A Salina trader, Christina Phillips Campbell, observed: "The hides that the white men brought in were stiff like boards. . . . With the Indians it was different; the hides they brought were soft and pliable." The women scraped the hides, then tanned them using buffalo brains. When Campbell began to stock her store with soap, Kanza women bought large quantities which they used in place of brains in processing the hides.[51]

In the spring, Kanza women went door-to-door in Emporia, selling baskets of gooseberries at twenty-five cents per basket. They often appeared at farmhouses, offering to trade blackberries, grapes, plums, and, sometimes, calico cloth for pork, flour, and other provisions. Topeka-area farmer Alan Coville acquired dressed buckskin, moccasins, and wild fruit at nearby Kanza camps. The women asked to leave their dried wild grapes and plums at his place while they went west to hunt bison. When the tribe returned, the women would bring a buffalo robe or some other present for keeping their fruit.

Kanza women frequently appeared on the streets of Council Grove bearing baskets of wild fruit. In May 1861, the *Press* reported "groups of staid matrons and shy maidens from the Kaw Nation busily engaged in peddling wild gooseberries, which are remarkedly fine for this season."[52]

In the spring of 1861, Council Grove was a small village of thirty houses and about 130 people. At the time, most of the 775 white inhabitants of Morris County lived in log huts tucked out of sight in the timbered margins of streams. Finally released from the clutches of the drought, the town's prospects were good. According to the *Council Grove Press*, the outbreak of war in April 1861 had little detrimental effect on Council Grove. Because of the abundant moisture, crops were plentiful and livestock were "luxuriating upon the rich grasses that now cover the prairies." The town was growing and many houses were under construction. Bernstein's saloon was enlarging, migration into the region continued unabated, plenty of good land was available for the taking, and the town was protected by a recently organized militia company—the Frontier Riflemen. Altogether the region was "a glorious picture of quiet and happy security."[53]

As for the obstacle posed to settlers by the Kanzas, two-thirds of the original Kanza Reservation was being appraised tantamount to the government offering this land for sale. Besides, proclaimed the May 18, 1861, *Council Grove Press*, the Kanzas "are docile as 'sheeps,' and don't do anything to nobody, not nary, but sell ponies and robes, and consume riffle whiskey. The 'Frontier Riflemen,' (of which they have a profound respect) will take care that the Kaws be liberally disposed of. Certainly no obstacle will be allowed to intervene between the poor benighted heathens, and 'manifest destiny.' 'Lo! the poor Indians,' he don't die hard, no sir-ee, he 'shuffles off this mortal coil' with commendable decency, and respect to the advancing hosts of civilization."[54]

This triumphant declaration expresses many attributes of a system of belief prevalent among white Americans of the nineteenth century now called "white colonialism." It exults at the successful intimidation of Indians by means of Euro-American armed might, sneers at them as drunken sots, deplores their "benighted" status as non-Christians, justifies invasion of Kanza land by invoking the unassailable doctrine of Manifest Destiny, and, above all, celebrates the Indians' vanishing as a vindication of the legitimacy of white conquest. The newspaper articulates the belief of many Americans at that time that, in the words of historian Reginald Horsman, "American Indians were doomed because of their own inferiority and that their extinction would further world progress." Absent is acknowledgment of a causal link between white aggression and Indian misery. The white American's rise to prosperity and power was unequivocally good, a demonstration of racial superiority. Indian suffering hardly merited comment, the natives' decline and inevitable disappearance a result of inherent racial weakness. More than just absolving Euro-Americans from any need to critically examine their own complicity in the demise of American Indians, the "Vanishing American" belief provided the ideological means to achieve the desired outcome of Indian extinction. "The belief in the Vanishing Indian," says Brian W. Dippie, author of *The Vanishing American*, "was the ultimate cause of the Indian's vanishing."[55]

The outbreak of the American Civil War posed no challenge to the Euro-American beliefs in their racial superiority and their providentially inspired mission to conquer the continent. If anything, the war reinforced the confidence of white Americans because it ushered in a period of prosperity for most northerners. Council Grove was well positioned to share in this war-induced economic growth. During the Civil War, government freighters traveled the Santa Fe Road to deliver huge amounts of commodities to the Union soldiers defending the American Southwest against both invading Confederate forces in 1861 and 1862 and uprisings by the Apaches and Navajos throughout the war. During the same period private freighters carrying a wide variety of cargoes expanded their operations. Before the war, Westport and Kansas City had been the leading shipping points on the eastern end of the trail, but with the onset of hostilities, cities to the north were considered safer starting points, with Leavenworth emerging as the major outfitting point for westbound trail traffic. The supply trains departing from Leavenworth joined the old Santa Fe Road near present-day Wilmington, Kansas. About two days later these wagons rolled into Council Grove, stimulating a brisk and lucrative business on Main Street, causing the period of war to be referred to as the "flush times of Council Grove."[56]

Merchant George M. Simcock recorded the volume of Santa Fe Road trade passing through Council Grove in 1862: 3,000 wagons, 618 horses, 20,182 oxen, 8,046 mules, 98 carriages, 3,072 men, and 15,000 tons of freight with an estimated value of $40 million. In May of that year, combined sales of the three Council Grove business houses catering to Santa Fe Road freighters totaled $22,022.04. A Missouri newspaper promoting the westward expansion of railroads estimated that in 1864, forty million pounds of freight had been hauled from the Missouri River to Utah, New Mexico, and Colorado, these shipments requiring nine thousand wagons, fifty thousand cattle, sixteen thousand horses and mules, and ten thousand men. A clerk in the Pioneer Store, William Shamleffer estimated that during this era his store alone sold $200,000 a year.[57]

While the Civil War enhanced the prosperity of Council Grove merchants, it also amplified the violence that had long festered in and around the Kanza Reservation. It was a time when authorities seemed unable to check the spread of terror. On July 1862, Hiram Farnsworth reported to Commissioner Dole that seven people, including two Kanzas, had been murdered near the Santa Fe Road crossing of Rock Creek in a nine-week period. State and military authorities had been notified of these violent acts but had done nothing. Many people fled, leaving the region even more unprotected. Farnsworth asked Dole for permission to enlist Kanza warriors to guard the agency.[58]

Throughout the spring of 1863, the people of Council Grove were in a continual state of apprehension about the possibility that the town might be raided by Missouri guerrillas. A local militia unit, the Morris County Rangers, was organized under the leadership of Captain Samuel Wood, but it proved ineffective in blocking rebel incursions into Morris County. In early May, a band of Missouri guerrillas headed by Dick Yeager encamped just south of town. When Yeager threatened to attack the town, Council Grove's border state heritage came into play. An avowed proslavery Democrat, Maryland native Malcolm Conn went to the camp to talk with Yeager, whom he had known before the war when the rebel leader was a freighter on the

Santa Fe Road. Conn spent several hours in the Missourians' camp, attempting to persuade the men to spare Council Grove. Writing in the early twentieth century, historian George Morehouse attributed Conn's success in fulfilling this mission to improvement of Yeager's disposition after a local doctor extracted a painful tooth from his mouth, the "number of southern sympathizers at Council Grove," and the merchant's employment of "a good supply of warming stimulants." However, after the forty-five men in Yeager's band dispersed, about a dozen of them rode west on the Santa Fe Road to Diamond Spring, where they killed storeowner Augustus Howell, wounded his wife, looted the store, and burned the buildings.[59]

The aftershock of what became known as the Yeager Raid was felt in the area throughout the summer. The return of the guerrillas was both feared and expected. "They will take us when we are not expecting them," warned the *Emporia News*. Then on August 21, 1863, news came of the raid on Lawrence in which a rebel guerrilla band led by William Quantrill killed around two hundred men and boys. "These are indeed times of trouble, and human life seems to be of no value," mourned the September 12 *Emporia News*. "We lay down at night not knowing whether we shall be permitted to enjoy the light of another day or not."[60]

Inevitably the Kanzas were caught up in this spate of violence. "Bloody Bill" Anderson and his brother, Ellis, were accused of killing Kanzas in separate incidents, both involving the Indians trying to get at whiskey possessed by the Andersons. Whiskey was again the pivotal factor in a May 1862 incident that left at least two Kanzas dead near J. L. French's "grocery" on Rock Creek in close proximity to A. I. Baker's residence. According to the May 10 *Emporia News*, about thirty Kanzas broke into French's store and helped themselves to the contents of a barrel of whiskey. French and some neighbors barricaded themselves inside French's nearby house, from where French began to shoot through a chink in the wall, wounding two Kanzas and killing one. The enraged Kanzas broke into the house as the whites escaped through a back window. During the ensuing chase another Kanza was killed. The actual number of Kanza deaths may have exceeded the two originally reported, as the May 17 *Emporia News* cited the discovery of six Kanza bodies in the woods near

French's house, vindicating Ishtalasea's later assertion that during this period seven Kanzas had been murdered by whites. French was indicted by federal authorities for selling whiskey to Indians in violation of the intercourse law. Farnsworth asserted that French had actually precipitated the incident by giving the Kanzas whiskey. Incredibly, in July 1863, French filed a claim against the Kanzas for losses he suffered during the incident. In response, the Kanza agent offered this assessment: "Having been a violator of law, and the cause of the mob, I do not think he is entitled to damage."[61]

*

The Indian Office's longstanding neglect of the Kanzas changed in 1861 when Hiram Farnsworth, a forceful, articulate, and politically well-connected Republican, was appointed Kanza agent. Realizing that the whites who had encroached on the reservation between 1856 and 1859 were likely to do violence to the Indians if they did not receive compensation for the improvements they had made while squatting on the reservation, Farnsworth and the Kanza chiefs agreed to terms in the 1862 treaty requiring the tribe to make such payments to the trespassers. Pursuant to the Treaty of 1859, the government allotted forty acres of the diminished reservation to each member of the tribe and constructed 138 stone huts for the Kanzas spread along stream valleys. On paper a linear grid denoting individual ownership was superimposed on land long regarded by the Kanzas as a common holding. On the landscape scattered farmhouses with adjoining plots of privately owned land were to replace the communal village habitations. This grid-based land ownership provided a symbolic means of rationalizing the conquest of the land and its natives. That conquest was also justified by the doctrine of the "Vanishing American," a widely held and self-reinforcing belief that as industrial civilization advanced across the continent, Indians would inevitably disappear because of their racial inferiority.

Responding to the threats posed by these various forms of aggression, the Kanzas became more productive farmers, increased trade with whites, and asserted more forceful leadership. Hard Chief's successor, Ishtalasea, formed an alliance with Farnsworth, and an unprecedented period of vigorous advocacy on behalf of the tribe began. This included a trip to Washington, D.C., where Ishtalasea and Farnsworth met with President Lincoln. Although stimulating economic prosperity for Council Grove merchants, the Civil War also spread lawless violence across the countryside, and inevitably the Kanzas were caught up in this. Despite the more forceful governmental and tribal leadership and a release from the grip of the encroachers, the Kanzas remained vulnerable to the destructive forces that gathered around their diminishing homeland. Sensing "endless trouble and quarrels" should they remain on their reservation, in 1864 Kanza chiefs indicated for the first time their willingness to move out of Kansas.

Stations of Kanza Troops, 1863–65. © 2014, University of Oklahoma Press.

CHAPTER 6

Some Were Decidedly Improved

During the tribe's occupation of the Neosho River reservation, the Kanzas frequently returned to their previous home in the Topeka area. In doing so, they followed the "Kaw Trail," one of four such trails so named in the eastern half of Kansas. From the Kanza Reservation, this Council Grove–Topeka "Kaw Trail" passed northeast up the Rock Creek watershed, crossed the divide between the Kansas and Neosho Rivers near present-day Eskridge, Kansas, then descended the Mission Creek valley to Uniontown, an early-day trading post located on the south bank of the Kansas River a few miles west of Topeka. At fifty-five miles, this trail was shorter than the route favored by Euro-Americans, which roughly followed the present-day Kansas Turnpike before joining the Santa Fe Road in the Wilmington area. White people who had traveled the Council Grove–Topeka Kaw Trail by animal-drawn wagons had little good to say about it. "I cannot recommend this route, especially for loaded teams," wrote a Lawrence man. "It is too hilly and rough. It is said to be shorter, however, than any other route." Four days were required for Euro-Americans to complete the trip from Council Grove to Topeka via Wilmington and the Santa Fe Road while the Kaw Trail required eight days. Having just completed a journey on the latter trail, a disillusioned man signing himself "Honas" wrote from Council Grove: "If you wish to do humanity and ox-flesh a kindness, advise everybody to come here by way of Wilmington."[1]

For Fool Chief the Younger and his Rock Creek band, however, the Council Grove–Topeka trail provided the best way for homecoming visits to their former village site. At least eight generations of Kanzas had lived and hunted in the Kansas River valley, so this was the place to visit the graves of their ancestors, a profoundly important spiritual undertaking, imbued with deeper significance because of the Kanza belief that the souls of their dead returned to "spirit villages" located where the tribe had previously dwelled. This means that the Kanzas who died on the Neosho reservation returned post-mortem to reoccupy their former homes in the Kansas River valley, a belief carrying obvious implications for the Council Grove area. Finally, the presence of a tribal holy place, the Prayer Rock near Shunganunga Creek, undoubtedly drew Kanza worshippers back to the region.[2]

When in Topeka, the Kanzas frequently traded with white merchants. In 1859, trade with ninety-four Kanzas produced a credit balance of $1,248.90 for Topeka businessman Harvey Young. Fool Chief was a good customer, patronizing Young's Topeka business five times in September, purchasing two hundred pounds of flour, sixteen pounds of sugar, twelve pounds of coffee, seven pairs of shoes, ten yards of calico, one blanket, one shirt, and four plugs of tobacco, running up a bill of $62.92. At that time, Fool Chief was responsible for feeding and clothing eight people sharing his lodge, including his wife, Hehojame, and two men, another woman, and three children.[3]

These visits were facilitated by the presence of a few mixed-blood Kanzas—Bellmards, Pappans, and other offspring of marriages of Kanza women and French traders—who continued to dwell into the early 1860s along the north bank of the Kansas River between Topeka and Lecompton on property assigned them by the 1825 treaty. Every summer, Tu pi k'e, the "potato-digging-place," served as a refugee center for hundreds of Kanzas during the years Euro-Americans had overrun the Neosho reservation.[4]

In May 1863, a farmer living near the Kaw Trail in the Mission Creek valley a few miles west of Dover witnessed an astonishing and graphic display of Kanza pedestrian speed and endurance. The farmer, William Beach, observed a large group of Kanzas accompanied by a recruiting officer walking past his farm en route to Topeka, where they were to be mustered into Company L, Ninth Kansas Cavalry. The next day about noon, Beach "looked over toward the road and saw a big Kaw Indian streaking it back toward Council Grove. He was moving right along at a good gait and every bit of clothing he wore was a new army hat." During the next couple of hours every Kanza recruit passed by in the nude, walking the trail back to the Neosho villages, where they proudly donned their new uniforms. Before setting out, they had stripped off their new clothing and bundled it for traveling so the uniforms would be clean when presented to the admiring gazes of fellow Kanzas. Within a day or two, all had rejoined their company at Fort Leavenworth, after a round trip of over 150 miles. Among the Kanzas and related tribes, such prodigious walking was not unusual.[5]

After being issued their uniforms in Topeka, the Kanza recruits reported to Fort Leavenworth where they were formally enlisted, received horses, and were organized into a cavalry company. At this time they were placed under the command of Lieutenant John I. Delashmutt, a former Council Grove hotelkeeper, who would lead Company L until the end of the war. On May 27, a Leavenworth newspaper praised the Kanza unit encamped near the fort: "It is well disciplined and will do good service under its gallant commander." When on June 19 they left Fort Leavenworth bound for Westport, there were about fifty Kanzas enlisted in Company L.[6]

Prior to the formation of Company L, Kanzas had unsuccessfully attempted to enroll in support of the Union cause, and the army had likewise unsuccessfully sought to gain Kanzas' services. One month after the war had begun, several Kanzas had offered to join the Frontier Riflemen, the Council Grove militia unit. "Unconditionally, they will go wherever called, and fight for their great Father at Washington," declared the *Council Grove Press*. Their offer was not accepted. On August 22, 1861, General James H. Lane wrote to the agents of the Sacs and Foxes, Shawnees, Delawares, Kickapoos, Potawatomies, and Kanzas, asking them to immediately send Indian troops to defend the southern border of Kansas against the threat of Confederate forces then organizing in Indian Territory. Agent Farnsworth's lukewarm response pointed out that the Kanzas had few guns, little ammunition, and no money or provisions. But by January 1862, the

Kanza agent appeared more receptive to Kanza enlistment, assuring Commissioner William Dole that he could supply about "150 vigorous warriors" from the tribe.[7]

By the war's end, eighty-seven Kanza warriors had served in Company L, Ninth Kansas Cavalry, and three mixed-bloods saw action with Company F, Fifteenth Kansas Volunteer Cavalry. At enlistment time these men ranged in age from eighteen through thirty-five, though most were in their early to mid twenties. When enlisting for a three-year term, each Kanza in Company L was required to take a Euro-American name, the most popular ones being names (or versions of names) of presidents and prominent local men. These included Thomas Jefferson, George Washington, Malcolm Conn, James Munkers, Sameul Wood, Seth Hayse (two Kanzas took this name), and Charles Withington. A few names retained a vestige of their Indian identity, among them Little Bear, White Feather, Eli Elkhorn, Joseph Kickapoo, and Little Thunder. Only one Kanza deserted and three were discharged before the end of their enlistment period. Twenty-four Kanza soldiers died during the war, most of diseases such as pneumonia, dysentery, measles, and bronchitis.[8]

During their first year of service, the men of Company L were stationed along the Kansas-Missouri border where they provided guard duty and periodically pursued the pro-Confederate Bushwhackers into Missouri. In July and early August 1863 they were stationed at Westport. Immediately following Quantrill's August 21 raid of Lawrence, Company L joined other Kansas cavalry units in pursuit of the guerrillas. This force caught up with a band of Quantrill's men in Missouri, killing several of the raiders and recapturing some of the property taken from Lawrence. By autumn, Company L had dropped south into Linn and Neosho Counties, and by December the Kanza soldiers were stationed at Fort Scott nearby. March 1864 found them briefly encamped on the north side of the Kansas River near Lawrence.[9]

During its second year, the Kansas Ninth operated as a more consolidated regiment, and Company L functioned as an extension of its regiment in solidifying the Union occupation of Confederate Arkansas. In April 1864, the Ninth Kansas Cavalry marched through the Missouri towns of Harrisonville, Clinton, and Springfield en route to Fort Smith, where the regiment encamped at Mazzard's Prairie until July. From this base, the Ninth conducted numerous raiding, scouting, and foraging expeditions, some resulting in skirmishes with the enemy. This activity drew praise from Brigadier General Eugene A. Carr, who described the seven hundred men in the unit as "good fighters." In July, the regiment was transferred to Little Rock. When the Confederate force commanded by Sterling Price invaded Missouri, the Ninth Cavalry both scouted and harassed the rebels. In October the regiment was sent to its final station, De Vall's Bluff, located fifty-four miles east of Little Rock. The arrival of the Ninth Kansas at De Vall's Bluff received this notice in the *United States Sanitary Commissioner Bulletin*: "Company L of this regiment is composed exclusively of Caw Indians. A finer body of men was never seen, and the officers of the regiment say they are the best and most reliable scouts, and most splendid horsemen." This was the final station of Company L and the point at which the Kanza soldiers were mustered out of service on July 17, 1865.[10]

The highest ranking Kanza of Company L was Sergeant Abram Munroe. His Kanza name was Nimjanogah. Known as Soldier Chief, he was among the nine Kanzas who were first to enroll as volunteers in Council Grove on March 12, 1863. At this time the enrolling officer, John Delashmutt, assigned him the rank of corporal. Shortly after the thirty-two-year-old Munroe enlisted at Fort Leavenworth, he was promoted to sergeant, a rank he retained throughout the duration of his service.[11]

Munroe comes alive to us through his letters to government officials. At Little Rock on July 31, 1864, he wrote to agent Farnsworth: "I just returned a few days ago from a scout & brought in four prisoners. When the Rebels see the Federals coming they always run and don't stop to show fight." Munroe and his fellow soldiers had learned that Ishtalasea and other chiefs were in Washington negotiating a treaty that presumably would remove the tribe from Kansas. The Kanza soldiers bristled at the notion that they "are down here exposed to danger both of being killed and dying from sickness while they [the chiefs] are lying at home doing nothing and now while we are away they want to sell our land. It is not right & the boys down here will never give their consent." In reference to the 1862 assignment of forty-acre allotments to individual Kanzas, Munroe wrote: "If any of the Chiefs are there tell them to go ahead & sell their own land if they want but not to interfere with ours for we don't care where they go."[12]

Munroe's high standing among his men is reflected in a petition signed by fifty-six of his fellow Kanza soldiers on December 3, 1864, urging President Lincoln to appoint Munroe head chief of the Kanzas. When forwarding this petition to his superiors in the Indian Office, agent Farnsworth characterized its recommendation as "impolitic," suggesting instead that the matter be postponed until after the Kanza soldiers returned home, at which time the whole Kanza nation could act if such a change was deemed desirable.[13]

At the time of his discharge on July 17, 1865, Munroe received praise from the commanders of both Company L and the Ninth Kansas. Captain James L. Arnold wrote that the sergeant "has been a prompt and energetic soldier, and by his truthfulness and honesty has won the respect and esteem of his commanding officers and all his fellow soldiers." Another officer described Munroe as "an honest, faithful and generous hearted man, fully deserving the confidence of all." In January 1866, Farnsworth recommended to the Indian Office that a high government official confer the title of chief on Abe Munroe. Although he never became head chief, after the war Abe Munroe's signature frequently appeared on documents signed by Kanza chiefs and headmen.[14]

In a January 1867 letter addressed to "My Great Father, Washington City," Munroe expressed the postwar disillusionment felt by many Kanza veterans living on the reservation:

I think you do not know that when the war broke out, a good many of our people, went to help drive back the Secesh from our country, and served as good soldiers all through the war. You sent us word that if the Secesh got all of our lands we would probably not get much to eat, so we went to the war—and the most of our men came home again, some of them died in the service, many after they came home. There is a number of Widows and orphans of our soldiers that our Great Father forgets. We think that our widows and orphans should not be forgotten by you. I was in a good many battles, one that lasted 4 days, and I was always ready to march even if the order came in the night. I am called the Soldier Chief and I want my great father to write a few lines to show me that he does not forget the soldiers and I would like to secure a medal from you.[15]

Particularly galling was the perception that the government was generous to their Plains Indian enemies, while ignoring the loyal Kanzas. Farnsworth noted that the tribes that had furnished soldiers to the Union army frequently complained that they had received "no valuable recognition" for their services, while those tribes "who have broken treaties, plundered our citizens, murdered our women and children and made war upon our nation, are loaded with the richest gifts."[16]

Despite Company L's record, white suspicions persisted on the Kansas frontier about the true loyalties and intentions of the Kanzas. They were, after all, Indians, and by July 1864 Indians were making war on white people in central and western Kansas. A Junction City newspaper attributed an August raid on settlements in northern Kansas to the usual tribes—Kiowas, Comanches, Arapahos, and Cheyennes—then added the Kanzas to its culprit list based on an eyewitness account that among the raiders were "shaved headed and painted Indians, which no doubt were the Kaws." In early September the same newspaper reported that the Osages, Sacs and Foxes, and Kanzas—all having provided warriors to the Union army—were holding a council on the Sac and Fox Reservation. "They need looking after in these troublesome times," was the ominous warning. Indeed, on October 8 a grand council of eastern Kansas tribes was held at the Sac and Fox Agency, where chiefs representing fifteen Kansas tribes pledged their loyalty to "the Great Father," President Lincoln.[17]

The Indian war on the Kansas plains prompted General Samuel Curtis to visit the Kanza Agency in early August, and there he informed Farnsworth that the Kanzas were forbidden to conduct their fall hunt because if they did go west to the buffalo country "they would be in danger from his troops." In protest, Farnsworth noted that all Indians were looked upon with suspicion and that "some bad men do all they can to create ill will towards them." The agent pointed out that without the hunt the tribe would be in a starving condition by the middle of October, in which case the Indian Office would be called upon to assist the Indians to prevent starvation. What followed was a rare display of prompt and effective action by government officials on behalf of the beleaguered Kanzas. The secretary of the Interior Department, J. P. Usher, interceded with the War Department on behalf of allowing the Kanzas and other "border tribes" to hunt that fall on the plains. The army relented, the Kanzas obtained protection papers from military authorities, and the tribe departed soon after the annuity payment in late September for the buffalo grounds, where they conducted a successful hunt.[18]

That autumn, the Kanzas established their hunting camps on Sharps Creek, the Little Arkansas, the Smoky Hill, and Big Turkey Creek. Meanwhile, rumors continued to circulate that the tribe was "having friendly intercourse with tribes hostile to the United States." In December, Farnsworth decided to investigate, visiting all of the Kanza bands. Arriving at one of the camps, the agent discovered that a large war party had gone out after the Cheyennes "to revenge their losses of men and stock" suffered from raids by that tribe. "I could not get the slightest evidence of any friendly feeling existing between these tribes," he reported. The agent concluded that the conduct of the Kanzas toward the whites "has invariably been friendly."[19]

When they returned to the reservation, the Kanza soldiers who had been fighting with the Union army discovered that their agent's confidence in their goodwill and behavior was conditional. Apparently unnerved by the prospect of well-armed Indian veterans filtering back to their reservations and rubbing shoulders with neighboring whites, in May 1865 Farnsworth recommended that the Indian Office impose selective gun control. According to the agent, several Kanzas, including three chiefs, were carrying revolvers, causing anxiety among both whites and Indians. He recommended that Indians not be allowed to carry revolvers, pistols, and knives larger than the common sheath knife. Commissioner of Indian Affairs Dole concurred, instructing agents to have these weapons taken out of the hands of the Indians. Apparently, however, disarming Indian combat veterans proved more difficult than anticipated, as subsequently the Indian Office moderated its policy, requiring Indians to deposit their arms with the agent only "when in public assemblies, at payments, or on the occasion of their visiting the towns." In anticipating problems with Indian veterans, Farnsworth had stimulated an anxious Indian Office to overreact. Against this background, the agent's terse postwar assessment of the Kanza veterans conveys an understated and poignant affirmation: "Their conduct," he wrote, "has been far better than was anticipated. Some were decidedly improved by their army experience."[20]

The absence of the able-bodied men serving in the army was cited by the government farmer, Thomas Huffaker, as a factor in the poor Kanza corn harvest of 1864. The major cause of crop failure, however, was a familiar nemesis. The Kanzas had planted three hundred fenced acres of corn, potatoes, and beans. Through mid-July the crops in the region appeared to flourish. Then two weeks of dry, hot weather seared the corn, ruining the fields beyond the help of rain. "A great and sad change," mourned the *Emporia News*. Because of the poor crop, the government was forced to intercede by purchasing $800 worth of seed corn for the spring 1865 planting. Worse still, the Kanza farmers still labored with insufficient implements and too few oxen. Farnsworth, however, placed some of the blame for crop failure on the Kanzas. He reported that less acreage had been improved and planted, the Kanzas had left the fields unattended during their summer hunt, weeds had overrun the fields, livestock had damaged the crops, and a large amount of fencing had been burned through carelessness. Despite the dry season, the agent insisted that with proper care the crop would not have been a failure. Their corn supply depleted, the Kanzas subsisted primarily on bison meat that winter.[21]

The successful winter hunt of 1864–65 initiated a prosperous period for the tribe in terms of agricultural production, bison hunting, and horse trading. That spring the Indians expanded their fields to four hundred acres, the weather proved benign, and best-ever crops were produced: 9,000 bushels of corn, 350 bushels of wheat, 500 bushels of oats, and 750 bushels of potatoes. There followed the best winter hunt in years, and then the Kanzas trading three thousand bison robes at seven dollars each, garnering the tribe $21,000. Buttressing the Kanzas' economic well-being was the horse trade conducted with their intermittent enemies, the Plains Indians who supplied horses that the Kanzas, in turn, sold to whites. In 1866, this trade amounted to at least $15,000 for the Kanzas, two-thirds of which was profit.[22]

Farnsworth provided an overview of his tribe's seasonal subsistence cycle during this period: those Kanzas able to make the autumnal trek one hundred miles west to the bison hunting camps "lived well and generally were healthy." The bison the Indians slaughtered provided meat, tallow, and robes, with enough of the latter sold in the winter to buy groceries and clothing. The balance was sold in the spring to support the Kanzas while they put in their crops. Then the horse trade carried them through the summer. In September 1866, after harvesting and storing their corn, it was not unreasonable that the tribe could expect another successful winter hunt, another year of relative prosperity. After all, during the previous four years, they had enjoyed three abundant crop harvests and four good winter hunts.[23]

This sanguine assessment was belied by the tribe's actual situation, which was far more complex and, as events proved, precarious. Population figures reveal a disturbing trend. In 1862 there were, according to Farnsworth, 866 Kanzas (460 males and 406 females). In 1866, there were 670 (319 males and 351 females), representing a decline of 23 percent during a period when there were no widespread epidemics. Farnsworth claimed that the Kanzas did not recover from disease as well as whites. "Men, seemingly robust, die from slight apparent causes," the agent reported in 1864. He also cited a high rate of mortality of both mothers and infants at birth. The high infant mortality rates were also noted by the superintendent of the Kanza Quaker school, Mahlon Stubbs, who attributed the Kanzas' decline to the likes of pneumonia, consumption (tuberculosis), scrofula (tuberculosis of the lymph nodes), liver complaints, and fevers, these caused by, in Stubbs's view, exposure, intoxicating liquors, and "irregular and filthy habits." Both the Kanza agent and school administrator vehemently denounced the "nefarious traffic" of the whiskey trade that in Stubbs's view caused "most, if not all, the Indian troubles."[24]

In council with Farnsworth in September 1864, the Kanza chiefs demanded that $250 of their agricultural fund be used for medical

Shingawassa chief of Kaw indian

Shingawassa, Kanza chief. Shingawassa's band established hunting camps on the Saline River west of Salina in the late 1850s and early 1860s. Courtesy Salina Public Library.

purposes, an amount not sufficient for the overall medical needs of the tribe but enough to provide basic medical care in the most difficult cases. Farnsworth frequently paid the doctors at his own expense rather than letting the Kanzas suffer and die when a physician might help them. In the spring of 1865, the Office of Indian Affairs approved $150 for medicine, but contrary to the wishes of the Kanzas it took this money out of the annuity fund rather than the agricultural assistance fund. From the federal bureaucracy's point of view, this was a minor accounting shuffle. However, the Kanzas, certain that agents Montgomery and Dickey had cheated them in 1858 and 1861, were bitterly opposed to any use of their money that diminished the full amount of their annuity, $8,000. Friction on this point surfaced again during the September 1865 annuity payment when the Indian Office, again ignoring both Farnsworth and the Kanzas, sent $7,760 to the tribe, subtracting from the annuity fund $240 for medicine.

In response, a council of chiefs and headmen insisted that the full $8,000 be paid. "They are so exceedingly tenacious on this point that I have yielded to their wishes," reported the agent. As a result, the paltry sum of sixty dollars was left for medicine.[25]

For many years, the fiscally conservative Indian Office had adversely affected the Kanzas by not providing funds for sufficient draft animals and implements needed to successfully practice agriculture. Each year the government set aside approximately $1,200 for Kanza agriculture. Of this amount, $600 was for the salary of the Kanza farmer, the position occupied by Huffaker from 1862–65. In addition to medical supplies, the remainder was to be spent for seed, fencing, implement repair and acquisition, and draft animals. In 1862, the Indian Office purchased twelve yoke of oxen for common use of 130 families. Three years later, nine of the draft animals were dead or lost, causing much delay in getting in the crops. Farnsworth recommended selling three aging oxen, the money from their sale to be used to purchase "small plows and plow harnesses" better adapted to ponies. Some Kanzas were already using ponies to plow their fields, the agent reported. Perhaps the entire tribe could be convinced to train their ponies to do farmwork. Concurring with the agent was Mahlon Stubbs, the newly appointed Kanza farmer who replaced Huffaker in January 1866. Stubbs found that of the twenty-four plows on hand, only six were the one-horse plows the Kanzas needed for their small ponies. He also found a deficiency in the number of harnesses, double and single trees, collars, trace chains, and hoes, the latter the main implement for tending their crops. Shortages of such items existed because white neighbors stole and purchased agricultural equipment from the Indians. To address these needs, Farnsworth immediately ordered $797.50 worth of implements and tools, especially small plows and cheap chain harnesses. These items were purchased by Stubbs in Kansas City. Back on the reservation he distributed the new hardware to the head of each Kanza household.[26]

It was not easy for the Kanzas to make the transition from employing oxen yoked and driven by the government farmer to draft ponies they were expected to work themselves. That first spring when making his rounds to the Kanza fields, Stubbs frequently found the collars wrong side to the horse and wrong end up. Never having worn a harness, the ponies so well adapted for chasing bison balked at pulling a plow. Frequently, a Kanza woman led a pony by the bridle bit while a man held the plow handles. Sometimes the pony would rear, plunge like a bucking bronco, and run away. A white passerby observed a Kanza man plowing: "He had his blanket off, and held the plow as for dear life. One squaw led the pony and another laid on the whip." Despite these understandable difficulties, in 1866 the Kanzas produced five thousand bushels of corn, a decline from the previous year but still a productive harvest. Farnsworth declared 1866 a successful farming year, with more Kanzas taking "considerable interest in their work. I think there is an increasing disposition with some men to do their part of the work."[27]

Three years before receiving his appointment as Kanza farmer, Stubbs had journeyed with his family from Iowa to the Neosho reservation where he began his assignment as superintendent of the new boarding school operated by the Quakers. Arriving in the spring of 1863, Stubbs was shocked to discover that the recently constructed school was filthy, without furnishings, and not provided with either a well or cistern. The Stubbs family worked for two months to clean and furnish the buildings. Agent Farnsworth then met with the Kanzas in council, informing them that they were expected to send their children to the boarding school when it opened in May. Some of the leading chiefs and warriors made strong objections. However, on the opening day, thirty-two boys and three girls appeared at the school, riding their ponies behind their parents. It was soon apparent that most of the enrollees were from the poorer families. Those parents whose families had plenty to eat and wear had not allowed their children to leave home. Stubbs reported that the children "were entirely in a wild, uncultivated condition, never having attended school," and none could speak English. Many were clad in calico shirts and little else. Stubbs made sure that each was scrubbed, combed, and rubbed with ointment. Blue denim clothing had been made for the children, but much of it did not fit, so when assembled the Kanza scholars were a motley-looking set.[28]

As was typical with almost all programs newly launched by the government on the Kanza Reservation, initial reports were full of optimism and observed progress. In this vein, Mahlon Stubbs wrote in September 1863 that the students "nearly all evince an aptness to learn, and a willingness to do most kinds of work that would not do discredit to white children of the same ages." Twelve could read easy lessons, all could spell three-letter words.[29]

The boys assisted in farming operations such as plowing and hoeing while the girls were instructed in homemaking. During the summer the older boys awoke at daybreak and immediately reported to the stable where they helped to milk the twelve cows. After breakfast, all of the boys were assembled, each was issued a hoe, and then they were marched to the cornfield or potato patch for an assault on weeds. By mid-morning the boys were seated in the classroom for the day's lessons. After the evening meal, they were once again marched to the fields. This "mission farm" was usually quite productive. The first year, the eighty-eight cultivated acres produced twenty-five hundred bushels of corn, two hundred bushels of spring wheat, an assortment of vegetables, and twenty-five tons of hay. The searing winds and heat of July 1864, however, reduced corn production by one-half. During the heat wave, the Quakers closed the doors and windows of the classroom and sprinkled water on the floor. In 1865, the mission farm comprised twenty-five acres of wheat, fifteen acres of oats, and forty-five acres of corn. By June 15 that year the Kanza boys had plowed the cornfield three times. The school's 1865 crops were described as "bountiful." After two years of observing the performance of the Kanza boys in the fields, Stubbs acknowledged that they "have been quite serviceable on the farm."[30]

The children's conduct in the classroom was reported as uniformly good. "I have found these children much easier governed than I have anticipated," wrote a white teacher in 1866. "When treated kindly, they seem to be of an affectionate disposition." Ranging in age from four to seventeen, the children were instructed in reading, writing, spelling, arithmetic, geography, and drawing, with the latter their favorite subject. After the second year, nine were reading (all but one of the students who had learned to read the first year failed to return for the second term), and five students could read pretty well in their text, *Wilson's Second Reader*. After the fourth year, twelve were again reported as being able to read and two could divide compound numbers. Exercises were done on blackboard, slate, and paper. A student named Mechushingah was the most advanced, reading proficiently in *Wilson's Second Reader*, performing "mental arithmetic," and writing in "a pretty good hand." Enrollment numbers remained fairly consistent during the four years the school operated: in 1863, thirty-two boys and three girls; in 1864, forty-seven boys and three girls; in 1865, thirty-three boys and seven girls; and in 1866, twenty-eight boys and five girls.[31]

As the years passed, official reports contained fewer descriptions of progress and more of difficulties, and the enrollment numbers were misleading. The school was plagued by turnover and irregular attendance. A male instructor reported that "some of the boys are pretty bad to run off, [and] it is pretty hard to keep them interested in school." After three years, Thomas Stanley replaced Stubbs as superintendent, holding this position during 1866, the school's final year of operation. Early that year, while the Kanzas were away hunting bison, only twenty-two students attended school regularly through the winter. When the Kanzas returned from the hunt in the spring, students went home to visit, came back to school, but after a short time "wished to go home again, and in some cases left without . . . consent." By May, just fifteen students attended the school. Having little enthusiasm for the institution, most of the Indian parents allowed their children to remain home. Other students were taken from school to assist with farm work at home. For the 1866 term, the average daily attendance was only 13.6 pupils.[32]

The list of reasons for the school's troubles, as provided by government and school officials, closely resembled explanations of the Methodist failure more than a decade before: the language barrier, lack of support by Indian parents, absence of the most promising children, limitations of the Quaker system of pedagogy, failure to Christianize the scholars and adults, and the early marriage of Kanza girls. In May 1866, Farnsworth and Stanley assembled a council to learn the Indians' views of the beleaguered school. The Kanzas complained that their children were not well fed and clothed and that the lessons were not presented in interesting, lively, and attractive ways. School officials promised improvements, but later that summer the Kanza agent declared the school a failure and on September 15 it was closed. While acknowledging that the Quaker educators were conscientious and sincere in their desire to help the Indians, the Kanza agent concluded that the children did not remain long enough in school to do any permanent good: "the scholars on leaving school become in all respects as much heathen as those children who have not been in school." The Kanza elders concurred, observing, as had their forebears, "that the young men who have been to school are the worst in the tribe."[33]

Just as the school was failing, Stanley and Farnsworth found themselves managing the Kanza Agency and school as a refugee camp for a group of women and children who had been captured during Kiowa and Comanche raids on settlements in Texas. The first group of freed captives—Mrs. Caroline McDonald and four children—arrived at the Kanza Agency in late October 1865, having been released by their Kiowa captors following the signing of the Little Arkansas Treaty near present-day Wichita. By the summer of 1866, the government had placed ten captives at the Kaw Mission, where they anxiously awaited return to their Texas homelands. All of these women and children had family members killed by Indians during raids in 1864 and early 1865. They all arrived at the Quaker school in poor condition.[34]

The older captive children were enrolled in the school, where they studied side-by-side with Kanza children. This arrangement met the disapproval of two of the women captives, who complained that the health of the Texas children—and by extension all of the captives— was jeopardized by their mixing with the Kanzas. The women also objected to all of the captives being housed in only two rooms in the school's dormitory. Throughout the spring and summer, the delay in returning the women and children to Texas was the source of much wrangling and contention between the captives and Indian Office officials. The gridlock persisted into August. The bureaucrats were especially concerned about the costs of retaining the Texans at the Kanza school. Finally Farnsworth drew on his political connections to arrange for the captives' return to their Texas homes. By September a five-wagon caravan bearing weary exiles and supplies was homeward bound, all arriving safely in Texas in October.[35]

From the earliest American history to the present, Indian captive stories have been prominently featured. For example, the October

1864 raids on Elm Creek, Texas, and the subsequent search for the captives—some of whom were among the Kanza Agency refugees—became the subject of at least one novel, various articles, and the famous 1956 western film *The Searchers*, directed by John Ford and starring John Wayne. A more recent treatment of the Indian captive theme is Jeff Brome's *Dog Soldier Justice: The Ordeal of Susanna Alderdice in the Kansas Indian War*, published in 2005. Brome's narrative of the 1867 and 1868 Cheyenne raids in north central Kansas focuses on the cruelties endured by the captive white women. This treatment is safely ensconced in the "settler history" tradition of viewing the tragic events of the Indian-white conflict solely through the point of view of the Euro-American participants. Because no attempt is made in the book to contextualize the raids in terms of understanding the Dog Soldiers' violence as a furious expression of a desperate people losing their land and a beloved way of life, *Dog Soldier Justice* reinforces the stereotype of Indians as less-than-human Other, a screaming, demonic presence, the faceless terrorists of their age.[36]

In *Everything You Know about Indians Is Wrong*, Indian author and cultural critic Paul Chaat Smith cites the belief of Cherokee artist Jimmie Durham "that no relationship in the Americas is more profound or more central than that between Indians and settlers, and that nothing is more lied about." In the case of the Kanzas, the distortion of this story cannot be attributed to unavailable historical sources, at least for the Neosho River period. For, in contrast to many facets of the tribe's history, the Indians' Euro-American contemporaries and their descendants left behind a fairly substantial body of narratives, mostly reminiscences, describing encounters with the Kanzas. An examination of these histories reveals, not surprisingly, a multiplicity of behaviors and attitudes manifested by both whites and Kanzas. Since all the chroniclers available to us are white, readers are hostage to how deeply the writers have cared to look into the humanity of the Kanzas with whom they associated—that is, how willing and able they were to relate to the Indians as subjects. That capacity for empathy allows us to experience the humanity of the Indians and that of their white neighbors with the humor, kindness, playfulness, folly, dignity, and sadness inherent in the human condition. Without empathy, as was often the case, especially in newspaper accounts, white chroniclers reduced the Kanzas to human caricatures, the better to keep them at a safe distance, and better yet to banish from their sight forever. This dark propensity is a pervasive and necessary theme of the Kanzas' history, but it does not contain the whole story. The following brief compendium of anecdotes may help right the balance.[37]

Christena Phillips Campbell came to the settlement of Salina in 1858. As a young bride, she took charge of a trading store. At this time Kanzas, having established hunting camps nearby on the Smoky Hill and Saline Rivers, were her frequent customers. At first, when she sold flour, sugar, and coffee to the Indians, Christena measured portions by weight. The Kanzas objected, shaking their heads and saying "no good." They insisted that the flour be measured using large tin pans and the sugar using large tin cups. One day three Kanza women trading in the store kept looking at Campbell's feet and shaking their heads. One approached, stooped down, and raised Campbell's skirt a little. When the hoops under her skirt was revealed, all of the Kanzas had a good, long laugh. Some time later, one spring evening, three Kanza women approached the cabin, asking to see their "white sister." Campbell went outside to meet them. They took her hand in theirs, saying, "Goodbye, goodbye,—home to Council Grove—one sleep—go home!" Then one of them unwrapped a little package, taking out a gold ring, and while saying good-bye, put it on her finger. "I do not know what I would have done if it had not been for the Indians," Campbell recalled. "I was with the Indians a good deal, and I had many good friends among them."[38]

Christena Campbell is but one of several pioneer women who established harmonious relationships with the Kanzas and left us a record of having done so. Men, on the other hand, seemed less inclined toward such friendships, although there were exceptions. Soon after Kansas became a U.S. territory in 1854, James R. McClure established a claim near the confluence of Lyon Creek and the Kansas River just southwest of present-day Junction City. McClure built his cabin near a camp frequented by the Kanzas, the tribe having hunted and fished in the area for many years. Regarded by the Indians as an intruder, McClure sought to diffuse tensions by making peace with the chiefs, in the process becoming acquainted with two—Pegahoshe and Fool

Chief the Younger. McClure described Pegahoshe, whom he called "Reg-e-kosh-ee," as a "fine specimen of physical manhood, a large, well-developed, proportioned Indian, with keen black eyes, commanding appearance, and the bearing of one who was born to lead." Pegahoshe, McClure believed, was perceptive, intelligent, honest, and well informed on many subjects. McClure often invited the old chief to dinner, and a friendship was formed. Commanding the respect of his tribe, Pegahoshe was effective in resolving difficulties arising between the settlers and the Indians.[39]

Fool Chief, in McClure's view, was the finest-looking Indian he had ever seen. The handsome young chief had a dignified and refined appearance and an aloof manner that reflected his rank and superiority. He put up his tipi some distance from others and had little interchange with other Kanzas apart from giving commands. Fool Chief repelled McClure's attempts to cultivate his friendship as the Kanza chief regarded himself as the white man's superior and "resented any intention on my part to form an intimate friendship with him." Fool Chief's wife, Hehojame, McClure reported, was intelligent, tall, beautiful, and far better dressed than the other women. Like her husband, she held herself aloof. The Fool Chief tipi was always neat and the best made in the camp. The Kanzas esteemed Fool Chief as a brave warrior and great hunter, and they admired him for his mental and physical qualities. McClure concluded: "I have never met an Indian who would compare with him in manner and appearance."[40]

Flowing parallel to Lyon Creek a few miles to the east was Clarks Creek. A few miles upstream from where the Clarks Creek joins the Kansas River (five miles west and one mile north of present-day White City) was a well-timbered place with a firm, flat, graveled streambed and nearby spring. This was a favorite crossing point and campsite of the Kanzas as they traveled to and from their hunting camps on the Smoky Hill and Saline Rivers west of Salina. In 1857 the Warneke family settled here and for the next decade became well acquainted with the tribe. When returning from hunts, the Kanzas often stopped at the Warneke cabin to trade buffalo meat for cornbread. The Warneke and Kanza children played together. Their favorite game was to hand wrestle while mounted on ponies, the victor the one able to get the other to fall off. During bitterly cold nights the family invited the Kanzas to sleep in their cabin, whereupon the floor would become a mat of Indians. One winter a Kanza band was returning from a successful hunt near Salina when the Indians were caught in a severe blizzard on Clarks Creek. In order to lighten their load for the return through the storm to Council Grove, they made arrangements with the Warnekes to store about ten thousand pounds of buffalo meat. The Indians then pushed on into the storm, returning a few days later in good weather to reclaim their meat.[41]

During this same winter hunt, the Kanzas had been joined by a group of settlers, a not infrequent arrangement. In the winter of 1855–56, a party of men from the area around Manhattan, Kansas, made a "meat trip" about one hundred miles west. Careful to keep clear of Cheyennes, these men relied on the Kanzas and Potawatomies, who "always ready for war in their hunting expeditions, usually kept the hostile Indians at a distance." Near the Little Arkansas in May 1857, some cavalry officers in Major John Sedgwick's column began to pursue what they thought were buffalo. These "buffalo" turned out to be Kanza hunters who were tracking buffalo themselves. The officers and Kanzas continued on together, overtaking a herd three miles later, where each party began its own hunt.[42]

Early in the Civil War, soldiers camped near Council Grove "had a world of fun" setting up target-shooting contests with the Kanzas. The targets were a staple of the army—the hard, square biscuits called hardtack, placed about twenty paces away. The Kanzas shot at them with bows and arrows, rarely missing the mark. With the exception of trade, target shooting was probably the most frequently recorded form of Kanza-white socialization, and the Indian shooters seldom failed to impress their observers with their accuracy. James Josiah Webb witnessed two bow-wielding Kanza boys shoot a small woodpecker out of a tall cottonwood tree. "They showed great skill with the bow, as they would scarcely ever miss any target we would set up for them," he wrote. During a shooting match in Emporia, a Kanza hit a nickel with an arrow at sixty-five feet. On Thanksgiving Day 1871, a "turkey shoot" was held on the main street in Atlanta, a recently established (though ultimately short-lived) town located near the Kanza winter hunting camp on Cow Creek in what is now Rice County. The contestants stood sixty-five yards from their prizes, live turkeys tethered to a cracker box. Because the Kanzas much preferred to shoot their muzzle-loading "squirrel rifles" from a kneeling position, contest managers required all shooters to stand upright. Each time the authorities relaxed this prohibition, they lost a turkey to a dead-eyed Indian.[43]

The Thomson family of Wabaunsee County always welcomed a visit by the Kanzas as a means of relieving the monotony of an isolated frontier existence on Dragoon Creek. One day a Kanza man and his wife stopped overnight en route to Topeka. When the Thomsons fed the couple, the Indians responded with smiles and "grunts of satisfaction." A few weeks later, after spending the day laboring in cornfields, the Thomson men and boys returned to their cabin where they found awaiting them a dish of fried venison provided by these same Kanzas "as a token of their appreciation of our kindness." In 1857, a few days after Quakers Thomas and Mary Stanley and their children arrived at their new home just south of the Kanza Reservation, one of their oxen wandered off and drowned in a swamp. After Stanley recovered the ox carcass with assistance from his neighbors, he walked to the nearest Indian village on Kahola Creek, where he shook hands with the Kanzas and invited them to help themselves to ox meat. The Indians received his offer enthusiastically, patting the stranger on the back, saying, "heap good, heap good; other white man say, 'go way, go way'; they *peshie* (no good)." During the ensuing sixteen years, the Kanzas often came to the Stanley home in times of need to partake of fruit from the orchard, vegetables from the garden, and milk from the cows. Frequently before setting out on their buffalo hunts, the Indians would place their aged and sick in tents on the Stanley premises, knowing they would be protected and cared for there.[44]

The harmonious relations suggested by these anecdotes should not obscure the well-documented and intractable fact that many Euro-Americans bore ill will toward their Kanza neighbors. Examples of this darker impulse, as we have seen, abound in the newspapers of the day. In the August 11, 1865, issue of the *Council Grove Press*, the editor buttressed his support for constructing a new school—a question to be determined by an upcoming election—by employing one of Council Grove's most frequently used and effective polemical tactics, Kanza baiting: "If you are anxious to make your presence felt for evil, vote down the school-house. If you don't want education, or civilization, unless you can have them for nothing, vote down the school-house. If you want to be a savage, try to get the Kaws back in Council Grove and vote down the school-house. Get the Kaws to vote—everyone of them will vote against it—would rather have the money to buy worthless trinkets, 'big whisky.'"[45]

By 1865, a lingering legal dispute regarding Council Grove land titles had been resolved. On September 1, 1863, a patent signed by President Lincoln was issued to the Council Grove Town Company. The company's proprietorship had been disputed in court by Jacob A. Hall, a Santa Fe Road mail contractor from 1850 through 1862. Having gained possession of the one-square-mile town site, the company could now begin to sell property, ushering in a period of growth and prosperity, especially for the company's board members.[46]

Council Grove in 1865 was still a raw frontier town. Side streets looked like cow paths and weeds grew so thick and high that bells were attached to cows so they could be found. The only man in town to own a buggy was one of the wealthiest, Malcolm Conn. Everyone else traveled by horseback or two-horse wagon. When it rained, the streets and walkways became muddy quagmires. But in 1866, the town company and individual entrepreneurs began to make substantial improvements to the constructed environment. The company installed six-foot-wide wooden sidewalks on both sides of Main Street for two blocks and graveled the pedestrian crossings. A new bridge was constructed across the Neosho. Health and safety issues were addressed. The *Council Grove Democrat* admonished its readers to treat sinks and outhouses with a solution of copperas (ferrous sulfate) and water as they become foul in hot weather. An ordinance was passed forbidding swimming in the Neosho within the town's limits.[47]

Numbers generated by the 1865 state census help bring into focus the Council Grove of the mid-1860s. Council Grove Township, whose inhabitants included farmers in the town's immediate vicinity, grew

Council Grove's Main Street, c. 1872. Courtesy Morris County Historical Society.

from 385 in 1860 to 586 in 1865. The actual town in 1865 had a population of 373, 178 females and 195 males. The average age of the females was 18.5, and the average age of males was 22.2. The African American population was zero in 1860, ten in 1865. Virtually equal numbers of adults in the township were born in free states (115) and slave states (114). There were three saloonkeepers, three blacksmiths, one minister, two teachers, two millers, and one "gentleman." In 1860, the seven wealthiest men in the township had combined personal estates of $42,000 out of a total of $84,099. By 1865, the personal estate value of the township had swelled to $218,815, half of which was possessed by seven men.[48]

Even as the fortunes of the Democratic Party declined precipitously in Kansas in the mid-1860s, Morris County, reflecting its border-state, pro-Southern heritage, continued to be that party's stronghold. In the presidential election of 1864, Morris was the only county in Kansas favoring Democrat George McClellan (98 votes) over incumbent

Republican Abraham Lincoln (70). In the 1865 county election, every Democratic candidate was elected. In 1866, the first postwar newspaper in Kansas to be unequivocally Democratic was the *Council Grove Democrat*. Consistent with the avowedly racist doctrine of its party, almost every extant edition of the *Democrat* carried articles vilifying African Americans, sometimes in the most racist terms imaginable. The Democrats' racialist extremism should not obscure the fact that the overwhelming majority of U.S. citizens of all classes and party affiliations enthusiastically embraced the ideology of white supremacy. In Kansas, white people may have rejected slavery but they were also adamantly opposed to black or Indian equality. The systematic racism that oppressed the Kanzas and other tribes, then, is but one expression of a pervasive racial inequality corroding relations between the dominant whites and a broad spectrum of racial minorities in all regions of nineteenth-century America.[49]

One hundred miles west of the Missouri border and approximately one hundred miles east of territory occupied by the Plains tribes, Council Grove was a strategic location on a busy military highway—the Santa Fe Road. The twin threats posed by Missouri guerrillas and "hostile" Indians transformed the town into a center of military activity during the last two years of the Civil War. A blockhouse was built and various units were stationed there. By autumn 1863, Council Grove was headquarters of the Seventh Regiment of the Kansas State Militia, Colonel Samuel N. Wood commanding. One of the ironies of Wood's stint as military commander was that this inveterate Indian hater benefited from intelligence the Kanzas supplied him about suspicious whites lurking around their camps. In March, Wood was promoted to brigadier general commanding the Fifth Brigade District of the Kansas State Militia, headquartered in Council Grove.[50]

Precipitated by the unprovoked killing of Cheyenne chief Lean Bear by cavalry troops in May 1864, the "Indian War of 1864–1865" erupted on the plains. In July, five wagon trains and 104 white men were besieged near the Cow Creek Crossing by a large force of Cheyenne, Arapaho, Kiowa, and Comanche warriors. Then on November 29, 1864, a Cheyenne/Arapaho village on Sand Creek in eastern Colorado was attacked by militiamen under Colonel John

Chivington. This infamous "Sand Creek Massacre" provoked a furious and sustained retaliation by the Plains tribes that made the already hazardous travel on the Santa Fe Road extremely dangerous. By spring 1865, military commanders ordered caravans to wait at Council Grove until they had assembled one hundred well-armed men before proceeding westward.[51]

In 1866, Council Grove merchants enjoyed yet another boom year of trade, this attributable to the sustained upsurge of commercial activity on the Santa Fe Road. The volume of trail traffic bore little resemblance to that of 1846 when four hundred commercial wagons, not counting government transportation, crossed the plains from the United States to Mexico. In 1866, the number of such wagons coming into New Mexico was five to six thousand. In the midst of this prosperous year, however, developments portended the loosening of Council Grove's grip on the road of commerce. The construction of the Union Pacific Railroad, Eastern Division, progressed westward up the Kansas River valley. At the onset of 1866, the tracks were completed to Topeka, and these reached Manhattan in August and Junction City by early November. Freighters now made more money locating the eastern terminals of their Santa Fe Road operations at the advancing end of the tracks because railroad shipping was more efficient than wagon trains. Once the rails were laid to Junction City, that town became the beginning of the trail, which then extended west up the Smoky Hill valley before crossing southwest to join the established trail route near the big bend of the Arkansas River. In consequence, when the wagons began to roll in the spring of 1867, the road to Santa Fe had circumvented Council Grove, and the town was never again the same.[52]

The Kanzas underwent a major transition as well when Ishtalasea, head chief since 1861, died on Friday night, September 29, 1865. Earlier that day he had received his annuity payment at the agency. Throughout September he had lived on short rations, and it was said that the sudden consumption of large quantities of food he had purchased that day caused his death. Ishtalasea was the last Kanza chief to have been born before 1800. When he was a young warrior, the powerful and feared Kanzas roamed freely throughout that portion of the central plains later called Kansas. "Our Great Father told us we were the richest of all the Indians; now we are poor," he had written to the commissioner of Indian Affairs in 1863. The Kanzas mourned his death in large numbers. He had been a sober and eloquent chief, and a good representative of his people. At the time of his death, Ishtalasea lived with his family in a two-story stone house one mile northwest of the agency. The limestone walls of his house, called by local people "the Chief's House," were still standing until the 1980s.[53]

One year elapsed after Ishtalasea's death before a new head chief was selected. After the annual payment in the fall of 1866, the Kanzas immediately headed west on the bison hunt, except for fifteen or twenty headmen who remained behind to sign annuity documents. Determined that a new head chief be designated, Farnsworth assembled the Kanza leaders at the council house and explained to them that they were to elect their new head chief. In response, almost every man stated the reasons he was best qualified to be chief, then voted for himself, so no clear favorite emerged. The Kanza agent then proposed that the election of a head chief be put on hold, and that Allegawaho, in his capacity as head chief of the Kahola village, be the first to sign the annuity document. After much discussion, this was agreed upon. Allegawaho stepped forward, his X was affixed at the top of the list Kanza names, and in consequence he became the undisputed head chief because the Kanzas by then had integrated the belief that the order of signatures on such documents was the final arbiter of their rank.[54]

Soon after Allegawaho's "election," Hiram Farnsworth resigned as the Kanza agent, a position he had occupied for over five years. In contrast to his two predecessors and counter to the "Indian agent as devil" theory espoused by many of his contemporaries and some modern historians, Farnsworth had performed his duties conscientiously, efficiently, and energetically. But his final months as agent were fraught with problems. Besides the school failure and contention surrounding the captives from Texas, he faced the federal government's meddling in the traders' system.[55]

When Farnsworth began his term as Kanza agent in the spring of 1861, he discovered that his tribe owed white traders $36,500. This debt saddled the Kanzas with the responsibility for settling these

Kanza chiefs Allegawaho, Fool Chief, and Watianga. Courtesy Kansas State
Historical Society.

accounts out of their common fund as prescribed by the Treaty of 1859. Much of this money was paid to the Council Grove traders for whom the annuity system worked well. Some local merchants boasted that within three days of the $8,000 annuity payments, $7,000 of it would end up in their hands. Some Indians would waste the payments "wantonly in gambling, drunkenness, or in some useless expenditure, doing no good to himself or family." Much to the consternation of the Kanzas, the annuity payments were frequently delayed. Scheduled for early September, the 1861 payment finally arrived in February 1862. Still reeling from the 1860–61 drought, the destitute Kanzas appealed to their new agent, who issued them $2,000 worth of supplies, the money coming out of his own pocket.[56]

In response to the system's multiple failings, the Indian Office assigned a trader to a store located at the Kanza Agency, and in November 1861 Commissioner William Dole authorized Farnsworth "to give orders." The new system empowered the agent to issue orders to the head of each Kanza household authorizing the purchase of flour, bacon, and other necessary items from the agency trader, who was required to supply such goods on credit until the amount assigned to each household was used up. By monitoring and regulating how the annuities were spent, the agent was able to put a cap on debt, negate the tendency of the Indians to use their annuities to purchase whiskey and trinkets, and channel money to the "fair-dealing" agency trader and away from potentially unscrupulous merchants. The agent issued the orders at payment time when the Kanzas bought clothing, provisions, rifles, and ammunition to outfit themselves for winter and the fall hunt. During Farnsworth's term, ten dollars was assigned to each household member. Usually large families took about half their annuity and small families nearly all of it. "The trader is at the pay table," wrote Farnsworth, "and settles his accounts with the head of each family as the money is paid to the Indian, the trader taking the amount of his just claim, and the Indian the balance."[57]

Powerful economic interests disapproved of the "orders system." Echoing modern conservative-liberal debates about government regulation of free markets, some congressmen expressed concerns about the stifling of the virtues of free competition. Allegations were made that the system was open to exploitation by collusive agents and their privileged traders. In June 1866, Congress mandated its abolishment. Once again the Indians would receive direct cash payments, releasing the annuity funds to the laissez faire marketplace. The Kanza agent's response was unequivocal: his impoverished and improvident tribe would consume their annuities in a few days, once again incur large debts, and go to the buffalo country with very limited means of support. No trader would take a license to trade at this agency, and the agent would become responsible for debts the Indians incurred with Council Grove merchants. These disappointments and the removal of his closest supporters from positions of influence in the government led to the Indian Office reassigning Farnsworth to other duties in September. With that, the Kanzas lost one of their few allies in the federal bureaucracy. Though not without shortcomings—including sharing the conventional wisdom of his contemporaries that improvement for Indians required destroying their culture—Farnsworth had consistently demonstrated that he was willing to listen to the Kanza headmen in council and to advocate forcefully on their behalf in the halls of government. By the end of 1866, the Kanzas faced the future without the leadership of their beloved chief Ishtalasea and trusted agent Farnsworth. What was headed their way was intimated by the December 29 *Emporia News*: the Union Pacific Railway, Southern Branch, was making "efforts to obtain as additional franchises to their road the Kaw Lands, lying near Council Grove."[58]

*

Although the tribe experienced the darkest period of its history from 1846 to 1873, the Kanzas' time of occupation of the Neosho River reservation was not one of unremitting gloom. There were instances when both the Kanzas and their Euro-American neighbors breached racial and cultural barriers to interact in modes of accommodation undergirded by recognition of their common humanity. Ironically, the Civil War provided an opportunity for young Kanza men steeped in warrior traditions to serve effectively as soldiers in the Union army. Some white settlers developed relationships with their Kanza neighbors based on mutual respect, at times even affection. The mid-1860s were a relatively prosperous time for the Kanzas. Finally freed from the inhibitions imposed by the presence of white encroachers, some Kanzas began to adopt Euro-American methods of farming and raised good crops. Four successive buffalo hunts were successful. Once again a school began to operate on the reservation, this one administered by dedicated and hardworking Quakers. Enumerating these promising developments cannot erase the lingering presence of darker forces: sickness continued to stalk the tribe, hostile whites cast their land-hungry eyes toward the diminished reserve, the great chief Ishtalasea died, and the best agent in the tribe's history resigned. Still, the nightmarish period begun by the 1855 smallpox epidemic and sustained by the six-year-long white occupation of the reservation by the mid-1860s had yielded to a sense of brighter prospects for the tribe's future. In retrospect, we can now imagine the potential emergence of a transformational period in white-Kanza relations. Would it be possible to establish a middle ground of accommodation on and around the Kanza Reservation? Could a zone of peaceful, mutually beneficial coexistence replace the prevailing geography of racism and violence?

CHAPTER 7

In No Condition to Compete with Their Formidable Enemies

In November 1867, a band of Kanzas was encamped on Plum Creek between present-day Great Bend and Ellsworth, Kansas, for their annual winter bison hunt. Later that month, a party of about forty Cheyennes professing peaceful intentions approached the camp, where they were received hospitably. When the Cheyennes departed, they encountered a lone Kanza herder, whom they killed and scalped within sight of the camp. Enraged, Kanza warriors mounted their ponies and rode out to meet the enemy. During the ensuing four-hour battle, fourteen Cheyennes and two Kanzas were killed, many on both sides were seriously wounded, and several ponies died. The Kanzas finally drove the Cheyennes from the field and collected scalps.[1]

Other Kanza bands camping in the area were notified of the battle. Anticipating that the powerful and better-armed Cheyennes would return in force, the entire tribe of Kanzas, population 658 according to a count by Kanza agent Elias S. Stover, began a hasty 110-mile flight back to their reservation. Most of the few ponies not exhausted in battle were mounted by men, as was the custom—horses provided men the mobility required to hunt game and compete with enemies. As the broken column advanced across the prairie, many Kanzas died, succumbing to the cold, exhaustion, and hunger. Most headed east-northeast, probably staying close to the recently abandoned Fort Riley–Fort Larned road. This route would take them by Fort Harker and near the budding settlements of Salina and Abilene

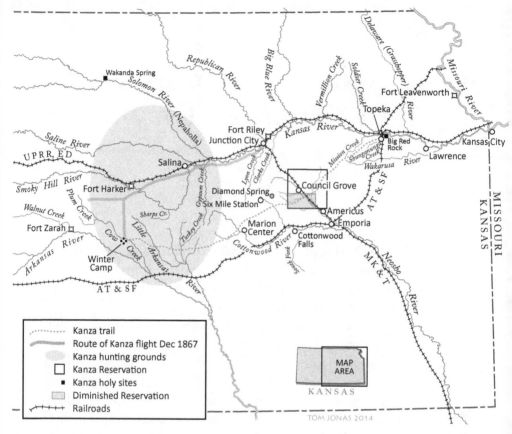

Kanza Homeland, 1865–73. © 2014, University of Oklahoma Press.

before ending at Fort Riley. It is likely that the Kanzas chose this route rather than their well-established southern trail (through present-day Rice, McPherson and Marion Counties) in hopes that the army forts, Union Pacific railroad line, and white settlements might afford them protection. By Christmas, all of the survivors had arrived at either Fort Riley or the agency near Council Grove.[2]

New Kanza agent Stover reported that the Kanzas had "suffered terribly" on their return march and that many of their horses had died. During the desperate flight, sixty-one Kanzas died, and many weakened by the ordeal died subsequently. To prevent starvation, Stover issued the destitute Indians small quantities of flour and beef.

Two days after their return, he met with the Kanzas in council. The agent found them in "most lamentable condition," with their children dying in great numbers.[3]

A close look at the agent's tabulations of the Kanza population in 1867 and 1868 reveals another grim aspect of the tragic march. "You can imagine what their sufferings were when, in the last year, they have decreased from 658 to 539, in one of the most healthy years known since the settlement of the west," the agent reported in September 1868. Stover's reported loss of 119 Kanzas represents an 18 percent decline in total population. A deeper analysis reveals a chilling pattern. In September 1867, Stover counted 298 males, while in 1868 there were 275 males, an 8 percent drop. Female numbers, on the other hand, decreased from 360 in 1867 to 264 in 1868, a 27 percent decline. Although the individuality of those frozen bodies left behind in the hills of central Kansas will always remain obscure, we can at least infer through the lens of gender their collective identity.[4]

As the Kanzas came straggling in, they established a camp on the south bank of the Smoky Hill River near Fort Riley. There, during the last week of December, they performed a series of dances attended by many men from Junction City and the fort. The Indians were desperate for cash, a majority of them having nothing to eat except what they could buy from the whites. "War dance" exhibitions had entertainment value to the whites and therefore generated revenue. The beginning of the dance was described by the *Junction City Union*: "The old men of the party were remorseless in their demands for more money while the young chief who led the dances had just whiskey enough in him to cause him to be exceedingly anxious to give us a first class entertainment." The ensuing manifestation of female rage proved memorable. Suddenly the young dance leader was assaulted by "an old squaw," reported the *Union*, "in a very bad humor, as her vinegar face indicated." The Kanza woman rushed into the dance circle and attacked the dance leader, knocking him down. Another observer described what happened next: "As fast as he got up he was thrown again by the little Amazon. This was done three times." The cheering and applause of the white audience provoked a chief to get up on a tree stump and gruffly order the white men to go home, which they did without argument.[5]

Neither of the two accounts of this event betrayed the slightest awareness of the Kanzas' recent ordeal nor did the white witnesses seem to understand that they were in the presence of a deeply traumatized people. To them the dance was merely entertainment spiced by the comedic assault. Context was of little interest. That context can now be outlined, of course, in broad historical terms, among which are several salient features. Two tribes, the Cheyennes and the Kanzas, were competing for a diminishing number of bison within a cultural framework of a deeply ingrained militarism, which elevated male warriors. The stress of white encroachment on hunting grounds was made manifest by increasing numbers of hide hunters, forts, trails, railroads, and, more recently, settlements extending into central Kansas. The land itself was suffering, the degradation of the plains caused in part by Indians (mainly because of market-driven overhunting of game and the subsistence requirements of their pony herds) and in part by climate, especially the increased frequency of drought after 1845. In short, by 1867 both the Cheyennes and the Kanzas inhabited a landscape of diminishing possibilities.[6]

The December 1867 Kanza march, then, emerges into view from a background of multifaceted and interwoven cultural and environmental influences. Such complexity does not make good melodrama, which means that this tragic event has little traction in our imaginations. Even the weather did not cooperate in providing conditions for a ready-for-Hollywood story. On November 25, Ellsworth received two inches of snow and three days later, on Thanksgiving Day, a strong snowstorm swept through central Kansas. But December 1867 was mild as Kansas Decembers go and there were no terrible blizzards. It was just cold enough to kill. A conventionally dramatic story requires a polar reduction: humans versus nature, good guys versus bad guys, cowboys and Indians, Custer and Crazy Horse, government bullies and Indian victims, and so on. Other American Indian marches attained considerable renown, among the most notable being the Cherokee "Trail of Tears," the Navajo "Long Walk" after their 1864 deportation from Arizona, the Nez Perce 1,600-mile "retreat" in 1877, Ponca chief Standing Bear's 1878 return to Nebraska, and the Northern Cheyenne trek home from Oklahoma to Montana in 1878–79. Although each of these tragic journeys—

all of which involved considerable suffering, injustice, and Indian heroism—has its own unique history, implicit in all is a direct and well-documented causal link between the tribes' forced exiles and the villainy of the U.S. government's Indian policies and practices. About them, books and articles have been written, songs sung, films made, posters hung, statues erected, historical associations formed, roadside markers installed, monuments dedicated, and national historic trails established. They have become, in varying degrees of visibility, national icons.[7]

Today almost no one in Kansas or outside the state knows anything about the Kanzas' death walk. A 1971 book surveying the tribe's history from 1673 through 1873 devotes three sentences to it.[8] Obviously, the 110-mile distance traversed by the Kanzas comes up short when compared to the more famous Indian marches. Perhaps more significant is that there were no witnesses to chronicle the details of the Kanzas' flight, no eloquent patriot chief articulating his people's loss. But the facts remain: ten percent of a people for whom the state of Kansas is named perished during a 110-mile winter walk through the heart of this state, a cataclysmic event by any standard of measurement.

These Kanza dead have no grave markers. Their lives were as evanescent as wind-driven cloud shadows drifting across the plains. We know they were disproportionately young and female, but we don't know their names. They are historical nonentities. During a few cold days in December 1867, they became too weak to go farther, dropped to the ground, then died—sixty-one of them—on the Kansas prairie.

Despite the tragic subsequent events, the Kanzas considered the battle with the Cheyennes a victory worthy of celebration. Soon after the tribe had all returned to the reservation, a "scalp dance" was held at the Big John Creek village not far from the Kanza Agency. Trader Joab Spencer attended this dance and provided a detailed description. The Cheyenne scalps were hung on a pole erected in the middle of the village. Aligned in single file, with knees bent and faces grave, the men shuffled and bobbed up and down without changing position. The dancers paid close attention to their work, and Spencer was impressed with the seriousness of the affair. He also was astonished

Drawing of a "Dog Dance" performed in the interior of a Kanza earth lodge while the artist, Samuel Seymour, was visiting the Kanzas' Blue Earth village in 1819. Courtesy Kansas State Historical Society.

at the dancers' endurance: "How men could endure such exercise for hours without recess, is hard to understand."[9]

The Kanza trader correctly understood this dance and all Kanza dances as religious ceremonies. Music was provided by a drum of rawhide stretched over the open end of a keg. Accompanying the drumming was a singer improvising songs that described and celebrated the brave deeds of warriors who had taken Cheyenne scalps in the battle. The drumming could be heard at a great distance. Spencer remained for a long time before he returned to his home at the agency, where far into the night he heard the drumbeat and singing. That the Kanzas could celebrate their victory in the wake of overwhelming tragedy must be understood within the deep-seated tradition of honoring triumphant warriors and giving thanks to Wakanda for the defeat of enemies. The performance of the scalp dance affirmed the regaining of Wakanda's favor, an essential dispensation at a point in time when the Kanzas were reeling from a disastrous year, as a brief review of 1867 events confirms.[10]

The year began inauspiciously when at daybreak on January 1, a party of Cheyennes raided Chief Watianga's hunting camp between the Smoky Hill and Little Arkansas Rivers, capturing forty-four ponies and mortally wounding a Kanza man. Subsequently, the Kanzas' fear of renewed Cheyenne aggression inhibited the tribe's ability to freely range over the plains in pursuit of bison and other game. By February, it was clear that the winter hunt had failed, and Farnsworth's short-term successor as Kanza agent, Forrest R. Page, requested that the Indian Office supply the tribe with blankets, flour, and beef at a cost of $2,150.[11]

On March 25, Allegawaho, Fool Chief, and Watianga wrote Commissioner of Indian Affairs Lewis Bogy, spelling out their grim situation: "Our people have been in the buffalo country, ever since last September & have never made so poor a hunt. They have been able to barely take enough game to keep them alive. The continued severe cold weather had destroyed more than half their ponies, usually we bring in large lots of robes, to exchange for provisions in the spring, but this season, there will not be two Robes to the family on average, and many will have none, in fact will have to come on foot home, a distance of 150 miles. Many left corn at home in caches, enough to do them for food for some time, but much of that, has been spoiled by the wet weather." Compounding these immense difficulties—after a four-year hiatus—was the reinvasion of the reservation by squatters. By autumn 1866, several white families lived on the reservation, some paying rent to the Kanzas and raising crops. After the tribe left for the winter hunt, according to the Kanza chiefs, "the whites came & took possession of our places & stole our plows, harnesses, & corn & hay that we had left here . . . & have broken out our windows & carried off the doors to our houses. The houses are now full of whites, & the Indians will be in, in a few days & will have no place to go to." Fearing their people would starve to death before raising a crop, the chiefs asked for more assistance, concluding the letter: "The thing we want, is that we may have something to save life."[12]

The whites' occupation of the Kanzas' diminished reservation in the winter of 1866–67 had been prompted by speculation that a recently negotiated treaty stipulating the final expulsion of the Kanzas would soon be ratified by the U.S. Senate. When in the spring of 1867 it became clear that the removal of the Kanzas was not imminent, most of the squatters left. In late May, Kanza chiefs and headmen, citing their peoples' destitution and suffering due to the failure of the winter hunt, once again wrote to the commissioner pleading for an early annuity payment. A few weeks later, the chiefs requested that $2,000 of their school fund be channeled to the purchase of flour to enable the Kanzas to subsist through the remainder of the year. Agent Stover approved the request, confirming that the tribe was indeed destitute. The Indian Office responded by sending Superintendent Thomas Murphy to the Kanza Agency on July 22 to oversee the annuity payment. Beginning in the morning and concluding by 1:00 p.m., the dispersal of $8,000 was made in a quiet and orderly manner with the Kanzas expressing their gratitude to "the Great Father" for being so prompt.[13]

While at the reservation, Murphy observed how the miserable conditions on the reservation bred strife within the tribe. Fool Chief, regarded by Murphy as the most intelligent Kanza man, had been subjected to various indignities by his people, including being whipped by women during a drunken brawl earlier in the year. When one of the men stabbed Fool Chief in the stomach, the chief shot his assailant dead with a revolver. Fool Chief fled to the agent's house, where his wounds were dressed and he was granted protection. A council was then held during which "covering the dead," the traditional form of mediating murder, was employed. The family of the deceased man demanded that Fool Chief surrender his chieftaincy of the Rock Creek village and give them abundant material presents, saying that he should otherwise be killed. Fool Chief agreed to these terms, dispensing to the family a large number of ponies, robes, and other valuable items, then retreated from his duties to suffer a period of disgrace. This was yet another violent act involving Kanza leaders. Two Kanza head chiefs—Fool Chief the Elder in 1846 and Hard Chief in 1861—had both been murdered by their own people. Crushed by the weight of unrelenting poverty and a sense of powerlessness, the edifice of Kanza social order appeared to be cracking, with modes of tribal civility all too often yielding to self-inflicted violence.[14]

By the summer of 1867—as agent Farnsworth had predicted when the orders system was abolished in 1866—the Kanzas were so indebted to the agency trader that he was no longer willing to sell them more. The tribe owed $6,000 to the trader, Joab Spencer. Acknowledging the justness of this debt, the chiefs explained that they were unable to make payment because doing so would leave their families without any means of support. They also cited how the hostility of the Plains Indians prevented them from hunting bison with success and safety. Ordinarily a summer hunt on the plains provided the Kanzas with meat, but, with many Kanzas intimidated by the Cheyennes, few hunters ventured out that summer.[15]

On October 9, most of the Kanzas departed the reservation for the winter hunt on the plains. With the pony herd greatly diminished, most were forced to travel on foot, limiting progress to about ten miles per day. Nevertheless, the tribe was accused of stealing horses from the Arapahos on October 17 while that tribe was encamped near the site of the peace councils conducted on the Medicine Lodge River in present-day Barber County, about 150 miles from the Neosho reservation. (Here, as a means of establishing peace on the southern plains, treaties were signed by the U.S. government and the Comanche, Kiowa, Arapaho, Cheyenne, and Kiowa-Apache tribes pledging the signees to cease hostilities and obligating the tribes to relocate to reservations in Indian Territory.) Vigorously denying the horse-theft charges, the Kanzas accused the Arapahos of stealing thirty-four of their horses while they were en route to the buffalo country. Tribal leaders demanded that they be compensated for the theft of their horses and complained bitterly about the way they had been treated by the Plains Indians. Stover conveyed to Murphy how the tribe felt betrayed by the federal government. By being compliant with the wishes of "the Great Father," the Kanzas had incurred the enmity of the Plains Indians who waged war against the whites. Meanwhile, the government furnished their enemies with arms, ammunition, and provisions used "to drive their people from the common hunting ground" and refused to hear the Kanza complaints or address wrongs.[16]

The Kanzas' sense of vulnerability to their Cheyenne and Arapaho enemies sheds light on their hasty and disastrous flight following the

Plum Creek battle in late November. They knew they could not hold their ground against the superior numbers of their well-equipped and mounted foes, whom the Indian Office at the Medicine Lodge treaty grounds had supplied with fresh arms and ammunition. The Kanzas, as Stover wrote to Murphy in December, "are compelled to rely upon their own resources in every thing of this kind which of course leaves them in no condition to compete with their formidable enemies."[17]

At the same time that the Kanzas were confronting and then re-coiling from their enemies on the plains, a familiar parasite returned to infest the Kanza Reservation. Taking advantage of the absence of the Indians and once again expecting ratification of a treaty that would remove the Kanzas, white squatters entered the reservation and took possession of Indian houses and lands, intending to make permanent settlements. This time the "settlers" were better orga-nized, banding together and parceling out to each other portions of the reservation and establishing "squatters laws" designed to pro-tect their claims to the land as soon as the anticipated treaty became law. "This high-handed outrage ought to be stopped immediately," Superintendent Thomas Murphy wrote to the Indian Office, "and the perpetrators punished to the full extent of the law."[18]

Stover warned that if the trespassers were not removed soon, the entire reservation would be fully settled within three months. The agent foresaw that the squatters were likely to duplicate what they had done the previous winter when they destroyed much Indian property, and knew that if fully ensconced on the reservation, they would prevent the Kanzas from planting their crops in the spring. The agent and the superintendent knew of only one effective solu-tion: military intervention. This time action was forthcoming, and it came from the top. On December 2, 1867, General Ulysses S. Grant, commanding general of the U.S. Army, wrote Lieutenant General William Tecumseh Sherman, commander of the Division of the Mis-souri, "in relation to the encroachments of white men on the lands of the Kansas Indians." Grant ordered Sherman "to take such steps as he may think advisable for maintain[ing] our treaty stipulations with the Indians." The army appeared to be focused primarily on the Osage Reservation, which was then occupied by hundreds of white squatters. At the request of Kansas governor Samuel Crawford, Grant's order was suspended, and for the following two years there is no mention in the official correspondence of the encroachment problem on the Kanza Reservation. It seems reasonable to conclude, then, that the threat of intervention by the army's most famous and powerful generals commanded the squatters' obedience for the time being.[19]

The events of 1868 were even more calamitous for the Kanzas. Their pony herd had been decimated and the survivors so "reduced in flesh" that in late December 1867 the chiefs had informed their agent that they would not be able to travel again until June. At about this time, the Department of the Interior, informed of Cheyenne intentions to exact revenge on the Kanzas, ordered the tribe to remain on the reservation. By late January the products of the 1867 harvest had all been consumed. The only option left was government relief. "It cannot be possible," wrote Stover, "that the Government will compel these Indians to remain upon their limited reservation and in the midst of a civilized and christian people die of starvation." Trader Joab Spencer issued provisions on credit up until April 15, when he announced that no additional provisions would be forthcoming. On May 14, the Kanza agent spelled out the situation to Murphy: the Kanzas were confined to the reservation, surrounded on all sides by white settlers, and unable to obtain food from their crops of corn, potatoes, beans, and peas until later in the fall. "There is," wrote Stover, "no game on the Reservation and not one single means of support left them."[20]

As early as late December 1867, the Cheyennes were reported to be planning to wage war on the Kanzas, with the intention "to scalp the whole tribe." A few months later, Cheyenne warriors, apparently unaware that their enemies were confined to the Neosho reservation, scoured the Arkansas River valley in search of the Kanzas. Cheyenne chiefs supported the warriors, asserting that as the aggrieved party they needed to strike their foes first before talking peace. By restricting the Kanzas to their reservation, government officials, fearful that large war parties would alarm settlers on the frontier and hoping to preserve the fragile peace arranged at Medicine Lodge, employed the strategy of separating the Indian foes. The Cheyennes, however, decided that if the Kanzas could not come to them, they would go to the Kanzas.[21]

Just before midnight on June 2, 1868, a messenger appeared at the door of the Kanza agent's house bearing an urgent message: a large party of Cheyenne warriors was headed toward Council Grove. Earlier that day, a force of from three to five hundred Cheyenne and Arapaho warriors led by Little Robe and Tall Bull had passed north of Marion Center, heading east toward the Kanza Reservation. Armed with rifles and revolvers, the formidable party was also well-mounted: reportedly each warrior possessed at least five sturdy ponies. Word of the impending attack was quickly spread to the three Kanza villages and Council Grove. Kanza warriors, estimates of their numbers ranging from sixty to one hundred, gathered their arms and painted themselves for battle. Older Kanza people gathered at the agency barn while the children were placed at the Quaker school for safety.[22]

Among the children was a mixed-blood, one-eighth Kanza—eight-year-old Charles Curtis. Having lost his mother to death in 1863 and being isolated from his itinerant father, Orren Curtis, Charlie moved from North Topeka to the reservation in 1866. For two years he lived with his maternal grandparents, Julie and Louis Pappan, who had recently established residency on their reservation allotments. On June 3, Stover dispatched the Kanza interpreter, Joseph James, to Topeka to convey news of the Cheyenne incursion to governor Samuel J. Crawford. Accompanying "Joe Jim" on this trip was Charlie Curtis, who, after arriving in Topeka, once again took up residence with his paternal grandparents, William and Permelia Curtis. Never again would Charles live on the Kanza Reservation. He went on to have an exceptionally successful political career, capped by his assuming the office of vice president of the United States in the administration of Herbert Hoover in 1929.[23]

At about 10:00 A.M. on June 3, a group of white Council Grove citizens met the Cheyenne and Arapaho warriors just west of town. The Indians stated that if the whites did them no injury, they would not harm them. Their real intention was "to clean out the Kaws." With this assurance, the citizens offered no resistance. That morning the Indians divided into two parties. About ninety Indians, one-third of them Arapahos, rode east through town on Main Street. The other group proceeded south to Four Mile Creek. At the time, whites in the region had little faith in the Kanzas' ability to counter this imposing force. The *Emporia News* assessed the tribes' battle prospects: "There are sixty Kaw warriors in arms. It is supposed that they can do nothing against the large force of Cheyennes."[24]

Around noon, the warriors passed through Council Grove and arrived in the vicinity of the agency. Riding bareback and each holding two revolvers, they charged the Kanza position. The Kanzas fired a few shots, prompting the Cheyennes and Arapahos to retreat and gather on a ridge a few hundred yards west of Little John Creek. Here they began peace talks with agent Stover and Albert G. Boone, a veteran Indian trader and agent who happened to be visiting the agency. While this group parleyed, they were shot at by the Kanzas, who were dug in among the timber fringing the west bank of the creek. Stover returned to the Kanzas while Boone and the Plains Indians fell back, still under Kanza fire. According to Boone, who had retreated to a high point to view the skirmish, the two sides fought mounted and on foot for about three or four hours, "charging, circling and maneuvering[,] both parties trying all the strategy they know to get the advantage." Hearing the firing, other whites gathered on a nearby ridge as spectators. "The chief then order[ed] the Bugler to sound a retreat which he did[,] not missing a note."[25]

Because the adversaries maintained a distance of four to five hundred yards throughout most of the skirmish, the estimated three thousand shots fired resulted in only one wounded warrior on each side. The Kanzas had refused to be drawn out into the open field of battle, a successful strategy derived, no doubt, from the presence of many battle-tested Civil War veterans in their ranks. When the Cheyennes began to withdraw, some observers suspected a ruse to lure the Kanzas into an ambush by the larger force of Cheyennes known to be nearby. Others speculated that the Indians had retreated when they observed that the number of white onlookers had grown to about 250. Once again, the Plains tribes rode through Council Grove on Main Street. West of town, they robbed at least three farmhouses and a trading post on Six Mile Creek. Finding no game in the area, the hungry warriors killed and butchered at least eleven cattle during the expedition. A few days after the battle, Little Robe admitted to the Cheyenne agent, Edward Wynkoop, that his party had committed some depredations and suggested that the aggrieved parties be compensated out of the tribe's annuities.[26]

During the battle, Kanza women had gathered behind the Kanza lines near the agency where, led by a woman named Mahunga, they had conducted a dance while singing a solemn chant. Observing the dance was trader Joab Spencer, who knew Mahunga well. Spencer's description is exceptional both because he actually found value in what Kanza women were doing and because he recognized and acknowledged the religious substance of their dance:

> Judge Huffaker, of Council Grove, and myself passed near the dancers, and the old woman looked at us as we passed, recognizing us, but no halt was made by the participants. Such an expression of earnestness, reverence and solicitude I think I have never witnessed in any one. She was in this act of worship invoking the help of Wah-kun-dah, the Supreme Being, in the then raging battle, for her people's success. Her whole soul was enlisted in this act of worship. As her tribe was successful in the conflict she doubtless felt that her efforts have been crowned with success; that the Great Spirit had been pleased with her service, and had answered her intercessions.
>
> I have never felt more respect for the religious devotions of any one than I did for that old heathen woman and her company of devotees.[27]

Although inconsequential as a military engagement, the "Cheyenne Raid of 1868" had important ripple effects on both whites and Indians. The raid terrified eastern Kansans, who were shocked that a band of "wild Indians" could penetrate into the settlements to attack a peaceful tribe on their reservation. "This is one of the boldest Indian movements on the frontier," declared the *Junction City Union*. Frightened settlers in Morris, Chase, Marion, Geary, Butler, Dickinson and Lyon Counties gathered in protective enclaves to grimly await the inevitable onslaught. At Cottonwood Falls, thirty-two women and children had spent the night of June 2 at Sam Wood's house while the men covered the floor of one of the outbuildings. "The women were so terrified at every little noise," wrote Mrs. Wood. "Some one would hop up, and look out, and waken the rest all up, to get ready to be murdered. I got but little sleep last night." After it became clear that settlers had suffered little injury, newspaper editors worried about the raid's effect on immigration.[28]

In response to demands by outraged citizens and state officials that the frontier be protected, the federal government took action through the twin instruments of the army and the Indian Office. A cavalry company was posted at the old Santa Fe Road crossing of the Cottonwood River. Troops patrolled the border from Fort Harker in present-day Ellsworth County south to Wichita. The Indian Office delayed the promised distribution of arms and ammunitions to the Cheyennes and Arapahos, stoking resentment among young warriors, especially those of the Dog Soldier band, who in mid-August launched a series of devastating attacks on settlements in north central Kansas. Reacting to these and other raids, various army units took to the field in pursuit of the Indians. On November 27, the Seventh Cavalry under command of Colonel George Armstrong Custer attacked Black Kettle's Cheyenne village in the Washita River valley (in present-day west central Oklahoma), assisted by six Kanza scouts.[29]

To insulate the Kanzas from the military operations on the plains and to separate the tribe from its enemies, the Office of Indian Affairs continued to forbid the Kanzas to leave their reservation. During their confinement, the Kanzas were subject to a steady stream of messages purporting the imminent return of an overwhelming force of Plains Indians intent on their extermination. In desperation, the Kanzas and their agent turned to the army for protection. In late June 1868, a company of Fifth Infantry troops was stationed near Council Grove under the command of Captain Martin Mullins. Mullins was under strict orders not to interfere with the Indians "so long as their hostility is confined to themselves, but should they attack white settlers you will at once take the aggressive." Additionally, Mullins was forbidden to protect government property at the agency or render assistance of any kind to agent Stover. The Kanzas asked for help from their allies and neighbors, the Sacs and Foxes. The Indian Office interceded by ordering the Sac and Fox agent to not permit his tribe "to take any part in these difficulties." Stung by the government's ingratitude, the Kanzas told Stover they remembered that when "the Great Father" was in trouble, they had left their families and homes to fight for him, "yet when they call upon him to assist them, he not only refuses, but assists their enemies, and prevents their old friends from coming to their assistance."[30]

This imposed confinement took a horrendous toll. Stover advised the Indians to concentrate in a strong position and make preparations to resist. "They might as well die by the hands of their enemies as to starve on the prairies," the Kanza agent wrote. "They are[,] with my assistance, making every preparation to give their enemies a warm reception." Even six weeks after the June 3 battle, the Kanzas were still reluctant to leave their fortified camp. Their neglected crops also suffered from another dry summer, reducing corn production to less than ten bushels for the entire reservation. Small children especially suffered. "Last night they begged so hard, and were suffering so badly, for something to eat," wrote Stover on July 10, "that I was compelled to purchase some Beef & flour for them."[31]

Despite the government's quarantine order, some bands of Kanzas escaped their confinement and headed back to their old haunts in the Kansas River valley. In mid-June, a Kanza band was encamped near Topeka where they were, according to a Topeka newspaper, "gobbling up the putrescent animal and vegetable matter about the city." In July and early August, destitute Kanzas appeared in Lawrence and Leavenworth, asking for clothes, money, tobacco, coffee, and food. In early August, forty-one Kanzas were reported camped on a hill west of Lawrence. Sometimes the Indians would demonstrate their prowess with bows and arrows in exchange for change, clothing, or food. The August 4 *Lawrence Daily Tribune* demanded that the city authorities "do something to abate the Kaw Indian nuisance." Not surprisingly, none of the frequent and exasperated Lawrence newspaper accounts of the Kanza presence during this period mentioned the miserable reservation conditions that compelled the desperate Indians to roam and beg.[32]

On October 10, 1868, Stover reported that although the Kanzas had tried to subsist on their own since the Cheyenne raid, they had been wholly dependent upon the Kanza agent "for the actual necessaries of life." That month the $8,000 annuity was paid to the Kanzas.

Ten dollars was assigned to each member of the tribe, with the remainder paid to chiefs and braves for the general use of the people. This and the payment of $3,000 for back pay and bounty owed to the heirs of deceased Civil War veterans helped to provide clothing and other necessary articles heading into winter. Nevertheless, Stover wrote to Thomas Murphy, once again calling attention to the tribe's destitution. In turn, the superintendent wrote to Commissioner of Indian Affairs Nathaniel Taylor, Lewis Bogy's replacement, asking that Congress appropriate a sufficient amount so that the Kanzas would have subsistence through May 1869. By late winter, the Kanzas contemplated a future of absolute deprivation. On February 12, 1869, Joab Spencer again informed the tribe in council that he would no longer supply provisions to them on credit. At this point, the tribe owed Spencer and his partner, James R. Mead, $27,718.45.[33]

Allegawaho, seven other chiefs, and ten Kanza men immediately wrote to agent Stover, pleading with him and Superintendent Murphy to intercede on their behalf. Regarding their prospects, the Kanza leaders did not mince words: "We are now out of anything to eat! We have barely enough provisions to last us till the last of the present month. After that our women & children must die of starvation without some assistance from the government. What can you do for us & will you present the matter to the Superintendent, and Commissioner, and ask them to help you in this matter? The Govt. should pay for our provisions, as they are feeding the Osages, & other Indians. We are peaceable and have sent our young men to the army and have tried to do every thing that the Govt. has required of us. We now ask Shall we starve?"[34]

On March 3, Congress appropriated $25,000 to be expended for the relief of the Kanzas. Immediately a political battle erupted about whether this money should be spent to retire the claims of traders Spencer and Mead or to pay for feeding the Indians to prevent further suffering. The traders gained the support of the Kansas congressional delegation. Opposing them were Indian Office bureaucrats. Ultimately Congress concurred with the Indian Office. Spencer and Mead would not receive payment until after the Kanzas sold their reservation, which required a new treaty. Once again, Kanza chiefs would be brought to Washington.[35]

During the winter of 1866–67, Allegawaho had been hunting buffalo with his Kahola band in central Kansas when a messenger arrived in camp to inform the recently designated head chief that he needed to return immediately to the reservation to meet with special commissioners about a proposed new treaty. By late January, Allegawaho and village chiefs Watianga and Fool Chief, accompanied by interpreters Joseph James and Thomas Huffaker, were passengers on a noisy machine chugging through the rapidly industrializing landscape of the eastern United States. On board with them was a delegation of about seventy Indians representing fourteen Kansas tribes, all summoned for a meeting in Washington, D.C., with Commissioner Bogy. The chiefs had been rounded up for a grand council that would pave the Indians' way out of Kansas and out of the way of the postwar immigration then inundating the state. "It is thought," proclaimed the *Lawrence Journal*, "that in the course of twelve or fifteen months there will be left no tribal organization in the state, and that the Indians will nearly all be removed to their new homes at the South."[36]

In 1867, Allegawaho was about fifty years old. He stood over six feet tall and was lean, with an angular face and thin lips. He was a member of the Small Hanga clan, or Chicken-hawk people. As an elder, he was a leader in war and mourning customs, a singer of sacred songs, and entrusted with handling and opening sacred bundles. "Allegawaho" is the Pawnee word for "Big Elk." As a young Kanza warrior, Allegawaho had killed a Pawnee chief with that name and then adopted "Allegawaho" for himself as a trophy. In the early 1860s, he shared a lodge with eight people including two wives, Wawgobah and Hoyah. In 1868, his household consisted of three women and seven children. Allegawaho's favorite wife was said to rival the wife of his cousin, Fool Chief, as the finest-looking woman in the tribe. Following Hard Chief's death in 1861, Allegawaho and Nopawia were considered equals as chiefs of the Kahola Creek village. The first time he is listed as the Kanza head chief is February 1867. This trip to Washington, then, was to be his initial test in that capacity.[37]

Delineating Allegawaho's character is elusive because of the paucity of anecdotal material about him. However, four of his Euro-American contemporaries left behind sketchy assessments of the man. Joab Spencer thought that Allegawaho was the only Kanza worthy of the position as head chief. "He was not a strong man intellectually, but he was honest, sober and truthful—the best man in the tribe. Physically, he was tall, straight, and in every way a typical Indian." Describing Allegawaho as "tall and stately," George Morehouse called him "a remarkable character, long trusted as the wisest leader of the tribe" and its most eloquent orator, a chief "considered safe and honest in his dealings." Addison Stubbs also remarked on Allegawaho's fierce oratory and powerful physical presence, remembering him as "a tall, rawboned, Roman-nosed Indian." John Maloy, who claimed to be well acquainted with Allegawaho, provided this description: "He was a tall, shapely Indian, possessing more than average intelligence. He was sociable and courteous, in a sort of aboriginal way, to those whom he liked but his disposition was not lovable, and, when displeased his conduct was not calculated to captivate the affections of even a peace commissioner from an eastern state."[38]

As disagreeable as it is to most Euro-American sensibilities, the Kanzas, like most tribes, were fond of consuming dog flesh. Morehouse told a story about this. While convalescing from a lengthy illness, Allegawaho's favorite wife asked him to procure her a canine meal to hasten her recovery. To gratify her wishes, he came to Council Grove, where he asked around for a fat dog. A citizen offered him one, but he could not afford the asking price of two dollars. Still determined to please his beautiful ailing spouse, he borrowed the money from a friend, and returned to the Kahola village with the doomed dog. Euro-Americans seem to have relished telling stories about dog-eating Kanzas. These stories accentuate the habits of the Indians that seemed strange and even bestial to them, confirming their otherness while attaching an implied moral superiority to themselves, the representatives of a "civilized" normality.[39]

Allegawaho's character is also revealed by what does not appear in the records. Ledgers of white Indian traders record several thousand dollars of debts incurred in the 1850s by hundreds of Kanzas. The ledgers list the names of all of the prominent Kanzas save one—Allegawaho.[40]

Soon after arriving in Washington, the assembled chiefs were told by the Indian Office that they had a choice: either stay in Kansas

and become U.S. citizens or move to Indian Territory to live as Indians. Of the tribal representatives present, only the Kanzas, Sacs and
Foxes, and some of the Potawatomies needed interpreters for these
meetings. The Kanzas and the Sacs and Foxes were singled out by
one official as the two tribes present who could be removed to Indian
Territory without much expense or trouble, as they "have not a great
deal of household furniture." In one of the later meetings, Commissioner Bogy withdrew the option of the tribes remaining in Kansas,
declaring the government's expectation that "you will move away
next spring."[41]

In a treaty signed on February 13, 1867, there were five main provisions. The Kanza agreed to cede their diminished reservation to
the United States for $100,000. The United States would sell the re-
maining trust lands, using this income to retire Kanza debts. The
new reservation in Indian Territory would be provided with an
agent's house, blacksmith shop, manual labor school, agricultural
implements, livestock, and a house for a physician. Allegawaho,
Fool Chief, Watianga, and Joseph James each would be granted 320
acres on the diminished reservation "in consideration of services
rendered." Considering the large cessions of land the Kanzas had
previously made while receiving little benefit from them, the United
States would pay the tribe a perpetual annuity of ten thousand
dollars.[42]

When news of the treaty signings reached Kansas, newspapers
were exultant. According to the *Junction City Union*, the treaties
had secured 1,071,946 acres in the state. "The Kaw Reserve contains
thousands of acres of good farming and timber land, the opening up
to settlement of which will be a great advantage and blessing to this
part of Kansas," declared the *Emporia News*. "It will be a blessing also
to get rid of these worthless dog eaters."[43]

By the mid-1860s, there were an estimated five hundred white
squatters occupying Kanza trust lands. From their standpoint, the
"vexed question" of the disposal of Kanza lands had long been a
thorn in their sides. The sale of 160,000 acres of trust lands in 1863
by means of sealed bids had gone badly awry. When the bids were
opened, it was discovered that Robert Corwin, a wealthy Washington insider and land speculator, had bid just slightly above his

(*On right*) Kanza chiefs Allegawaho (*standing*), Fool Chief, and Watianga, and (*on left*) five Sac and Fox chiefs in conference with Commissioner of Indian Affairs Lewis V. Bogy (*standing*) and Indian Affairs official Charles E. Mix in Washington, D.C., January 1867. Courtesy Morris County Historical Society.

competitors on seventy-five of the best claims. The squatters' worst fears were confirmed: the government had rigged the sale to the advantage of well-connected speculators. The ensuing squatter backlash forced the Indian Office to cancel the bids. Then the treaty of June 1864 promised to make the lands available, but it failed to be ratified. In 1866, when informed about the proposal to sell eighty thousand acres of the Kanza Reservation to the Union Pacific Railway, Southern Branch (UPRSB), the squatters once again mounted a thunderous outburst of opposition, and the proposed sale was never authorized. In the meantime, the situation became even more complicated when wealthy outsiders, led by a group of Boston financiers, engaged in rampant speculation in the Kanza land scrip. Final resolution was promised by the February 1867 treaty, but it too failed to be ratified, defeated by various powerful interest groups—squatters, speculators, merchants, the Indian Office, and the railroad—pulling at cross purposes and producing a political paralysis that stymied another effort by the railroad to acquire Kanza trust lands in 1868.[44]

During the 1860s, still more people squatted on the Kanza trust lands. They built homes, established productive farms, and raised families. They were gamblers. Possessing no legal title to their property, they lived in fear that the fruit of their labor and tenuous hold on their lands would be whisked out from under them by powerful outside forces. All the while, these settlers sustained livelihoods free of the burdens of land payments and taxes. When it finally came time to purchase the land, they banked on the collective clout of their peers as organized in the claims association to protect their interests.[45]

The government's inability to expedite the sale of the trust lands imposed additional financial burdens on the Kanzas. As early as 1863, agent Farnsworth, citing the tribe's huge debt obligations from 1850s traders' claims ($36,494.47) and the 1861–62 construction of huts, agency, and school ($111,878.60), estimated that it would be twenty-five years before the money garnered from reservation land sales could be applied to improving the Indians' living conditions. Not mentioned by the agent was the $26,918.63 the Kanza were obligated by treaty to pay the squatters for "improvements" they had made while trespassing on the reservation. From June 1866 through March 1869, the tribe had accumulated other debts of forty thousand dollars owed traders who provided subsistence on credit while the Kanzas' ability to hunt was crippled by the outlying presence of their Cheyenne enemies and the Kanzas' subsequent confinement to the reservation. Then there was the accrual of interest on the Kaw scrip issued as certificates of indebtedness. This amount growing at 5–6 percent per year would eventually total $129,432.64. Other costs the Kanzas were made to pay included depredation claims and costs associated with the appraisal, advertising, and sale of their lands. Staggering under this enormous debt load and unable to derive income from the stagnant land sales, the tribe sought a single buyer capable of a prompt delivery of a cash payment. At about that time, one such prospect was headed their way.[46]

As the Kanza land question remained unresolved, the UPRSB (renamed in 1869 the Missouri, Kansas, and Texas Railroad, which would become known as the "Katy") prepared to build a line from Junction City down the Neosho valley through Council Grove all the way to the Osage Reservation line in southeastern Kansas. The railroad was to traverse the Kanzas' diminished reservation. On August 24, 1867, an advance party of officials, contractors, and promoters of the UPRSB stopped at the Kanza Agency. Agent Stover escorted his visitors to the nearby agency trading store, where, to their surprise, they found awaiting them a group of Kanzas arranged in a semicircle. In the center was a chief, Pahanle-gaqli.[47]

The chief stepped out to extend his hand to the group's leader, railroad contractor "Major" A. F. Beach of Ballston Spa, New York, and then with "appropriate enunciation and graceful gestures," delivered an eloquent speech. "Father," the chief said,

> a few years ago the Kansas Nation was great in numbers, their lodges counted more than other tribes, their wealth in horses and furs were greater, and their lands extended from beyond the great river on the East to the headwaters of the Kansas, and from the Kansas to the pale river of the North. Now they are few in number and poor in property, and their land has diminished to a small piece, which afford them no game, and upon which they do not wish to remain.
>
> Father, the Kansas has always been the friends of the white, and wishes always to be. As an evidence of their friendly feeling, the Kansas presents you the Pipe of Peace, cut from the sacred red stone quarry of the north. Where this pipe goes the arrow of the Kansas will not fly.[48]

At the conclusion of the speech, Pahanle-gaqli presented Beach with an elegant red-stone pipe. Following handshakes all around, the Kanzas gave members of the party a number of dressed skins, robes, moccasins, and other handcrafted items. This gifting, like the invoking of "Father" to begin each statement, made the railroader guests their kin, a form of bonding, as we have seen, deeply seated in Kanza culture. The chronicler of this encounter, probably Robert McBratney of Junction City, while acknowledging that many whites persisted in calling the Kanzas a "bare-headed, bare-legged, hungry, starving, begging band of lazy thieves," demonstrated some empathy for the Indians by providing a brief overview of the history of the drastic diminishment of the tribe's land holdings. The writer also offered this: "How like a farce this looks upon paper, and how strongly am I tempted to strike it from the journal of the trip down the Neosho valley, and yet, in fact, how like it is to the approaching *finale* of a great tragedy."[49]

Although this meeting did nothing to transform the Kanza situation, it signals how the tribe's situation had been transformed. As representatives of the railroad, the touring party introduced the Kanzas to the most powerful instrument of American capitalism at the time, which would bring sweeping changes to the Kanza homeland and the Great Plains region environmentally, economically, and technologically. The railroads enhanced agricultural production, increased land values, stimulated immigration, introduced new technologies, expanded the power of capital, and, in the words of historian William Robbins, "accelerated the commodification of nature." An industrial juggernaut was now loosed on the Kanzas. Pahanle-gaqli's eloquence, the gifts, and the evocations of kinship were trifling relics of a rapidly receding past when whites and Indians had sometimes met in a middle ground of mutual respect and affirmation. Such ritualistic gestures were now viewed as "farce," and the solemn and eloquent chief—when measured against the powerful economic and technological forces now brought to bear on his people—was the embodiment of a pathetic and doomed people hardly worth mentioning.[50]

Two months after the railroad party visited the Kanza Agency, a ground-breaking ceremony in Junction City officially began the construction of the UPRSB. However, little progress was made until the spring of 1869, when Robert S. Stevens—the contractor for the 1861–62 construction on the reservation—was appointed manager of the railroad building effort.[51]

In an attempt to establish the necessary legal groundwork before construction began, the Indian Office once again entered into treaty negotiations with the Kanzas. Assembled at the Kanza Agency on March 13, 1869, ten chiefs and fourteen other Kanza men signed a treaty document providing for the sale of their eighty-thousand-acre diminished reservation to the UPRSB at a cost of $120,000. Additionally, the unsold portion of the trust lands, then consisting of 135,000 acres, was to be sold to the railroad at eighty-seven and a half cents per acre. The agreement resembled earlier treaties with the Potawatomies, Kickapoos, and Delawares, which authorized the selling of reservations to railroads. The squatters' worst fears were realized. The treaty of 1869, however, would become the third Kanza treaty in five years not to be ratified.[52]

That spring, work on the railroad proceeded at a furious pace. By May, seven hundred workers were cutting and hauling ties, grading the road, and laying track. The Kanzas granted a contractor access to their timber to furnish the railroad ties at a rate of twenty cents per tie. Grading on the diminished reserve commenced in June, with a number of Kanza men assisting in this work. According to their agent, "Many of them show a desire to labor and assist themselves." That summer, a farmer south of the reservation was unable to find laborers to assist him during wheat harvest. He went to the Kanza villages and hired several men, who "did well and bound wheat equal to a white man."[53]

In July, Stevens secured a right of way through both the trust lands and the diminished reservation. Meanwhile the influx of railroad workers onto the reservation brought trouble. Superintendent Enoch Hoag noted that because the railway was contiguous to the Kanzas' homes, the Indians were "exposed to many evils." The presence of so many roughneck workers increased the Kanzas' consumption of intoxicating drink. The draft animals used by the workers roamed the reservation at night destroying the all-important corn crop. The Indians complained almost every day to their new agent, Mahlon Stubbs, who had replaced Elias Stover, that the railroad workers were ruining their land by cleaning out all timber suitable for ties within two miles of the roadbed, this deforestation facilitated by the continuous operation of two sawmills.[54]

Timber cutting on the reservation had long been a sore point with the Kanzas. As early as 1857, Kanza chiefs had protested the "spoliations committed, by cutting and destroying timber" by trespassing whites. In each of the three unratified treaties of the 1860s, the Kanzas insisted on provisions requiring an investigation into losses sustained by the tribe due to unlawful destruction of their timber. But some timber removal had been sanctioned by their agents. In the mid-1860s, whites had contracted with the Indians for the cutting of some of the best timber, primarily bur oak and walnut, for firewood and shingles. One of these contracts had stipulated the cutting and delivery of thirty cords of reservation timber. Hiram Farnsworth justified this arrangement by pointing out the Indians were very needy and the timber was going to waste. During their last years on the reservation, the Kanzas, some of whom were quite handy with an axe, were induced by agent Stubbs to cut and sell their abundant treetops and down timber for firewood at three dollars per cord.[55]

The wielding of Indian and settler axes and saws, however, was but the nibbling of mice compared to the railroad's onslaught. The Indian Office and the railroad clashed over the quantity of timber harvested for ties. According to Enoch Hoag, a federal superintendent appointed by President Grant, the Indian Office and the Kanzas did not wish any more timber taken from the reservation "than the necessary amount to complete their Road through the same." At twenty-five hundred ties per mile, the ten-mile span of the Diminished Reserve required a total of twenty-five thousand ties. The railroad harvested 104,591 ties from the reserve, an amount sufficient to construct thirty additional miles of track beyond its boundaries. But the timber contract of July 14, 1869, vindicates the railroad's position. The agreement granted the railroad "the right to enter upon any of the lands within said diminished Reserve and take therefrom whatever timber for ties and other purposes, it may desire."[56]

Consisting of oak, locust, mulberry, black walnut, and red elm, the ties were six inches square and eight feet long. At twenty cents per tie, the total owed the Kanzas was $20,918.20. Another $2,400 was owed them as a right-of-way payment. Never accounted for were the trees harvested to build bridges. The railroad denied harvesting timber for bridges, a claim disputed by agent Stubbs, who had observed "a large amount of such timber sawed and removed." Further exacerbating the situation was the railroad's delinquency in making full payment. In February 1871, the Indian Office reported that the Katy had paid only $11,000. In March 1871, Allegawaho and ten other chiefs and other Kanza men requested that the railroad pay the tribe the money due, saying, "We know of no other funds we can look to to relieve our wants while we are raising our crops." Katy officials refused to make full payment, arguing that the twenty cents per tie rate was much too high, although that was the exact amount stipulated in the contract. However, the railroad did make a $3,000 payment in June.[57]

At the Kanza Agency on June 24, 1872, Allegawaho concluded a speech to Superintendent Hoag with a succinct overview of the tribe's history with the railroad: "You made a contract 3 years ago with the Rail Road company for Right of way—and Ties & timber to build the Road. We did not want the Road to go through our land— You advised us to consent and told us they would pay 20 cents a piece for the ties and pay the money every month. We have not received near all that is due us—We are very poor—and want you to get it for us immediately—it has been due 3 years."[58]

Three months later the railroad finally made a payment of $7,563.09, but the combined total of $21,563.09 paid to the Kanzas was still approximately $1,750 less than the amount specified by the contract.[59]

While the devastating impact of the railroad construction dismayed the Kanzas, Council Grove citizens were giddy with excitement at the railroad's long-anticipated arrival in their town. When, at noon on October 27, 1869, excursionists from Junction City, Manhattan, Fort Riley, and Topeka unloaded from their five railcars in Council Grove, they were greeted by a group of lively and festive hosts. An hour later, a dinner for 250 was served on tables "loaded with good things of the country—chickens, pies, cakes, and everything desired by the hungry celebraters." After the whites were fed, the Kanzas "carried off the remainder, and all of them acted as though they were well filled." Following the meal, champagne corks popped and dignitaries made speeches.[60]

The arrival of the railroad was the most exciting event in Council Grove in three years. In 1867 and 1868, visitors had reported that the town was stagnating. At that time Council Grove was reeling from three blows: the discontinuance of long-distance wagon trains passing through town, the decision to route the main line of the Atchison, Topeka, and Santa Fe Railway through Emporia and Chase County instead of Council Grove, and the failure of a succession of proposed treaties to deliver the Kanza Reservation into the settlers' hands. To be sure, in 1867 a few Indian traders operated at Council Grove and occasionally a wagon train would pass through. A July 31 letter comparing Emporia to Council Grove noted on the streets of the Morris County town "a more profuse sprinkling of dark, swarthy faces, and glittering eyes, indicating Mexican origin, and a greater proportion of red blankets and deerskin moccasins." This lingering racial diversity echoes Council Grove during its recent trail-era heyday, when Main Street was a stage for the intersecting of Mexican and Anglo traders with the Kanzas, producing a cultural mosaic of diverse languages, customs, goods, and ideas then flourishing on the American frontier.[61]

In June 1869, a recently completed church building in Council Grove provided the setting for performances of a popular musical, *The Flower Queen*. "The ladies looked fully as sweet as the flowers they represented," raved the *Emporia News*. One performance was attended by a former secretary of war and future commander of the U.S. Army, General John M. Schofield, and his retinue of army officers. In early August, another party of officers toured Council Grove, Emporia, and Americus. Among them was George Armstrong Custer, then stationed at Fort Hays. In partnership with Amos S. Kimball, Custer bought several lots in Americus and paid $1,750 for 120 acres on the south edge of Council Grove. Custer's investments reflected how the coming of the railroad and the anticipated removal of the Kanzas had sparked a resurgence of land speculation in the region. That fall, Council Grove appeared revitalized by its commercial prospects. An Emporia visitor reported that every man he saw was in a hurry. "The wagons and buggies go rushing about just like the cars had arrived. Business of all kinds is reviving. Somebody will get rich."[62]

At about the same time, the Kanzas too enjoyed a brief burst of prosperity. When the Kanzas returned from the winter hunt of 1869–70, they brought home as much meat and robes as their horses could carry. Some ponies staggered under the weight of their packs. Others dragged two long poles fastened to their sides, bearing a huge load of fresh or dried meat, frequently mounted by a woman or child. Upon their return, the Kanza villages erupted in unrestrained celebration, and for good reason. This successful hunt followed three years of miserable failure that had plunged the Kanzas into unprecedented destitution, debt, and dependency. A productive, mostly self-sufficient, and much-beloved way of life—reliant on the yearly cycle of the bison hunt—had crumbled. The numbers tell part of the story. The winter hunt of 1865–66 had netted the tribe $21,000 in robes and furs. At that time 670 Kanza full-bloods possessed a total of four hundred horses. The next three winter hunts produced a combined total of $2,000 in robes and furs. By September 1869, the full-blood population had shrunk to 525, and the pony herd numbered two hundred. But then the hunt of 1869–70 earned the tribe $6,000. This income, combined with the railroad payments, finally released the tribe from dependence on government relief throughout 1870. That spring the Kanzas celebrated, and it would not be possible to overstate their joy.[63]

The winter hunts had been a feature of the tribe's annual cycle since around 1830. Before then, each autumn the Kanzas dispersed in small bands and hunted deer and other small game in present-day northeastern Kansas and northwestern Missouri. In the summer, the tribe journeyed west to present central Kansas to hunt bison. But by 1830, their eastern hunting grounds were occupied by emigrant tribes such as the Delawares, and game there was greatly reduced, so the Kanzas shifted their winter hunts west to the bison hunting grounds. At about the same time, the Kanzas benefited from the robe trade being established on the central plains.[64]

Before factionalism infected the tribe and diseases decimated their population, Kanza bison hunts were highly organized communal events requiring the cooperation of the whole band. The clan system integrated the tribe during these hunts, as each clan had a specific location in the camp circle, which was divided by a wide avenue usually open on the east end. Eight of the sixteen clans, called Yata People, camped on the left side of the avenue and the other eight clans, known as Ishtonga People, camped on the right side of the avenue. The Kanzas would not proceed with the hunt without the consent of the Cedonga (Buffalo) clan. A general council selected a hunt leader, a tremendous honor conferred only on men of exceptional

Kanza hunting camp on the Saline River. Courtesy Salina Public Library.

character. An *akida*, a police force of twenty proven warriors, ensured that the hunt was well regulated and that everyone obeyed
the leader.[65]

The men were expert buffalo hunters. The Kanzas' hunting tech-
niques were closely observed by James R. Mead, a hunter and trader
who, from 1859 through 1864, lived near the tribe's hunting camps
northwest of Salina. According to Mead, the Indians, although possessing firearms, almost always used a bow, which, they said, "was
always loaded." Mead claimed that the bow and arrow was a more
effective bison hunting weapon than the muzzle-loading rifle. He
had witnessed mounted Indians using bows and arrows killing
thousands of bison. Another observer provided this description of
a Kanza hunter: "Astride a good horse, beside a bellowing band of
wild beef, leaning forward upon the neck, and drawing his limbs
close to the sides of his horse, the naked hunter uses his national

weapon with astonishing dexterity and success. Not unfrequently, when hitting no bones, does he throw his arrows quite through the buffalo." Danger always lurked, however, because in the middle of the chase a pursuing horse might step into a prairie dog or badger hole. Mead had witnessed an Indian poised to shoot a bison cow thrown to the ground when his horse suddenly fell. Before the hunter could recover, the cow turned and killed him.[66]

The Kanzas' hunting prowess extended to small game. Mead was especially impressed with the Indians' success in hunting raccoons. Accompanied by their many dogs, they would examine tree trunks for claw marks made by climbing raccoons. Then they would cut down a small tree nearby, leaving its branches to protrude a few inches as footholds. Leaning this "ladder tree" against the trunk, they would climb the big tree, and then, using a small axe, cut into the hollow where the coon was hiding, either killing it there or prodding it out. An old Kanza hunter named Pahgahne perfected a method of hunting prairie chickens, birds that flourished on the reservation throughout the time it was occupied by the Kanzas. Armed with a long muzzle-loading rifle, Pahgahne would preserve the meat value of his quarry by shooting the tips of the chickens' wings so they could not fly. Many frosty mornings Pahgahne would appear with six perfectly preserved prairie chickens dangling from his belt.[67]

By the late 1860s, however, most game—once so abundant in the upper Neosho valley—was depleted. As a result, bison hunting became even more crucial to the tribe's well-being. Access to the bison country southwest and west of the Kanza Reservation was provided by a network of well-established trails. One of them extended from the three Kanza villages south through Chase County, crossing the Cottonwood River between Elmdale and Strong City. From here it struck south over the uplands to Sycamore Springs near present-day Eldorado. A branch of this trail headed west up the Cottonwood River valley, passing by present-day Clements, Cedar Point, Florence, and Peabody, then heading straight west. This trail was used extensively by the Kanzas when squatters occupied their reservation during the late 1850s and early 1860s. The well-timbered valleys of the Cottonwood River and Middle and Diamond Creeks provided comfortable winter campsites off the reservation.[68]

The principal Kanza trail was a one-hundred-mile-long track stretching from the Kanza Reservation villages to the Cow Creek campsite in present Rice County. Traced relative to modern features, this trail passed through the village of Diamond Springs in Morris County; clipped one section of northwestern Chase County; crossed Marion County diagonally two miles south of Lincolnville, through the Marion Reservoir and Hillsboro; extended east–west in McPherson County a couple miles north of Moundridge, then passed near Inman; and ended at the confluence of Big and Little Cow Creeks a couple miles south of Lyons. This Kanza trail ran roughly parallel to—and from three to nine miles south of—the Santa Fe Road.[69]

In his article "Along the Kaw Trail," George P. Morehouse claimed that this Kanza trail had better grass and water than the Santa Fe Trail, an assertion that is probably correct, given the environmental impact of the heavily used and long-lived commercial route. Morehouse also described the trail as straight as a ruler's edge, "going up and down hills, across sharp ridges, when a slight detour would have avoided heavy pulls." In fact, early-day surveys indicate that the trail did not form a rigid line across the landscape. It trends in a fairly straight line west-southwest between the Neosho villages and present-day Hillsboro, then sags gently to the south for a few miles, before heading slightly north of west from near present-day Moundridge. The route also meandered in response to landscape features such as springs and sloping ridges affording the best campsites and easiest passage across valleys.[70]

Every fall and frequently in the summer the Kanzas journeyed en masse over this trail, leaving behind in their lodges only those too frail or sick to travel and a few caregivers. In 1869, the six hundred or so Kanzas possessed an estimated two hundred ponies, the best of them mounted by men. Some of the women and children rode on the travois poles dragged by the horses and others walked. Proceeding in single file, they seldom covered less than ten miles per day. However, Morehouse observed that the trail was not a single path but cut into the ground in several places, creating a corridor up to thirty feet wide. As a laborsaving measure, the Kanzas would often leave the poles of their small tents intact at streamside campsites, ready to be quickly covered by skins during future visits.[71]

Although Cow Creek was their preferred camping site, upon arriving in buffalo country the tribe often dispersed in bands across central Kansas. The Kanzas are known to have established hunting camps on the Little Arkansas River, Plum Creek, Turkey Creek, Smoky Hill River, Solomon River, and Saline River. Sometimes the vagaries of weather, bison migrations, and the threatening presence of enemies compelled the Kanzas to locate their camps east of the usual bison range.[72]

While in camp, Kanza women prepared large quantities of "buffalo jerk." They cut or "jerked" the meat into strips, plaited them into mats, then either hung them on scaffolds, wound them around sticks stuck in the ground, or spread them over willow frames surmounting a small fire. When dry, the meat was black as ink, very brittle, but quite tasty. Although these "jerks" were desirable commercial articles in the white settlements, most of the dried meat was packed back to the Neosho River villages for the tribe's winter and spring sustenance. The women also kept busy tanning and dressing buffalo robes and furs the men brought in from their hunt. The hunts were crucial to the survival of the Kanzas for two additional reasons. First, the buffalo hides and furs processed by the women earned the Kanzas as much as $25,000 a year in trade value. Second, in the winter the short buffalo and grama grasses of central Kansas were more nutritious than the bluestem grasses of the Flint Hills, thus providing vital nourishment at a critical time to the pony herds.[73]

Ordinarily the Kanzas returned to the reservation over the same trail, arriving at their villages sometimes as early as Christmas and sometimes as late as April, the month of their homecoming in 1870. During the joyous celebration that spring, they must have known that they did not have many hunts left. "You know our condition," wrote Allegawaho and five Kanza chiefs to a government official in July 1870. "The game is all out of the country and we are hard pressed to provide our subsistence."[74]

✳

In postwar Kansas, powerful demographic, technological, and environmental forces erupted across the landscape with furious energy. Kansas was transformed by a rapid influx of settlement, railroad building, and capital. The army established a formidable presence in central and western Kansas, and the buffalo pastures swarmed with white hide hunters. These changes placed crushing pressures on the Indians of Kansas. As the herds diminished in number and range, more conflict erupted between the Kanzas and their Plains Indian enemies, especially the Cheyennes. After a four-year hiatus, once again white encroachers invaded the reservation. In response to the Cheyenne Raid of 1868, the government ordered the Kanzas confined to the reservation, a disastrous decision that caused a precipitous decline in tribal living conditions. As debt and dependency mounted, Kanza morale and health plummeted. Although the construction of the railroad through the diminished reservation in 1869 provided the Kanzas with much-needed cash payments, it also left in its wake an immense destruction of hardwood timber. Three successive winter hunts were unsuccessful, the all-important pony herd was depleted, and the reservation was bereft of game. The dominant culture's progress and improvement meant the Kanzas' demise. As never before, industrial civilization had access to instruments enabling the Euro-Americans to impose their will on the Indians and their homeland. The Kanzas inhabited a damaged country of dwindling possibilities.

CHAPTER 8

THE DARKEST PERIOD

In the summer of 1869, the newly elected president of the United States, Ulysses S. Grant, adopted a "Peace Policy" regarding the Indians. Aiming to clean up the corruption endemic in the Indian Office and to "civilize" the Indians by nonmilitary means, the president turned to churches to nominate officials to implement his new policy. In the "Central Superintendency," the administrative region that included all the Kansas tribes and some in Indian Territory, the newly appointed superintendent, Enoch Hoag, and all of the agents were members of the Society of Friends (Quakers). In the autumn of 1870, a Quaker medical doctor, William Nicholson, visited each agency in the Central Superintendency to report on the tribes. On October 4, he began his three-month-long inspection tour at the Kanza Agency, remaining seven days, recording in a diary his observations of the Kanzas' condition and progress. Singular in their detail and—considering the standards of the period—objectivity, Nicholson's diary entries provide a rare glimpse of the Kanzas during the tribe's final days in Kansas.[1] He covered topics ranging from modes of dress, use of tobacco, living arrangements, and marriage, to interactions with traders and funerary practices.

According to Nicholson, while some of the Kanza men were stout and muscular, most were undersized and lean, reflecting a lack of proper nutrition. All the Kanzas wore blankets, shirts, and leggings, the latter made of either buffalo skin or flannel. Their moccasins, highly ornamented with beadwork, did not keep the feet dry. The

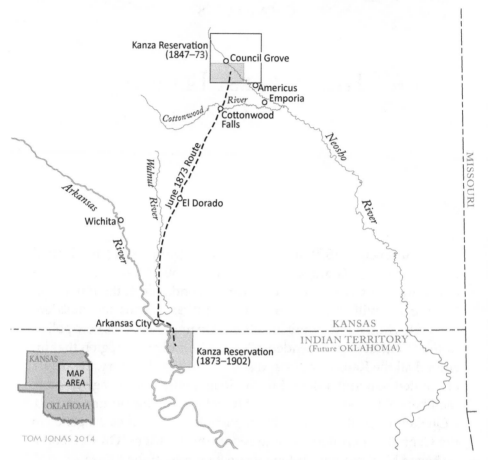

Route of Removal, 1873. © 2014, University of Oklahoma Press.

men wore breechcloths and cut their hair short or shaved their heads except for a tuft of hair left on top. The women wore their hair long, Nicholson wrote, but "dress[ed] much as the men." Both sexes perforated each ear with four holes that were sometimes loaded with trinkets. Faces were painted red with blue and black streaks. The men pulled out their whiskers with coiled wires. The Kanza preferred their clothing to white men's, and were, in general, "quite indisposed to adopt the habits of civilized life."[2]

Nicholson was fascinated with how the Kanzas smoked tobacco, noting its use by nearly all the men but few women. When they gathered, the Indians often puffed "the first whiff of smoke upwards as an offering of thankfulness to the Great Spirit." The men would pass the pipe around, inhaling the smoke into their lungs, then exhaling it through their noses. They smoked a mixture of tobacco and sumac leaves. Sometimes their tomahawks served this purpose: the pipe tomahawk had a bowl hollowed out opposite its cutting edge, and a canal extending the length of the hickory handle was the stem, the end of which was shaped into a mouthpiece.[3]

While a few of the Kanzas lived separately in stone houses, most lived in huts grouped together in three villages. These huts were covered with bark or buffalo hides, Nicholson reported, with an opening at the top for admitting light and emitting smoke. The larger huts had entrances on each side, these covered by buffalo skins when necessary. There were no cattle, few pigs, but lots of ponies and dogs. Horse racing with attendant betting was a passion, the wagers consisting of ponies, blankets, and shirts. In early October 1870, the Kanzas were busy drying the abundant corn, beans, and pumpkins they had raised that summer, a task they had to finish before leaving for the winter hunt.[4]

Girls often married as early as age twelve. The marriage ceremony was simple and straightforward. The parents of the groom offered presents to the prospective bride's parents. If these were accepted, a crier then called for objections. If none were forthcoming, a wedding feast soon took place. The Kanzas were polygamous, and divorce— initiated by both men and women—was fairly common. If a man stole another's wife, he was subject to summary vengeance. Observing that conjugal attachment was not very strong among the Kanzas, Nicholson suggested that "parental and filial affection is well developed." In contradiction to previous reports, Nicholson found that childbirth was no more difficult or dangerous for Kanza mothers than for white mothers. The Quaker physician, however, disapproved of how the Kanza mothers tied their infants "upon a board for some months & then tucked [them] under the blanket between the woman's shoulders."[5]

Because provisions had been scarce during the previous winter, the Kanzas had already obligated their annuities to the agency trader by purchasing on credit items such as flour, coffee, and sugar.

When the annuity monies were distributed on October 6, almost all of the funds went directly into the hands of the trader. This provoked resentment among Allegawaho and the council men, who insisted that before they would sign the payroll, the trader needed to distribute gifts as had been the tradition. The trader finally obliged by dispensing tobacco and crackers, which the headmen divided equally among the people. During a lengthy speech delivered the next day, Allegawaho complained that his people "merely *saw* their money but never handled it—that the trader got it all."[6]

On October 10, the chiefs, headmen, and a large number of the tribe listened carefully as agent Stubbs explained a proposal for Kanza removal to Indian Territory. The Kanzas then requested that the white men leave while they discussed the matter among themselves. When they reconvened, Allegawaho rose to speak. Nicholson recorded his statement:

> They had concluded to send a delegation of the Kaws & half breeds with the Agent to view the country & if they liked it they would be willing to go. They wished to see the country & know if it would bring corn &c— that they wanted good land so they could walk the white man's road, follow the plow &c—that if their Great Father could move their present land and river and timber all down there, they would go altogether at once but as they would have to leave their present good land they wanted to see whether they could find more as good as that is. They wanted to sell their land directly to their Great Father. Did not want to bargain with any body else &c. They wanted to go down there to see the country at once while the leaves were green & did not want to wait until they would have to dig under the snow to see what kind of soil it was. [Allegawaho] wanted to live like white men and did not wish to have anything to do with the wild southern red men, alluding to Cheyennes, Arapahoes, Kiowas, Comanches &c—said they would come and eat with the Kaws out of the same spoon & sit by the same fire & then go off & shoot them. He did not want to mix with them. He wanted to follow his plow with the white man & if the wild Indians killed him at his plow, he wanted his children still to follow the plow & be the white man's friend.[7]

Other chiefs spoke in confirmation of Allegawaho's words. They then agreed to return the next day to sign the enrollment forms. Finally, after several unsettled days, everyone departed in good humor.[8]

During his week among the Kanzas, Nicholson observed their funerary practices, noting that the tribe buried their dead without coffins, putting clothing, bows and arrows, a plate of food, and other small items in the grave, a custom observed by several other Euro-Americans. Nineteenth-century ethnologist Lewis Henry Morgan described the burial site as consisting of "a bow and arrow on the left side, a little brass or earth kettle between the legs or feet, containing corn or beans or dried buffalo meat, and their tobacco pouch and pipe." Often a warrior's gun, tomahawk, knife, saddle, bridle, blankets, and moccasins were buried with him. Dishes were frequently put on a Kanza woman's grave. These useful and beloved belongings were placed with the body in anticipation of the spirit's long afterlife journey, a passage facilitated by the Kanzas' primary means of mobility—the horse. The Kanzas sometimes killed the favorite mounts of the deceased on their graves. An Emporia man, Will Irwin, had befriended a Kanza man. When the Indian's daughter died, Irwin was invited to the little girl's funeral. She was "buried with her beloved trinkets and food for her journey. Then after burial, three Indians seized her pony and strangled it—leaving it upon the top of the grave."[9]

Ordinarily the Kanzas took measures to secure a body against animal scavengers, as illustrated by Morgan's description of a Kanza grave: "The hole in the ground is about one foot deep, the body is set up erect, and covered with bark, this is then covered with dirt lightly after which stones are piled up around the body loose so as [to] cover the body fully about one or two feet over their head." Morgan's assertion that the Kanzas were buried "in a sitting posture facing the west" is contradicted by early-twentieth-century ethnologist Alanson Skinner, who stated that the body, after being carefully wrapped in a buffalo robe, was placed in a grave covered with stones "not over three or four deep, at full length, head to the east." A traveler in the Kansas River valley came across the grave of a young Kanza

Sketch of a Kanza burial practice, "Digging the Grave," *Harper's Weekly*, November 14, 1868. Courtesy Kansas State Historical Society.

male covered by stones and a "heap of sods," and "surrounded with a pen of small logs, within which were set up two poles." Two scalps taken by the warrior were mounted on one of the poles, some ornaments of his horse on the other.[10]

Although the Kanzas knew how to prevent wolves and other animals from penetrating their graves, they were less successful in defending against the violation by Euro-Americans. When Judge J. H. Watson discovered several Indian graves on the brow of a hill overlooking Kanza campsites on the Cottonwood River and Middle Creek in western Chase County in 1860, he proceeded to desecrate them. "These [the graves] are formed by piling up stones over the dead body," wrote Watson. "On removing a few of these, I perceived the moldering bodies of the once proud savage, an old rusty tin cup, and the decayed remains of what was once a bow and arrow."[11]

"It is perfectly easy to procure skulls . . . in the Kaw [country], if it is managed prudently," noted Lewis Henry Morgan. "The graves are heaps of stones, or a pile of timber which can be easily opened at the top and the skull taken out, without much of any labor and without much disturbance." Morgan reported that he could secure "any quantity" of Kanza skulls at the bargain rate of $1 each. Watson and Morgan were not run-of-the-mill grave robbers. Watson was one of the most respected citizens of Emporia and narrowly missed becoming a justice of the state supreme court. Morgan is considered by many to be the father of American anthropology and among the most eminent scientists of the nineteenth century. The interests of science, presumably, granted him license to remove skulls from Indian graves so that they might be taken back east to museums or other scientific institutions, where they would be studied, catalogued, and stored.[12]

To gain perspective on Morgan's cold-blooded assault on the Kanza dead requires understanding that in the mid-nineteenth century the scientific community embraced a belief in the inherent inequality of the races. Evidence to confirm this was ascertained by means of "anthropometry," or anatomical measurement, particularly of the cranium. Racial comparisons of skull, head, and face required amassing a collection of diverse specimens for study, and all the research pointed toward the same conclusion. "A long series of well-conceived experiments has established the fact," wrote Dr. Josiah C. Nott, "that the capacity of the crania of the Mongol, Indian, and Negro, and all dark-skinned races, is smaller than that of the pure white man. And this deficiency seems to be especially well-marked in those parts of the brain which have been assigned to the moral and intellectual faculties."[13]

At that time, "science" was employed to confirm the racialist convictions of ordinary white people in every region of America. Being a superior race, however, placed a special responsibility on the whites, who had, in the words of a Kansas settler, John Hawkins Clark, "taken upon [themselves] the charge of this beautiful country." Clark spoke for all classes of Euro-Americans when he declared that Indians must submit to rule by whites. "Manifest Destiny," Clark wrote, "is spreading the white race broadcast throughout the fair fields of the great west, shedding the light of science, of civilization, and of religion, covering the dark savage superstition of the native race in the grave of the past." Although during the territorial period, Kansans had fought over the legal status of African Americans, they were, in the words of historian Kristen Tegtmeier Oertel, "simultaneously united on the ground of white supremacy over the Indians." A scientifically endorsed sense of racial superiority and the providential mission of conquest implicit in Manifest Destiny licensed white Kansans to subject the Kanzas and other tribes to grave desecration, abusive language, intimidation, physical assault, theft of reservation land, eradication of native cultural beliefs, elimination of game, massive slaughter of trees, and the poisoning of Indian bodies with alcohol.[14]

Ethnologist J. Owen Dorsey supplied a counterpoint to the conventional wisdom of the period, which relegated the Kanzas to the netherworld of "dark savage superstition." In the winter of 1882–83, ten years after the tribe's removal to Indian Territory, Dorsey observed a Kanza funeral ritual. In his *Mourning and War Customs of the Kansas*, Dorsey describes an intricate ceremony in which clan identities and functions were hugely important. The lengthy and detailed process involved sacred songs, venerated objects such as a sacred shell and pipe, gift exchange, and elaborate prayers to Wakanda. What is clear in Dorsey's account is the complexity and depth of the Kanza funerary traditions. Understandably, the settlers fixated on mourners' wailing, burial site structures, and horse sacrifices, but Kanza mourning rituals manifested expressions as spiritual, venerable, complicated, and culturally integrated as those of their Euro-American counterparts.[15]

Kanzas mourned the dead frequently during their last years in Kansas. As a physician, Nicholson examined the causes of the tribe's high mortality rate. He attributed the Kanzas' poor health, in part, to "protracted exposure to inclemencies of weather and irregularities in the supply of wholesome food." Moccasins, blankets, and leggings, in his view, did not protect them from the elements nearly as well as Euro-American coats and pantaloons. He noted that most adult deaths occurred in spring, and pneumonia was the most fatal disease. Many children died in infancy and the survivors frequently suffered from scrofula, tuberculosis of lymph nodes, especially in the neck. He strongly disapproved of how the Kanzas treated a sick man by covering him closely in blankets so as to "almost suffocate him to death[,] rather helping him along to the happy hunting ground."[16]

In July 1870, agent Stubbs alerted the Indian Office that tribal mortality was double the number of births within the previous year. The agent attributed this deplorable condition to the insufficient allocation of fifty dollars quarterly for medical purposes, an amount too small to hire a competent physician capable of providing proper medical treatment. The inadequate medical fund had been a sore point for Stubbs's predecessors, Farnsworth and Stover. Farnsworth in particular had reported large numbers of Kanzas dying for want of medical attention. Stubbs requested $150 to cover medical expenses for the third quarter of 1870, and this amount included the costs of vaccination. A year later, citing concern that the unusual amount of sickness that spring would continue into the third quarter, the agent raised his request to $300. In October he reported that the additional money had helped to relieve much suffering and saved lives.[17]

In April 1871, Dr. William Hunt, a Quaker physician, began to practice medicine at the Kanza Agency. Charging low fees and furnishing his own medicines, the unsalaried Hunt saved several Kanza lives. When in November 1872 the Indian Office challenged Stubbs about the quarterly $300 medical fund and the presence of an unauthorized physician, the agent pointed out that before Hunt's arrival the tribe had received little benefit from its meager medical funds because no physician lived closer than four miles from the agency and that each medical visit to the Indians cost an average of six dollars. Observing that the Kanzas had become very unhealthy and "are fast decreasing," the agent concluded with a plea that the enhanced medical fund be sustained.[18]

Dr. Hunt's services were especially required in 1872, as that year the Kanzas suffered a series of health setbacks. The vaccinations administered the year before had failed, and with the close proximity of proven disease vectors—railroad workers—a new round of vaccinations was needed. Stubbs reported that the Indians' meager diet was "very unwholesome and will cause sickness and death unless it can be remedied." Pneumonia and scrofula were listed as the most fatal diseases. The agent noted that Kanza men were more susceptible to death than women and that there was "not a man living in the tribe over fifty five years of age." He also reported that some of the tribe "persist in employing an Indian Doctor." (An order of Kanza shamans, called "Wakandagi," employed ritual and magic to channel the power of Wakanda to the tribe and to heal the sick and wounded.)[19]

In lobbying the Indian Office to increase medical funding, Stubbs frequently cited the tribe's "fast decreasing" numbers. Without a doubt, the Kanzas were an unhealthy people, and Stubbs, observing death and decay all around him, was moved to act to relieve suffering. However, the Quaker agent's assertions of tribal population decline are not confirmed by his annual censuses. In September 1868, there were 539 Kanzas (275 males, 264 females). In September 1873, the total number was 533 (279 males, 254 females). The decline in population during the twenty-one years before Stubbs became the Kanza agent—from 1,600 to 539—had indeed been precipitous. The unprecedented stabilization of Kanza numbers during the tribe's final five years on the Neosho reservation is partially a reflection of the efficacy of Stubbs's long-overdue efforts to provide the Indians with substantive medical attention.[20]

A cornerstone of President Grant's "Peace Policy" was a renewed emphasis on education as a supposedly benign means of assimilating Indian children into Euro-American society. When former school superintendent Stubbs was appointed Kanza agent in July 1869, one of his top priorities was to reopen the school for the Kanzas that had stood empty and unused since September 1866. He contracted with a fellow Quaker, Nathan Pinson, to oversee the operation of the Kaw Indian Manual Labor School, and in December the school once again opened its doors. During the 1869–70 term, forty boys and five girls attended.[21]

The new Quaker school faced the same difficulties as its predecessors. "The Indians are not as much in favor of a school as I should like to see them," Stubbs observed. Contributing to this lack of enthusiasm was the recurring observation of the Kanzas that their children who had attended school became the dregs of the tribe. The agent also cited the obstacles of language limitations, little contact with civilizing influences, and the proximity of "a village where intoxicating liquors are kept for retail." The schoolchildren frequently ran away and those who attended were made fun of by their friends when they returned to their villages, causing them to drop English and "go back to Indian habits." There were also logistical problems. The two main buildings, with windows broken and plaster falling off, were now practically unusable. Only one room of the school building was functional, and the boarding house was "not decent or comfortable." The well yielded no water, the yard fence was down, none of the shade or fruit trees planted on the high rocky prairie had survived, and generally, reported Stubbs, "things look very uninviting about the place."[22]

By the end of the second year, the bleak evaluations began to yield to more tempered assessments. In response to pleas from Pinson and Stubbs for more funding, the Society of Friends donated $1,000 to the school, supplementing the $2,500 annual operating budget furnished by the government. The improving financial situation mirrored general improvement in the school's operations. Stubbs reported that the progress of scholars was very satisfactory. Enhanced Kanza support for the school during 1871 is indicated by two long-desired outcomes: more girl enrollees (eight) and the attendance of Albert Taylor, son of head chief Allegawaho. A year later, of the forty-three Kanzas in attendance, twelve were girls. By September 1872, a major change had taken place. The older Kanza adults previously "averse to the education of their children," Stubbs reported, "are not only willing but anxious, and use their influence to keep them in school."[23]

This turnaround can be attributed, in part, to the cohesion and dedication of the Quaker agent and school staff members. A measure of the Quaker commitment is indicated in 1872 by the unprecedented total of nine Quakers listed as staff members of the Kanza Agency and school. The primary cause of this "radical change" on the part of the Kanza adults, however, had more to do with the Indians' evolving understanding of their situation in the early 1870s. In May 1871, Allegawaho uttered these prophetic words: "I believe my people will soon be impoverished. This I do not want to see. This

Quaker families at the Kanza Agency, 1871. Fourth from right in the row of standing people is the young interpreter Addison W. Stubbs. His father, agent Mahlon Stubbs, is seated third from left in the front row. Courtesy Kansas State Historical Society.

is the darkest period in our history." Faced with shrinking options, the Kanzas were willing to choose white man's education, at least experimentally, as the only apparent path out of the darkness.[24]

The second Quaker school for Kanzas ceased operations in May 1873. Stubbs's final report could not have been more positive: "The progress of the children was all we could ask, and many of them gave evidence by their daily life that they had received a knowledge of the plan of salvation, and were living up to it." As early as May 1872, Stubbs and Hoag had urged the Indian Office to immediately begin construction of new mission school buildings for the Kanzas in Indian Territory "to avoid interrupting their education." Later that year, Stubbs extracted a promise from the Kanzas that when they relocated to Indian Territory, they would leave their children behind to attend the school in Kansas until suitable buildings were in place on their new reservation. However, as the time for removal approached, the Indians decided to take the children with them. For over a year after their arrival in Indian Territory, the Kanzas had no school. By

August 1873, Kanza children were coming to the agency in Indian Territory every day begging to come to school. The agent's urgent request that a building be constructed in time for the winter term was ignored. Finally, in August 1874, a "substantial and commodious" school opened with fifty-four pupils in attendance.[25]

In response to the overwhelming pressures to conform to the demands of the dominant white society during their waning years in Kansas, the Kanzas had finally embraced one of the cornerstones of the government's assimilation program—white schooling. All the same, while living on the Neosho reservation, the Kanzas never fully acquiesced to the prescribed eradication of their culture, and this resiliency of the tribe's cultural conservatism is perhaps nowhere better illustrated than in the Kanzas' relations with other tribes.

In June 1872, following a journey of about two hundred miles from their villages in east central Nebraska, Pawnee visitors had sent an emissary to Allegawaho's village on Kahola Creek announcing their presence and mission of peace. Allegawaho called a council in which the Kanza chiefs decided to reciprocate. Soon all of the tribe was busy preparing for the ceremonial meeting. Warriors painted their bodies and ponies in ways that expressed peaceful intentions. Then the Kanzas rode in single file to where the Pawnees were camped on the uplands not over two miles south of Council Grove. They dismounted, left their ponies behind in the care of boys, and advanced toward the line of waiting Pawnees in a solemn procession, chanting a song of peace. When the column of Kanzas got within about five yards of the Pawnees, they stopped, then retreated, walking backward while facing the visitors. As the Kanzas receded, the Pawnees advanced, singing their songs of friendship. This back-and-forth movement was repeated several times, then suddenly stopped.[26]

It must have been an extraordinary sight, the Kanza and Pawnee warriors standing silent and motionless on the prairie of the Kanza Reservation, face-to-face in two lines. As the ancient adversaries looked into each other's eyes, a Kanza chief stepped forward with great dignity and drew a pipe from his belt. The Pawnee chief stepped up to the Kanza chief, the two meeting in the middle. The Kanza took a whiff of his own pipe and handed it to the Pawnee chief, who drew from it as well. The visiting chief then puffed on his own pipe, then passed it to the Kanza chief, who drew smoke from it. Each chief then walked to the end of his tribe's column, passing the other's pipe to each man, who smoked from it in turn, the chiefs accompanying the pipe as it advanced along the line. When at the end of the line, each chief took the pipe and smoked it one last time, thus concluding the initial ceremony.[27]

Everyone then mounted their ponies and rode to the place where the Kanza women had prepared a great feast. The Pawnees remained on the Kanza Reservation for about ten days. Much entertainment was enjoyed and many gifts were exchanged. The Kanzas showered their guests with ponies, guns, and other valuables. So generous were the hosts that when the Pawnees departed the Kanzas were almost bankrupt.[28]

This peace-making encounter was a variant of an ancient and elaborate ceremony known as the Hako by the Pawnees and Wa-wa-thon by the Osages and Kanzas. Also known as the calumet ceremony, the ritual was widely practiced by tribes in the central plains and along the Mississippi valley. It may have originated on the plains in prehistoric times, and the ancestors of the Pawnees and other Caddoan groups may have been originators of this ritual. The primary symbolic instrument was the calumet, a pipe made of a wooden stem and Catlinite (pipestone) bowl. The pipe smoking, gift exchanges, and songs were ceremonial means of fitting real or potential enemies into a kin structure so they could be communicated with peacefully.[29]

By 1872, the Pawnees were reeling from poverty, epidemics, chronic hunger, the hostility of Plains Indians, and the loss of their land. The tribe's population had declined from 8,000 in the 1830s to 2,447. The aggression of their powerful Sioux enemies had left the Pawnee demoralized and destitute. Surrounding settlers, though less overtly violent than the Sioux, were relentlessly determined to excise the Pawnees from their homeland. In desperation, the Pawnees turned to their enemies to form alliances. Weakened from similar circumstances, the Kanzas welcomed the peaceful overture. That these beleaguered tribes rallied their energies and meager resources to enact this venerable form of Indian diplomacy is a testament to the durability of the Indians' culture.[30]

A major impetus bringing enemy tribes together to resolve their conflicts was President Grant's "Peace Policy." Quaker administrators in the Indian Office in Nebraska, Kansas, and parts of Indian Territory convened a peace council of warring tribes on February 25, 1870, on the North Canadian River. Accompanied by agent Stubbs, Kanza chiefs met with Cheyenne, Arapaho, Kiowa, and Comanche chiefs. A few months later, Stubbs reported that the long-standing enmity between the Kanzas and the Cheyennes had finally been resolved. Contributing to the Cheyennes' receptivity to the government's peace initiative was the crushing defeat of the militant Dog Soldier band by a force of U.S. cavalry troops and Pawnee scouts in July 1869 at Summit Springs, Colorado. After this battle, the Kanzas were freed from the threat of Cheyenne attacks during their buffalo hunts, a change that undoubtedly contributed to the tribe's successful hunts from the autumn of 1869 through the summer of 1871.[31]

One by one during the post–Civil War period, the Kanzas' Indian neighbors were compelled to submit to either a radical diminishment of their reservations, or, more commonly, a removal to Indian Territory. Still, long-standing intertribal antagonisms and alliances persisted, frequently manifesting in the long-established traditions of pony theft and trade. In August 1869, a delegation of three Omahas accompanied by their agent visited the Kanza Agency to regain eighteen ponies the Kanzas had stolen earlier that spring. Initially the Omahas suspected the Otoes of the theft and had captured twenty-five of that tribe's ponies. The Otoes responded with a raid, retaking their ponies while killing several Omahas. The Kanzas acknowledged committing the theft, explaining that they believed that the Omahas had previously stolen horses from them. Now convinced of the Omahas' innocence, the Kanzas returned the stolen ponies to the visitors, and the two tribes parted on good terms. A month later, several Kanzas visited the Osages, trading blankets and other goods to their allies in exchange for a number of ponies.[32]

In late June 1869, about one hundred Kanzas joined a party of Sacs and Foxes of Mississippi for a short buffalo hunt, the first time the tribe had been allowed to venture onto the plains since December 1867. The experiences of the Sacs and Foxes closely resembled those of the Kanzas. They had been ravaged by liquor, rent with factionalism, subject to repeated encroachments by whites, and suffered a steep decline in population. They too had undergone a diminishment of their reservation, allotment of their land, and construction of a large number of unwanted stone huts by contractor Robert S. Stevens. That summer hunt with the Kanzas was the tribe's last in Kansas, and in December 1869, when most of the Sacs and Foxes migrated to Indian Territory, the Kanzas lost their closest Indian neighbors and one of their most loyal allies. Before the Sacs and Foxes left, squatters invaded their reservation, breaking down fences and tearing down houses. One band led by Chief Mokohoko refused to leave. Every night, whites pelted the doors of the Indian huts with rocks.[33]

As Indians vacated Kansas, whites poured in. During the 1860s, Kansas more than tripled in population, from 107,206 to 364,339. The population of the counties near or immediately west of the Kanza Reservation grew rapidly. The Kanzas did not need population counts—they could see what was happening. In July 1870, Allegawaho assessed the situation: "White men are all around us and we are cramped and pressed on every hand."[34]

On May 31, 1870, fifty men drove their wagons onto the diminished Kanza Reservation and began to select claims. Agent Stubbs confronted the men and ordered them to leave at once. They shrugged him off, claimed that five hundred more squatters would arrive the next day, and said that they would hold the land by force and not obey orders from an Indian agent or a U.S. marshal. The situation was ripe for political demagoguery. A few days later, Lieutenant Governor Charles V. Eskridge of Emporia climbed atop a wagon bed in the vicinity of Fool Chief's village on Rock Creek and began to speak to hundreds of white people gathered there. He told them the Kanza Reservation was "only possessed by the Indians[,] not occupied." Squatters had waited long enough for Congress to remove the Kanzas. Now the people were justified to stake claims. "The land is yours. If you are here first the land is yours; possession is nine points of law." As for the Indians, Eskridge recommended that each squatter pay the tribe five dollars.[35]

Throughout most of its history, the Kanza Reservation was either overrun by encroachers or so threatened. By late May 1870, outraged citizens, learning that Congress had once again adjourned without approving a Kanza treaty mandating the removal of the tribe, moved boldly to resolve the Kanza land question themselves. At this time, the squatters and Eskridge were encouraged by what had recently transpired in southern Kansas, where thousands of settlers in defiance of the law had occupied the Osage Reservation. As for the Kanza Reservation, it was land unsettled, uncultivated, and untaxed. A newspaperman traveling by rail through the Kanza Reservation found "as beautiful a country as lies in the Neosho Valley, and yet it lies uncultivated, the home of a squalid, dirty, idle, mischievous race of Indians." Even while acknowledging that the reservation squatters were in violation of the law, the paper urged others to "swell the number, it will hasten the removal of the Indians."[36]

The squatters' mettle was soon tested by U.S. troops. On Saturday morning, June 19, a squad of soldiers boarded a special train at Fort Riley bound for the Kanza Reservation "for the purpose of driving the settlers off." They remained for two or three days, but they found no squatters.[37]

Less than a year later, the squatters returned. On March 3, 1871, Stubbs reported that squatters had recently held meetings and passed resolutions "advising the immediate settlement" of the reservation. This time, encroachers described as "Kentuckians" occupied several huts, built fences, broke ground, and planted potatoes. Stubbs reported that soldiers were on the way to evict the squatters, but it is unclear if this actually happened. Later that spring, the Kanza agent was absent from the reservation for several weeks while on a special assignment for the Indian Office. Upon returning in mid-June, he discovered "several persons . . . making improvements by building houses—breaking ground" on the diminished reservation. "I am at a loss to know what course to pursue in the premises," he wrote to Superintendent Hoag.[38]

A pervasive factor in settler encroachment was the perennial "vexed question" of Kanza Reservation land sales. Although, by the terms of the Treaty of 1859, the secretary of the Interior had authority to sell Kanza trust lands and diminished reservation lands not allotted to the Indians, no land had been sold since June 1865. This paralysis stemmed from the congressional failure to ratify the three treaties negotiated with the Kanzas that would have provided for the sale of the Kanza Reservation and the removal of the tribe. By April 1871, approximately 218,000 acres of the reservation lands remained unsold. That month, Secretary Columbus Delano, perceiving that the question was once again mired, directed that the reservation land sale proceed.[39]

When Delano decided to expedite the sale, he failed to consult one vital stakeholder. "The whites have made attempts to buy my lands, but I have refused to listen to them," declared Allegawaho on May 22, 1871. "And I am opposed to selling it in parts[;] when we sell I want to sell it altogether." The Kanza head chief demanded to be taken to Washington to meet with "the Great Father" himself. "I wish to go immediately for the longer I delay the poorer my people get." The land question "cannot be settled otherwise," for "I have never yet asserted that I wished to sell my lands. This idea originated with the President." Allegawaho concluded his speech with this statement: "What I have said is not mine but my people's." A month later, the Kanzas instructed their agent to ask the Indian Office "to have the sale stopped at once."[40]

On October 3, the Kanza chiefs assembled in council were informed that after the bids had been opened in Washington, 62,733 acres of their poorest lands remained unsold. Foreseeing that, if the bids were accepted, these unsold parcels scattered throughout the reservation would be surrounded by white owners and therefore greatly reduced in value, Allegawaho, Nopawia, Abe Munroe, William Johnson, and six other chiefs wrote a letter to Superintendent Hoag requesting that all the bids be rejected. The chiefs recommended that the reservation land be appraised and sold either in parcel or aggregate to the highest bidder or bidders, thereby making the land available to a single buyer, always the Indians' preference.[41]

The 1871 Kanza land sale clearly illustrated why a single buyer was in the tribe's best interest. The firm of Smith and Van Doren bid an aggregate of $449,532.30 for all of the available reservation land. The Interior Department, however, rejected this bid on the basis that it violated article 4 of the 1859 treaty requiring that the land be sold in 160-acre parcels. The valid individual bids on quarter sections totaled $274,613, or $174,919.30 less than the bid for all the lands taken together. Enoch Hoag wrote that if the Kanzas lost this amount, they would "be left with insufficient means to purchase and establish themselves on new homes with any degree of comfort." Hoag endorsed the Kanza chiefs' recommendations that the reservation be appraised and sold at no lower than the appraised value to the highest bidders or bidder "in parcels or in whole."

Pointing out that the Kanza lands were equal in value to Chippewa and Munsee lands in Kansas that recently had sold at $4.81 per acre, Hoag asserted that the Kanza lands should be sold at no less than $500,000. On October 31, Secretary Delano declared that all bids were rejected.[42]

That month the Kanza chiefs agreed to remove to the Indian Territory on the condition that "when there we shall be made secure from future encroachments." Otherwise, the chiefs declared their intention to remain on the Kansas reservation. Shortly afterward, a delegation of Kanza headmen and Stubbs traveled to Indian Territory to select a new home. The Kanzas were pleased with a tract of Osage Reservation land adjacent to the Kansas border. Stubbs reported that the tribe could be induced to move there, but would probably refuse to move farther south into Indian Territory.[43]

The proposed removal was facilitated by two acts of Congress; one affected all Indians and the other applied to the Kanzas alone. In 1871, Congress abolished the treaty-making system. Henceforth, until the Indian Reorganization Act of 1934, Indian peoples would no longer be treated as sovereign nations but rather as subjects of the U.S. government. However, land cessions still required the consent of the tribes. Subsequently, on May 8, 1872, Congress passed the "Kaw Land Bill" providing for the removal of the Kanzas to Indian Territory and the sale of their Kansas lands in 160-acre tracts at not less than the appraised value. "Bona fide" settlers were granted an opportunity to purchase the land they occupied. Demonstrating the settlers' political clout, the legislation ignored the advice of the Indian Office and the wishes of the chiefs favoring a single-buyer option. Predictably, the local response was overwhelmingly positive. "Soon we shall have settlers rushing from every direction to this fine body of land," predicted the *Council Grove Democrat.*"[44]

A couple of weeks before the bill's passage, the Interior Department sent its chief executive to the Neosho reservation to initiate the process of securing the Kanzas' approval. On Sunday, April 21, a southbound train stopped on the railroad tracks about one-half mile west of the Kanza Agency. Standing on the slightly elevated ground of the agency, about two dozen Kanza chiefs and headmen saw, in the distance, a small party disperse from one of the cars and begin to walk up the road toward where the Indians, some agency employees, and a couple of Council Grove citizens awaited. As the group of well-dressed dignitaries approached, the onlookers could see that each man gripped a briefcase. One man, accompanied by his wife, possessed the bearing of authority. He was Columbus Delano, secretary of the Department of the Interior.[45]

Soon everyone assembled for a council. Delano spoke first in a mild and persuasive tone. He said the Kanzas would be better off in a new country where game was plentiful. They would live in Indian Territory near their kin, the Osages. Their reservation land would be sold at full value, providing a surplus of money to purchase new land, build homes, and acquire stock and implements needed to farm. He counseled the usual government litany: give up hunting, send their children to school, and begin farming like white people. In glowing terms, he pictured a future when the Kanzas would live far better than at present.[46]

Everyone then turned to the Kanza head chief. Allegawaho arose, folded his blanket beneath his arms, and in a slow and measured cadence, as if measuring every word, began his reply. It was, in Addison Stubbs's view, a lengthy, detailed, and accurate portrayal of the history of the relations between his tribe and the Euro-Americans. The chief protested against giving up the land where Kanza "dead are sleeping on the hill-tops, where they have their homes and their little fields." Finally, Allegawaho, standing straight as an arrow, looked the secretary in the eye, and, in Stubbs's words, spoke an earnest and eloquent appeal: "Be-che-go ('My Grandfather') you treat my people like a flock of Turkeys. You come into our dwelling places and scare us out. We fly over and alight on another stream but no sooner do we get well settled, than again you come along and drive us farther and farther. Ere long we shall find ourselves across the great Bah-do-tunga (mountains) landing in the Ne-skah-tunga (ocean)."[47]

After Allegawaho sat down, other chiefs arose to speak, some in favor of the removal and some opposed. Delano then responded, his emphatic and authoritative tone granting no room for argument. "It is my duty to say to you," declared Delano, "that you must sell your lands here and select a new reservation in Indian Territory." At that point the secretary terminated the meeting and his party briskly departed for the train.[48]

On June 24, Enoch Hoag visited the Kanza Reservation to explain the provisions of the Kaw Land Bill to the chiefs and headmen and to gain their assent to section 4, providing for the sale of the diminished reservation. The contents of the bill were carefully read and interpreted to the Indians. Allegawaho responded with these words: "My people don't want to lose any of the value of our land—and what I say is law—I speak for all of my people—we want to sell our land—and we want to sell all of it—We want $650,000 for it—because we have been offered that amount for it—and it is worth it—I want to take some of my people and the agent and go to Washington and see the President, and look after our business there—I do not want to cross the Arkansas River for a new home—but want land first selected on the Cana [Caney] River—while I am chief I want to look after the interest of my people—I want the women and children to have enough to eat and wear and the children to go to school."[49]

On this occasion, the Kanza chiefs presciently expressed their fears that they might not receive just compensation in the impending sale of their reservation because the appraisers would undervalue the land. They, reported Hoag, "desired that their interest herein be protected." The Quaker officials responded with a promise that would prove abysmally empty when tested by subsequent events: "We assured them that the Secretary of the Interior would set aside an unjust appraisal." The meeting ended with nine Kanza chiefs signifying the tribe's acceptance of the Kaw Land Bill by "touching the pen."[50]

While wrangling over the land question preoccupied the Kanza chiefs during the tribe's final years in Kansas, the tribe as a whole struggled to subsist. The successful winter hunt of 1869 was followed by a good hunt in the summer that brought home another supply of meat. Nevertheless, until the crops matured in the fall, the

Kanzas eked out a precarious existence by "trading in wild fruit, selling horses, and cutting and hauling wood" to nearby Council Grove and Americus. The planted acreage expanded that spring after the tribe received twenty-five one-horse plows and one hundred hoes. The Indians also built a considerable amount of fencing, though Stubbs considered their barriers "of rather a temporary character." Despite a dry summer, the Kanzas raised 4,513 bushels of corn and 357 bushels of potatoes. In the good years the surplus crops were dried and stored in cache pits near the lodges.[51]

Among the five Kanzas listed by physician William Nicholson as the most productive farmers of 1870 was Mahunga, the woman who had led the dancers at the agency during the June 1868 skirmish with the Cheyennes. Also known as "Margaret" and "Machutesah," she had farmed three acres, producing sixty bushels of corn and six bushels of potatoes. Although agriculture had long been the traditional occupation of Kanza women, their horticultural plots were small. Mahunga's emergence as a successful commercial farmer indicates that the range of socioeconomic possibilities available to Kanza women exceeded the reductive roles typically assigned them by white observers. While observing Kanza females in 1819 laboring in the fields, carrying wood and water, and preparing the food, Thomas Say also noted that the eldest wife commanded the lodge and that the fields and the camp were the domain of the women. The furnishings, food, clothing, and utensils inside the lodge all belonged to her. Mahunga's powerful spiritual presence while leading the dance illustrates how female agency extended to the religious realm as well. Ethnologist James Owen Dorsey identified two Kanza woman as tribal shamans, or wakandagi. Sansile performed various acts of shamanistic magic such as swallowing grass, then drawing a green snake from her mouth. Another woman shaman used a small pebble and a clam shell as medicine objects in her "mystery acts."[52]

Recently, scholars have reexamined how nineteenth-century white observers portrayed the division of labor between Indian women and men. Typically, Indian women were pitied as domestic drudges while men were scorned as lazy drones. In *Confronting Race: Women and Indians on the Frontier, 1815–1915*, Glenda Riley points out that while white commentators had many opportunities to watch Indian women toiling at domestic tasks in and near the village, they seldom viewed men in the demanding and dangerous tasks of warfare and hunting. By reducing Indian women to slavish beasts of burden, Euro-Americans reinforced their bias about the essential savagery of Indians. Riley's point is amplified by Kristen Tegtmeier Oertel in *Bleeding Borders: Race, Gender, and Violence in Pre-Civil War Kansas.* Conventionally reductive references to Indians as "squaw drudges" and "lazy braves" accomplished two necessary ideological tasks: demonstrating white superiority and rationalizing dispossession.[53]

Despite the government's intent to supplant Kanza women with men in the fields, women continued to be engaged in the new forms of farming. In the summer of 1871, the Kanzas realized a 100 percent increase in crop production over 1870: 8,750 bushels of corn, 700 bushels of potatoes, and 50 tons of hay. Three wagons purchased with $400 the tribe had netted through the sale of its defunct sawmill facilitated the farming that year. The wagons were especially useful in building fences, as previously the Kanzas had had to carry the fence rails from the woodlots on their shoulders. Although the harvest was bigger, the acreage planted decreased because the Kanzas had fewer ponies to help break the ground as draft animals. While they were in central Kansas for the winter hunt of 1870–71, the tribe suffered the loss of fifty ponies to severe cold weather. The hunt, however, was successful, with the Kanzas selling $4,500 worth of robes and furs. It would be their final good winter hunt in Kansas.[54]

In October 1871, the Kanzas regrouped at the reservation for the annuity payment. In early November, about two-thirds of the tribe once again followed their trail to buffalo country. It was to be a brief, disastrous, and terminal winter hunt. When they arrived at their old camps in Rice County, they found the grass had been eaten by Texas cattle or burned off, and there were no buffalo. Winter weather started on November 18. Sleet fell, and then a heavy snow followed by bitter cold. About one-third of their ponies perished, and soon their possessions gave out. By December 15, ten lodges had returned to the reservation while the remainder of the destitute tribe scattered in central Kansas. By mid-January, most Kanzas had reoccupied the reservation, where they lived on dried corn and by selling firewood. Unfortunately, most of the remaining ponies were too weak to haul wood, the railroad would not buy any, and the firewood "commanded a very poor price." Magnifying the crisis was that before leaving on the hunt, the Kanzas had sold a large portion of their corn. In desperation, Stubbs wrote to his supervisor: "What course shall I pursue to relieve their wants? An early reply is solicited."[55]

By March 1872, many Kanzas were wandering throughout Kansas begging and "living on corn and what dead animals they can pick up." That spring, the Indian Office finally furnished the tribe subsistence and clothing, spending $7,563.09 on relief before the year ended, the money coming from the railroad's timber payments. Both Stubbs and Hoag recommended that the Kanzas be removed to Indian Territory the coming winter in time to plant crops at their new homes in the spring. The agent commented on "the discouraging effect" the prospect of losing their land and being removed had had on the Indians "for the last eight years." In fact, uncertainty about where they were to live had hovered over the Kanzas since 1858.[56]

According to the Kanza agent, the leading men of the tribe realized that they needed to engage more extensively in agricultural pursuits and depend less on hunting. The Kanzas demanded more agricultural implements and seeds and expanded their fields to 250 acres. In 1872, the tribe enjoyed its best harvest ever: ten thousand bushels of corn, eight hundred bushels of potatoes, and fifty tons of hay. Soon after the crops were planted, the younger people went on a successful buffalo hunt, procuring a supply of meat and skins for moccasins. In December, Stubbs reported that the annuity payment of November 5 "came opportunely," as the Indians were destitute of clothing. He also noted that the summer's bountiful crop had temporarily placed the Indians in comfortable circumstances. However, the few Kanzas that had gone on the winter hunt found their hunting grounds settled by whites and their favorite campsites denuded of timber and no longer fit for habitation.[57]

In mid-December 1872, the Indian Office ordered the cessation of the Kanzas' practice of cutting wood in large quantities and selling it to surrounding whites. Because this timber had been included in the recently completed appraisal of reservation lands, the government felt obligated to protect it in anticipation of the upcoming land sale. Having no robes to sell, the Kanzas had depended on the firewood business for their winter subsistence. On December 18, "in view of their being directed to stop cutting and selling wood," Stubbs submitted an estimate of $12,000 for the subsistence of the five hundred members of the tribe at twenty cents per capita for 120 days. The winter was unusually severe. Snow covered the ground from December 20 through the end of February. Finally, on March 22, Secretary Delano authorized $10,000 "for the removal and immediate relief of the Kansas Indians."[58]

While the Kanzas lingered on the brink of removal, just beyond the reservation's northern boundary Council Grove continued to expand. Businesses and houses were erected and culverts, sewers, and sidewalks built. Street lamps were installed and Main Street macadamized. The development extended to the east side of the Neosho, formerly the location of the dense grove of huge hardwood trees, now yielding to "building and other improvements underway," among them a bakery, grain mill, lumberyard, railroad office, and boardinghouse. A fleeting reminder of the region's wild past surfaced in late December, when a "ferocious looking" mountain lion that "offered fight" was trapped and killed within two miles of Council Grove. But domestication held sway: citizens organized a temperance society and a baseball club, the Council Grove Social Club sponsored a hop, and a new brass band gave a concert. In February 1872, Council Grove had a population of over seven hundred, while the populations of nearby Americus and Emporia were three hundred and twenty-five hundred respectively.[59]

By spring 1872, Council Grove had embraced the "coal excitement," a speculative phenomenon that would hold the town in its grip for two years. It was thought that a rich vein of coal had been discovered one mile west of town. Almost every issue of the *Council Grove Democrat* reported signs of coal being brought up from the mine shaft. "Now there is nothing that would benefit our town and country adjacent more!" declared the editor. Samples from the mine shaft were produced and passed around town. In February 1873, Council Grove was suddenly made wild with excitement by the rumor that the coal-boring operations had perforated a coal vein about forty inches in thickness. "The consequence was a general stampede to the scene of operations."[60]

"Kaw Indian: The Warrior Galloping across the Fields," sketched c. January 1873, shortly before the Kanzas were removed from Kansas and relocated to a reservation in Indian Territory. Courtesy Edward King Collection, Oklahoma Historical Society Research Division.

That same month, Seth Hays died in his home at the age of sixty-two. "He was in fact the father of our city," the *Council Grove Democrat* proclaimed, "and none watched more jealously the working out of its 'manifest destiny.' His history for the past twenty-five years is so interwoven with our town." Hays was buried by the side of his ex-slave, Sarah Taylor. With the frontier rapidly receding over the western horizon, his death signified that Council Grove's days of prominence were fading into memory. The financial fates of Seth

Hays and his fellow frontier-era merchants such as Simcock, Conn, Shamleffer and Huffaker were summarized by local historian John Maloy in the 1880s: "Fortunes were made but they are gone, and most ever man who was then in such easy circumstances" was now "poor as the traditional church mouse."[61]

Beginning in the autumn of 1873, the fortunes of the local elites were ravaged by a series of calamities not unlike unforgiving biblical plagues. On September 18, the failure of the national brokerage firm of Jay Cooke precipitated a depression that gripped the United States for five years. On November 13, 14, and 15, "one of the most terrible and disastrous prairie fires that ever visited our State" raged through western Morris County. In August 1874 "came the myriads of grasshoppers, devouring every green substance that came in their path and leaving the country behind them a bleak and gloomy waste." Perhaps the worst blow of all was that by the end of 1874, the coal mine was finally recognized as fraudulent, the mine shaft having been salted with coal taken from a local blacksmith shop. Council Grove investors lost about $35,000. "Many of our business men were irreparably done for," wrote Maloy.[62]

Reeling from these catastrophic events and desperately needing economic solace, Council Grove leaders turned their eyes toward the long coveted 218,000 acres of unsold Kanza Reservation lands. The process of securing the reservation for the settlers was well underway in January 1873 when an appraisal commission chaired by Mahlon Stubbs sent its report to the Indian Office in Washington. The crux of the commission's report was this: the trust lands were appraised at $2.28 per acre, and the diminished reservation land was appraised at $3.88 and 3/4 per acre, the general average being about $2.87 per acre. The significance of this document stemmed from the Kaw Land Bill that required the selling of the reservation land at prices no less than the appraised value. Quaker administrators and the Kanzas both recognized the critical necessity of receiving "full value" for the reservation lands as a means of paying off the tribe's substantial debts, purchasing the new reservation from the Osages, and having enough left to make a fresh start on their new reservation.[63]

While Stubbs was away appraising the trust lands, a large number of the stone houses built for the Indians were destroyed by both

Indians and whites. If the huts had been left intact, Stubbs observed, the Kanzas would have benefited monetarily and the whites would have had ready-made homes when they occupied the diminished reservation.[64]

In March 1873, the Kanza agent received orders to remove the Kanzas as soon as possible. In mid-May, Stubbs reported that "the Indians are afraid to move for fear there will be nothing there [in Indian Territory] to subsist on." To feed the Kanzas for four months, Stubbs requested thirty thousand pounds of flour, sixty thousand pounds of beef, ten thousand pounds of bacon, and one hundred pounds of tobacco. The chiefs informed their agent that three tribal headmen who "do not want to go like paupers" needed six ponies for the trip south.[65]

On the eve of their final departure, many Kanzas appeared in Council Grove to say good-bye to their white friends. These meetings frequently involved an exchange of gifts, with the Indians presenting whites with tomahawks, pipes, bows and arrows, and photographs of themselves. All of the leading men, according to Maloy, expressed to him their regret "that they were compelled to go, and wondered how long it would be until they would have to go on further."[66] In his farewell to the Kanzas published in the June 3 *Council Grove Democrat*, Maloy acknowledged the tribe's legacy and obliged his readers with the requisite racist commentary:

> Kansas owes much to the Kaws or Kansas Indians. Our state bears the name of the tribe, as well the principal river. Our capital city, Topeka, we believe, is a name derived from their language. They have in fact left their impress upon our state, and have afforded us names for streams and towns all over it, and long after the Kaws shall have wrestled with the great spirit their history will be perpetuated by association if by no other means.
>
> To Morris county their removal has long been a looked for blessing. They occupied one of the finest bodies of land in the state, mostly embraced within our county limits. The land is now in market, will soon be settled up, and instead of a few hundred lazy, filthy Indians, we will ere long have a dense community of farmers, living upon land that will add to the taxable wealth of our county.[67]

In the weeks preceding their departure, Kanza women made trips at dawn and dusk to the hilltops where their loved ones were buried. Each gravesite was marked by a patch of sunflowers that would bloom in late summer. "Seated with backs to the sun," wrote Addison Stubbs, "they wept and howled, until their pitiful wails could be heard for miles."[68]

The 533 remaining full-blooded members of the tribe left the Kansas reservation on June 4. Mahlon Stubbs hired about forty white men with teams to carry the tribe's poorer members and their belongings. Those with ponies packed their own belongings and provided their own transport. On June 12, 1873, the Indians reached El Dorado, Kansas, where they gave a "war dance" attended by almost every person in town. They arrived at their new reservation on June 21. No Kanzas died en route, and, according to their agent, they had no difficulty with the whites or among themselves.[69]

After the Kanza removal, the settlement of the reservation involved a decade-long struggle between familiar stakeholders: settlers, local entrepreneurs, three appraisal commissions, the Indian Office, Quaker neighbors sympathetic to the Kanzas, outside speculators, national and state politicians, and the Indians. Adding to the complexity was conflict within these factions. Take, for example, the reservation settlers. "Lawsuits were plenty," wrote Maloy, "and there are but few men now living on claims taken at that time but what were enjoined or had some one else enjoined from interfering with somebodys right of possession."[70]

A summary review of events centered on the tribe's former Kansas homeland indicates that their relocation to Indian Territory extended the Kanzas' darkest period. In the summer of 1873, the sale of the 80,640-acre diminished reservation was unsuccessful. Claiming that the appraisal of the Stubbs Commission was too high, most settlers boycotted the sale, and only 1,838 acres were purchased. The Interior Department disallowed the bids, rejected the appraisal of the Stubbs Commission, and appointed a new commission headed by T. C. Jones of Ohio. This decision was vehemently protested by Superintendent Hoag, who reminded his superiors in Washington that the Kanzas had argued that they wanted to remain in Kansas until their reservation lands were sold and paid for and had reluctantly agreed to move to Indian Territory only after Hoag and Stubbs had assured them "that their interest would be protected in their absence." Hoag warned the Indian Office that the tribe's "interests would not only be 'not protected' but would be endangered by reduced appraisal and forced sale this autumn."[71]

In the autumn of 1873, after viewing the reservation land, T. C. Jones informed the commissioner of Indian Affairs that the Stubbs Commission's appraisement was "a fair and just one," that reappraisal would be an injustice imposed on the Kanzas, and that the land should be sold upon the basis of the appraisement already made. In response, the secretary of the Interior dissolved the new appraisal commission and restored the appraisal of the Stubbs Commission. However, the question was referred to Congress.[72]

With stipulations that the Stubbs Commission appraisal was "so high that neither settlers nor purchasers were able to pay the same," acts of Congress dated June 23, 1874, and July 5, 1876, mandated a reappraisal of the Kanza Reservation. In April 1877, agent Cyrus Beede reported that he had met in full council with the Kanzas, and—for the second time—the Indians had declined to give their assent to reappraisal. Finally, during a May 31 council, the Kanzas, under immense pressure from government officials, agreed to the reappraisal stipulation.[73]

In December 1878, a new reappraisal commission, chaired by Thomas Sears Huffaker, submitted its final report. The Huffaker Commission reduced the Stubbs Commission appraisal of Kanza lands by approximately 40 percent. Table 2 compares the two appraisals exclusive of improvements and the actual sales of the unsold aggregate reservation lands.

In November 1878, Huffaker had been rewarded for his efforts on behalf of his constituents by being elected to serve a second term in the Kansas House of Representatives. Four years later, decimated by disease and neglect, the Kanza population had dwindled to 285. Predictably, the reduced appraisal of their Kansas land and the serial postponements in its dispensation had produced little income to relieve the heavily indebted Kanzas. That year, 1882, Huffaker received a letter from former Kanza interpreter Joseph James. The two men were well acquainted, having collaborated as translators

Table 2. Appraisals and Actual Sales of Kanza Lands

	Total Acres	Per Acre	Total Value
1872 Stubbs Commission:	218, 652	$2.87	$626,651.78
1878 Huffaker Commission:	216,378.5	$1.72	$372,531.21
Actual Sales:	216,481	$1.92	$417,101.75

Sources: U.S. House of Representatives, *Report of Kaw Commission and Estimate of Appropriation for Settlement of Certain Claims,* H.R. document no. 169, 58th Cong., 3rd sess., 1905, 15–16, 80; Jones to Smith, September 16, 1873, LR, OIA, Kansas Agency; *Annual Report of the United States Commissioner of Indian Affairs* (1879): 183.

on various occasions, including two trips together to Washington, D.C. Like Huffaker, James was no friend of Mahlon Stubbs, the agent having fired the Kanza mixed-blood for drunkenness and neglect of duty in 1871. "You used to call me my friend," James wrote. "I used to help you & do you favors. I wish you to do me the same." James inquired about the sale of the tribe's Kansas lands, pleading with Huffaker "to help us to get what is due to us. We ask you a favor. Please try to do something for us."[74]

*

The contention of this book that the zone of interaction between Kanzas and Euro-Americans was replete with racism and violence finds no better illustration than the assault on the Kanza dead. Adept at preventing wolves and other animals from penetrating their graves, the Kanzas were unable to prevent the enthusiastic and widespread desecration of their people's gravesites by both scientists collecting skulls and common grave robbers. Other forms of aggression visited on the Kanzas during the tribe's final years on the Neosho reservation were timber thievery, demagoguery by local politicians, ubiquitous land encroachment, and betrayal by presumed Indian "friends" in the protracted appraisal of reservation land. Ironically, President Grant's "Peace Policy" instituted in 1869 did result in a more effective and humane administration of Kanza affairs by dedicated Quaker agents and teachers. The Quaker school operating from 1869 through 1873 was much more successful than its two predecessors.

The Quakers also made improvements in the areas of agriculture, medical care, and advocacy on behalf of the Kanzas within the Office of Indian Affairs. This sanguine assessment of the merits of the Society of Friends' administration should be tempered, however, by acknowledging that while the Quakers defended the human rights of the Kanzas, they had no interest in defending the rights of the tribe to be Indians. In the final outcome, both the Quaker administrators and Kanza chiefs were unable to defend the tribe's vital interests against their powerful adversaries. On the contentious and crucial matter of reservation land appraisal and sales, the forces of Manifest Destiny once again triumphed.

Notes

ABBREVIATIONS USED IN THE NOTES

Dorsey Papers	James Owen Dorsey Papers, Kansa (c. 1882), National Anthropological Archives, Washington, D.C.
KDWP	Kansas Department of Wildlife and Parks
KHC	*Kansas Historical Collections*
KHQ	*Kansas Historical Quarterly*
LR, OIA, Central Superintendency	Letters Received by the Office of Indian Affairs, Central Superintendency, National Archives and Records Administration, 1871, Record Group 75, M856, R 34
LR, OIA, Fort Leavenworth Agency	Letters Received by the Office of Indian Affairs, Fort Leavenworth Agency, National Archives and Records Administration, Record Group 74, Microfilm 234
LR, OIA, Kansas Agency	Letters Received by the Office of Indian Affairs, Kansas Agency, National Archives and Records Administration, Record Group 74, Microfilm 234
LR, OIA, Osage River Agency	Letters Received by the Office of Indian Affairs, Osage River Agency, National Archives and Records Administration, Record Group 74, Microfilm 234
LR, OIA, Potawatomie Agency	Letters Received by the Office of Indian Affairs, Potawatomie Agency, National Archives and Records Administration, Record Group 74, Microfilm 678

LR, OIA, Schools   Letters Received by the Office of Indian
                                        Affairs from Schools, 1850–51, National
                                        Records and Archives Administration,
                                        Record Group 74, Microfilm 234
LR, OIA, St. Louis Superintendency   Letters Received by the Office of Indian
                                        Affairs, St. Louis Superintendency,
                                        1824–1851, National Archives and Records
                                        Administration, Record Group 74, Micro-
                                        film 234
RUSCIA   *Annual Report of the United States Commis-
                                        sioner of Indian Affairs*

INTRODUCTION

1. As one of many historical spellings of this tribe's name ("Kaw" and "Kansa" have been prevalent terms), "Kanza" is used in this book in conformance with the Kaw Nation's preferred nomenclature in its recent publications.

2. Wilson Hobbs, "The Friends Establishment in Kansas Territory," *Kansas Historical Collections* [hereafter cited as *KHC*] 8 (1904): 258–59.

3. Ibid.

4. Glenn Albrecht, "Psychoterratic Conditions in a Scientific and Technological World," in *Ecopsychology: Science, Totems, and the Technological Species*, ed. Peter H. Kahn, Jr., and Patricia H. Hasbach (Cambridge: MIT Press, 2012), 255–57.

5. Johnny Rae McCauley talk, video recording by Deb Pryor, Kaw Mission State Historic Site (June 1996).

6. Elliot West, *Contested Plains: Indians, Goldseekers, and the Rush to Colorado* (Lawrence: University Press of Kansas, 1998), 336; Kristen Tegtmeier Oertel, *Bleeding Borders: Race, Gender and Violence in Pre-Civil War Kansas* (Baton Rouge: Louisiana State University, 2009), 10.

1. A NEW HOME FOR THE KANZAS

1. Kanza agent Richard W. Cummins to Superintendent Thomas Harvey, July 17, 1847, Letters Received by the Office of Indian Affairs, Fort Leavenworth Agency, National Archives and Records Administration, Record Group 74, Microfilm 234 [hereafter cited as LR, OIA, Fort Leavenworth Agency]; Robert Rankin, "Kanza Place Names from the Dorsey Files," unpublished paper, July 2012; Louise Barry, *The Beginning of the West: Annals of the Kansas Gateway to the American West, 1540–1854* (Topeka: Kansas State Historical Society, 1972), 622.

2. Barry, *The Beginning of the West*, 668.

3. Charles J. Kappler, comp., *Indian Affairs: Laws and Treaties*. Vol. 2 (Washington, D.C.: Government Printing Office, 1904), 552–54.

4. Luke Lea, commissioner of Indian Affairs, 1850–53, quote from Francis Paul Prucha, *The Great Father: The United States Government and the American Indians* (Lincoln: University of Nebraska Press, 1984), 112–13.

5. Jay H. Buckley, *William Clark: Indian Diplomat* (Norman: University of Oklahoma Press, 2008), 87–88.

6. Roger L. Nichols, ed., *The Missouri Expedition 1818–1820: The Journal of Surgeon John Gale with Related Documents* (Norman: University of Oklahoma Press, 1969), 39. Here and throughout the book, extracts and shorter quotations are generally presented verbatim, with spelling and punctuation oddities intact. I occasionally use brackets to indicate my changes in capitalization, punctuation, etc., for the sake of comprehensibility.

7. Kappler, *Indian Affairs*, 222, 554; Fool Chief and Hard Chief to "My Father," January 23, 1844, LR, OIA, Fort Leavenworth Agency.

8. Cummins to Harvey, March 6, 1844, LR, OIA, Fort Leavenworth Agency; Barry, *The Beginning of the West*, 516, 564; Cummins to OIA, September 21, 1844, quote from "High Waters in Kansas," *KHC* 8 (1903–1904): 476–77; "Fatal Malady at the Kaw Village," *Niles National Register* 69 (November 1, 1845): 134.

9. Kappler, *Indian Affairs*, 554.

10. Ibid., 552–54.

11. John C. Fremont to Secretary of War William Wilkins, August 28, 1844, LR, OIA, Fort Leavenworth Agency; Cummins to Harvey, July 17, 1847, LR, OIA, Fort Leavenworth Agency; Kanza agent Elias. S. Stover to Superintendent Thomas Murphy, December 5, 1867, Letters Received by the Office of Indian Affairs, Kansas Agency, National Archives and Records Administration, Record Group 74, Microfilm 234 [hereafter cited as LR, OIA, Kansas Agency], Roll 367.

12. Cummins to Harvey, July 17, 1847, LR, OIA, Fort Leavenworth Agency.

13. Ibid.; Kappler, *Indian Affairs*, 552.

14. Cummins to Harvey, July 17, 1847, LR, OIA, Fort Leavenworth Agency.

15. "Pike's Journal, Part II," repr., *Wagon Tracks* 17 (August 2003): 29; Kate L. Gregg, *The Road to Santa Fe: The Journal and Diaries of George Champlin Sibley* (Albuquerque: University of New Mexico Press, 1968), 16–32.

16. Thomas Jefferson Farnham, *Travels in the Great Western Prairies, the Anahuac and Rocky Mountains, and in the Oregon Territory* (1843; repr., London: British Library, Historical Print Editions, 2011), 7–8, 14–16; David White, ed., "Obadiah Oakley, 1839," in *News of the Plains and Rockies, 1803–1865*, vol. 2 (Spokane: Arthur H. Clark, 1996), 279, 282–83; James Josiah Webb, *Adventures in the Santa Fe Trade* (Glendale, Calif.: Arthur H. Clark, 1931), 46, 168–69.

17. Cummins in *Annual Report of the United States Commissioner of Indian Affairs* [hereafter cited *RUSCIA*] (1845), 542; Harvey to Commissioner of Indian Affairs William Medill, February 7, 1846, LR, OIA, Fort Leavenworth Agency; Cummins to Harvey, February 23, 1846, LR, OIA, Fort Leavenworth Agency.

18. Mason Wade, ed., *The Journals of Francis Parkman*, vol. 2 (New York: Harper, 1947), 420–21; Dr. Augustus M. Heslep letter, July 8, 1849, in *Southern Trails to California in 1849*, ed. Ralph P. Bieber (Glendale, Calif.: Arthur H. Clark, 1937), 366.

19. Cummins in *RUSCIA* (1845), 542; Harry C. Myers, ed., "Captain William Becknell's Journal of Two Expeditions from Boon's Lick to Santa Fe," *Wagon Tracks* 11 (May 1997): 22; Barry, *Beginning of the West*, 663; Michael L. Tate, *Indians and*

Emigrants: Encounters on the Overland Trails (Norman: University of Oklahoma Press, 2006), 27–28.

20. J. J. Lutz, "The Methodist Missions among the Indian Tribes in Kansas," *KHC* 9 (1905–1906): 198–99; Cummins to Harvey, January 14, October 30, 1847, LR, OIA, Fort Leavenworth Agency; Harvey to Medill, April 27, 1847, LR, OIA, Fort Leavenworth Agency; Cummins to Medill, September 5, 1847, LR, OIA, Fort Leavenworth Agency.

21. Ladd H. Schwegman, ed., "Memoirs of a Mexican War Volunteer: Charles Henry Buercklin," *Wagon Tracks* 11 (May 1997): 14; David Clapsaddle, "Four Foot Soldiers on the Trail: An Illinois Odyssey," *Wagon Tracks* 22 (November 2007): 21–22; Harvey to Medill, July 3, 1846, LR, OIA, Fort Leavenworth Agency.

22. Cummins to Harvey, July 17, 1847, LR, OIA, Fort Leavenworth Agency.

23. Harvey to Medill, August 11, 1847, LR, OIA, Fort Leavenworth Agency; Cummins to Harvey, July 17, 1847, LR, OIA, Fort Leavenworth Agency.

24. Cummins to Harvey, July 17, 1847, LR, OIA, Fort Leavenworth Agency.

25. Harvey to Medill, September 8, October 29, 1847, LR, OIA, Fort Leavenworth Agency.

26. Josiah Gregg, *Commerce of the Prairies* (1844; repr., Norman: University of Oklahoma Press, 1990), 10–12; Bieber, *Southern Trails*, 366.

27. Gregg, *Commerce*, 10.

28. Ibid., 332.

29. Leo E. Oliva, "The Army's Attempts at Freighting during the Mexican War, 1846–1848," *Wagon Tracks* 23 (November 2008): 20–21; Craig Crease, "Boom Times for Freighting on the Santa Fe Trail, 1848–1866," *Wagon Tracks* 23 (February 2009): 17.

30. Oliva, "The Army's Attempts," 24; Crease, "Boom Times," 17.

31. Barry, *Beginning of the West*, 671–72; Katie Davis, "Seth M. Hays and the Council Grove Trade," *Wagon Tracks* 2 (November 1987): 10; "Diary of Philip Gooch Ferguson," in Adam Robinson Johnston, Marcellus Ball Edwards, and Philip Gooch Ferguson, *Marching with the Army of the West, 1846–1848*, ed. Ralph P. Bieber, Southwest Historical Series 4 (Glendale, Calif.: Arthur H. Clark, 1936), 299–300.

32. Harvey to Medill, January 25, 1848, Letters Received by the Office of Indian Affairs, St. Louis Superintendency, 1824–1851, National Archives and Records Administration, Record Group 74, Microfilm 234 [hereafter cited as LR, OIA, St. Louis Superintendency]; Harvey to Medill, January 26, 1848, LR, OIA, Fort Leavenworth Agency; Kanza agent Solomon Sublette to Harvey, February 19, 1848, Letters Received by the Office of Indian Affairs, Osage River Agency, National Archives and Records Administration, Record Group 74, Microfilm 234 [hereafter cited as LR, OIA, Osage River Agency], Roll 643.

33. Robert W. Frazer, ed., *Over the Chihuahua and Santa Fe Trails, 1847–1848: George Rutledge Gibson's Journal* (Albuquerque: University of New Mexico Press, 1981), 93, 96.

34. Bieber, *Southern Trails*, 52; Barry, *Beginning of the West*, 761–62; William Y. Chalfant, *Dangerous Passage: The Santa Fe Trail and the Mexican War* (Norman: University of Oklahoma Press, 1994), 271.

35. Robert L. Duffus, *The Santa Fe Trail* (1931; repr., New York: David McKay, 1975), 223; Kanza agent Charles Handy, "List of Persons employed," September 30, 1849, LR, OIA, Osage River Agency; Mamie Stine Sharp, "Home-coming Centennial Celebration at Council Grove, June 27 to July 2, 1921," *KHC* 16 (1923–25): 556.

36. George P. Morehouse, *The Kansa or Kaw Indians and Their History* (Topeka, Kans.: State Printing Office, 1908), 37; Barry, *Beginning of the West*, 781; Ray E. Merwin, "The Wyandot Indians," *KHC* 9 (1905–1906): 84; William E. Connelley, "The First Provisional Constitution of Kansas," *KHC* 6 (1900): 103–104.

37. *RUSCIA* (1848), 448, 454; Barry, *Beginning of the West*, 763.

38. Donna C. Roper, "The Pawnee in Kansas: Ethnohistory and Archaeology," in *Kansas Archaeology*, ed. Robert J. Hoard and William E. Banks (Lawrence: University Press of Kansas, 2006), 235–38; Richard White, *The Roots of Dependency: Subsistence, Environment, and Social Change among the Choctaws, Pawnees, and Navajos* (Lincoln: University of Nebraska Press, 1983), 153–55; Willard H. Rollings, *The Osage: An Ethnohistorical Study of Hegemony on the Prairie-Plains* (Columbia: University of Missouri Press, 1992), 148–49; Louise Barry, "The Kansa Indians and the Census of 1843," *Kansas Historical Quarterly* 39 [hereafter cited as *KHQ*] (Winter 1973): 490.

39. Franklin G. Adams, ed., "Reminiscences of Frederick Chouteau," *KHC* 8 (1903–1904): 429, 431; Addison Stubbs, "Script No. 5 in Radio Talk Series" (n.d.), Addison W. Stubbs Papers, box 1, Kansas Historical Society, 1; John Francis McDermott, ed., *Tixier's Travels on the Osage Prairies* (Norman: University of Oklahoma Press, 1940), 223; Gene Weltfish, *The Lost Universe: Pawnee Life and Culture* (Lincoln: University of Nebraska Press, 1965), 309.

40. Adams, "Reminiscences of Frederick Chouteau," 429.

41. Ibid., 427.

42. Ibid.; James Owen Dorsey, *A Study of Siouan Cults*, Eleventh Annual Report of the Bureau of American Ethnology (1889–90; repr., Whitefish, Mont.: Kessinger Publishing, n.d.), 374, 376, 386; William Johnson, "Letters from the Indian Missions in Kansas," *KHC* 16 (1923–25): 230; Benjamin Y. Dixon, "Furthering Their Own Demise: How Kansa Death Customs Accelerated Their Depopulation," *Ethnohistory* 54 (Summer 2007): 493; White, *Roots of Dependency*, 153; Roper, "The Pawnee in Kansas," 238; James N. Leiker and Ramon Powers, *The Northern Cheyenne Exodus in History and Memory* (Norman: University of Oklahoma Press, 2011), 24.

43. William Johnson, "Letters from the Indian Missions," 232–34; Barry, *Beginning of the West*, 421, 423, 451–52, 477, 526–27; William E. Smith, "The Oregon Trail through Pottawatomie County," *KHC* 17 (1926): 439; Edwin Bryant, *Rocky Mountain Adventures* (New York: Hurst, n.d.): 53; *RUSCIA* (1849), 1094–95.

44. Thomas S. Huffaker, Letters, Thomas S. Huffaker Papers, Kansas Historical Society archives, summary of May 3, 1906 interview; T. C. Henry, *Dickinson County Chronicle*, July 14, 1876; Matt Thomson, *Early History of Wabaunsee County, Kansas* (1901; repr., Manhattan, Kans.: Ag Press, 1979), 101–103.

45. George P. Morehouse, "History of the Kansa or Kaw Indians," *KHC* 10 (1907–1908): 351; Hiram Martin Chittenden and Alfred Talbot Richardson, eds., *Life, Letters, and Travels of Father Pierre-Jean De Smet, S. J. 1801–1878*, vol. 1 (1905; repr., New York: Kraus Reprint, 1969), 285.

46. Harvey to Medill, January 26, 1848, LR, OIA, Fort Leavenworth Agency; *RUSCIA* (1848), 396, 454.

47. Cummins in *RUSCIA* (1845), 542; Handy in *RUSCIA* (1849), 1094–95; Bieber, *Southern Trails*, 368.

48. Harvey to Medill, May 12, 1848, LR, OIA, Osage River Agency.

49. Harvey to Medill, February 7, 1848, LR, OIA, Fort Leavenworth Agency; Barry, *Beginning of the West*, 744; Harvey to Medill, March 31, May 12, 1848, LR, OIA, Osage River Agency; John Haverty to Medill, May 26, 1848, LR, OIA, Osage River Agency.

50. Barry, *Beginning of the West*, 775, 788, 790–91; William B. Claycomb, "James Brown: Forgotten Trail Freighter," *Wagon Tracks* 8 (February 1994): 4–5.

51. Dan Flores, *The Natural West: Environmental History in the Great Plains and Rocky Mountains* (Norman: University of Oklahoma Press, 2001), 66; Rolfe D. Mandel, "Late Quaternary and Modern Environments in Kansas," in *Kansas Archaeology*, ed. Robert J. Hoard and William E. Banks (Lawrence: University Press of Kansas, 2006), 26; West, *The Contested Plains*, 89–90; Elliott West, *The Way to the West: Essays on the Central Plains* (Albuquerque: University of New Mexico Press, 1995), 40; Barry, *Beginning of the West*, 892, 972, 982.

52. Handy to Superintendent David D. Mitchell, August 29, 1849, LR, OIA, Osage River Agency; Barry, *Beginning of the West*, 808; "The Emigrants by the Santa Fe Route from the Cincinnati *Dispatch*," *KHQ* 12 (August 1943): 324 (reprint of anonymous June 7, 1849 letter).

53. Barry, *Beginning of the West*, 829–31, 864–65; Ramon Powers and James N. Leiker, "Cholera among the Plains Indians: Perceptions, Causes, Consequences," *Western Historical Quarterly* 29 (Autumn 1998): 321–22, 331–35; Ramon Powers and Gene Younger, "Cholera on the Overland Trails, 1832–1869," *Kansas Quarterly* 5 (Spring 1973): 39.

54. Handy in *RUSCIA* (1850), 57.

2. ONE OF THE MOST DIFFICULT TRIBES

1. Clinton E. Brooks and Frank D. Reeve, eds., *Forts and Forays: James A. Bennett, A Dragoon in New Mexico, 1850–1856* (Albuquerque: University of New Mexico Press, 1948), 11; Barry, *Beginning of the West*, 671, 949–50.

2. Lutz, "Methodist Missions," 201; Lela Barnes, ed., "Letters of Allen T. Ward, 1842–1851: From the Shawnee and Kaw (Methodist) Missions," *KHQ* 33 (Autumn 1967): 370, 372.

3. Barnes, "Letters of Allen T. Ward," 372, 375; Lutz, "Methodist Missions," 201; Barry, *Beginning of the West*, 962.

4. Thomas Johnson to commissioner of Indian Affairs, October 12, 1851, Letters Received by the Office of Indian Affairs from Schools, 1850–51, National Records and Archives Administration, Record Group 74, Microfilm 234 [hereafter cited as LR, OIA, Schools], Roll 785; Johnson to commissioner of Indian Affairs, January 21, 1852, LR, OIA, Schools, Roll 786.

5. Harvey in *RUSCIA* (1846), 71; Robert F. Berkhofer, Jr., *Salvation and the Savage: An Analysis of Protestant Missions and American Indian Response, 1787–1862* (Lexington: University of Kentucky Press, 1965), 15; Francis Paul Prucha, *The Great Father: The United States Government and the American Indians*, abridged ed. (Lincoln: University of Nebraska Press, 1986), 102.

6. David Wallace Adams, *Education for Extinction: American Indians and the Boarding School Experience, 1875–1928* (Lawrence: University Press of Kansas, 1995), 15.

7. Ibid., 21.

8. Harvey to Medill, February 7, 1848, LR, OIA, Fort Leavenworth Agency; Harvey in *RUSCIA* (1847), 108.

9. William E. Unrau, *The Kansa Indians: A History of the Wind People, 1673–1873* (Norman: University of Oklahoma Press, 1971): 119–22.

10. Lutz, "Methodist Missions," 195–96; "Letters from the Indian Missions," 227–28, 237–38, 240; Martha B. Caldwell, comp., *Annals of Shawnee Methodist Mission and Indian Manual Labor School*, second ed. (Topeka: Kansas State Historical Society, 1977), 11; Unrau, *Kansa Indians*, 128.

11. Caldwell, *Annals*, 21; Lutz, "Methodist Missions," 196–97; "Letters from the Indian Missions," 229–30, 240, 259–60; Willard Hughes Rollings, *Unaffected by the Gospel: Osage Resistance to the Christian Invasion (1673–1906): A Cultural Victory* (Albuquerque: University of New Mexico Press, 2004), 100–101; Morehouse, *The Kansa*, 32.

12. Dorsey, *A Study of Siouan Cults*, 366–67, 374–76, 379–80, 385–86, 418–19; Rollings, *The Osage*, 29–30; Garrick A. Bailey, ed., *The Osage and the Invisible World: From the Works of Francis La Flesche* (Norman: University of Oklahoma Press, 1995), 9, 30–35; Alanson Skinner, "Societies of the Iowa, Kansa and Ponca Indians," *Anthropological Papers of the American Museum of Natural History* 11 (1915): 769–70.

13. "Letters from Indian Missions," 230–35, 259–60; Caldwell, *Annals*, 44; Lutz, "Methodist Missions," 197–99; Adams, "Reminiscences of Frederick Chouteau," 428; Morehouse, *The Kansa*, 24.

14. Lutz, "Methodist Missions," 201; Caldwell, *Annals*, 72; Eli Sewall, November 17, 1862, LR, OIA, Kansas Agency; obituary of Thomas Huffaker, *Council Grove Republican*, July 14, 1910; Thomas Huffaker to J. J. Lutz, May 17, 1905, Thomas Huffaker Papers, Kansas Historical Society, Topeka.

15. "Descendants of Christopher Huffaker," Huffaker Genealogical Papers, Kaw Mission State Historic Site, Council Grove, Kansas; Frederick A. Norwood, *The Story of American Methodism* (Nashville: Abingdon Press, 1974), 201–202.

16. Bill of Sale, March 31, 1853, Thomas Huffaker Papers; James R. McClure, "Taking the Census and Other Incidents in 1855," *KHC* 8 (1903–1904): 234; Territorial Census, 1855, District 8, Kansas Historical Society, www.territorialkansasonline.org/, item no. 102171 (accessed February 1, 2012); Huffaker to Lutz, May 17, 1905.

17. E. H. Stanford, February 24, 1862, LR, OIA, Kansas Agency; Lutz, "Methodist Missions," 202.

18. Thomas Johnson, January 21, 1852, LR, OIA, Schools; Johnson in *RUSCIA* (1852), 377; Adams, "Reminiscences of Frederick Chouteau," 425–26; George P.

Morehouse, "Along the Kaw Trail," *KHC* 8 (1903–1904): 207, 209; Rollings, *Unaffected by the Gospel*, 74.

19. Huffaker to Lutz, May 17, 1905; Morehouse, *The Kansa*, 32; Gordon F. Davis to "Old Kaw Mission," June 26, 1960, letter, quote from Frank Haucke and others, "The Kaw Mission of Council Grove, Kansas," manuscript (n.d.), Kaw Mission State Historic Site.

20. Caldwell, *Annals*, quote from G. Douglas Brewerton (December 18, 1855): 94.

21. George P. Morehouse, "Probably the First School in Kansas for White Children," *KHC* 9 (1905–1906): 233.

22. Harriett Bidwell Shaw, *Crossing the Plains: The Journal of Harriett Bidwell Shaw in 1851*, Kansas Memory, Kansas Historical Society, www.kansasmemory.org/item/209694 (accessed December 21, 2012); "Julius Froebel's Western Travels, Part IV," *Wagon Tracks* (November 2010): 27; Hobbs, "The Friends Establishment," 258; Barry, *Beginning of the West*, 1153, 1199.

23. C. B. Boynton and T. B. Mason, *A Journey through Kansas Describing the Country, Climate, Soil, Minerals, Manufacturing, and Other Resources* (Cincinnati: Moore, Wilstach, Keys, 1855), 117.

24. *Weekly Kansas Herald* (Leavenworth), November 10, 1854; John Maloy, *History of Morris, County, 1820 to 1890* (Council Grove, Kans.: Morris County Historical Society, 1981), 6.

25. Rollings, *Unaffected by the Gospel*, 91, 95, 141; John W. Whitfield in *RUSCIA* (1853), 324.

26. Barry, *Beginning of the West*, 1185; Cummins to Pilcher, October, 1839, LR, OIA, St Louis Superintendency; *RUSCIA* (1845), 542; Jay Griffiths, "Let Them Drink Coke," *Orion* (January/February 2011): 13.

27. Maloy, *Morris County*, 24; Johnson to Luke Lea, January 21, 1852, LR, OIA, Schools; Johnson in *RUSCIA* (1852), 378.

28. Michael L. Tate, *Indians and Emigrants: Encounters on the Overland Trails* (Norman: University of Oklahoma Press, 2006), 84–88.

29. Johnson, January 21, 1852, LR, OIA, Schools; *RUSCIA* (1852), 377; W. G. Ewing Sr., July 9, 1852, Letters Received by the Office of Indian Affairs, Potawatomie Agency, National Archives and Records Administration, Record Group 74, Microfilm 678 [hereafter cited as LR, OIA, Potawatomie Agency]; Francis W. Lea in *RUSCIA* (1852), 377.

30. David D. Mitchell in *RUSCIA* (1852), 66.

31. Whitfield in *RUSCIA* (1853), 324; Kanza agent John Montgomery in *RUSCIA* (1855), 434.

32. Harvey in *RUSCIA* (1847), 841; "Letters from Indian Missions," 266.

33. Harvey in *RUSCIA* (1847), 841; Edwin James, Thomas Say, Steven Harriman Long, *Account of an Expedition from Pittsburgh to the Rocky Mountains* (1823; repr., Charleston, S.C.: Bibliolife, 2010), 124.

34. Clara Gowing, "Life among the Delaware Indians," *KHC* 12 (1911–12): 186; Caldwell, *Annals*, quote from Brewerton, 94; Rollings, *Unaffected by the Gospel*, 95.

35. Lutz, "Methodist Missions," quote from George P. Morehouse, 201–202; Whitfield in *RUSCIA* (1853), 324; William Nicholson, "Quaker Committee Report," *KHQ* 3 (August 1934): 295; Rollings, *Unaffected by the Gospel*, 152; Morehouse, "First School," 233.

36. Dorsey, "Study of Siouan Cults," 369; Rollings, *Unaffected by the Gospel*, 112; Mahlon Stubbs to Enoch Hoag, January 6, 1870, LR, OIA, Kansas Agency.

37. Whitfield in *RUSCIA* (1853), 324; Kanza agent George Clark, November 13, 1854, LR, OIA, Potawatomie Agency; Kanza chiefs and Commissioner of Indian Affairs James Denver, transcript of meeting, July 22, 1857, LR, OIA, Kansas Agency; Kevin Abing, "Before Bleeding Kansas: Christian Missionaries, Slavery, and the Shawnee Indians in Pre-Territorial Kansas, 1844–1854, *Kansas History* 24 (Spring 2001): 61–63, 69; Barry, *Beginning of the West*, 994; Caldwell, *Annals*, 71.

38. Clark, November 13, 1854, LR, OIA, Potawatomie Agency; Abing, "Before Bleeding Kansas," 67; Huffaker, March 1, 1857, LR, OIA, Kansas Agency.

39. Montgomery in *RUSCIA* (1855), 434; Boynton, *Journey through Kansas*, 118.

40. David Waldo, James Brown, and others, Memorial to the President of the United States, January 10, 1851, LR, OIA, Osage River Agency.

41. Adams, "Reminiscences of Frederick Chouteau," 432; Percival Lowe, *Five Years a Dragoon, and Other Adventures on the Great Plains* (Norman: University of Oklahoma Press, 1965), 37; Barry, *Beginning of the West*, 981.

42. Indian agent A. R. Woolley, July 4, 1851, LR, OIA, Potawatomie Agency.

43. The ensuing description of this incident is based on Lowe's *Five Years a Dragoon*, 109–14.

44. James et al., *Account of an Expedition*, 122–23; Robert H. Lowie, *Indians of the Plains* (Garden City, N.Y.: American Museum of Natural History, 1965), 113; Waldo Wedel, "The Kansa Indians," *Transactions of the Kansas Academy of Science* 49 (June 1946): 27–28.

45. Adams, "Reminiscences of Frederick Chouteau," 428; Justin McBride, director of the Kaw Nation Language Project, Kaw Mission State Historic Site, "6 Kaw Chiefs," letter to Ron Parks, September 18, 2002; Bryant, *Rocky Mountain Adventures*, 52; Morehouse, *The Kansa*, 29.

46. Bryant, *Rocky Mountain Adventures*, 52–53.

47. Kappler, *Indian Affairs: Laws and Treaties*, 225; Barry, *Beginning of the West*, 166–67, 281.

48. Barry, *Beginning of the West*, 183, 250–51, 354; Barry, "Kansa Census of 1843," 484.

49. Smith, "Oregon Trail through Pottawatomie County," 439; Barry, *Beginning of the West*, 542; Bryant, *Rocky Mountain Adventures*, 52–53.

50. Barry, *Beginning of the West*, 357; Adams, "Reminiscences of Frederick Chouteau," 429.

51. Adams, "Reminiscences of Frederick Chouteau," 429–31; Fool Chief and Hard Chief to "My Father," January 23, 1844, LR, OIA, Fort Leavenworth Agency.

52. Adams, "Reminiscences of Frederick Chouteau," 425; list of claimants, July 12, 1862, LR, OIA, Kansas Agency.

53. Ledger of trader Christopher Columbia, February 5, 1862, LR, OIA, Kansas Agency.

54. Ronald T. Takaki, *Iron Cages: Race and Culture in Nineteenth-Century America* (New York: Knopf, 1979), 61.

3. WHITE MEN NOW LIVING AMONGST US

1. *Kanza News,* July 24, 1858.

2. Ibid.; Farnsworth, receipt for payment, February 8, 1862, LR, OIA, Kansas Agency; Improvements on Diminished Reserve, LR, OIA, Kansas Agency, April 16, 1862.

3. *Kanza News,* July 24, 1858.

4. Denver to Charles Mix, March 25, 1858, LR, OIA, Kansas Agency.

5. Paul Wallace Gates, *Fifty Million Acres: Conflicts over Kansas Land Policy, 1854–1890* (Ithaca: Cornell University Press, 1954), 39–42, 222; Montgomery to Cumming, June 5, 1856, LR, OIA, Kansas Agency; Montgomery to Captain William Walker, First Cavalry, July 1, 1856, LR, OIA, Kansas Agency.

6. Captain William Walker to Lieutenant R. Riddick, June 24, 1856, LR, OIA, Kansas Agency; Montgomery to Cumming, June 30, July 9, 1856, LR, OIA, Kansas Agency; Montgomery to Captain Walker, July 1, 1856, LR, OIA, Kansas Agency; Montgomery to Colonel Edwin V. Sumner, July 5, 1856, LR, OIA, Kansas Agency; Montgomery to A. J. Isaacs, U.S. attorney general in Kansas Territory, July 5, 1856, LR, OIA, Kansas Agency; Montgomery to Denver, June 14, 1857, LR, OIA, Kansas Agency.

7. Montgomery to Cumming, July 24, 1856, LR, OIA, Kansas Agency; Alfred Thayer Andreas, with William G. Cutler, *The History of the State of Kansas,* vol. 1 (1883; repr., Atchison, Kans.: Atchison County Historical Society, 1976), 791; Cumming to Manypenny, August 12, November 20, 1856, LR, OIA, Kansas Agency; Montgomery, eviction notice, November 25, 1856, LR, OIA, Kansas Agency; Charles Columbia and others to Montgomery, July 12, 1856, LR, OIA, Kansas Agency; Whitfield to Manypenny, July 15, 1856, LR, OIA, Kansas Agency; "Committee of People" to Manypenny, July 19, 1856, LR, OIA, Kansas Agency; Charles Columbia and others, petition to K. T. Governor John W. Geary, December 5, 1856, LR, OIA, Kansas Agency; *Herald of Freedom,* May 30, 1857; Montgomery to Commissioner John W. Denver, June 14, 1857, LR, OIA, Kansas Agency.

8. Huffaker, Baker, Mosier, Columbia, and others, Depositions, July 19, 1856, LR, OIA, Kansas Agency.

9. *Weekly Kansas Herald,* November 24, 1854; Huffaker, Deposition, July 19, 1856, LR, OIA, Kansas Agency; William E. Unrau, "The Civilian as Indian Agent: Villain or Victim?" *Western Historical Quarterly* 3 (October 1972): 417.

10. List of settlers and appraisal, May 16, 1862, LR, OIA, Kansas Agency; Census of Kansas Territory, "Morris County," July 11, 1859; William Michael Shimeall, "Arthur Inghram Baker: Frontier Kansan" (master's thesis, Emporia State University,

1978), 127, 142; Andreas, *History of Kansas*, 1, 846; *Emporia News*, May 5, 1860; *Kanza News*, July 31, 1858, quote from *Western Metropolitan* (Kansas City).

11. West, *Contested Plains*, 13, 115–16; W. F. Pride, *History of Fort Riley* (1926; repr., Fort Riley, Kans.: U.S. Cavalry Museum and the Fort Riley Historical and Archaeology Society, 1987), 121; Montgomery to Denver, June 14, 1857, LR, OIA, Kansas Agency.

12. Kappler, *Indian Affairs*, 553; Charles Columbia and others to Geary, petition, December 5, 1856, LR, OIA, Kansas Agency; letter of 57 "settlers" to Commissioner Denver, May 12, 1857, LR, OIA, Kansas Agency.

13. John C. McCoy, "Survey of Kansas Indian Lands," *KHC* 4 (1886–88): 306; Kenneth W. McClintock to Ron Parks, letter, July 11, 2002), "Shawnee Reservation Boundaries in Morris County."

14. Huffaker et al., Depositions, July 19, 1856, LR, OIA, Kansas Agency.

15. Manypenny to Secretary of the Interior Robert McClelland, May 9, 1856, LR, OIA, Kansas Agency; Montgomery to Denver, June 14, 1857, LR, OIA, Kansas Agency.

16. Robert W. Baughman, *Kansas in Maps* (Topeka: Kansas State Historical Society, 1961), 26; Columbia and citizens to Geary, petition, December 5, 1856, LR, OIA, Kansas Agency; Letter of 57 "settlers" to Denver, May 12, 1857, LR, OIA, Kansas Agency.

17. *Kanza News*, July 24, 1858; Montgomery to Cumming, July 24, 1856, LR, OIA, Kansas Agency.

18. Gates, *Fifty Million Acres*, 58.

19. Montgomery to Denver, June 14, 1857, LR, OIA, Kansas Agency.

20. Ibid.

21. Hard Hart, The Wolf, and other Kanza chiefs and headmen to Commissioner Denver, July 22, 1857, LR, OIA, Kansas Agency.

22. Ibid.; *Kanza News*, July 25, 1857; *Herald of Freedom*, August 8, 1857.

23. Hard Hart, The Wolf, and other Kanza chiefs and headmen to Commissioner Denver, July 22, 1857, LR, OIA, Kansas Agency; Hard Hart and Kanza headmen, conference with K. T. Governor James Denver, March 25, 1858, LR, OIA, Kansas Agency.

24. Northrup and Chick to Cumming, May 9, 1857, LR, OIA, Kansas Agency; Montgomery to Denver, June 14, 1857, LR, OIA, Kansas Agency.

25. Huffaker to Cumming, May 15, 1857, LR, OIA, Kansas Agency; Hard Chief and other chiefs to Denver, March 19, 1858, LR, OIA, Kansas Agency.

26. Thomas H. Stanley to Charles Mix, August 23, 1858, LR, OIA, Kansas Agency.

27. Montgomery to Denver, June 14, 1857, LR, OIA, Kansas Agency; Kanza agent Milton C. Dickey in *RUSCIA* (1859), 523; West, *Way to the West*, 45.

28. Montgomery to Denver, June 14, 1857, LR, OIA, Kansas Agency.

29. Kenneth McClintock, "When Council Grove Began," manuscript (January 31, 1995), 1–2; *Kanza News*, August 6, 1859.

30. *Kansas Press*, July 25, 1859; *Kanza News*, July 16, 1859.

31. *Kansas Press* (Council Grove), September 26, 1859, quote from *Lawrence Republican*; Mark L. Gardner, "Malcolm Conn: Merchant on the Trail," *Wagon Tracks* 1 (February 1987): 7–8; Kathryn Davis Gardner, "Conn and Hays: Council Grove's Trail Merchants," *Journal of the West* 18 (April 1989): 32–33, 36.

32. Crease, "Boom Times," 21; *Kansas Press*, October 17, 1859; *Kansas State Record* (Topeka), July 28, 1860, quote from *Council Grove Press*.

33. *Kansas Press*, October 17, 1859.

34. Kappler, *Indian Affairs*, 800, 803; Anna Heloise Abel, "Indian Reservations in Kansas and the Extinguishment of Their Title," *KHC* 8 (1903–1904): 98.

35. Greenwood in *RUSCIA* (1859), 17; Robert M. Kvasnicka and Herman J. Viola, eds., *The Commissioners of Indian Affairs: 1824–1977* (Lincoln: University of Nebraska Press, 1979), 59, 85; Prucha, *Great Father*, 113; Alexander Saxton, *The Rise and Fall of the White Republic: Class Politics and Mass Culture in Nineteenth-Century America* (London: Verso, 1990), 56–57.

36. Kappler, *Indian Affairs*, 800–802.

37. Ibid., 801–802.

38. Robinson in *RUSCIA* (1859), 482.

39. Kappler, *Indian Affairs*, 553.

40. Superintendent H. B. Branch, July 12, 1862, LR, OIA, Kansas Agency; Prucha, *Great Father*, 76.

41. Dickey to Robinson, February 15, 1860, LR, OIA, Kansas Agency; Kappler, *Indian Affairs*, 800.

42. *Kansas Press*, October 10, 17, 31, 1859; November 7, 1859; Patricia Nelson Limerick, *The Legacy of Conquest: The Unbroken Past of the American West* (New York: W. W. Norton, 1987), 42.

43. *Kansas Press*, October 10, 31, 1859; November 7, 1859.

44. Ibid., October 10, 17, 31, November 7, 1859; Samuel. N. Wood and others, petition to the President of the United States and the U.S. Senate, May 7, 1860, LR, OIA, Kansas Agency; S. N. Wood and others, memorial to Commissioner Albert B. Greenwood, June 4, 1860, LR, OIA, Kansas Agency.

45. Robert S. Stevens to Samuel N. Wood, April 2, 1860, Samuel Newitt Wood Papers, Kansas Historical Society; Abel, "Indian Reservations," 98; Kappler, *Indian Affairs*, 800–801.

46. Dickey to Mix, July 27, 1860, LR, OIA, Kansas Agency; Kanza chiefs, statement (endorsement note about), October 15, 1860, LR, OIA, Kansas Agency; Kappler, *Indian Affairs*, 800.

47. Dickey to Greenwood, December 11, 1860, LR, OIA, Kansas Agency.

48. *Kansas Press*, April 30, May 14, 1860.

49. West, *Contested Plains*, 117–20, 145–46.

50. Leroy R. Hafen, ed., "Diary of Charles C. Post," *To the Pike's Peak Gold Fields, 1859* (Lincoln: University of Nebraska Press, 2004), 33.

51. West, *Contested Plains*, 89, 191–92, 230–32; Donald J. Berthrong, *The Southern Cheyennes* (Norman: University of Oklahoma Press, 1963), 101, 225; Flores, *Natural*

West, 67–70; James E. Sherow, "Workings of the Geodialectic: High Plains Indians and Their Horses in the Region of the Arkansas River Valley, 1800–1870," in *A Sense of the American West: An Anthology of Environmental History*, James Sherow, ed. (Albuquerque: University of New Mexico Press, 1998), 96–107.

52. During the 1860s the Dog Soldiers, originally a warrior society, became the most numerous and powerful band among the Cheyennes.

53. West, *Contested Plains*, 192–93; Berthrong, *Southern Cheyennes*, 93, 259–60; John H. Monnett, "Reimagining Transitional Kansas Landscapes: Environment and Violence," *Kansas History* 34 (Winter 2011–12): 259–60, 268–69, 273; Dickey, February 6, 1860, LR, OIA, Kansas Agency.

54. Stephen Jackson Spear, "Reminiscences of the Early Settlement of Dragoon Creek, Wabaunsee County," *KHC* 13 (1913–14): 351; *Kansas Press*, May 30, 1859; *Emporia News*, June 2, 1860.

55. West, *Contested Plains*, 178–79.

56. Barbara M. Burgess, *Kansas Historical Markers* (Topeka: Kansas State Historical Society, 2001), 25.

57. Donald L. Blakeslee, *Holy Ground, Healing Water: Cultural Landscapes at Waconda Lake, Kansas* (College Station: Texas A&M University Press, 2010), 160–61.

58. Barry, *Beginning of the West*, 1168; John Rydjord, *Kansas Place-Names* (Norman: University of Oklahoma Press, 1972), 109; Warren G. Hodson, "Geology and Ground-Water Resources of Mitchell County, Kansas," State Geological Survey of Kansas Bulletin 140 (April 1959): 37–39; G. E. Patrick, "The Great Spirit Spring," *Transactions of the Kansas Academy of Science* 7 (1906): 22–26; *Waconda Springs*, pamphlet, Kansas Department of Wildlife and Parks [hereafter KDWP], Waconda State Park; Blakeslee, *Holy Ground*, 99; Ada Swineford and John C. Frye, "Notes on Waconda or Great Spirit Spring, Mitchell County, Kansas," *Transactions of the Kansas Academy of Science* 58 (1955): 265–70.

59. Isaac McCoy, *History of Baptist Indian Missions* (1840; repr., Springfield, Mo., Particular Baptist Press, 2003), 411–42; Douglas R. Parks and Waldo Wedel, "Pawnee Geography: Historical and Sacred," *Great Plains Quarterly* 5 (Summer 1985): 155–58, 175; Walter R. Schoewe, "The Geography of Kansas, Part III—Hydrogeography," *Transactions of the Kansas Academy of Science* 56 (June 1953): 131–90; Blakeslee, *Holy Ground*, 99–103.

60. Gregg Doud, "Waconda Springs, the Indian's Holy Place, the White Man's Health Spa, Today's Memories," text of speech published in *Solomon Valley Post*, June 15, 1989; *Waconda Springs*, pamphlet, KDWP; Blakeslee, *Holy Ground*, 165–67.

61. George P. Morehouse, "Religion of the Indians, Especially of the Kansa or Kaws," Biennial Report of the Kansas State Historical Society, no. 27 (1928–30) (Topeka, Kans.: State Printer, 1931), 40, 42; Dorsey, "Mourning and War Customs of the Kansas," *American Naturalist* 19 (July 1885): 676; Rex Buchanan, ed., *Kansas Geology* (Lawrence: University Press of Kansas, 1984): 58; Rex C. Buchanan and James R. McCauley, *Roadside Kansas* (Lawrence: University Press of Kansas, 1987): 115–16, 160; James R. Shortridge, *Kaw Valley Landscapes* (Lawrence: University Press of Kansas, 1977), 183.

62. Morehouse, "Religion of the Indians," 40–46; Dorsey, "Mourning and War Customs," 676. In "The Sacred Red Rock of the Kansa" (unpublished manuscript, May 1, 2007), Patricia J. O'Brien, Ph.D., suggests that this "Prayer Rock" may, in fact, have been a large red quartzite rock located a few miles north of Topeka.

63. Morehouse, "Religion of the Indians," 45.

64. Dorsey, *Siouan Cults*, 366–67, 372; Say in *Account of an Expedition*, ed. James, Say, and Long, 125–26.

65. Morehouse, "Religion of the Indians," 40, 42; Tonda Rush, "Folklore Offers Insights about Kanza Indians," *Lawrence Journal-World*, November 8, 1979.

66. Monnett, "Reimagining Transitional Kansas Landscapes," 264; Gary R. Entz, "Religion in Kansas," *Kansas History* 28 (Summer 2005): 124–26; Blakeslee, *Holy Ground*, 89–93.

4. THIS UNFORTUNATE AND NEGLECTED TRIBE

1. *Herald of Freedom*, February 28, 1857; Lewis Henry Morgan, *The Indian Journals, 1859–1862*, Leslie A. White, ed. (1959; repr., New York: Dover Publications, 1993), 92; *Kanza News*, July 24, 1855.

2. Montgomery in *RUSCIA* (1855), 434; Morehouse, *The Kansa*, 33; Hartman Lichtenhan, "Reminiscences of Hartman Lichtenhan," *KHC* 9 (1905–1906): 549; Clark, November 13, 1854, LR, OIA, Potawatomie Agency; Montgomery, November 9, 1857, LR, OIA, Kansas Agency; Wedel, "The Kansa," 27; W. J. Griffing, "Committee on Explorations," *KHC* 8 (1903–1904): 134–35; *Weekly Kansas Herald* (Leavenworth), July 14, 1855.

3. William E. Unrau, "Epidemic Disease and the Impact of the Santa Fe Trail on the Kansas Indians," *Heritage of the Great Plains* 17 (Spring 1984): 3, 4, 6–7; Clyde D. Dollar, "The High Plains Smallpox Epidemic of 1837–38," *Western Historical Quarterly* 8 (January 1977): 16–17; Donald R. Hopkins, *Princes and Peasants: Smallpox in History* (Chicago: University of Chicago Press, 1983), 3–5.

4. Montgomery in *RUSCIA* (1855), 434; Powers and Leiker, "Cholera among the Plains Indians," 335–37.

5. Unrau, "Epidemic Disease," 2, 6; Paul Shepard, *The Only World We've Got* (San Francisco: Sierra Club Books, 1996), 138; Wedel, "The Kansa," 26–27.

6. Montgomery in *RUSCIA* (1855), 434; Manypenny in *RUSCIA* (1855), 435.

7. Kappler, *Indian Affairs*, 553.

8. Barry, *Beginning of the West*, 1201; Superintendent Andrew Cumming to Commissioner of Indian Affairs George Manypenny, June 23, August 29, 1854, LR, OIA, Potawatomie Agency; C. H. Strieby, interviewed by William E. Connelley, July 7, 1910, Connelley Papers, box 13, Kansas Historical Society, 12; *Emporia News*, February 13, 1864; Alfred Thayer Andreas, *The History of the State of Kansas*, 1 (1883; repr., Atchison, Kans.: Atchison County Historical Society, 1976), 120, 126, 144.

9. Unrau, "Civilian as Indian Agent," 413–14, 419–20; Montgomery, quarterly statement, March 31, 1856, LR, OIA, Kansas Agency.

10. Manypenny in *RUSCIA* (1855), 327.

11. James R. McClure, "Taking the Census and Other Incidents in 1855," *KHC* 8 (1903–1904): 235; Sharp, "Home-coming," 567; "Diary of Samuel A. Kingman at Indian Treaty in 1865," *KHC* 17 (1926–28): 450; *Council Grove Press*, February 16, 1861; David K. Clapsaddle, "A Frail Thin Line: Trading Establishments on the Santa Fe Trail, Part I," *Wagon Tracks* 24 (February 2010): 23, 25; Clapsaddle, "Frail Thin Line: Trading Establishments on the Santa Fe Trail," Part II, *Wagon Tracks* 24 (May 2010): 15–16, 19; R. M. Wright, "Personal Reminiscences of Frontier Life in Southwestern Kansas," *KHC* 7 (1901–1902): 48; William E. Unrau, *Indians, Alcohol, and the Roads to Taos and Santa Fe* (Lawrence: University Press of Kansas, 2013), 106; H. B. Mollhausen, "Over the Santa Fe Trail through Kansas in 1858," *KHQ* 16 (November 1948): 354; Hezekiah Brake, *On Two Continents: A Long Life's Experience* (Topeka, Kans.: published by author, 1896), 123, 178.

12. Asahel Beach, statement (August 22, 1859) in "Miscellaneous" folder, Maxine L. Kinton Papers, Manuscripts, Kansas Historical Society; Asahel Beach to Samuel N. Wood (November 1, 1860) Samuel N. Wood Papers, Manuscripts, Kansas Historical Society; William E. Unrau, *White Man's Wicked Water: The Alcohol Trade and Prohibition in Indian Country, 1802–1892* (Lawrence: University Press of Kansas, 1996), 49; *49th Congress, 1st Session, H. Ex. Doc. No. 125* (Ser. 2399), Claim No. 151, p. 12.

13. Unrau, *The Kansa*, 160; Cummins to Harvey, December 21, 1847, LR, OIA, Fort Leavenworth Agency; Unrau, *White Man's Wicked Water*, 57.

14. Harvey in *RUSCIA* (1848), 441.

15. Cummins, December 21, 1847, March 20, 1848, LR, OIA, Fort Leavenworth Agency.

16. Handy in *RUSCIA* (1850), 57; W. G. Ewing Sr. to Commissioner Luke Lea, July 28, 1851, July 9, 1852, LR, OIA, Potawatomie Agency; David Waldo, James Brown, et al., memorial to the president of the United States, January 10, 1851, LR, OIA, Osage River Agency.

17. Adams, "Reminiscences of Frederick Chouteau," 427; Barry, *Beginning of the West*, 534, 1063; Huffaker, "Fool Chief—A Reminiscence," *Council Grove Republican*, June 10, 1887; George W. Martin, "The Territorial and Military Combine at Fort Riley," *KHC* 7 (1901–1902): 378; Jeanne P. Leader, "The Pottawatomies and Alcohol: An Illustration of the Illegal Trade," *Kansas History* 2 (Autumn 1979): 160.

18. Burton A. James in *RUSCIA* (1854), 312; Montgomery in *RUSCIA* (1855), 434; *RUSCIA* (1856), 682; *RUSCIA* (1857), 474; *RUSCIA* (1858), 474.

19. Unrau, *White Man's Wicked Water*, 45; Sac and Fox agent C. C. Hutchinson in *RUSCIA* (1862), 107; "Apparent Per Capita Alcohol Consumption: National, State, and Regional Trends, 1850–2007," National Institute on Alcohol Abuse and Alcoholism, http://pubs.niaaa.nih.gov/publications/survelliance87/CONS07.pdf (accessed December 12, 2012), data from Merton M. Hyman, M. Zimmerman, C. Gurioli, and A. Helrich, *Drinkers, Drinking and Alcohol-Related Mortality and Hospitalizations: A Statistical Compendium* (New Brunswick, N.J.: Rutgers University, 1980); W. J. Rorabaugh, *The Alcoholic Republic: An American Tradition* (New York: Oxford University Press, 1979), 11, 248; West, *Contested Plains*, 147; "Territorial Census, 1855, District 8,"

Kansas Historical Society, www.territorialkansasonline.org/, item no. 102171 (accessed April 15, 2011); U.S. Bureau of the Census, "Morris County," in *Eighth Census of the United States, 1860* (Washington, D.C.: Government Printing Office, 1864); Raymond B. Wrabley, Jr., "Drunk Driving or Dry Run? Cowboys and Alcohol on the Cattle Trail," *Kansas History* 30 (Spring 2007): 40.

20. Sharp, "Home-coming," 567; *Council Grove Press*, September 1, 1860, May 4, 1861; Kanza agent Hiram W. Farnsworth in *RUSCIA* (1861), 666.

21. James R. Mead, *Hunting and Trading on the Great Plains, 1859–1875* (Norman: University of Oklahoma Press, 1986), 102.

22. William E. Unrau, *The Rise and Fall of Indian Country, 1825–1855* (Lawrence: University Press of Kansas, 2007), 146–49.

23. Thomas H. Gladstone, *The Englishman in Kansas; or, Squatter Life and Border Warfare* (1857; repr., Lincoln: University of Nebraska Press, 1971), 43.

24. Hutchinson in *RUSCIA* (1862), 107; *Kansas State Record*, March 3, June 16, July 21, 1860.

25. Robert M. Utley, *High Noon in Lincoln: Violence on the Western Frontier* (Albuquerque: University of New Mexico Press, 1987), 176.

26. Denver to Mix, March 25, 1858, LR, OIA, Kansas Agency; Thomas White, Thomas Huffaker, and James H. Bradford, Depositions, March 12, 1862, LR, OIA, Kansas Agency; Allen Crowley, Deposition, March 15, 1862, LR, OIA, Kansas Agency.

27. Adam Helm and John Back, Affidavits, January 27, 1862, LR, OIA, Kansas Agency; *Kanza News*, August 14, 1858.

28. *Kanza News*, August 14, 1858; H. J. Espy, *Kansas Press*, July 11, 1859.

29. Joseph Keasting, Price Piles, A. T. Wood, and Peter Windle, Depositions, January 16, 1860, LR, OIA, Kansas Agency; Kanza agent Milton C. Dickey to Superintendent A. M. Robinson, February 24, 1860, LR, OIA, Kansas Agency.

30. Dickey to Commissioner of Indian Affairs A. B. Greenwood, October 15, 1859, LR, OIA, Kansas Agency; *Freeman's Champion* (Prairie City, Kansas), March 4, 1858, quote from Gideon Elias letter of February 11, 1858; *Council Grove Press*, May 11, 1861; Stubbs to Hoag, December 15, 1871, LR, OIA, Kansas Agency; Dickey to Robinson, February 6, 1860, LR, OIA, Kansas Agency.

31. Dickey in *RUSCIA* (1860), 337.

32. Farnsworth to Commissioner of Indian Affairs William P. Dole, June 13, August 13, 1861, LR, OIA, Kansas Agency.

33. Francis Tymoney in *RUSCIA* (1858), 472; Perry Fuller in *RUSCIA* (1860), 335; James Clifton, *The Prairie People: Continuity and Change in Potawatomi Indian Culture, 1665–1965* (Iowa City: University of Iowa Press, 1977): 368.

34. J. L. Gillis in *RUSCIA* (1860), 317; *Kansas Press*, June 13, 20, 1859.

35. Gates, *Fifty Million Acres*, 82; *Herald of Freedom* (Lawrence, Kansas), October 24, 1857.

36. Tom Hill, *Kansas Press*, June 27, 1859.

37. H. J. Espy, *Kansas Press*, July 11, 1859.

38. Huffaker to Dickey, August 9, 1859, LR, OIA, Kansas Agency; Dickey to Robinson, August 10, 1859, LR, OIA, Kansas Agency.

39. "Seth Hays' 'Register,'" *Kansas Press*, June 13, 1859.

40. Dickey, August 10, 1859, LR, OIA, Kansas Agency.

41. Hill, *Kansas Press*, June 27, 1859; Espy, *Kansas Press*, July 11, 1859; Kristen Tegtmeier Oertel, "'The Free Sons of the North' versus 'The Myrmidons of Border Ruffianism': What Makes a Man in Bleeding Kansas?" *Kansas History* 25 (Autumn 2002): 176.

42. Hill, *Kansas Press*, June 27, 1859; Espy, *Kansas Press*, July 11, 1859.

43. Hill, *Kansas Press*, June 27, 1859; Espy, *Kansas Press*, July 11, 1859; Huffaker, August 9, 1859, LR, OIA, Kansas Agency.

44. Hill, *Kansas Press* June 27, 1859; Thomas Huffaker response to questionnaire from Kansas State Historical Society, (c. 1900), Thomas Huffaker Papers, Kansas Historical Society; Richard White, *The Middle Ground: Indians, Empires, and Republics in the Great Lakes Region, 1650–1815* (Cambridge: Cambridge University Press, 1991), 76–77.

45. Espy, *Kansas Press*, July 11, 1859; Hill, *Kansas Press*, June 27, 1859.

46. Hill, *Kansas Press*, June 27, 1859; Kenneth W. McClintock to Ron Parks, May 25, 2009; Huffaker, August 9, 1859; Thomas Huffaker response to questionnaire, Kansas Historical Society.

47. Utley, *High Noon in Lincoln*, 172–73; John N. Mack, "United We Stand: Law and Order on the Southeastern Kansas Frontier, 1866–1870," *Kansas History* 30 (Winter 2007–2008): 242, 245–46.

48. Hill, *Kansas Press*, June 27, 1859.

49. Ibid.; Dickey, August 10, 1859; Maloy, *Morris County*, 24.

50. *Kansas Press*, July 11, 1859.

51. Andreas, *History of the State of Kansas*, 797–98; Lalla Maloy Brigham, *The Story of Council Grove on the Santa Fe Trail* (1921; repr., Council Grove, Kans.: Morris County Historical Society, n.d.), 19–20; Alice Strieby Smith, "Through the Eyes of My Father," *KHC* 17 (1926–28): 712–15; Frank Haucke, "The Kaw or Kansa Indians," *KHQ* 20 (February 1952): 44–45.

52. James Hall, *Sketches of History, Life, and Manners in the West*, vol. 2 (Philadelphia: Harrison Hall, 1835), 74–76; White, *Middle Ground*, 389; Richard Slotkin, *The Fatal Environment: The Myth of the Frontier in the Age of Industrialization, 1800–1890* (1985; repr., Norman: University of Oklahoma Press, 1998), 253; Tom Dunlay, *Kit Carson and the Indians* (Lincoln: University of Nebraska Press, 2000), 153–54; Takaki, *Iron Cages*, 81–84.

53. *Herald of Freedom*, May 30, 1857.

54. *Emporia News*, August 18, 1860; *Kansas State Record*, July 14, 1860; West, *Contested Plains*, 327.

55. *Topeka Tribune*, March 3, 1860; *Lawrence Republican*, March 22, 1860.

56. *Council Grove Press*, July 30, August 6, 27, 1860; *Topeka Tribune*, July 14, 1860.

57. *Topeka Tribune,* September 29, 1860, quote from *Council Grove Press.*

58. *Emporia News,* February 16, 1861.

59. Dickey to Mix, July 27, 1860, LR, OIA, Kansas Agency; Dickey in *RUSCIA* (1860), 337; Mead, *Hunting and Trading,* 80; *Lawrence Republican,* August 30, 1860; *Kansas State Record,* October 6, 1860, quote from letter of "H. L. J., Salina," September 27, 1860.

60. Greenwood to Dickey, October 10, 1860, LR, OIA, Kansas Agency; Dickey to Greenwood, March 1, 1861, LR, OIA, Kansas Agency; Farnsworth in *RUSCIA* (1861), 666.

61. Joseph G. Gambone, "Economic Relief in Territorial Kansas, 1860–1861," *KHQ* 36 (Summer 1970): 150–51.

62. *Emporia News,* August 18, 1860; *Emporia News,* September 22, 1860, quote from *Leavenworth Daily Times; Topeka Tribune,* September 8, 1860.

63. Gambone, "Economic Relief," 163–64; *Topeka Tribune,* November 10, 1860, quote from *Council Grove Press;* Rita G. Napier, "Rethinking the Past; Reimagining the Future," *Kansas History* 24 (Autumn 2001): 231.

64. *Emporia News,* December 22, 1860; George W. Glick, "The Drought of 1860," *KHC* 9 (1905–1906): 484; Gambone, "Economic Relief," 173; Farnsworth to Dole, June 13, 1861, LR, OIA, Kansas Agency; Thomas Senior Berry, *Western Prices before 1861: A Study of the Cincinnati Market* (Cambridge: Harvard University Press, 1943), 154.

65. *Council Grove Press,* February 16, 1861.

5. ENDLESS TROUBLE AND QUARRELS

1. "Census Roll and Appraisement, Kansa, 1862," Records Relating to the Kansas Trust Lands and Diminished Reserve, National Archives and Records Administration, M234, R 445; Joab Spencer, "The Kaw or Kansas Indians: Their Customs, Manners, and Folk-lore," *KHC* 10 (1907–1908): 373; Dickey in *RUSCIA* (1859), 523; Farnsworth in *RUSCIA* (1861), 666.

2. Kanza Language Project, *The Kanza Clan Book* (Kaw City, Oklahoma: Kaw Nation, 2002): 7–8; Rollings, *The Osage,* 23; Alice C. Fletcher and Francis La Flesche, *The Omaha Tribe,* vol. 1 (Lincoln: University of Nebraska Press, 1992): 135–37; Skinner, "Societies of the Iowa, Kansa and Ponca Indians," 763.

3. David I. Bushnell, Jr., "Villages of the Algonquian, Siouan, and Caddoan Tribes West of the Mississippi," *Bulletin 77* (Washington, D.C.: Bureau of American Ethnology, 1922): 97; *Herald of Freedom,* May 8, 22, 1858; Farnsworth to Dole, January 21, 1862, LR, OIA, Kansas Agency.

4. James Owen Dorsey, "Kansa Indian Place Names, Map and Notes," Manuscript 389, Dorsey Papers, Smithsonian Institution National Anthropological Archives, Washington D.C.; "Explanation of Map," *KHC* 9 (1905–1906): 571.

5. James F. Hoy, "Controlled Pasture Burning in the Folklife of the Kansas Flint Hills," *Great Plains Quarterly* 9 (Autumn 1989): 233; Allen M. Coville, "Incidents Relative to the Early History of Kansas," Coville Papers, Kansas Historical Society, 4–5;

Waldo R. Wedel, "Notes on the Prairie Turnip (*Psoralea esculenta*) among the Plains Indians," *Nebraska History* 59 (Summer 1978): 9; Sara T. L. Robinson, *Kansas: Its Exterior and Interior Life: Including a Full View of Its Settlement, Political History, Social Life, Climate, Soil, Production, Scenery, Etc.* (Boston: Crosby, Nichols, 1856), 65; Mead, *Hunting and Trading*, 78; Addison Stubbs, "Material concerning Kansas Indians," Addison W. Stubbs Papers, box 1, Kansas Historical Society, 21; Skinner, "Societies," 775; Fletcher and La Flesche, *Omaha Tribe*, 134.

6. "Houses Built at the Kaw Agency," handwritten notes, accessed at the Kaw Mission Historic Site, Stevens Family Papers, #1210, Division of Rare and Manuscript Collections, Cornell University Library, Ithaca, New York; "Census Roll and Appraisement, Kansa, 1862."

7. Julie Wilson, "Kansas Über Alles! The Geography and Ideology of Conquest, 1870–1900," *Western Historical Quarterly* 27 (Summer 1996): 180.

8. Farnsworth to Dole, June 13, 1861, January 27, 1862, LR, OIA, Kansas Agency.

9. Farnsworth to Senator Samuel Pomeroy, July 22, 1861, LR, OIA, Kansas Agency.

10. Contracts, Caleb B. Smith and Robert S. Stevens, August 9, 1861, LR, OIA, Sac and Fox Agency, National Archives and Records Administration, Record Group 74, Microfilm 234, Roll 440; Dickey to Greenwood, February 26, 1861, LR, OIA, Kansas Agency; *Emporia News*, February 9, 1861; *Kansas State Record*, January 26, March 2, 1861; *Council Grove Press*, March 16, April 13, 1861; Farnsworth to Dole, June 13, 1861, LR, OIA, Kansas Agency.

11. S. N. Wood to Martin Conway, February 19, 1861, LR, OIA, Kansas Agency; *Emporia News*, February 23, 1861; *Council Grove Press*, March 16, June 1, 1861; Rufus Briggs to Caroline Stevens Briggs, March 31, 1861, Robert S. Stevens Papers, 1856–75, Kansas Historical Society, Series 2, Letters 1860–1869, microfilm roll MS 2890, no. 610331 IN; Robert C. Stevens, *Thunderbolt from a Clear Sky: The Irrepressible Life of Robert W. S. Stevens*, abridged ed. (Rochester, N.Y.: WME Books, 2006), 32.

12. *Emporia News*, February 2, April 27, 1861; Dickey to Greenwood, February 23, 26, 1861, LR, OIA, Kansas Agency; Farnsworth to Dole, June 13, July 30, October 31, November 2, 11, 25, 1861, LR, OIA, Kansas Agency; Stevens to Dole, November 12, 1861, LR, OIA, Kansas Agency; James Kersey and Jeremiah Hadley to Superintendent Harrison B. Branch, June 6, 1861, LR, OIA, Kansas Agency.

13. Contract, August 9, 1861, LR, OIA, Sac and Fox Agency; contract, Smith and Stevens, December 28, 1861, Letters Received by the Office of Indian Affairs, Central Superintendency, National Archives and Records Administration, Record Group 34, Microfilm 856 [hereafter cited as LR, OIA, Central Superintendency]; Dole in *RUSCIA* (1861), 12–13; W. G. Coffin, superintendent of Indian Affairs, Southern Superintendency, to Dole, December 20, 1861, LR, OIA, Kansas Agency; Farnsworth to Dole, January 17, 1862, LR, OIA, Kansas Agency; *Emporia News*, January 4, 1862.

14. "Houses Built at the Kaw Agency," Stevens Family Papers.

15. John Montgomery and Charles Withington, Contract, April 25, 1858, LR, OIA, Kansas Agency; Stubbs to Hoag, January 23, 1871, LR, OIA, Kansas Agency; Coffin to Dole, December 20, 1861, LR, OIA, Kansas Agency; Donald Cress and F. J. Revere,

interview by author, Allegawaho Memorial Heritage Park, Kaw Nation, July 4, 2008. The agency house stood on the west side of present-day Morris County Road 525 until its destruction around 1940.

16. "Houses Built at the Kaw Agency," Stevens Family Papers; Haucke, "The Kaw or Kansa Indians," 46; Stubbs to Hoag, January 23, 1871, LR, OIA, Kansas Agency; Denver to Mix, March 25, 1858, LR, OIA, Kansas Agency; Thomas Stanley to Mix, August 23, 1858, LR, OIA, Kansas Agency; Montgomery in *RUSCIA* (1858), 475; A. M. Robinson in *RUSCIA* (1859), 482; Dickey to Robinson, February 6, 1860, LR, OIA, Kansas Agency; Farnsworth to Dole, January 17, 1862, LR, OIA, Kansas Agency; Herb Pankratz and Mike Ruppert, archaeological survey field notes, Kansas Historical Society (July 18, 1974); Farnsworth to Spencer, Bill of Sale, "Frame Storehouse," Records of Morris County Register of Deeds, September 10, 1867; Revere and Cress, July 4, 2008; *Council Grove Democrat,* June 9, 1874. The walls of the interpreter's house were stabilized by the Kaw Nation in 2003 with funding provided by the Heritage Trust Fund, which is administered by the Kansas Historical Society from revenues generated by the state of Kansas. The shell of the interpreter's house—often mistakenly identified as the agent's house and office—is the only structure still standing of the six or seven buildings that once formed the Kanza Agency complex.

17. Kanza agent Mahlon Stubbs to Superintendent Enoch Hoag, January 23, 1871, LR, OIA, Kansas Agency; Farnsworth to Branch, August 13, 1863, LR, OIA, Kansas Agency; Farnsworth to Branch, September 16, 1863, LR, OIA, Central Superintendency.

18. Farnsworth, quarterly report, June 18, 1862, LR, OIA, Kansas Agency; Farnsworth to Dole, January 20, 1863, LR, OIA, Kansas Agency; Farnsworth to Branch, March 16, 1863, LR, OIA, Kansas Agency; Farnsworth in *RUSCIA* (1862), 277.

19. Special commissioner Edward Wolcott to Dole, April 4, 1862, LR, OIA, Kansas Agency; Farnsworth to Dole, October 18, 1861.

20. Farnsworth to Dole, December 20, 1861, LR, OIA, Kansas Agency.

21. *Council Grove Press,* June 22, 1861.

22. Ibid., July 20, 1861; Abel, "Indian Reservations in Kansas," 99; Kappler, *Indian Affairs,* 801–802, 829.

23. Kappler, *Indian Affairs,* 829–30; Thomas Huffaker, Affidavit, March 12, 1862, LR, OIA, Kansas Agency; Wolcott to Dole, March 19, 1862, LR, OIA, Kansas Agency.

24. Farnsworth to Dole, March 29, 1862, LR, OIA, Kansas Agency; Wolcott to Dole, April 4, 1862, LR, OIA, Kansas Agency; special commissioner S. Brady to Dole, April 10, 1862, LR, OIA, Kansas Agency; Huffaker to Farnsworth, September 9, 1862, LR, OIA, Kansas Agency.

25. Huffaker to Farnsworth, September 9, 1862, LR, OIA, Kansas Agency; Farnsworth to Dole, January 20, 27, 1863, LR, OIA, Kansas Agency; Farnsworth, quarterly report, June 18, 1862, LR, OIA, Kansas Agency.

26. Huffaker to Farnsworth, September 9, 1862, LR, OIA, Kansas Agency; Farnsworth to Dole, November 7, 1862, March 3, 1863, LR, OIA, Kansas Agency; Farnsworth in *RUSCIA* (1862), 276.

27. Farnsworth to Dole, January 20, 1863, LR, OIA, Kansas Agency; Shimeall, "Arthur Inghram Baker," 50; Farnsworth and Huffaker in *RUSCIA* (1863), 376–77.

28. Farnsworth to Dole, January 20, 1863, LR, OIA, Kansas Agency.

29. Ibid.

30. *Council Grove Press*, April 27, May 11, 1861; Morehouse, *The Kansa*, 30; Addison Stubbs, *Star Times* article, manuscript (n.d.), Addison W. Stubbs Papers, box 1, p. 4; Ishtalasea and chiefs to Dole, July 17, 1863, LR, OIA, Kansas Agency.

31. Barry, "The Kansa Indians and the Census of 1843," 484; Annuity Census, November 9, 1857, LR, OIA, Kansas Agency; Kappler, *Indian Affairs*, 554; "Census Roll and Appraisement," Kansa, 1862.

32. Claims of traders Christopher Columbia and Alexander Kennedy, February 5, 1862, LR, OIA, Kansas Agency; Farnsworth to Dole, July 24, 1862, LR, OIA, Kansas Agency; Farnsworth and Huffaker, statement, May 29, 1863, LR, OIA, Kansas Agency.

33. Ishtalasea and chiefs to Commissioner Dole, July 17, 1863, LR, OIA, Kansas Agency.

34. Farnsworth to Dole, April 12, 1862, LR, OIA, Kansas Agency; Branch to Dole, December 15, 1862, LR, OIA, Kansas Agency; Prucha, *Great Father*, 62–63.

35. Huffaker, *Council Grove Republican*, June 10, 1887; Hard Hart to Denver, July 22, 1857, LR, OIA, Kansas Agency; White, *The Middle Ground*, 179; Louis Burns, *A History of the Osage People* (Tuscaloosa: University of Alabama Press, 2004), 130; "Letters from Indian Missions in Kansas," 263–64; White Plume to General William Clark, May 17, 1827, Thomas S. Huffaker Papers.

36. Farnsworth to Dole, January 24, May 17, 1863, LR, OIA, Kansas Agency; Ishtalasea to Dole, July 17, 1863, LR, OIA, Kansas Agency; A. V. Blacklidge to Department of Interior, August 29, 1863, LR, OIA, Kansas Agency.

37. Farnsworth to Dole, July 17, 1863, LR, OIA, Kansas Agency.

38. Farnsworth to Dole, July 31, 1861, June 13, October 12, November 11, 1863, LR, OIA, Kansas Agency.

39. Unratified Kanza Treaty of 1864, "Documents relating to the negotiation of an unratified treaty of June 11, 1864, with the Kaw Indians" (June 11, 1864) http://digicoll.library.wisc.edu/ (accessed December 21, 2012); Farnsworth to Dole, November 11, 1863, LR, OIA, Kansas Agency.

40. Unratified Kanza Treaty of 1864.

41. Ibid.

42. *Council Grove Press*, June 25, 1864. The Kanzas and other tribes referred to high-placed government officials in Washington, D.C., especially the commissioner of Indian Affairs and the president, as "Great Father" as a traditional way of showing respect and forming alliances through invocations of kinship.

43. Ibid.

44. Muster-Out Roll of Company L, Ninth Kansas Cavalry, June 30, 1865, LR, OIA, Kansas Agency.

45. *Council Grove Press*, June 25, 1864.

46. *Emporia News,* July 2, 1864; Unrau, *Kansa Indians,* 201–203.

47. Sharp, "Home-Coming," 568–69.

48. Ibid., 567; *Council Grove Press,* March 16, 23, 1861; *Kansas State Record,* March 2, 1861, quote from *Council Grove Press;* Loretta Fowler, *The Columbia Guide to American Indians of the Great Plains* (New York: Columbia University Press, 2003), 72.

49. Huffaker to Farnsworth, September 9, 1862, LR, OIA, Kansas Agency; *RUSCIA* (1860), 337; *RUSCIA* (1863), 508; *RUSCIA* (1864), 511; Farnsworth to Dole, June 10, 1864, LR, OIA, Kansas Agency; Christopher Columbia, claims, February 5, 1862, LR, OIA, Kansas Agency.

50. Coville, "Incidents," 19; Nicholson, "Tour of Indian Agencies," 295; John Kirk Townsend, *Narrative of a Journey across the Rocky Mountains to the Columbia River* (1839; repr., Corvallis: Oregon State University Press, 1999), 18–19; *Emporia News,* May 14, 1859; Orville W. Mosher, "Three Indian Villages Were Once Located in This Area," *Lyon County Historical Museum* (1965) [compilation of historical articles written by Mosher and published in the *Emporia Gazette* 1950–67]: 58; Luke F. Parsons Diary—1859, 1860, 1861," Manuscript, *Kansas Collection,* Salina Public Library, 11; *Smoky Hill and Republican Union* (Junction City, Kansas), January 28, 1863; Rodney Staab, "Kansa Presence in the Upper Kansas Valley," *Kansas Anthropologist* 16 (1995): 40, 41.

51. "Material concerning Kansas Indians," Addison W. Stubbs Papers, box 1, p. 1; George P. Morehouse, "Along the Kaw Trail," *KHC* 8 (1903–1904): 207; Julia Shellabarger Porter, "My Grandmother, from the Record of Christina Phillips Campbell," Manuscript, *Kansas Collection,* Salina Public Library, 32.

52. Mosher, "Three Indian Villages," 59; Coville, "Incidents," 19; *Council Grove Press,* May 18, 1861.

53. *Council Grove Press,* February 16, 1861; Government Land Office, Survey Notes (January 1861), Kansas Society of Land Surveyors, compact disk #23, Range 8 to 9 East (Duke West Interactive Graphics, Inc., Leavenworth); U.S. Census, 1860, "Morris County"; *Council Grove Press,* May 4, 11, 18, 25, June 1, 1861.

54. *Council Grove Press,* May 18, 1861.

55. Reginald Horsman, *Race and Manifest Destiny: The Origins of American Racial Anglo-Saxonism* (Cambridge, Mass.: Harvard University Press, 1981), 207, 210; Glenda Riley, *Confronting Race: Women and Indians on the Frontier, 1815–1915* (Albuquerque: University of New Mexico Press, 2004), 221–24; Brian W. Dippie, *The Vanishing American: White Attitudes and U.S. Indian Policy* (Lawrence: University Press of Kansas, 1982), 71.

56. Crease, "Boom Times," 20, 21; Leo E. Oliva, *Soldiers on the Santa Fe Trail* (Norman: University of Oklahoma Press, 1967), 139; Walker Wyman, "Freighting: A Big Business on the Santa Fe Trail," *KHQ* 1 (November, 1931): 24–25; Wood, *The Old Santa Fe Trail,* 224; Maloy, *Morris County,* 46.

57. Maloy, *Morris County,* 46; *Council Grove Press,* June 15, 1863, quote from *Leavenworth Times;* James E. Hudson, "Camp Nichols: Oklahoma's Outpost on the Santa Fe Trail," quote from *Daily Missouri Democrat* (St. Louis), May 11, 1845, in *Wagon Tracks* 14 (November 1999): 13; Sharp, "Home-Coming," 567.

58. Farnsworth to Dole, July 23, 1862, LR, OIA, Kansas Agency.

59. *Council Grove Press*, May 18, 1863; Maloy, *Morris County*, 45–46; Connelley, interview of C. H. Strieby (July 7, 1910), Connelley Papers, box 13, pp. 12–13; George P. Morehouse, "Diamond Springs, 'The Diamond of the Plain,'" *KHC* 14 (1915–18): 799–800.

60. *Emporia News*, May 16, September 12, 1863.

61. *Emporia News*, May 10, 17, 1862; William E. Connelley, interview of Eli M. Sewell (July 7, 1910), Connelley Papers, box 13, Kansas Historical Society, 2, 4; Ishtalasea to Dole, July 17, 1863, LR, OIA, Kansas Agency; Farnsworth to Dole, July 14, 1863, LR, OIA, Kansas Agency.

6. SOME WERE DECIDEDLY IMPROVED

1. Barry, *Beginning of the West*, 817, 857, 886–87; Thomson, *Early History of Wabaunsee County*, 5; Gregory M. Franzwa, *Maps of the Santa Fe Trail* (St. Louis: Patrice Press, 1989), 57–61; *Emporia News*, May 7, 1864; *Topeka Tribune*, November 19, 1859.

2. James Owen Dorsey, "Dhegiha Language Papers in the Smithsonian Institution c. 1870–1890," James Owen Dorsey Papers, Kansa (c. 1882), National Anthropological Archives, Washington, D.C. [hereafter cited as Dorsey Papers]; Dorsey, "Sketch Map of Arkansas River, Neosho River and Kansas River," Dorsey Papers; Dorsey, *Siouan Cults*, 422.

3. Harvey G. Young, Affidavits, February 26, 1862, LR, OIA, Kansas Agency.

4. Fannie E. Cole, "The Kansas Indians in Shawnee County after 1855," *KHC* 8 (1903–1904): 481; Anna Maria Morris, "A Military Wife on the Santa Fe Trail," in *Covered Wagon Women: Diaries & Letters from the Western Trails, 1840–1890*, vol. 2, *1850*, ed. Kenneth L. Holmes (Glendale, Calif.: Arthur H. Clark, 1983): 23; James Owen Dorsey, "Kansas Indian Place Names, Map and Notes," Dorsey Papers; Morgan, *Indian Journals*, 33, 78.

5. "They Walked Then," *Topeka Journal*, October 23, 1916; McDermott, *Tixier's Travels*, 248.

6. *Council Grove Press*, March 16, 1861; "Consolidated Morning Reports, March 1862–December, 1864," Fort Leavenworth, microfilm roll MS 803.01, Archives, Kansas Historical Society, Topeka; *Leavenworth Daily Conservative*, May 27, June 9, 1863.

7. *Council Grove Press*, May 25, 1861; James H. Lane to Indian agents, August 22, 1861, LR, OIA, Kansas Agency; Augustus Wattles to Farnsworth, August 25, 1861, LR, OIA, Kansas Agency; Farnsworth to Dole, January 21, 1862, LR, OIA, Kansas Agency.

8. Muster Roll, Company L, Ninth Kansas Volunteer Cavalry, LR, OIA, Kansas Agency; "Roster of Officers and Enlisted Men of Kansas Volunteers, Fifteenth regiment Cavalry, Company F," in *Report of the Adjutant General of the State of Kansas, 1861–1865* (Topeka: Kansas State Printing Company, 1896), 514, 515.

9. *War of the Rebellion: A Compilation of the Official Record of the Union and Confederate Armies*, series 1, vol. 22, part 2 (Washington, D.C.: Government Printing Office, 1893), 420, 761; "Ninth Kansas Cavalry Regiment," *American Civil War Research*

Database, subscription database (accessed September 1, 2011); *Kansas Daily Tribune* (Lawrence), March 25, 31, 1864.

10. *War of the Rebellion: A Compilation of the Official Record of the Union and Confederate Armies*, Series 1, Vol. 41, Part 2 (Washington D.C.: Government Printing Office, 1893), 23, 504, 836, 889, 1008; Benjamin Woodward, "Report from Duvall's Bluff, Arkansas," *United States Sanitary Commission Bulletin* 3 (1866): 859.

11. Muster Roll, Ninth Kansas, LR, OIA, Kansas Agency; Petition of Kanza soldiers, December 3, 1864, LR, OIA, Kansas Agency; Abram Munroe to "My Great Father," January 19, 1867, LR, OIA, Kansas Agency.

12. Munroe to Farnsworth, July 31, 1864, LR, OIA, Kansas Agency.

13. Petition of Kanza soldiers, December 3, 1864, LR, OIA, Kansas Agency; Farnsworth to Dole, January 7, 1865, LR, OIA, Kansas Agency.

14. James L. Arnold, letter, July 17, 1865, LR, OIA, Kansas Agency; Alexander Shaler, letter, July 18, 1865, LR, OIA Kansas Agency; Farnsworth to Superintendent Thomas Murphy, January 15, 1866, LR, OIA, Kansas Agency.

15. Munroe to "My Great Father," January 19, 1867, LR, OIA, Kansas Agency.

16. Farnsworth to Dole, August 11, 1864, LR, OIA, Kansas Agency.

17. Albert Castel, *A Frontier State at War: Kansas 1861–1865* (Ithaca, N.Y.: Cornell University Press, 1958): 216–17; *Smoky Hill and Republican Union*, August 27, September 3, 1864; Farnsworth to Dole, August 11, 1864, LR, OIA, Kansas Agency; Farnsworth to Dole, January 7, 1865, LR, OIA, Kansas Agency. The Kanza did not attend this council, having already left for the fall hunt. However, in December, fifteen chiefs and other men of the tribe signed this document pledging loyalty to the United States.

18. Farnsworth to Dole, August 11, 1864, LR, OIA, Kansas Agency; Farnsworth in *RUSCIA* (1864), 511; Dole to Secretary of Interior John P. Usher in *RUSCIA* (1864), 514; Castel, *Frontier State at War*, 217; Farnsworth to Dole, January 9, 1865, LR, OIA, Kansas Agency.

19. Farnsworth to Dole, January 9, 1865, LR, OIA, Kansas Agency.

20. Farnsworth to Dole, May 10, 1865, LR, OIA, Kansas Agency; Dole to Superintendent William M. Albin, June 2, 1865, LR, OIA, Kansas Agency; Murphy in *RUSCIA* (1865), 211; Farnsworth in *RUSCIA* (1866), 275.

21. Huffaker in *RUSCIA* (1864), 512; *Emporia News*, July 30, 1864; Farnsworth, quarterly report, December 17, 1864, LR, OIA, Kansas Agency; Farnsworth in *RUSCIA* (1864), 510.

22. Farnsworth in *RUSCIA* (1865), 214, 580; Farnsworth in *RUSCIA* (1866), 274, 350.

23. Farnsworth in *RUSCIA* (1866), 274.

24. *RUSCIA* (1862), 356; *RUSCIA* (1864), 511; *RUSCIA* (1866), 346; Mahlon Stubbs, superintendent of Kaw Mission-School, response to questionnaire, July 25, 1865, in U.S. Senate, "Appendix," in *Doolittle Commission Report*, Senate Report, No. 156, 39th Congress, Second Session, serial 1279, 1867, 484–85.

25. *RUSCIA* (1864), 511; Farnsworth to Dole, January 9, 1865, LR, OIA, Kansas Agency; Farnsworth to Mix, May 10, 1865, LR, OIA, Kansas Agency; Farnsworth

to Murphy, September 6, 1865, LR, OIA, Kansas Agency; Farnsworth in *RUSCIA* (1866), 275.

26. Farnsworth to Dole, May 20, 1865, LR, OIA, Kansas Agency; Stubbs to Farnsworth, January 31, 1866, LR, OIA, Kansas Agency; Farnsworth to Dole, June 18, 1863, LR, OIA, Kansas Agency; Farnsworth to Branch, July 28, 1863, LR, OIA, Kansas Agency; Farnsworth to Murphy, February 1, 1866, LR, OIA, Kansas Agency.

27. Addison Stubbs, "Sketch of the Life of Mahlon Stubbs," Manuscript (n.d.), Addison W. Stubbs Papers, box 1, Kansas Historical Society, p. 8; Addison Stubbs, "Historical Address Delivered by Addison W. Stubbs at the Reunion in Council Grove, July 1, 1921," Manuscript, Addison W. Stubbs Papers, box 1, Kansas Historical Society, p. 2; Addison Stubbs, "Material Concerning Kansas Indians," 2; *Emporia News*, April 30, 1869; Farnsworth in *RUSCIA* (1866), 274.

28. Addison Stubbs, "Historical Address," 3–4; Farnsworth to Branch, September 16, 1863, in *RUSCIA* (1863), 376–77; Stubbs to Farnsworth, September 17, 1863, in *RUSCIA* (1863), 377–78.

29. Addison Stubbs, "Historical Address," 5–6; *Emporia News*, January 2, 1864; Stubbs in *RUSCIA* (1863), 378.

30. Samuel J. Spray to Joseph Newby, June 15, 1865, J. H. Newby Papers, Kansas Historical Society; Stubbs in *RUSCIA* (1863), 378, 506; Farnsworth in *RUSCIA* (1864), 512; Addison Stubbs, "Historical Address," 6; Stubbs in *RUSCIA* (1864), 512.

31. Stubbs in *RUSCIA* (1864), 512; Margaret H. Watkins to Farnsworth in *RUSCIA* (1866), 276; Spray to Newby, June 15, 1865 in *RUSCIA* (1863), 378, 506; *RUSCIA* (1865), 577.

32. Stubbs in *RUSCIA* (1864), 511; Spray to Newby, June 15, 1865; Stanley to Farnsworth in *RUSCIA* (1866), 275; Watkins to Farnsworth in *RUSCIA* (1866), 276; Farnsworth to Murphy in *RUSCIA* (1866), 276.

33. Farnsworth in *RUSCIA* (1866), 274, 276; Stanley in *RUSCIA* (1866), 275; Spray to Newby, June 15, 1865; Farnsworth in *RUSCIA* (1864), 510; Stubbs in *RUSCIA* (1864), 511–12.

34. Barbara Neal Ledbetter, *Fort Belknap Frontier Saga: Indians, Negroes and Anglo-Americans on the Texas Frontier* (Burnet, Tex.: Eakin Press, 1982), 141, 143, 146–47, 149; Gregory Michno, "The Search for the Captives of Elm Creek," *Wild West* (April 2009): 46, 49–50; Kenneth F. Neighbours, "Elm Creek Raid," *Handbook of Texas Online*, Texas State Historical Association, www.tshaonline.org/handbook/online/articles/bte01 (accessed August 16, 2011); Farnsworth to Murphy, November 18, 1865, LR, OIA, Kansas Agency; Murphy to Commissioner of Indian Affairs Dennis Cooley, November 21, 1865, LR, OIA, Kansas Agency.

35. Ledbetter, *Fort Belknap*, 147, 163–79; Michno, "The Search," 49–51; Farnsworth to Murphy, November 18, 28, 1865, April 14, June 5, 1866, LR, OIA, Kansas Agency; Murphy to Cooley, November 21, December 2, 1865, April 18, June 8, 1866, LR, OIA, Kansas Agency; Farnsworth, financial reports, January, September, 1866, LR, OIA, Kansas Agency; receipt, work performed by Elizabeth Ann Sprague [Fitzpatrick], September 1866, LR, OIA, Kansas Agency; W. H. Watson to Cooley, June 26, 1866, LR, OIA, Kansas Agency.

36. Jeff Brome, *Dog Soldier Justice: The Ordeal of Susanna Alderdice in the Kansas Indian War* (Lincoln, Kans.: Lincoln County Historical Society, 2005); Monnett, "Reimagining Traditional Kansas Landscapes," 274.

37. Paul Chaat Smith, *Everything You Know about Indians Is Wrong* (Minneapolis: University of Minnesota Press, 2009), 136.

38. Porter, "My Grandmother," 27, 29–31.

39. James R. McClure, "Taking the Census," 231–32, 240, 246–48; Dorsey, "Kansas Indian Place Names, Map and Notes"; Clara M. Fengel Shields, "Lyon Creek Settlement," *KHC* 14 (1915–18): 147.

40. McClure, "Taking the Census," 247–48; Morehouse, *The Kansa*, 30.

41. Dorsey, "Kansa Indian Place Names, Map and Notes"; *Warneke Stories*, manuscript compiled by descendants of John and Barbara Warneke, and made available to the Kaw Mission State Historic Site by Ken and Shirley McClintock.

42. *Warneke Stories*; Kevin G. W. Olson, *Frontier Manhattan: Yankee Settlement to Kansas Town, 1854–1894* (Lawrence: University Press of Kansas, 2012), 88; William Y. Chalfant, *Cheyennes and Horse Soldiers: The 1857 Expedition and the Battle of Solomon's Fork* (Norman: University of Oklahoma Press, 2002): 79; Dickey to Greenwood, January 24, 1860, LR, OIA, Kansas Agency.

43. Albert Robinson, "Campaigning in the Army of the Frontier," *KHC* 14 (1915–18): 285; Webb, *Adventures in the Santa Fe Trade*, 167; *Emporia News*, March 10, 1860; "Met the Indians," *Lyon Daily News*, August 17, 1946.

44. Thomson, *Wabaunsee County*, 115; H. Pearl Dixon, *Sixty Years among the Indians: A Short Life Sketch of Thomas H. and Mary W. Stanley Quaker Missionaries to the Indians* (privately printed, 1922), 20, 38, 40.

45. Maloy, *Morris County*, 51.

46. Questionnaire, Huffaker Papers; Kenneth McClintock, "Council Grove Town Co. Patent," manuscript, (n.d.), Kaw Mission State Historic Site; Maloy, *Morris County*, 44; Barry, *Beginning of the West*, 1207; Farnsworth testimony, November 17, 1862, LR, OIA, Kansas Agency; David L. Richards, editor, "Charles W. Fribley's Trail Diary and Letters, 1857–1859, Part I," *Wagon Tracks* 12 (August 1998): 22; *Council Grove Press*, October 19, November 30, December 14, 1863. The Jacob Hall case was resolved in 1877 when the U.S. Supreme Court denied Hall's claim, then being litigated by his heirs.

47. Sharp, "Home-coming," 537, 555; *Council Grove Democrat*, March 2, 9, April 6, May 5, 18, June 15, July 28, August 4, September 15, November 17, December 1, 1866.

48. First Census, State of Kansas, 1865, "Morris County," Council Grove Public Library, microfilm; U.S. Bureau of the Census, "Morris County."

49. Maloy, *Morris County*, 50, 51, 53; *Council Grove Democrat*, January 26, 1866–December 1, 1866; Oertel, *Bleeding Borders*, 4–10, 110–15, 133–34; Zachary J. Lecher, "Are We Ready for the Conflict? Black Abolitionist Response to the Kansas Crisis, 1854–1856," *Kansas History* 31 (Spring 2008): 26–27, 31; Eric Foner, *Free Soil, Free Labor, Free Men: The Ideology of the Republican Party before the Civil War* (New York:

Oxford University Press, 1970), 262–97; James N. Leiker, "Race Relations in the Sunflower State," *Kansas History* 25 (Autumn 2002): 218–24.

50. Sharp, "Home-coming," 555; Joseph F. Meany, Jr., "Jeremiah Stokes: A Case Study in Family History," *Wagon Tracks* 18 (May 2004): 13; *Council Grove Press*, February 15, March 7, May 7, 28, June 11, July 23, August 20, 1864; *Emporia News*, April 2, August 13, 1864.

51. David K. Clapsaddle, "For Whom the Bell Tolls?" *Wagon Tracks* 21 (August 2007): 6; Beverly Carmichael Ryan, "Under Siege at the Cow Creek Crossing, July 1864," *Wagon Tracks* 14 (August 2000): 6–9; Beverly Carmichael Ryan, "Under Siege at the Walnut and Cow Creek Trail Crossings, July 1864," *Wagon Tracks* 18 (August 2004): 7; Stokes, "A Case Study," 13.

52. *Council Grove Democrat*, March 2, April 27, May 4, June 1, 15, July 6, 20, August 18, 1866; Duffus, *The Santa Fe Trail*, 255; Joseph W. Snell and Robert W. Richmond, "When the Union and Kansas Pacific Built through Kansas, Part 1," *KQH* 32 (Summer 1966): 180–86; Maloy, *Morris County*, 54; Amy L. Sanderson, "The Faults of Memory: J. L. Sanderson, His Family, and the Santa Fe Trail," *Wagon Tracks* 22 (August 2008): 12; *Junction City Union*, July 21, 1866; David K. Clapsaddle, "The End of the Trail: Rail-Roads, Commission Houses, and Independent Freighters," *Wagon Tracks* 23 (February 2009): 22.

53. *Council Grove Press*, October 6, 1865; *Junction City Union*, November 11, 1865; Maloy, *Morris County*, 50; Spencer, "The Kaw," 381; Morehouse, "History of the Kansa," 354; Ishtalasea and chiefs to Dole, July 17, 1863, LR, OIA, Kansas Agency.

54. Spencer, "The Kaw," 381–82.

55. Unrau, "The Civilian as Indian Agent," 407–408, 411, 414, 418.

56. Branch, July 12, 1862, LR, OIA, Kansas Agency; Farnsworth to Murphy, June 8, 1866, LR, OIA, Kansas Agency; *RUSCIA* (1866), 18.

57. Farnsworth to Murphy, June 8, 1866, LR, OIA, Kansas Agency; Donald Chaput, "Generals, Indian Agents, Politicians: The Doolittle Survey of 1865," *Western Historical Quarterly* 3 (July 1972): 278.

58. *Emporia News*, March 8, 1862, December 29, 1866; Stubbs, *Doolittle Commission Report*, 485; Unrau, "The Civilian as Indian Agent," 415; Chaput, "Generals, Indian Agents, Politicians," 278; Farnsworth to Murphy, June 8, 1866, LR, OIA, Kansas Agency.

7. IN NO CONDITION TO COMPETE WITH THEIR FORMIDABLE ENEMIES

1. Agent Elias S. Stover in *RUSCIA* (1868), 260–61; Stover to Murphy, December 5, 27, 1867, LR, OIA, Kansas Agency; William Y. Chalfant, *Hancock's War: Conflict on the Southern Plains* (Norman, Okla.: Arthur H. Clark, 2010): 507.

2. Stover, December 27, 1867, LR, OIA, Kansas Agency; Stover in *RUSCIA* (1868), 260–61; David Clapsaddle, "Conflict and Commerce on the Santa Fe Trail: The Fort Riley–Fort Larned Road, 1860–1867," *Kansas History* 16 (Summer 1993): 128, 134–37.

Today the route of the Kanza retreat would roughly follow Highway 156 through southwestern Ellsworth County to Ellsworth, there joining Highway 140 eastbound all the way to Junction City.

3. Stover in *RUSCIA* (1868), 260–61; Stover, December 27, 1867, LR, OIA, Kansas Agency.

4. Stover in *RUSCIA* (1868), 261, 355; Stover in *RUSCIA* (1867), 378, 396.

5. Stover, December 27, 1867, LR, OIA, Kansas Agency; *Junction City Union*, January 4, 1868; Jean Lindsey, comp., *John R. Wells Discovers Kansas* (Stockton, Kans.: n.p., 1998); "Hunted Buffalo in Plug Hat," *Rooks County Record*, June 28, 1917.

6. West, *The Contested Plains*, 77, 89–90, 191–94, 197–200, 232; Flores, *Natural West*, 67–70; Sherow, "Workings of the Geodialectic," 96–107; Andrew C. Isenberg, *The Destruction of the Bison* (Cambridge: Cambridge University Press, 2000), 121–22.

7. *Emporia News*, November 22, 29, December 13, 27, 1867.

8. Unrau, *Kansa Indians*, 209.

9. Spencer, "The Kaw," 375–76.

10. Ibid.

11. Stover to Murphy, May 17, 1867, May 14, 1868, LR, OIA, Kansas Agency; Kanza agent Forrest R. Page to Commissioner of Indian Affairs Lewis Bogy, LR, OIA, Kansas Agency, February 18, March 7, 1867.

12. Allegawaho, Fool Chief, and Watianga to Bogy, March 25, 1867, LR, OIA, Kansas Agency; Page to Murphy, November 27, 1866, LR, OIA, Kansas Agency.

13. *Emporia News*, April 5, 19, 1867; Page to Commissioner of Indian Affairs Nathaniel Taylor, April 10, 1867, LR, OIA, Kansas Agency; Allegawaho and chiefs to Taylor, May 27, 1867, LR, OIA, Kansas Agency; Stover to Murphy, June 6, 1867, LR, OIA, Kansas Agency; Murphy to Taylor, July 29, 1867, LR, OIA, Kansas Agency.

14. Murphy to Taylor, July 29, 1867, LR, OIA, Kansas Agency; Morehouse to George W. Martin, April 16, 1904, George P. Morehouse Papers.

15. Murphy to Taylor, June 13, 1867, LR, OIA, Kansas Agency; Farnsworth to Taylor, May 13, August 7, 1867, LR, OIA, Kansas Agency; Stover to Murphy, May 14, 1868, LR, OIA, Kansas Agency.

16. Stover to Murphy, December 30, 1867, LR, OIA, Kansas Agency; Berthrong, *Southern Cheyennes*, 296–97.

17. Stover to Murphy, December 27, 30, 1867, LR, OIA, Kansas Agency.

18. Stover to Murphy, November 16, 1867, LR, OIA, Kansas Agency; Murphy to Charles Mix, November 21, 1867, LR, OIA, Kansas Agency.

19. Stover to Murphy, November 16, December 5, 1867, LR, OIA, Kansas Agency; Murphy to Mix, November 21, 1867, LR, OIA, Kansas Agency; General Ulysses S. Grant to Secretary of the Interior J. D. Cox, December 2, 1867, LR, OIA, Kansas Agency; Raymond L. Welty, "The Policing of the Frontier by the Army," *KHQ* 7 (August 1938): 248.

20. Stover to Murphy, January 25, May 14, December 27, 1867, LR, OIA, Kansas Agency.

21. Stover to Murphy, December 27, 1867, LR, OIA, Kansas Agency; Berthrong, *Southern Cheyennes*, 299–302.

22. Sondra Van Meter, *Marion County Kansas Past and Present* (Hillsboro, Kans.: M. B. Publishing House, 1972), 15, 18; Andreas, *History of Kansas*, vol. 1, 1256; Thomas Huffaker, *Kansas State Record*, June 9, 1868; Morehouse, *The Kansa*, 36; *Kansas Daily Record*, June 6, 1868; *Junction City Union*, June 6, 1868; Berthrong, *Southern Cheyennes*, 304; William E. Unrau, *Mixed-Bloods and Tribal Dissolution: Charles Curtis and the Quest for Indian Identity* (Lawrence: University Press of Kansas, 1989), 72–73.

23. Unrau, *Mixed-Bloods*, 64, 66, 73–75; Samuel J. Crawford, *Kansas in the Sixties* (Chicago: A. C. McClurg, 1911), 288–89.

24. Huffaker, *Kansas State Record*, June 9, 1868; *Kansas Daily Record*, June 6, 1868; *Emporia News*, June 5, 1868; Maloy, *Morris County*, 59–60.

25. Huffaker, *Kansas State Record*, June 9, 1868; Haucke, "The Kaw," 49; Albert G. Boone to Murphy, June 4, 1868, LR, OIA, Kansas Agency.

26. *Emporia News*, June 12, 1868; "About the Indians," *Kansas State Record*, June 9, 1868; Huffaker, *Kansas State Record*, June 9, 1868; Stover to Murphy, June 13, 1868, LR, OIA, Kansas Agency; Stover in *RUSCIA* (1868), 261; Andreas, *History of Kansas*, vol. 1, 800–801; Morehouse, *The Kansa*, 36; Maloy, *Morris County*, 60; Indian agent Edward Wynkoop to Murphy, June 12, 1868, LR, OIA, Kansas Agency; Berthrong, *Southern Cheyennes*, 303–304.

27. Spencer, "The Kaw," 375.

28. *Junction City Union*, June 6, 1868; *Kansas State Record*, June 8, 1868; *Kansas Daily Record*, June 7, 1868; *Emporia News*, June 12, 1868; "About the Indians," *Kansas State Record*, June 9, 1868; Andreas, *History of Kansas*, vol. 1, 1256; Van Meter, *Marion County*, 15, 18; Jessie Perry Stratford, *Butler County's Eighty Years, 1855–1935* (El Dorado, Kans.: Butler County News, 1934), 24, 42; *Chase County Sketches*, vol. 1, 329; Thomas F. Doran, "Kansas Sixty Years Ago," *KHC* 15 (1919–22): 491; Morehouse, *The Kansa*, 36; Marvin H. Garfield, "Defense of the Kansas Frontier, 1868–1869," *KHQ* 1 (November 1932): 454–55.

29. Huffaker, *Kansas State Record*, June 9, 1868; Garfield, "Defense of the Kansas Frontier," 455; Berthrong, *Southern Cheyennes*, 304–306, 310, 326–28; George Armstrong Custer to Crosby, December 22, 1868, U.S. Senate, *Senate Executive Document No. 40*, 40th Cong., 3rd sess., 3; William E. Connelley, ed., "John McBee's Account of the Expedition of the Nineteenth Kansas," *KHC* 17 (1928): 369; Mrs. Frank C. Montgomery, "Fort Wallace and Its Relation to the Frontier," *KHC* 17 (1928): 237; *Junction City Union*, April 17, 1869.

30. General Alfred Sully to Colonel T. C. English, telegram, July 7, 1868, LR, OIA, Kansas Agency; Stover to Murphy, June 20, July 10, 15, 1868, LR, OIA, Kansas Agency; *Lawrence Daily Tribune*, July 16, 22, 1868; Captain M. Howard, Fort Riley, to Captain Martin Mullins, July 8, 1868, LR, OIA, Kansas Agency; Sac and Fox agent Albert Wiley to Stover, July 8, 1868, LR, OIA, Kansas Agency.

31. Stover to Murphy, July 10, 15, October 10, 1868; Stover in *RUSCIA* (1868), 261.

32. *Kansas State Record*, June 25, 1868; *Lawrence Daily Tribune*, July 14, August 2, 4, 5, 12, 1868; *Emporia News*, August 7, 1868.

33. Stover to Murphy, July 10, 15, October 10, 1868, LR, OIA, Kansas Agency; Stover in *RUSCIA* (1868), 261; Murphy to Taylor, August 5, November 14, 1868, LR, OIA, Kansas Agency; J. H. McWilliams to Charles Mix, August 6, 1868, LR, OIA, Kansas Agency; T. C. English to Adjutant General, U.S. Army, October 5, 1868, LR, OIA, Kansas Agency; Joab Spencer to Taylor, March 18, 1869, LR, OIA, Kansas Agency.

34. Allegawaho, chiefs, and others to "Our Father, Major E. S. Stover," February 12, 1869, LR, OIA, Kansas Agency.

35. Stover to Taylor, January 12, 1869; Stover to Murphy, March 6, 1869, LR, OIA, Kansas Agency; "Act of Congress for the Relief of the Kaw Indians in Kansas," March 3, 1869, LR, OIA, Kansas Agency; J. W. McMillan to Representative Benjamin F. Butler, March 9, 1869, LR, OIA, Kansas Agency; McMillan to commissioner of Indian Affairs, March 11, 1869, LR, OIA, Kansas Agency; Murphy to Taylor, March 11, 12, April 21, 1869, LR, OIA, Kansas Agency; Senator Pomeroy to Taylor, March 6, 1869, LR, OIA, Kansas Agency; Senator Ross to Taylor, March 5, 1869, LR, OIA, Kansas Agency; Spencer to Taylor, March 13, 1869, LR, OIA, Kansas Agency.

36. Page to Bogy, February 12, 1867, LR, OIA, Kansas Agency; *Emporia News*, January 26, February 2, 1867; *Junction City Union*, December 29, 1866, February 2, 16, 1867; Unratified Kanza Treaty of 1864.

37. Bradford Koplowitz, *Kaw Indian Census and Allotments* (Bowie, Md.: Heritage Books, 1996), 3; Dorsey, "Mourning and War Customs," 672–74; Robert Rankin, interview with author, August 6, 2012; Census and Appraisement, Kansa, 1862, LR, OIA, Kansas Agency; Kaw Census, October 3, 1868, LR, OIA, Kansas Agency; Morehouse, *The Kansa*, 29; Farnsworth to Dole, January 24, November 11, 1863, LR, OIA, Kansas Agency; Kanza chiefs to Bogy, February 28, 1867, LR, OIA, Kansas Agency.

38. Spencer, "The Kaw," 382; Morehouse, *The Kansa*, 29; Addison Stubbs, "Historical Facts Pertaining to the Kaw or Kansas Indians," script of talk given August 12, 1925, Addison W. Stubbs Papers, box 1, Kansas Historical Society, 9; Maloy, *Morris County*, 24.

39. Morehouse, *The Kansa*, 29–30; Haucke, "The Kaw," 40; Brake, *On Two Continents*, 203; Alan Coville, "Incidents Relative to the Early History"; Addison Stubbs, "Material concerning Kansas Indians," 4; Mosher, "Lyon County Historical Museum," 18.

40. Branch, "Traders' Debts," July 12, 1862, LR, OIA, Kansas Agency.

41. Unratified Kanza Treaty of 1867, "Documents relating to the negotiation of an unratified treaty of February 13, 1867, with the Kaw Indians and the Sauk and Fox of Missouri Indians" (February 13, 1867), http://digital.library.wisc.edu/ (accessed October 13, 2011), 5, 21, 26, 40, 47–48.

42. Ibid., 98–108.

43. *Junction City Union*, March 23, 1867; *Emporia News*, February 22, 1867.

44. Gates, *Fifty Million Acres*, 148–50; Unrau, "Council Grove Merchants," 277–80; Sam Wood to Dole, April 7, 1863, LR, OIA, Kansas Agency; Unrau, "Indian Water Rights to the Middle Arkansas: The Case for the Kaws," *Kansas History* 5 (Spring

1982): 57, 60; Abel, "Extinction of Reservation Titles," 98–99; Maloy, *Morris County*, 42–44, 54; *Junction City Union*, quote from *Topeka Record*, March 23, 1867; *Emporia News*, February 8, 1867; Hoag in *RUSCIA* (1869), 359.

45. Maloy, *Morris County*, 42–44, 57, 66–67; Farnsworth to Dole, July 22, 1867, LR, OIA, Kansas Agency; Blacklidge to Dole, April 17, 1863, LR, OIA, Kansas Agency; Murphy to Mix, November 16, 1867, LR, OIA, Kansas Agency.

46. Branch, List of Kanza Traders' Debts, July 12, 1862, LR, OIA, Kansas Agency; Farnsworth to Dole, January 20, 1863, LR, OIA, Kansas Agency; U.S. House of Representatives, *Report of Kaw Commission and Estimate of Appropriation for Settlement of Certain Claims*, H.R. document no. 169, 58th Cong., 3rd sess. (1905), 24, 26, 27, 32, 35; Unratified Kanza Treaty of 1869, "Documents relating to the negotiation of an unratified treaty of March 13, 1869, with the Kaw Indians" (March 13, 1869), http://digital.library.wisc.edu/ (accessed October 13, 2011), 29.

47. "Down the Neosho!," *Junction City Union*, August 31, 1867.

48. Ibid.

49. Ibid.

50. William G. Robbins, *Colony and Empire: The Capitalist Transformation of the American West* (Lawrence: University Press of Kansas, 1994), 77, 171.

51. *Emporia News*, October 10, 1869; Stevens, *Thunderbolt*, 62.

52. Unratified Kanza Treaty of 1869, 25, 28–30; Gates, *Fifty Million Acres*, 117–20, 128–31, 136–38.

53. *Emporia News*, May 19, July 23, 1869; Stevens to Cox, June 12, 1869, LR, OIA, Kansas Agency; Kanza chiefs and Joab Spencer, contract, May 15, 1869, LR, OIA, Kansas Agency; Stover to Superintendent Enoch Hoag, July 1, 1869, LR, OIA, Kansas Agency.

54. Stevens and Hoag, Contract, July 14, 1869, LR, OIA, Kansas Agency; Hoag to Commissioner of Indian Affairs Ely Parker, August 12, 1869, LR, OIA, Kansas Agency; Kanza agent Mahlon Stubbs to Hoag, September 1, October 1, 1869, LR, OIA, Kansas Agency.

55. Hard Hart and Kanza chiefs to Denver, July 22, 1857, LR, OIA, Kansas Agency; Farnsworth to Dole, July 28, 1863, LR, OIA, Kansas Agency; Page to Murphy, November 15, 27, 28, 1867, LR, OIA, Kansas Agency; Allegawaho, Fool Chief, and Watianga to Bogy, February 28, 1867, LR, OIA, Kansas Agency; Farnsworth to Bogy, March 6, 1867, LR, OIA, Kansas Agency; Huffaker to Bogy, March 6, 1867, LR, OIA, Kansas Agency; Addison Stubbs, "Kansas Indians: Address Delivered by Addison W. Stubbs at the Reunion," 9–10; Addison Stubbs, "Historical Facts Pertaining to the Kaw," 7–8.

56. Ties Delivered on Kaw Reserve (n.d.), LR, OIA, Kansas Agency; Hoag to Parker, February 14, May 4, 1871, LR, OIA, Kansas Agency; Hoag to Commissioner of Indian Affairs Francis A. Walker, June 4, 1872, LR, OIA, Kansas Agency; Stevens and Hoag, contract, July 14, 1868, LR, OIA, Kansas Agency.

57. "Notice for Railroad Ties," *Emporia News*, August 13, 1869; Stubbs to Hoag, March 4, 1871, LR, OIA, Central Superintendency, 1871; Hoag to Walker, June 4,

1872, LR, OIA, Kansas Agency; Kanza chiefs and councilmen to Hoag, March 15, 1871, LR, OIA, Kansas Agency; Kanza chiefs and Joab Spencer, contract, May 15, 1869, LR, OIA, Kansas Agency; Stevens to Hoag, May 22, 1872, LR, OIA, Kansas Agency; Hoag and Stevens, contract, July 14, 1868, LR, OIA, Kansas Agency; U.S. House of Representatives, *Report of Kaw Commission*, 47.

58. Allegawaho to Hoag, June 24, 1872, LR, OIA, Kansas Agency.

59. U.S. House of Representatives, *Report of Kaw Commission*, 47.

60. *Emporia News*, October 29, 1869; *Kansas State Record*, October 29, 1869.

61. *Emporia News*, March 29, 1867.

62. *Emporia News*, January 29, February 26, July 2, August 6, 20, November 5, 1869; Maloy, *Morris County*, 63; Conn to Custer & Kimball, Warranty Deed, Register of Deeds, Morris County Courthouse, August 4, 1869. In 1881, Custer's widow, Elizabeth, sold the property for $1,976.

63. *RUSCIA* (1870), 259–60, 274, 333, 341; Maloy, *Morris County*, 61; Morehouse, "Kaw Trail," 208–209; *RUSCIA* (1866), 53, 274, 346, 364; *RUSCIA* (1867), 378, 388, 396; *RUSCIA* (1868), 256, 259, 260–62, 355, 364–65; *RUSCIA* (1869), 360, 378, 470. Maloy mistakenly places the celebration in the spring of 1869.

64. Dixon, "Furthering Their Own Demise," 479, 486–87.

65. Kanza Language Project, *Kanza Clan Book*, 5, 9–11; Dorsey, "Kansa Ethnographic and Linguistic Notes," Dorsey Papers; Skinner, *Kansa Organizations*, 747.

66. Mead, *Hunting and Trading*, 87; Farnham, *Travels in the Great Western Prairies*, 15.

67. Mead, *Hunting and Trading*, 78; Addison Stubbs, "Indian Hunters," Manuscript (n.d.), Addison W. Stubbs Papers, box 1, Kansas Historical Society, 2–3.

68. Stover to Murphy, May 14, 1868, LR, OIA, Kansas Agency; Allegawaho and chiefs to J. W. McMillan, July 14, 1870, LR, OIA, Kansas Agency; *Chase County Historical Sketches*, vol. 1, 15; John Madden, "Along the Trail," *KHC* 8 (1903–1904): 70; Van Meter, *Marion County*, 16, 21; *Emporia News*, January 28, February 4, 1860.

69. Morehouse, "Along the Kaw Trail," 206–208; Government Land Office, "Survey Notes and Maps," 1857–61.

70. Morehouse, "Along the Kaw Trail," 207–208; Government Land Office, "Survey Notes and Maps," 1857–61.

71. Morehouse, "Along the Kaw Trail," 207–209; *RUSCIA* (1869), 461, 463, 470.

72. Mead, *Hunting and Trading*, 71, 90, 102, 104; Farnsworth to Dole, January 1, 1865, LR, OIA, Kansas Agency; T. C. Henry, *Dickinson County Chronicle*, July 14, 1876; Edna Nyquist, *Pioneer Life and Lore of McPherson County, Kansas* (McPherson: Democrat-Opinion Press, 1932): 13–14; Government Land Office, notes and maps of the original Government Land Office surveys of Kansas, March 1861.

73. Mead, *Hunting and Trading*, 85; Farnham, *Travels in the Great Western Prairies*, 15; Addison Stubbs, "Material concerning Kansas Indians," 1; Stover, October 10, 1868, LR, OIA, Kansas Agency; Morehouse, "Along the Kaw Trail," 207; Joseph V. Hickey, *Ghost Settlement on the Prairie: A Biography of Thurman, Kansas* (Lawrence: University Press of Kansas, 1995), 152; White, *Roots of Dependency*, 182.

74. Allegawaho and chiefs to McMillan, July 14, 1870, LR, OIA, Kansas Agency.

8. THE DARKEST PERIOD

1. Robert M. Utley, *The Indian Frontier 1846–1890* (Albuquerque: University of New Mexico Press, 1984), 131–32; Nicholson, "Tour of Indian Agencies," 289–93.

2. Nicholson, "Tour of Indian Agencies," 295–96.

3. Ibid., 296–97.

4. Ibid., 294.

5. Ibid., 295–96.

6. Ibid., 297–99.

7. Ibid., 299–300.

8. Ibid., 300.

9. Ibid., 296; Morgan, *Indian Journals*, 92; Spencer, "The Kaw," 378; *Warneke Stories*; *Council Grove Press*, May 19, 1861; Mosher, *Lyon County Historical Museum*, 65.

10. Morgan, *Indian Journals*, 92; Skinner, *Kansa Organizations*, 772; "Letters from Indian Missions," 263.

11. J. V. Brower, *Memoirs of Explorations in the Basin of the Mississippi*, vol. 1, *Quivira* (St. Paul, Minn.: n.p., 1898), 52–53; J. H. Watson, "A Trip to the Great Plains," *Emporia News*, August 18, 1860.

12. Morgan, *Indian Journals*, 90; Tate, *Indians and Emigrants*, 137–39.

13. Horsman, *Race and Manifest Destiny*, 43–61, 116–38.

14. Louise Barry, ed., "Overland to the Gold Fields of California in 1852: The Journal of John Hawkins Clark," *KHQ* 11 (August 1942): 242; Oertel, *Bleeding Borders*, 10; Albert K. Weinberg, *Manifest Destiny: A Study of Nationalist Expansionism in American History* (Baltimore: Johns Hopkins Press, 1935), 72–90; Tate, *Indians and Emigrants*, 205–208.

15. Dorsey, "Mourning and War Customs," 670–80.

16. Nicholson, "Tour of Indian Agencies," 295–96; Unrau, "The Depopulation of the Dheghia-Siouan Kansa," *New Mexico Historical Review* 48 (October 1973): 322.

17. Stubbs to Hoag, October 1, 1869, July 23, 1870, July 16, October 9, 1871, LR, OIA, Kansas Agency; Bradford and Neal, physicians' bill, January 1, 1871, LR, OIA, Kansas Agency; Andreas, *History of Kansas*, vol. 2, 805; Farnsworth to Dole, June 18, 1862, January 20, 1863, LR, OIA, Kansas Agency; Stover to Murphy, July 26, 1867, LR, OIA, Kansas Agency.

18. Mahlon Stubbs, response to medical circular, July 1873, LR, OIA, Kansas Agency; Stubbs to Hoag, November 13, 1871, LR, OIA, Kansas Agency.

19. Stubbs to Hoag, January 8, March 18, December 2, 1872, LR, OIA, Kansas Agency; Stubbs, medical circular, July 1873, LR, OIA, Kansas Agency; Dorsey, *Study of Siouan Cults*, 418–19.

20. *RUSCIA* (1868), 355; *RUSCIA* (1873), 334.

21. Stubbs to Hoag, January 10, 1871, LR, OIA, Central Superintendency, 1871; *RUSCIA* (1870), 274, 333.

22. Stubbs, *RUSCIA* (1869), 377; Stubbs, *RUSCIA* (1870), 274; Stover to Murphy, January 5, 1869, LR, OIA, Kansas Agency; Stubbs to Hoag, September 1, 1869, January 23, 1871, LR, OIA, Kansas Agency; Nicholson, "Tour of Indian Agencies," 297.

23. Stubbs to Hoag, February 16, 1871, LR, OIA, Central Superintendency, 1871; *RUSCIA* (1871), 495, 612, 662; school superintendent Nathan Pinson to Stubbs, October 14, 1871, LR, OIA, Kansas Agency; *RUSCIA* (1872), 232, 387, 435.

24. *RUSCIA* (1872), 387; Allegawaho and chiefs to McMillan, July 14, 1870, LR, OIA, Kansas Agency; Allegawaho to "My Friends," May 22, 1871, LR, OIA, Kansas Agency.

25. *RUSCIA* (1872), 32; Hoag to Walker, May 29, 1872, February 2, 1873, LR, OIA, Kansas Agency; Stubbs to Hoag, December 2, 1872, August 18, 1873, LR, OIA, Kansas Agency; school superintendent Uriah Spray to Stubbs, (n.d.), LR, OIA, Kansas Agency; *RUSCIA* (1873), 201–202, 334–35; Kanza agent Isaac T. Gibson, *RUSCIA* (1874), 228.

26. Spencer, "The Kaw," 380–81.

27. Ibid.

28. Ibid.

29. Donald J. Wishart, *An Unspeakable Sadness: The Dispossession of the Nebraska Indians* (Lincoln: University of Nebraska Press, 1994), 32; Francis La Flesche, *War Ceremony and Peace Ceremony of the Osage Indians*, U.S. Bureau of American Ethnology Bulletin 101 (Washington, D.C.: Government Printing Office, 1939), 204; Weltfish, *Lost Universe*, 31, 175–76; Fletcher and La Flesche, *The Omaha Tribe* 2, 376–401; Rollings, *The Osage*, 37; Donald J. Blakeslee, "The Origin and Spread of the Calumet Ceremony," *American Antiquity* 46 (October 1981): 759–68.

30. Wishart, *Unspeakable Sadness*, 75, 91–93, 131, 180–81, 190–91.

31. Stubbs in *RUSCIA* (1870), 274; Stubbs to Hoag, February 1, 1870, LR, OIA, Kansas Agency; *Junction City Union*, January 8, 1870; Addison Stubbs, "Grant's Peace Policy," Manuscript, (n.d.), Addison W. Stubbs Papers, box 1, Kansas Historical Society, p. 17; Addison Stubbs, "Life of Mahlon Stubbs," 2; *Junction City Union*, April 8, 1871; Berthrong, *Southern Cheyennes*, 342–43, 351–52, 358, 361–62, 364.

32. *Junction City Union*, August 28, 1869; Stubbs to Hoag, October 1, 1869, LR, OIA, Kansas Agency; H. Craig Miner and William E. Unrau, *The End of Indian Kansas: A Study of Cultural Revolution, 1854–1871* (1978, repr., Lawrence: University Press of Kansas, 1990), 100–101.

33. Stover to Hoag, July 1, 1869, LR, OIA, Kansas Agency; William T. Hagan, *The Sac and Fox Indians* (Norman: University of Oklahoma Press, 1958): 229–30, 238–44; Joseph B. Herring, *The Enduring Indians of Kansas: A Century and a Half of Acculturation* (Lawrence: University Press of Kansas, 1990), 100; Miner and Unrau, *End of Indian Kansas*, 105, 137.

34. U.S. Bureau of the Census, "Population of States and Counties of the United States: 1790–1990," http://www.ipsr.ku.edu/ksdata/ksah/population/2pop16.pdf (accessed November 1, 2011); Allegawaho and chiefs to McMillan, July 14, 1870, LR, OIA, Kansas Agency.

35. A. C. Farnham, chief clerk, Central Superintendency of Indian Affairs, to Commissioner of Indian Affairs Ely Parker, June 1, 1870, LR, OIA, Kansas Agency; Stubbs to Farnham, June 7, 1870, LR, OIA, Kansas Agency.

36. Lt. Gov. Eskridge to Senator Pomeroy, "An Open Letter," *Emporia Tribune*, May 18, 1870; Penny T. Linsenmayer, "A Study of Laura Ingalls Wilder's *Little House on the Prairie*," *Kansas History* 24 (Autumn 2001): 174; *Emporia News*, May 20, 1870.

37. *Junction City Union*, June 25, 1870, quote from *Topeka Commonwealth*.

38. Stubbs to Hoag, March 2, 27, 1871, LR, OIA, Kansas Agency; Levi Parsons to Parker, March 16, 1871, LR, OIA, Kansas Agency; *Junction City Union*, March 11, 1871; Stubbs to Hoag, March 4, June 16, 1871, LR, OIA, Central Superintendency, 1871.

39. G. M. Simcock and "committee of citizens" to Secretary of the Interior Columbus Delano, c. April 1871, LR, OIA, Kansas Agency; *RUSCIA* (1879), 183; Parker to Delano, March 27, 1871, LR, OIA, Kansas Agency; Delano to Parker, April 29, 1871, LR, OIA, Kansas Agency.

40. Allegawaho to "My Friends," April 22, 1871, LR, OIA, Kansas Agency; Stubbs to Hoag, June 19, 1871, LR, OIA, Kansas Agency.

41. Allegawaho and chiefs to Hoag, October 3, 1871, LR, OIA, Kansas Agency.

42. Hoag to Delano, October 24, 1871, LR, OIA, Kansas Agency; *Junction City Union*, October 14, November 11, 1871; Delano to acting commissioner of Indian Affairs H. K. Clum, October 31, 1871, LR, OIA, Kansas Agency.

43. Allegawaho and chiefs to Hoag, October 3, 1871, LR, OIA, Central Superintendency, 1871; Stubbs in *RUSCIA* (1871), 495.

44. Prucha, *Great Father*, 165–66; *Council Grove Democrat*, May 9, 16, 1871.

45. *Council Grove Democrat*, April 25, 1872; Addison Stubbs, "Material Concerning Kansas Indians," 4.

46. Addison Stubbs, "Historical Facts Pertaining to the Kaw," 8; Stubbs, "Questionnaire," answer no. 18, Addison W. Stubbs Papers, box 1, Kansas Historical Society; *Council Grove Democrat*, April 25, 1872.

47. Addison Stubbs, "Historical Address Delivered by Addison W. Stubbs at the Reunion," 9.

48. Stubbs, "Questionnaire," answers no. 19 and 20; Addison Stubbs, "Historical Facts Pertaining to the Kaw or Kansas Indians," 9–10.

49. Hoag to Walker, June 25, 1872, LR, OIA, Kansas Agency; Allegawaho to Hoag, speech, June 24, 1872, LR, OIA, Kansas Agency.

50. Hoag to Walker, June 25, 1872, LR, OIA, Kansas Agency; Allegawaho, chiefs, and councilmen to President Ulysses S. Grant, June 24, 1872, LR, OIA, Kansas Agency; *Junction City Union*, July 13, 1872.

51. Stubbs in *RUSCIA* (1870), 274, 341.

52. Nicholson, "Tour of Indian Agencies," manuscript, (n.d.), Addison W. Stubbs Papers, box 1, Kansas Historical Society, 10; Morehouse, "The Kansa," 35; Waldo Wedel, "Prehistory and Environment in the Central Great Plains," *Transactions of the Kansas Academy of Science* 50 (June 1947): 7–8; Say in James, Say, and Long, *Account of an Expedition*, 123; Dorsey, *Study of Siouan Cults*, 418.

53. Riley, *Confronting Race*, 89–94; Oertel, *Bleeding Borders*, 35; Alice B. Kehoe, "The Shackles of Tradition," in *The Hidden Half: Studies of Plains Indian Women*, eds. Patricia Albers and Beatrice Medicine (New York: University Press of America, 1983), 69; Robert H. Lowie, *Indians of the Plains* (Garden City, N.Y.: American Museum of Natural History, 1965), 80–81; Sam Dicks, ed., "'A Sower Went Forth': Lyman Beecher Kellogg and Kansas State Normal," *Kansas History* 24 (Winter 2001–2002): 268.

54. *RUSCIA* (1871), 495, 622; Stubbs to Hoag, April 28, June 3, 1870, January 30, 1871, LR, OIA, Kansas Agency; Allegawaho and chiefs to Hoag, March 15, 1871, LR, OIA, Kansas Agency.

55. *Marion County Record*, November 11, December 9, 1871; Stubbs to Hoag, December 15, 1871, January 12, 1872, LR, OIA, Kansas Agency.

56. Stubbs to Hoag, March 18, 1872, LR, OIA, Kansas Agency; Hoag to Walker, May 10, June 28, 1872, LR, OIA, Kansas Agency; Stubbs in *RUSCIA* (1872), 232; Hoag in *RUSCIA* (1872), 227.

57. Stubbs in *RUSCIA* (1872), 232; Stubbs to Hoag, December 2, 1872, LR, OIA, Kansas Agency.

58. Stubbs to Hoag, December 2, 18, 1872, January 11, 1873, LR, OIA, Kansas Agency; *Council Grove Democrat*, December 26, 1872, February 25, 1873; Hoag to Walker, January 11, 1873, LR, OIA, Kansas Agency; Delano to the acting commissioner of Indian Affairs, March 22, 1873, LR, OIA, Kansas Agency.

59. *Junction City Union*, January 13, 1872; *Council Grove Democrat*, November 16, December 21, 28, 1871, February 22, 29, May 9, 1872; Maloy, *Morris County*, 67; special commissioner T. C. Jones to Commissioner of Indian Affairs Edward P. Smith, September 16, 1873, LR, OIA, Kansas Agency.

60. *Council Grove Democrat*, April 18, November 28, 1872, February 13, 20, 1873; Maloy, *Morris County*, 70–71.

61. *Council Grove Democrat*, February 26, 1873; Maloy, *Morris County*, 54–55, 79; Brigham, *Story of Council Grove*, 13.

62. Arthur M. Schlesinger, Jr., ed., *The Almanac of American History* (New York: Putnam, 1983), 324–25; Maloy, *Morris County*, 77, 79; "Letter from North Morris," *Council Grove Democrat*, November 18, 1874, February 4, 1875.

63. Hoag to Walker, January 3, 1873, LR, OIA, Kansas Agency; Stubbs to Walker, December 28, 1872, LR, OIA, Kansas Agency; T. C. Jones to Edward P. Smith, September 16, 1873, LR, OIA, Kansas Agency.

64. Stubbs to Walker, December 18, 1872, LR, OIA, Kansas Agency.

65. *RUSCIA* (1873), 22; *Junction City Union*, March 22, 1873; *Council Grove Democrat*, April 1, 1873; Stubbs to Hoag, May 13, 15, 1873, LR, OIA, Kansas Agency.

66. Maloy, *Morris County*, 75–76.

67. *Council Grove Democrat*, June 3, 1873.

68. Addison Stubbs, "Material Concerning Kansas Indians," 6–7.

69. Stubbs in *RUSCIA* (1873), 202, 334; Addison Stubbs, "Material Concerning Kansas Indians," 6; *Walnut Valley Times* (El Dorado, Kansas), June 13, 1873.

70. Maloy, *Morris County*, 74.

71. U.S. House of Representatives, *Report of Kaw Commission*, 14; Hoag to Delano, August 9, 1873, LR, OIA, Kansas Agency.

72. Jones to Smith, September 16, 1873, LR, OIA, Kansas Agency; Smith in *RUSCIA* (1873), 15, 23.

73. U.S. House of Representatives, *Report of Kaw Commission*, 15; Indian agent Cyrus Beede to Superintendent William Nicholson, April 13, 1877, LR, OIA, Osage and Kansas Agencies.

74. Stubbs to Hoag, August 10, 1871, LR, OIA, Central Superintendency, 1871; Kanza and Osage agent L. J. Miles in *RUSCIA* (1882), 72; Joseph James to Judge Thos. Hofacre [Huffaker], Dorsey Papers.

Bibliography

ARCHIVAL COLLECTIONS AND GOVERNMENT DOCUMENTS

Annual Report of the United States Commissioner of Indian Affairs. Washington, D.C.: Government Printing Office, 1845–74, 1879, 1884.

Census of the Territory of Kansas, 1859. "Morris County." Archives, Kansas Historical Society.

Census Roll and Appraisement. Kansas Tribe, 1862, Record Group 75 (R 445), National Archives and Records Administration, Washington, D.C.

Deed Records. Morris County Register of Deeds. Morris County Courthouse, Council Grove, Kansas.

First Census, State Of Kansas, 1865. "Morris County." Council Grove (Kansas) Public Library. Microfilm.

Fort Leavenworth Records. "Consolidated Morning Reports, March, 1862–December, 1864." Roll no. 803.01. Records loaned to Kansas Historical Society by the Fort Leavenworth Museum, Fort Leavenworth, Kansas.

Government Land Office. Notes and maps of the original Government Land Office surveys of Kansas. Kansas Society of Land Surveyors. 33 disc set. Duke West Interactive Graphics, Inc., Leavenworth.

James Owen Dorsey Papers, Kansa (c. 1882). National Anthropological Archives, Smithsonian Institution, Washington, D.C.

Kansas Historical Society
William E. Connelley Papers.
Alan M. Coville Papers.
Thomas S. Huffaker Papers.
Maxine L. Kinton Papers.
George P. Morehouse Papers.
Joseph H. Newby Papers.
Robert S. Stevens Papers.

Addison W. Stubbs Papers.

Samuel N. Wood Papers.

Kaw Mission State Historic Site

Davis, Gordon F. Letter to "Old Kaw Mission," June 26, 1960.

Huffaker Genealogical Papers.

McClintock, Kenneth. Unpublished papers.

Mosher, Orville Watson, Jr. Compilation of Kanza-related articles, 1950–67, published in *Emporia Gazette*, Lyon County Historical Museum.

Pankratz, Herb, and Mike Ruppert. Archeological survey field notes about Kaw Reservation area, July 18, 1974.

Kaw Reservation camp. Post Returns, June 1868. Company E, 5th Infantry. (M 617, R 1517) MS 683. National Archives and Records Administration, Washington, D.C.

Letters Received, Office of Indian Affairs (RG 75, M 234). National Archives and Records Administration, Washington, D.C.

Central Superintendency (M 856, R 34). "Letters Received Relating to the Cherokee, Choctaw and Chickasaw, Creek, Kansas (Kaw), Kickapoo, Kiowa, and Neosho (the Indian Territory and Kansas) Agencies," 1871.

Fort Leavenworth Agency, 1824–48 (R 300–302).

Kansas Agency, 1851–73 (R 364–369).

Osage River Agency (R 643–644).

Potawatomie Agency, 1851–60 (R 678–681).

Sac and Fox Agency, 1861 (R 440).

Schools, 1850–52 (R 785–786).

St. Louis Superintendency, 1824–1851 (R 74).

"Luke F. Parson's Diary—1859, 1860, 1861." Manuscript. Kansas Collection. Salina (Kansas) Public Library.

Porter, Julia Shellabarger. "My Grandmother, from the Record of Christina Phillips Campbell." Manuscript. Kansas Collection. Salina (Kansas) Public Library.

Smith, Frank A. "Tomah-Shinga." N.d., Geary County Historical Museum archives, Junction City, Kansas.

Stevens Family Papers, #1210. Division of Rare and Manuscript Collections. Cornell University Library, Ithaca, New York.

Territorial Census, 1855, District 8. Kansas Historical Society. Available at www.territorialkansasonline.org/ (item no. 102171).

Unratified Kanza Treaty of 1864. "Documents relating to the negotiation of an unratified treaty of June 11, 1864, with the Kaw Indians" (June 11, 1864), http://digicoll.library.wisc.edu/ (accessed December 21, 2012).

Unratified Kanza Treaty of 1867. "Documents relating to the negotiation of an unratified treaty of February 13, 1867, with the Kaw Indians and the Sauk and Fox of Missouri Indians" (February 13, 1867), http://digital.library.wisc.edu/ (accessed October 13, 2011).

Unratified Kanza Treaty of 1869. "Documents relating to the negotiation of an unratified treaty of March 13, 1869, with the Kaw Indians" (March 13, 1869), http:// digital.library.wisc.edu/ (accessed October 13, 2011).

U.S. Bureau of the Census. "Morris County." In *Eighth Census of the United States, 1860*. Washington, D.C.: Government Printing Office, 1864. Council Grove (Kansas) Public Library. Microfilm.

U.S. Bureau of the Census. "Population of States and Counties of the United States: 1790–1990." Available at Institute for Policy and Social Research, University of Kansas, http://www.ipsr.ku.edu/ksdata/ksah/population/2pop16.pdf (accessed November 1, 2011).

U.S. House of Representatives. *Report of Kaw Commission and Estimate of Appropriation for Settlement of Certain Claims*. H.R. document no. 169, 58th Cong., 3rd sess., 1905.

U.S. Senate. "Appendix." In *Doolittle Commission Report*. Senate Report no. 156, 39th Cong., 2d sess., serial 1279, 1867.

U.S. Senate. *Senate Executive Document No. 40*. 40th Cong., 3rd sess., 1868.

Warneke Stories. Undated manuscript compiled by the descendants of John and Barbara Warneke. Courtesy of Ken and Shirley McClintock, Council Grove, Kansas.

BOOKS, ARTICLES, AND THESES

Abel, Anna Heloise. "Indian Reservations in Kansas and the Extinguishment of Their Title." *Kansas Historical Collections* 8 (1903–1904): 72–109.

Adams, David Wallace. *Education for Extinction: American Indians and the Boarding School Experience, 1875–1928*. Lawrence: University Press of Kansas, 1995.

Adams, Franklin G., ed. "Reminiscences of Frederick Chouteau." *Kansas Historical Collections* 8 (1903–1904): 423–34.

Albers, Patricia C., and Beatrice Medicine, eds. *The Hidden Half: Studies of Plains Indian Women*. New York: University Press of America, 1983.

Albrecht, Glenn. "Psychoterratic Conditions in a Scientific and Technological World." In *Ecopsychology: Science, Totems, and the Technological Species*, edited by Peter H. Kahn, Jr., and Patricia H. Hasbach, 255–57. Cambridge: MIT Press, 2012.

Andreas, Alfred Thayer, with William G. Cutler. *The History of the State of Kansas*. 2 vols. 1883. Reprint, Atchison, Kans.: Atchison County Historical Society, 1976.

"Apparent Per Capita Alcohol Consumption: National, State, and Regional Trends, 1850–2007," National Institute on Alcohol Abuse and Alcoholism, http://pubs .niaaa.nih.gov/publications/survelliance87/CONS07.pdf (accessed December 12, 2012), data from Merton M. Hyman, M. Zimmerman, C. Gurioli, and A. Helrich, *Drinkers, Drinking and Alcohol-Related Mortality and Hospitalizations: A Statistical Compendium* (New Brunswick, N.J.: Rutgers University, 1980).

Bailey, Garrick A., ed. *The Osage and the Invisible World: From the Works of Francis La Flesche.* Norman: University of Oklahoma Press, 1995.

Barnes, Lela, ed. "Letters of Allen T. Ward, 1842–1851: From the Shawnee and Kaw (Methodist) Missions." *Kansas Historical Quarterly* 33 (Autumn 1967): 321–76.

Barry, Louise. *The Beginning of the West: Annals of the Kansas Gateway to the American West.* Topeka: Kansas State Historical Society, 1972.

———. "The Kansas Indians and the Census of 1843." *Kansas Historical Quarterly* 39 (Winter 1973): 478–90.

Baughman, Robert W. *Kansas in Maps.* Topeka: Kansas State Historical Society, 1961.

Berkhofer, Robert F., Jr. *Salvation and the Savage: An Analysis of Protestant Missions and American Indian Response, 1787–1862.* Lexington: University of Kentucky Press, 1965.

Berry, Thomas Senior. *Western Prices before 1861: A Study of the Cincinnati Market.* Cambridge: Harvard University Press, 1943.

Berthrong, Donald J. *The Southern Cheyennes.* Norman: University of Oklahoma Press, 1963.

Bieber, Ralph P., ed. *Journal of a Soldier under Kearny and Doniphan, 1846–1847.* Glendale, Calif.: Arthur H. Clark, 1935.

———, ed. *Southern Trails to California in 1849.* Glendale, Calif.: Arthur H. Clark, 1937.

Blakeslee, Donald J. *Holy Ground, Healing Water: Cultural Landscapes at Waconda Lake, Kansas.* College Station: Texas A&M University Press, 2010.

———. "The Origin and Spread of the Calumet Ceremony." *American Antiquity* 46 (October 1981): 759–68.

Boynton, C. B., and T. B. Mason. *A Journey through Kansas Describing the Country, Climate, Soil, Minerals, Manufacturing, and Other Resources.* Cincinnati: Moore, Wilstach, Keys, 1855.

Brake, Hezekiah. *On Two Continents: A Long Life's Experience.* Topeka, Kans.: printed by author, 1896.

Brigham, Lalla Maloy. *The Story of Council Grove on the Santa Fe Trail.* 1921. Reprint, Council Grove, Kans.: Morris County Historical Society, n.d.

Brooks, Clinton E., and Frank D. Reeve, eds. *Forts and Forays: James A. Bennett, A Dragoon in New Mexico, 1850–1856.* Albuquerque: University of New Mexico Press, 1948.

Brower, J. V. *Memoirs of Explorations in the Basin of the Mississippi.* Vol. 1, *Quivira.* St. Paul, Minn., 1898.

Bryant, Edwin. *Rocky Mountain Adventures.* New York: Hurst, 1885.

Buchanan, Rex, ed. *Kansas Geology.* Lawrence: University Press of Kansas, 1984.

Buchanan, Rex, and James R. McCauley. *Roadside Kansas.* Lawrence: University Press of Kansas, 1987.

Buckley, Jay H. *William Clark: Indian Diplomat.* Norman: University of Oklahoma Press, 2008.

Burns, Louis. *A History of the Osage People.* Tuscaloosa: University of Alabama Press, 2004.

Bushnell, David I., Jr. "Villages of the Algonquian, Siouan, and Caddoan Tribes West of the Mississippi." *Bureau of American Ethnology Bulletin 77* (1922): 89–97.

Caldwell, Martha B. *Annals of the Shawnee Methodist Mission*. 1939. Reprint, Topeka: Kansas State Historical Society, 1977.

Castel, Albert. *A Frontier State at War: Kansas 1861–1865*. Ithaca, N.Y.: Cornell University Press, 1958.

Chalfant, William Y. *Cheyennes and Horse Soldiers: The 1857 Expedition and the Battle of Solomon's Fork*. Norman: University of Oklahoma Press, 2002.

———. *Dangerous Passage: The Santa Fe Trail and the Mexican War*. Norman: University of Oklahoma Press, 1994.

———. *Hancock's War: Conflict on the Southern Plains*. Norman: University of Oklahoma Press, 2010.

Chaput, Donald. "Generals, Indian Agents, Politicians: The Doolittle Survey of 1865." *Western Historical Quarterly* 3 (July 1972): 269–82.

Chase County Historical Sketches. Volume 1. N.p.: Chase County (Kansas) Historical Society, 1940.

Chittenden, Hiram Martin and Alfred Talbot Richardson, eds. *Life, Letters, and Travels of Father Pierre-Jean De Smet, S. J. 1801–1878*, volume 1. 1905. Reprint, New York: Kraus Reprint, 1961.

Clapsaddle, David. "Conflict and Commerce on the Santa Fe Trail: The Fort Riley–Fort Larned Road, 1860–1867." *Kansas History* 16 (Summer 1993): 124–37.

———. "End of the Trail: Rail-Roads, Commission Houses, and Independent Freighters." *Wagon Tracks* 23 (February 2009): 22–24.

———. "For Whom the Bell Tolls?" *Wagon Tracks* 21 (August 2007): 6–7.

———. "Four Foot Soldiers on the Trail: An Illinois Odyssey." *Wagon Tracks* 22 (November 2007): 19–24.

———. "A Frail Thin Line: Trading Establishments on the Santa Fe Trail, Part I." *Wagon Tracks* 24 (February 2010): 21–26.

———. "A Frail Thin Line: Trading Establishments on the Santa Fe Trail, Part II." *Wagon Tracks* 24 (May 2010): 14–23.

Claycomb, William B. "James Brown: Forgotten Trail Freighter." *Wagon Tracks* 8 (February 1994): 4–6.

Clifton, James. *The Prairie People: Continuity and Change in Potawatomi Indian Culture, 1665–1965*. Iowa City: University of Iowa Press, 1977.

Cole, Fannie E. "The Kansas Indians in Shawnee County after 1855." *Kansas Historical Collections* 8 (1903–1904): 481–83.

Connelley, William E. "The First Provisional Constitution of Kansas." *Kansas Historical Collections* 6 (1900): 97–113.

———. "John McBee's Account of the Expedition of the Nineteenth Kansas." *Kansas Historical Collections* 17 (1926–28): 361–74.

Crawford, Samuel J. *Kansas in the Sixties*. Chicago: A. C. McClurg, 1911.

Crease, Craig. "Boom Times for Freighting on the Santa Fe Trail 1848–1866." *Wagon Tracks* 23 (February 2009): 16–21.

Danziger, Edmund J., Jr. "The Office of Indian Affairs and the Problem of Civil War Indian Refugees in Kansas." *Kansas Historical Quarterly* 35 (Autumn 1969): 257–75.

Davis, Katie. "Seth M. Hays and the Council Grove Trade." *Wagon Tracks* 2 (November 1987): 10–11.

DeBuys, William. *Enchantment and Exploitation: The Life and Hard Times of a New Mexico Mountain Range*. Albuquerque: University of New Mexico Press, 1985.

"Diary of Samuel A. Kingman at Indian Treaty in 1865." *Kansas Historical Collections* 17 (1926–28): 442–50.

Dicks, Sam, editor. "'A Sower Went Forth': Lyman Beecher Kellogg and Kansas State Normal." *Kansas History* 24 (Winter 2001–2002): 252–75.

Dippie, Brian W. *The Vanishing American: White Attitudes and U.S. Indian Policy*. Lawrence: University Press of Kansas, 1982.

Dixon, Benjamin Y. "Furthering Their Own Demise: How Kansa Death Customs Accelerated Their Depopulation." *Ethnohistory* 54 (Summer 2007): 473–508.

Dixon, H. Pearl. *Sixty Years among the Indians: A Short Life Sketch of Thomas H. and Mary W. Stanley, Quaker Missionaries to the Indians*. Privately printed, 1922.

Dollar, Clyde D. "The High Plains Smallpox Epidemic of 1837–38." *Western Historical Quarterly* 8 (January 1977): 15–38.

Doran, Thomas F. "Kansas Sixty Years Ago." *Kansas Historical Collections* 15 (1919–22): 482–501.

Dorsey, James Owen. "Mourning and War Customs of the Kansas." *American Naturalist* 19 (July 1885): 670–80.

———. *A Study of Siouan Cults*. Eleventh Annual Report of the Bureau of American Ethnology (1889–1890). 1894. Reprint, Whitefish, Mont., Kessinger Publishing, 2006.

Duffus, Robert L. *The Santa Fe Trail*. 1931. Reprint, New York: David McKay, 1975.

Dunlay, Tom. *Kit Carson and the Indians*. Lincoln: University of Nebraska Press, 2000.

"The Emigrants by the Santa Fe Route from the *Cincinnati Dispatch*." Reprint of letter of June 7, 1849. *Kansas Historical Quarterly* 12 (August 1943): 324.

Entz, Gary R. "Religion in Kansas." *Kansas History* 28 (Summer 2005): 120–45.

"Explanation of Map." *Kansas Historical Collections* 9 (1905–1906): 566–78.

Farnham, Thomas Jefferson. *Travels in the Great Western Prairies, the Anahuac and Rocky Mountains, and in the Oregon Territory*. 1843. Reprint, London: British Library, Historical Print Editions, 2011.

"Fatal Malady at the Kaw Village." *Niles National Register* 69 (November 1, 1845): 134.

Fletcher, Alice C., and Francis La Flesche. *The Omaha Tribe*. Vols. 1 and 2. Lincoln: University of Nebraska Press, 1992.

Flores, Dan. *The Natural West: Environmental History in the Great Plains and Rocky Mountains*. Norman: University of Oklahoma Press, 2001.

Foner, Eric. *Free Soil, Free Labor, Free Men: The Ideology of the Republican Party before the Civil War*. New York: Oxford University Press, 1970.

Fowler, Loretta. *The Columbia Guide to American Indians of the Great Plains*. New York: Columbia University Press, 2003.

Franzwa, Gregory M. *Maps of the Santa Fe Trail*. St. Louis: Patrice Press, 1989.

Frazer, Robert W., ed. *Over the Chihuahua and Santa Fe Trails, 1847–1848: George Rutledge Gibson's Journal*. Albuquerque: University of New Mexico Press, 1981.

Gambone, Joseph G. "Economic Relief in Territorial Kansas, 1860–1861." *Kansas Historical Quarterly* 36 (Summer 1970): 149–74.

Gardner, Kathryn Davis. "Conn and Hays: Council Grove Trail Merchants." *Journal of the West* 18 (April 1989): 31–38.

Gardner, Mark. "Malcolm Conn: Merchant on the Trail." *Wagon Tracks* 1 (February 1987): 7–8.

Garfield, Marvin H. "Defense of the Kansas Frontier, 1868-1869." *Kansas Historical Quarterly* 1 (November 1932): 451–73.

Garrard, Lewis H. *Wah-to-yah and the Taos Trail*. Norman: University of Oklahoma Press, 1955.

Gates, Paul Wallace. *Fifty Million Acres: Conflicts over Kansas Land Policy, 1854–1890*. Ithaca, N.Y.: Cornell University Press, 1954.

Gladstone, Thomas H. *The Englishman in Kansas; or, Squatter Life and Border Warfare*. 1857. Reprint, Lincoln: University of Nebraska Press, 1971.

Glick, George W. "The Drought of 1860." *Kansas Historical Collections* 9 (1905–1906): 480–85.

Gowing, Clara. "Life among the Delaware Indians." *Kansas Historical Collections* 12 (1911–12): 183–93.

Gregg, Josiah. *Commerce of the Prairies; or, The Journal of a Santa Fe Trader*. Two vols. 1844. Reprint, Norman: University of Oklahoma Press, 1990.

Gregg, Kate L. *The Road to Santa Fe: The Journal and Diaries of George Champlin Sibley*. Albuquerque: University of New Mexico Press, 1968.

Griffing, W. J. "Committee on Explorations." *Kansas Historical Collections* 8 (1903–1904): 134–35.

Griffiths, Jay. "Let Them Drink Coke." *Orion* (January/February 2011): 12–13.

Hafen, LeRoy R., ed. *To the Pike's Peak Gold Fields, 1859*. Lincoln: University of Nebraska Press, 2004.

Hagan, William T. *The Sac and Fox Indians*. Norman: University of Oklahoma Press, 1958.

Hall, James. *Sketches of History, Life, and Manners in the West*. Vol. 2. Philadelphia: Harrison Hall, 1835.

Haucke, Frank. "The Kaw or Kansa Indians." *Kansas Historical Quarterly* 20 (February 1952): 36–60.

Hickey, Joseph V. *Ghost Settlement on the Prairie: A Biography of Thurman, Kansas*. Lawrence: University Press of Kansas, 1995.

"High Waters in Kansas." *Kansas Historical Collections* 8 (1903–1904): 472–81. Excerpts from Jotham Meeker's diary and letters, May–December 1844.

Hiss, Tony. *The Experience of Place: A New Way of Looking at and Dealing with Our Radically Changing Cities and Countryside*. New York: Random House, 1990.

Hobbs, Wilson. "The Friends Establishment in Kansas Territory." *Kansas Historical Collections* 8 (1904): 250–71.

Hodson, Warren G. "Geology and Ground-Water Resources of Mitchell County, Kansas." *State Geological Survey of Kansas Bulletin* 140 (April 1959): 37–39.

Hopkins, Donald R. *Princes and Peasants: Smallpox in History*. Chicago: University of Chicago Press, 1983.

Horsman, Reginald. *Race and Manifest Destiny: The Origins of American Racial Anglo-Saxonism*. Cambridge: Harvard University Press, 1981.

Hoy, James F. "Controlled Pasture Burning in the Folklife of the Kansas Flint Hills." *Great Plains Quarterly* 9 (Autumn 1989): 231–38.

Hudson, James E. "Camp Nichols: Oklahoma's Outpost on the Santa Fe Trail." *Wagon Tracks* 14 (November 1999): 12–17.

Hyman, Merton M., M. Zimmerman, C. Gurioli, and A. Helrich. *Drinkers, Drinking and Alcohol-Related Mortality and Hospitalizations: A Statistical Compendium*. New Brunswick, N.J.: Rutgers University, 1980.

Isenberg, Andrew C. *The Destruction of the Bison*. Cambridge: Cambridge University Press, 2000.

James, Edwin, Thomas Say, and Stephen Harriman Long. *Account of an Expedition from Pittsburgh to the Rocky Mountains*. 1823. Reprint, Charleston, S.C.: Biblio-Life, 2010.

Johnston, Adam Robinson, Marcellus Ball Edwards, and Philip Gooch Ferguson. *Marching with the Army of the West, 1846–1848*. Edited by Ralph P. Bieber. Southwest Historical Series, 4. Glendale, Calif.: Arthur H. Clark, 1936.

"Julius Froebel's Western Travels, Part IV." *Wagon Tracks* 25 (November 2010): 27–28.

Kanza Language Project. *The Kanza Clan Book*. Kaw City, Okla.: Kaw Nation, 2002.

———. *Compiled Kanza Texts*. Kaw City, Okla.: Kaw Nation, 2009.

Kappler, Charles J., comp., *Indian Affairs: Laws and Treaties*. Vol. II, *Treaties*. Washington, D.C.: Government Printing Office, 1904.

Keckeisen, Robert Joseph. "The Kansa 'Half-Breed' Lands: Contravention and Transformation of United States Indian Policy in Kansas." Master's thesis, Wichita State University, 1977.

Koplowitz, Bradford. *The Kaw Indian Census and Allotments*. Bowie, Md.: Heritage Books, 1996.

Kvasnicka, Robert M., and Herman J. Viola, eds. *The Commissioners of Indian Affairs, 1824–1977*. Lincoln: University of Nebraska Press, 1979.

La Flesche, Francis. *War Ceremony and Peace Ceremony of the Osage Indians*. U.S. Bureau of American Ethnology Bulletin 101. Washington, D.C.: Government Printing Office, 1939.

Leader, Jeanne P. "The Pottawatomies and Alcohol: An Illustration of the Illegal Trade." *Kansas History* 2 (Autumn 1979): 157–65.

Lecher, Zachary J. "Are We Ready for the Conflict? Black Abolitionist Response to the Kansas Crisis, 1854–1856." *Kansas History* 31 (Spring 2008): 14–31.

Ledbetter, Barbara Neal. *Fort Belknap Frontier Saga: Indians, Negroes and Anglo-Americans on the Texas Frontier*. Burnet, Tex.: Eakin Press, 1982.

Leiker, James N. "Race Relations in the Sunflower State." *Kansas History* 25 (Autumn 2002): 214–36.

Leiker, James N., and Ramon Powers. *The Northern Cheyenne Exodus in History and Memory.* Norman: University of Oklahoma Press, 2011.

"Letters from the Indian Missions in Kansas." *Kansas Historical Collections* 16 (1923–25): 227–71. Correspondence from Methodist missionaries William and Thomas Johnson, Jerome C. Berryman, and others (1831–1845).

Lichtenhan, Hartman. "Reminiscences of Hartman Lichtenhan." *Kansas Historical Collections* 9 (1905–1906): 548–52.

Limerick, Patricia Nelson. *The Legacy of Conquest: The Unbroken Past of the American West.* New York: W. W. Norton, 1987.

Lindsey, Jean, compiler. *John R. Wells Discovers Kansas.* Stockton, Kans.: n.p., 1998. Available at Port Library, Beloit, Kansas.

Linsenmayer, Penny T. "Kansas Settlers on the Osage Diminished Reserve: A Study of Laura Ingalls Wilder's *Little House on the Prairie.*" *Kansas History* 24 (Autumn 2001): 168–85.

Lowe, Percival. *Five Years a Dragoon ('49 to '54) and Other Adventures on the Great Plains.* 1906. Reprint, Norman: University of Oklahoma Press, 1991.

Lowie, Robert H. *Indians of the Plains.* Garden City, N.Y.: American Museum of Natural History, 1965.

Lutz, J. J. "The Methodist Missions among the Indian Tribes in Kansas." *Kansas Historical Collections* 9 (1905–1906): 160–235.

Mack, John N. "United We Stand: Law and Order on the Southeastern Kansas Frontier, 1866–1870." *Kansas History* 30 (Winter 2007–2008): 234–51.

Madden, John. "Along the Trail." *Kansas Historical Collections* 8 (1903–1904): 67–71.

Magoffin, Susan Shelby. *Down the Santa Fe Trail and into Mexico: The Diary of Susan Shelby Magoffin, 1846–1847.* New Haven, Conn.: Yale University Press, 1962.

Maloy, John. *History of Morris County, 1820–1890.* Council Grove, Kans.: Morris County Historical Society, 1981.

Mandel, Rolfe D. "Late Quaternary and Modern Environments in Kansas." In *Kansas Archaeology,* edited by Robert J. Hoard and William E. Banks, 10–27. Lawrence: University Press of Kansas, 2006.

Marshall, James O. "The Kansa." In *Kansas Archaeology,* edited by Robert J. Hoard and William E. Banks, 219–32. Lawrence: University Press of Kansas, 2006.

Martin, George W. "The Territorial and Military Combine at Fort Riley." *Kansas Historical Collections* 7 (1901–1902): 361–90.

Masterson, Vincent V. *The Katy Railroad and the Last Frontier.* 1952. Reprint, Columbia: University of Missouri Press, 1988.

McClure, James R. "Taking the Census and Other Incidents in 1855." *Kansas Historical Collections* 8 (1903–1904): 227–50.

McCoy, Isaac. *History of Baptist Indian Missions.* 1840. Reprint, Springfield, Mo.: Particular Baptist Press, 2003.

McCoy, John C. "Survey of Kansas Indian Lands." *Kansas Historical Collections* 4 (1886–1888): 298–311.

McDermott, John Francis, ed. *Tixier's Travels on the Osage Prairies*. Norman: University of Oklahoma Press, 1940.

Mead, James R. *Hunting and Trading on the Great Plains, 1859–1875*. Norman: University of Oklahoma Press, 1986.

Meany, Joseph F., Jr. "Jeremiah Stokes: A Case Study in Family History." *Wagon Tracks* 18 (May 2004): 10–15.

Merwin, Ray E. "The Wyandot Indians." *Kansas Historical Collections* 9 (1905–1906): 73–88.

Michno, Gregory. "The Search for the Captives of Elm Creek." *Wild West* (April 2009): 46–52.

Middlesworth, Charles Lynn Van. "The Kansa: Cultural Construction and Preservation of Traditional Culture under Acculturation." Master's thesis, Eastern New Mexico University, 1975.

Miner, H. Craig, and William E. Unrau. *The End of Indian Kansas: A Study of Cultural Revolution, 1854–1871*. 1978. Reprint, Lawrence: University Press of Kansas, 1990.

Mollhausen H. B. "Over the Santa Fe Trail through Kansas in 1858." *Kansas Historical Quarterly* 16 (November 1948): 337–80.

Montgomery, Mrs. Frank C. "Fort Wallace and Its Relation to the Frontier." *Kansas Historical Collections* 17 (1928): 189–283.

Morehouse, George Pierson. "Along the Kaw Trail." *Kansas Historical Collections* 8 (1903–1904): 206–12.

———. "Diamond Springs, 'The Diamond of the Plain.'" *Kansas Historical Collections* 14 (1915–18): 794–804.

———. "History of the Kansa or Kaw Indians." *Kansas Historical Collections* 10 (1908): 327–68.

———. *The Kansa or Kaw Indians and Their History*. Topeka, Kans.: State Printing Office, 1908.

———. "Probably the First School in Kansas for White Children." *Kansas Historical Collections* 9 (1905–1906): 231–35.

———. "Religion of the Indians, Especially of the Kansas or Kaws." Biennial Report of the Kansas State Historical Society, no. 27 (1928–30): 40–50.

Morgan, Lewis Henry. *The Indian Journals, 1859–1862*. 1959. Reprint, New York: Dover, 1993.

Morris, Anna Maria. "A Military Wife on the Santa Fe Trail." In *Covered Wagon Women: Diaries & Letters from the Western Trails, 1840–1890*. Vol. 2, *1850*, edited by Kenneth L. Holmes. Glendale, Calif.: Arthur H. Clark, 1983.

Myers, Harry C., ed. "Captain William Becknell's Journal of Two Expeditions from Boon's Lick to Santa Fe." *Wagon Tracks* 11 (May 1997): 1, 20–24.

Napier, Rita G. "Rethinking the Past; Reimagining the Future." *Kansas History* 24 (Autumn 2001): 218–49.

Neighbours, Kenneth F. "Elm Creek Raid." *Handbook of Texas Online*. Texas State Historical Association. www.tshaonline.org/handbook/online/articles/bte01 (accessed August 16, 2011).

Nichols, Roger L., ed. *The Missouri Expedition 1818–1820: The Journal of Surgeon John Gale with Related Documents*. Norman: University of Oklahoma Press, 1969.

Nicholson, William. "A Tour of Indian Agencies in Kansas and the Indian Territory in 1870." *Kansas Historical Quarterly* 3 (August 1934): 289–326.

"Ninth Kansas Cavalry Regiment." *American Civil War Research Database*. Subscription database (accessed September 1, 2011).

Norwood, Frederick A. *The Story of American Methodism*. Nashville: Abingdon Press, 1974.

Nyquist, Edna. *Pioneer Life and Lore of McPherson County, Kansas*. McPherson: Democrat-Opinion Press, 1932.

O'Brien, Patricia J. "The Sacred Red Rock of the Kansa." Unpublished paper, May 1, 2007, draft.

Oertel, Kristen Tegtmeier. *Bleeding Borders: Race, Gender and Violence in Pre-Civil War Kansas*. Baton Rouge: Louisiana State University, 2009.

———. "'The Free Sons of the North' versus 'The Myrmidons of Border Ruffianism': What Makes a Man in Bleeding Kansas?" *Kansas History* 25 (Autumn 2002): 174–89.

Oliva, Leo E. "The Army's Attempts at Freighting during the Mexican War, 1846–1848." *Wagon Tracks* 23 (November 2008): 17–24.

———. *Soldiers on the Santa Fe Trail*. Norman: University of Oklahoma Press, 1967.

Oliva, Leo, and Bonita Oliva, eds. "Katie Bowen Letters, 1851: Part VI." *Wagon Tracks* 18 (August 2004): 16–20.

Olson, Kevin G. W. *Frontier Manhattan: Yankee Settlement to Kansas Town, 1854–1894*. Lawrence: University Press of Kansas, 2012.

Parks, Douglas R., and Waldo Wedel. "Pawnee Geography: Historical and Sacred." *Great Plains Quarterly* 5 (Summer 1985): 143–76.

Patrick, G. E. "The Great Spirit Spring." *Transactions of the Kansas Academy of Science* 7 (1906): 22–26.

"Pike's Journal, Part II." *Wagon Tracks* 17 (August 2003): 24–30.

Powers, Ramon, and Gene Younger. "Cholera on the Overland Trails, 1832–1869." *Kansas Quarterly* 5 (Spring 1973): 32–49.

Powers, Ramon, and James N. Leiker. "Cholera among the Plains Indians: Perceptions, Causes, Consequences." *Western Historical Quarterly* 29 (Autumn 1998): 317–40.

Pride, W. F. *History of Fort Riley*. 1926. Reprint, Fort Riley, Kans.: U.S. Cavalry Museum and the Fort Riley Historical and Archaeology Society, 1987.

Prucha, Francis P. *The Great Father: The United States Government and the American Indians*. Abridged ed. Lincoln: University of Nebraska Press, 1984.

"Recollections of James Francis Riley, Part II." *Wagon Tracks* 9 (May 1995): 11–16.

Richards, David L., ed. "Charles W. Fribley's Trail Diary and Letters, 1857–1859, Part I." *Wagon Tracks* 12 (August 1998): 1, 14–23.

Riley, Glenda. *Confronting Race: Women and Indians on the Frontier, 1815–1915*. Albuquerque: University of New Mexico Press, 2004.

Robinson, Albert. "Campaigning in the Army of the Frontier." *Kansas Historical Collections* 14 (1915–18): 285.

Robinson, Sara T. L. *Kansas: Its Exterior and Interior Life: Including a Full View of Its Settlement, Political History, Social Life, Climate, Soil, Production, Scenery, Etc.* Boston: Crosby, Nichols, 1856.

Rollings, Willard Hughes. *The Osage: An Ethnohistorical Study of Hegemony on the Prairie-Plains.* Columbia: University of Missouri Press, 1992.

———. *Unaffected by the Gospel: Osage Resistance to the Christian Invasion (1673–1906): A Cultural Victory.* Albuquerque: University of New Mexico Press, 2004.

Roper, Donna C. "The Pawnee in Kansas: Ethnohistory and Archaeology." In *Kansas Archaeology*, edited by Robert J. Hoard and William E. Banks, 233–47. Lawrence: University Press of Kansas, 2006.

Rorabaugh, W. J. *The Alcoholic Republic: An American Tradition.* New York: Oxford University Press, 1979.

"Roster of Officers and Enlisted Men of Kansas Volunteers, Fifteenth Regiment Cavalry, Company F." In *Report of the Adjutant General of the State of Kansas, 1861–1865.* Topeka: Kansas State Printing Company, 1896.

Rush, Tonda. "Folklore Offers Insights about Kanza Indians." *Lawrence Journal-World*, November 8, 1979.

Ryan, Beverly Carmichael. "Under Siege at the Cow Creek Crossing, July 1864." *Wagon Tracks* 14 (August 2000): 5–9.

———. "Under Siege at the Walnut and Cow Creek Trail Crossings, July 1864." *Wagon Tracks* 18 (August 2004): 5–9.

Rydjord, John. *Kansas Place-Names.* Norman: University of Oklahoma Press, 1972.

Sanderson, Amy L. "The Faults of Memory: J. L. Sanderson, His Family, and the Santa Fe Trail." *Wagon Tracks* 22 (August 2008): 8–17.

Saxton, Alexander. *The Rise and Fall of the White Republic: Class Politics and Mass Culture in Nineteenth-Century America.* London: Verso, 1990.

Schlesinger, Arthur M., Jr., ed. *The Almanac of American History.* New York: Putnam, 1983.

Schoewe, Walter R. "The Geography of Kansas, Part III—Hydrogeography." *Transactions of the Kansas Academy of Science* 56 (June 1953): 131–90.

Schwegman, Ladd H., ed. "Memoirs of a Mexican War Volunteer: Charles Henry Buercklin." *Wagon Tracks* 11 (May 1997): 10–19.

Sharp, Mrs. Mamie Stine. "Home-coming Centennial Celebration at Council Grove, June 27 to July 2, 1921." *Kansas Historical Collections* 16 (1923–25): 528–69.

Shaw, Harriett Bidwell. *Crossing the Plains: The Journal of Harriett Bidwell Shaw in 1851.* Kansas Memory, Kansas Historical Society, www.kansasmemory.org/item/209694 (accessed December 21, 2012).

Shepard, Paul. *The Only World We've Got.* San Francisco: Sierra Club Books, 1996.

Sherow, James E. "Workings of the Geodialectic: High Plains Indians and Their Horses in the Region of the Arkansas River Valley, 1800–1870." In *A Sense of the American West: An Anthology of Environmental History*, edited by James Sherow, 91–112. Albuquerque: University of New Mexico Press, 1998.

Shields, Clara M. Fengel. "The Lyon Creek Settlement." *Kansas Historical Collections* 14 (1915–18): 143–70.

Shimeall, William Michael. "Arthur Inghram Baker: Frontier Kansan." Master's thesis, Emporia State University, 1978.

Shortridge, James R. *Kaw Valley Landscapes*. Lawrence: University Press of Kansas, 1977.

Skinner, Alanson. "Societies of the Iowa, Kansa and Ponca Indians." *Anthropological Papers of the American Museum of Natural History* 11 (1915): 741–75.

Slotkin, Richard. *The Fatal Environment: The Myth of the Frontier in the Age of Industrialization, 1800–1890*. 1985. Reprint, Norman: University of Oklahoma Press, 1998.

Smith, Alice Strieby. "Through the Eyes of My Father: Fragments of Council Grove Frontier History." *Kansas Historical Collections* 17 (1926–28): 708–18.

Smith, Paul Chaat. *Everything You Know about Indians Is Wrong*. Minneapolis: University of Minnesota Press, 2009.

Smith, William E. "The Oregon Trail through Pottawatomie County." *Kansas Historical Collections* 17 (1926–28): 435–64.

Snell, Joseph W., and Robert W. Richmond. "When the Union and Kansas Pacific Built through Kansas, Part I." *Kansas Historical Quarterly* 32 (Summer 1966): 161–86.

Spear, Stephen Jackson. "Reminiscences of the Early Settlement of Dragoon Creek, Wabaunsee County." *Kansas Historical Collections* 13 (1913–14): 345–63.

Spencer, Joab. "The Kaw or Kansas Indians: Their Customs, Manners, and Folklore." *Kansas Historical Collections* 10 (1907–1908): 373–82.

Staab, Rodney. "Kansa Presence in the Upper Kansas Valley, 1846–1867." *Kansas Anthropologist* 16 (1995): 24–45.

Stevens, Robert C., and Betty Adams. *Thunderbolt from a Clear Sky: The Irrepressible Life of Robert W. S. Stevens*. Abridged ed. Rochester, N.Y.: WME Books, 2006.

Stratford, Jessie Perry. *Butler County's Eighty Years, 1855–1935*. El Dorado, Kans.: Butler County News, 1934.

Swineford, Ada, and John C. Frye. "Notes on Waconda or Great Spirit Spring, Mitchell County, Kansas." *Transactions of the Kansas Academy of Science* 58 (1955): 265–70.

Takaki, Ronald T. *Iron Cages: Race and Culture in Nineteenth-Century America*. New York: Knopf, 1979.

Tate, Michael L. *Indians and Emigrants: Encounters on the Overland Trails*. Norman: University of Oklahoma Press, 2006.

Thomson, Matt. *Early History of Wabaunsee County*. 1901. Reprint, Manhattan, Kans.: Ag Press, 1979.

"Touring Kansas and Colorado in 1871: The Journal of George C. Anderson." *Kansas Historical Quarterly* 22 (Autumn 1956): 193–219.

Townsend, John Kirk. *Narrative of a Journey Across the Rocky Mountains to the Columbia River*. 1839. Reprint, Corvallis: Oregon State University Press, 1999.

Unrau, William E. "The Civilian as Indian Agent: Villain or Victim?" *Western Histori-cal Quarterly* 3 (October 1972): 405–20.

———. "The Council Grove Merchants and Kansas Indians." *Kansas Historical Quar-terly* 34 (Autumn 1968): 266–81.

———. "The Depopulation of the Dhegiha-Sioux." *New Mexico Historical Review* 48 (October 1973): 313–28.

———. "Epidemic Disease and the Impact of the Santa Fe Trail on the Kansas Indi-ans." *Heritage of the Great Plains* 17 (Spring 1984): 1–9.

———. *Indians, Alcohol, and the Roads to Taos and Santa Fe.* Lawrence: University Press of Kansas, 2013.

———. "Indian Water Rights to the Middle Arkansas: The Case for the Kaws." *Kan-sas History* 5 (Spring 1982): 52–69.

———. *The Kansa Indians: A History of the Wind People, 1673–1873.* Norman: Univer-sity of Oklahoma Press, 1971.

———. *Mixed-Bloods and Tribal Dissolution: Charles Curtis and the Quest for Indian Identity.* Lawrence: University Press of Kansas, 1989.

———. *The Rise and Fall of Indian Country, 1825–1855.* Lawrence: University Press of Kansas, 2007.

———. *White Man's Wicked Water: The Alcohol Trade and Prohibition in Indian Country, 1802–1892.* Lawrence: University Press of Kansas, 1996.

Utley, Robert M. *High Noon in Lincoln: Violence on the Western Frontier.* Albuquerque: University of New Mexico Press, 1987.

———. *The Indian Frontier 1846–1890.* Albuquerque: University of New Mexico Press, 1984.

Van Meter, Sondra. *Marion County Kansas Past and Present.* Hillsboro, Kans.: M. B. Publishing House, 1972.

Walker, Wyman. "Freighting: A Big Business on the Santa Fe Trail." *Kansas Historical Quarterly* 1 (November 1931): 17–27.

War of the Rebellion: A Compilation of the Official Record of the Union and Confederate Armies, series 1, volumes 22, 41, part 2. Washington D.C.: Government Printing Office, 1893.

Webb, James Josiah. *Adventures in the Santa Fe Trade.* Glendale, Calif.: Arthur H. Clark, 1931.

Wedel, Waldo R. "The Kansa Indians." *Transactions of the Kansas Academy of Science* 49 (June 1946): 1–35.

———. "Notes on the Prairie Turnip (Psoralea esculenta) among the Plains Indi-ans." *Nebraska History* 59 (Summer 1978): 1–25.

———. "Prehistory and Environment in the Central Great Plains." *Transactions of the Kansas Academy of Science* 50 (June 1947): 1–18.

Weinberg, Albert K. *Manifest Destiny: A Study of Nationalist Expansionism in American History.* Baltimore: Johns Hopkins Press, 1935.

Weltfish, Gene. *The Lost Universe: Pawnee Life and Culture.* Lincoln: University of Ne-braska Press, 1965.

Welty, Raymond L. "The Policing of the Frontier by the Army." *Kansas Historical Quarterly* 7 (August 1938): 246–57.

West, Elliott. *The Contested Plains: Indians, Goldseekers, and the Rush to Colorado.* Lawrence: University Press of Kansas, 1998.

———. *The Way to the West: Essays on the Central Plains.* Albuquerque: University of New Mexico Press, 1995.

White, David, ed. *News of the Plains and Rockies, 1803–1865.* Vol. 2, *Santa Fe Adventurers, Settlers, Artists.* Spokane: Arthur H. Clark, 1996.

White, Mrs. S. B. "My First Days in Kansas." *Kansas Historical Collections* 11 (1909–10): 550–60.

White, Richard. *The Middle Ground: Indians, Empires, and Republics in the Great Lakes Region, 1650–1815.* Cambridge: Cambridge University Press, 1991.

———. *The Roots of Dependency: Subsistence, Environment, and Social Change among the Choctaws, Pawnees, and Navajos.* Lincoln: University of Nebraska Press, 1983.

White, William Allen. *The Autobiography of William Allen White.* New York: MacMillan, 1946.

Wilson, Julie. "Kansas Über Alles! The Geography and Ideology of Conquest, 1870–1900." *Western Historical Quarterly* 27 (Summer 1996): 170–87.

Wishart, David J. *An Unspeakable Sadness: The Dispossession of the Nebraska Indians.* Lincoln: University of Nebraska Press, 1994.

Wood, Dean Earl. *The Old Santa Fe Trail from the Missouri River.* Kansas City, Mo.: E. L. Mendenhall, 1951.

Woodward, Benjamin. "Report from Duvall's Bluff, Arkansas." *United States Sanitary Commission Bulletin* 3 (1866).

Wrabley, Raymond B., Jr. "Drunk Driving or Dry Run? Cowboys and Alcohol on the Cattle Trail." *Kansas History* 30 (Spring 2007): 36–51.

Wright, R. M. "Personal Reminiscences of Frontier Life in Southwestern Kansas." *Kansas Historical Collections* 7 (1901–1902): 47–83.

NEWSPAPERS

Council Grove Democrat, 1866, 1872–75.

Council Grove Press, 1860–61, 1863–65.

Council Grove Republican, 1887, 1910.

Daily Kansas State Record (Topeka), 1868.

Dickinson County Chronicle, 1876.

Emporia News, 1859–70.

Freeman's Champion (Prairie City, Kansas), 1858.

Herald of Freedom (Lawrence, Kansas), 1855–57.

Junction City Union, 1865–73.

Kansas Daily Tribune (Lawrence), 1864.

Kansas Press (Cottonwood Falls), 1859.

Kansas Press (Council Grove), 1859–60.

Kansas State Record (Topeka), 1860–61, 1868.
Kanza News (Emporia), 1858–59.
Lawrence Daily Tribune, 1868.
Lawrence Republican, 1860.
Leavenworth Daily Conservative, 1863.
Lyon Daily News, 1946.
Marion County Record, 1871.
Rooks County Record, 1917.
Smoky Hill and Republican Union (Junction City, Kansas), 1863–64.
Topeka Journal, 1916.
Topeka Tribune, 1859–60.
Walnut Valley Times (El Dorado, Kansas), 1873.
Weekly Kansas Herald (Leavenworth), 1854–55.

INTERVIEWS, RECORDINGS, AND PERSONAL COMMUNICATIONS

Cress, Donald, and F. J. Revere. Interview by author, Allegawaho Memorial Heritage Park, Kaw Nation, Kansas, July 4, 2008.
McBride, Justin (Kaw Nation Language Project). Letter to Ron Parks, September 18, 2002.
———. E-mail to Ron Parks and Pauline Sharp, October 14, 2009.
McCauley, Johnny Rae. Video recording of talk. Kaw Mission State Historic Site, Council Grove, Kansas, June 1996.
McClintock, Kenneth. Letters to Ron Parks, May 25, 2009 ("Site of June 1859 hanging"); July 11, 2002 ("Shawnee Reservation—Boundaries in Morris County").
Rankin, Robert. Interview by author, Pottawatomie County, Kansas, August 6, 2012.

INDEX

Abilene, Kans., 182

African Americans, 24, 43, 173, 174, 221, 222

Agencies, locations of, 95–96, 128

Agency, Neosho reservation, 96, 234; buildings, description of, 127–28, 266nn15–16; construction of, 77, 125, 127–28; farm, 124, 128; traders at, 176, 178–79, 189, 217, 218

Agents, Indian, 53, 65, 94–97, 112, 126–27, 176; duties of, 95, 98–99, 112; theft allegations against, 136, 140, 161

Agnes City, Kans., 63

Agriculture, Euro-American, 47, 61, 73, 205; drought, impact on, 116–17

Agriculture, Kanza, 11, 14, 19, 31–32, 73, 74, 78, 132, 133–34, 148, 162–63, 191, 246; adoption of Euro-American methods of, 159, 162–63, 180, 238, 246; crop production, 134, 159, 163, 196, 236, 237, 238; crops, 14, 19, 23, 46–47, 73, 133–34, 159–60, 180, 191, 196, 217; destruction of crops by railroad construction, 205; drought, effects on, 116–17, 134; farmer, government, 19, 132, 134, 159, 162–63; gender roles in, 46, 163, 236–37; hired

laborers on Euro-American farms, 134, 205; implements, draft animals, and tools used in, 19, 46, 78, 81, 132–34, 136, 159, 162–63, 236; thievery of implements by Euro-Americans, 162, 187

Albrecht, Glenn, 6

Alcohol, 29, 33, 48, 97–103, 107, 119, 144, 160, 172, 178, 183, 188, 222, 225, 229; French "grocery" incident, 147–48; railroad workers enhance consumption of, 205; Santa Fe Road, as vector of, 97–99, 101–102; stimulant of in-group violence, 99–100, 188

Alcohol, Euro-American: consumption of, 100–101; stimulant of in-group violence, 102–103

Allegawaho ("Big Elk"), 74, 77, 107, 120, 137, 139, 177, 187, 197, 213, 227, 230; "darkest period" statement by, 6, 94, 179, 225, 243; Delano, meeting with, 234–35; description of, 198–99; at grand council in Washington, D.C., 198–201; head chief, selection as, 176; letters and speeches of, 187, 197, 218–19, 225–26, 230, 232, 234, 235;

Lawrence Journal, 198
Lawrence Republican, 76
Lea, Francis W., 48, 96
Lea, Luke, 11–12
Lean Bear, 174
Leavenworth, Kans., 46, 76, 145, 153,
  196; whiskey sales at, 100
Leavenworth and Pike's Peak stage
  line, 82
Lecompton, 63, 72, 152
Leiker, James, 93
Lincoln, Abraham, 126, 140–41, 149,
  156, 157, 172, 174
Lincoln County, Kans., 15–16
Lincolnville, Kans., 212
Linn County, Kans., 154
Little Arkansas crossing, 97
Little Arkansas River, 32, 158, 170, 187,
  213
Little Arkansas Treaty, 166
Little Bear, 154
Little Ice Age, 32
Little John Creek, 122, 128; "Cheyenne
  Raid" at, 193
Little Robe, 192, 194
Little Rock, Ark., 155
Little Thunder, 154
Lost Spring, 97
Lowe, Percival G., 54–55
Lutz, Joseph Anthony, 39
Lyon County, Kans., 61, 66, 194
Lyon Creek, 168
Lyons, Kans., 97, 212

Mahunga, 194, 236
Majors, Alexander, 32
Maloy, John, 6, 46, 113, 241, 242, 243;
  Allegawaho, description of, 199;
  legacy of Kanzas, description of,
  242
Manhattan, Kans., 170, 175, 207
Manifest Destiny, 7, 34, 65, 119, 144,
  145, 221–22, 240, 246

Mansfield, William, 136
Manypenny, George P., 68, 70, 78, 94,
  97
Marion Center, Kans., 192
Marion County, Kans., 182, 194, 212
Marion Reservoir, 212
Marriage, 50, 165, 217
Marshall, John, 79
Mazzard's Prairie, Ark., 155
McBratney, Robert, 203
McCauley, Johnny Rae, 7
McClellan, George, 174
McClelland, Robert, 68
McClure, James R., 168–69
McCoy, Isaac, 67
McDonald, Caroline, 166
McGee, Fry, 97
McPherson, Kans., 16
McPherson County, Kans., 102, 182,
  212
Mead, James R., 101, 102; Indian
  hunters, description of, 210; Kanza
  indebtedness to, 197
Mechushingah, 165
Medical assistance, 130, 135, 140,
  161–62, 223–24, 246; physicians, 103,
  135, 140, 161, 223. See also Disease
Medicine Lodge Treaty, 189–90, 191
Medill, William, 20, 21, 30
Meriwether, David, 45
Methodist Episcopal Church South, 33,
  37, 41, 42; slavery, position on, 42
Mexican-American War, 5, 21, 22, 34
Mexican freighters. See Santa Fe Road
  (Trail)
Miami tribe, 24
Middle Creek, 211, 220
Mills (gristmills and sawmills), 14, 81,
  125, 127, 135, 136, 205, 239
Minghoci Oizkanka (Grand Point), 9
Minneapolis, Kans., 9, 67
Mission Creek, 19, 57; Treaty of 1846,
  negotiations at, 14

243, 244; as appraisal commissioner, 241; as government farmer, 162–63; as school superintendent, 160, 163–65
Sublette, Solomon, 23, 96
Summit Springs, Colo., 229
Surveys, land, 67, 124; of the Kanza Reservation, 67, 68, 69, 75, 124
Sycamore Springs, Kans., 211

Tall Bull, 192
Taylor, Albert, 225
Taylor, Nathaniel, 197
Taylor, Sarah ("Aunt Sally"), 43, 240
Tecumseh, Kans., 87
Territorial Relief Committee, 118. *See also* Destitution, Euro-Americans
Texas, captives from, 166–67
Thomson family, 171
Timber: destruction of by Euro-Americans, 72, 73, 140, 214; disputes about railroad payments for, 206–207; firewood, sold for, 206; hardwoods, 11, 15–16, 20–21, 35, 37, 46, 206, 214, 239; income source for Kanzas, 206, 236, 237, 238, 239; objections to Euro-American timber-cutting, 205–207; railroad ties, made from, 205–206; skill of Kanzas in cutting, 206
Tobacco, 215, 216–17
Topeka, Kans., 11, 13, 40, 87, 89, 115, 150, 152–53, 171, 175, 192, 196, 207, 242
Topeka Tribune, 115, 117
Townsend, John Kirk, 143,
Trade and Intercourse Act, 98, 99, 102, 112, 148
Trade with Euro-Americans, 13, 20, 24, 36, 48, 52–53, 58–60, 69–70, 79, 98–99, 102, 112, 136, 141–44, 152, 168, 199, 202, 215; fruits and berries in, 143–44, 236; horses in, 59, 105, 142, 159–60, 236; "jerks" in, 213; Kanza Agency, trader located at, 128, 176, 178–79,

189, 203, 217, 218; robes, hides, and furs in, 46–47, 59, 142–44, 184, 187, 208, 209, 213, 237; trading posts on Santa Fe Road in, 97; women, role of, 143–44, 168, 213, 236. *See also* Debts
Treaties, unratified, 207; 1864, 139–41, 200; 1867, 200–202; 1869, 204–205
Treaty of 1859, 79–82, 123, 131, 148, 178, 231, 232; amendment (1860) to, 81; opposition to, 80–81, 130–31
Treaty of 1846, 11, 13, 17, 59, 63, 67, 77, 78, 79, 94, 135, 138; summary of, 14; timber provision in, 15–16
Treaty of 1862, 131, 148; Huffaker land acquisition, 132; "Kaw scrip," 130–32
Treaty of 1825 (St. Louis), 13, 57, 63–64, 152
Treaty of 1825 (Turkey Creek), 16
Trust lands, 78, 130, 131, 200–202, 205; sale of, 200–202, 204–205, 231–35, 241; squatters on, 130, 201–202, 205
Turkey Creek, 81, 84; treaty signed at, 16

Union Pacific Railroad, Eastern Division, 175, 182. *See also* Railroads
Union Pacific Railway, Southern Branch (Katy), 179, 201–207; acquisition of Kanza reservation land by, 201–202, 204–205; construction of railroad by, 204–207, 214; criticisms of, 205–207; Kanza laborers employed by, 205; meeting of Kanza chiefs and railroad officials, 202–204; timber cutting by, 205–207, 214; Treaty (unratified) of 1869, 204–205. *See also* Railroads
Uniontown, 150
United States Sanitary Commission Bulletin, 155
Unrau, William E., 6, 65
Usher, J. P., 158
Utley, Robert, 103

CPSIA information can be obtained
at www.ICGtesting.com
Printed in the USA
LVHW021503261021
701602LV00002B/237